① Methad. main, Clin.
Tx. Cln. com
713-468-0536   9320 Westuw, Dr#10

125 70

Methdn. A-Action Clinic
713 694 8100
6311 Fulton St.

Shamsi Manazir MD Tx
713- 468 -0536
9320 W
open Til 5PM

John Lyons is recognised internationally as one of the most influential scholars in modern linguistics. This volume contains essays spanning many years of his thought and research, in addition to previously unpublished pieces. Chapters 2, 3 and 4 make their first appearance here, and set out the view of linguistics and linguistic theory which underlies the content of this and a companion volume (forthcoming).

The remaining six chapters have been either extensively revised or annotated to provide the reader with their historical context and to bring them in line with the author's current thinking.

This collection will be widely read both for the previously published material brought together here, and for the new chapters and many notes containing insights and arguments now available for the first time.

Natural language and universal grammar

Natural language and universal grammar

Essays in linguistic theory, volume I

JOHN LYONS

Trinity Hall, Cambridge

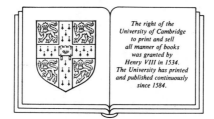

The right of the
University of Cambridge
to print and sell
all manner of books
was granted by
Henry VIII in 1534.
The University has printed
and published continuously
since 1584.

Cambridge University Press

Cambridge

New York Port Chester

Melbourne Sydney

HOUSTON PUBLIC LIBRARY

Published by the Press Syndicate of the University of Cambridge
The Pitt Building, Trumpington Street, Cambridge CB2 1RP
40 West 20th Street, New York, NY 10011, USA
10 Stamford Road, Oakleigh, Melbourne 3166, Australia

© Cambridge University Press 1991

First published 1991

Printed in Great Britain at the University Press, Cambridge

A catalogue record for this book is available from the British Library

Library of Congress cataloguing in publication data applied for

ISBN 0 521 24696 2 hardback

For Chloë and Edward: *vive la différence!*

Contents

Preface

Natural language and universal grammar is the first of two volumes with the common subtitle *Essays in linguistic theory* (henceforth *Essays*). Volume II, entitled *Semantics, subjectivity and localism*, will be published shortly.

The title that I have given to *Essays I* is not as innocent as it might appear to be at first sight; and there are those of my colleagues who might see it as being almost wilfully provocative. One of my general aims, in bringing the various chapters of *Essays* together, is to demonstrate that the expressions 'natural language' and 'universal grammar' are often employed nowadays loosely and uncritically (if not equivocally) in the case of the former and tendentiously in the case of the latter. What is (or, in my view, ought to be) meant by linguists when they use the highly ambiguous phrase 'natural language' (either generically or non-generically) is a question that is directly addressed in Chapter 4 of *Essays I*. All the chapters in both volumes are concerned with the structure of what are normally, but imprecisely, referred to as natural languages. Almost all of them, also, are concerned with (so-called) natural languages within the framework of what would be referred to traditionally as universal grammar. But, as I explain in Chapter 7 of *Essays I* (and, in greater detail, in one or two of the chapters in *Essays II*), my view of universal grammar differs from the generativist or Chomskyan view, which currently holds sway in linguistic theory and is propagated (all too often uncritically) in many textbooks. What is (or ought to be) meant by 'linguistic theory' (in contrast with 'theoretical linguistics') is discussed in some detail in Chapter 2 of *Essays I*.

Of the nine chapters in *Essays I*, three (Chapters 2, 3 and 4) have not been published before (though Chapter 2 incorporates a revised version of part of an earlier article) and have been written up in such a way that they are interrelated both with one another and with some of the previously unpublished chapters of *Essays II*. My guiding principle in writing them up in their present form has been to set forth a particular view of linguistics and linguistic theory which informs most, if not all, of the other chapters in both volumes.

The view of linguistics and linguistic theory that I currently hold is one which, in its essentials, I have held (and have not yet seen good reason to change) ever since I came into linguistics in the mid-1950s. My earlier training had been in classics (and historical and comparative philology). When I became familiar with Chomskyan generative grammar in 1957, I immediately integrated it, on the one hand, with traditional grammar and, on the other, with a rather eclectic blend of European and American structuralism. I did not realize, when I wrote some of my earlier articles and, more particularly, my book *Introduction to Theoretical Linguistics* (1968), that my view of the relation between traditional grammar and generative grammar and between structuralism and generative grammar was very much a minority view and one that was not shared by Chomsky and most of his followers. (Generative grammar was still relatively new and not always well understood, even by linguists.) That there was this difference between my view of generative grammar and the view of many other linguists did not become clear to me until the late 1960s or the very early 1970s, when Chomskyan generative grammar had come to be much more definitely associated with cognitive psychology and a particular kind of universalism than it had been previously. I now find it necessary to draw a distinction between generative grammar, properly so called, to which (as I explain in Chapters 2 and 3 of *Essays I*) I am as fully committed now as I have been since 1957, and generativism, about much of which, including its cognitivism and its notion of universal grammar, I am professionally, and I think properly, agnostic. But my agnosticism, unlike that of many critics, has nothing to do with the philosophical or psychological plausibility of generativism. For me, this is irrelevant. Taken on its own terms, Chomskyan generativism seems to me to be eminently defensible (even if much of the detailed empirical argument associated with it is not). But, in my view, linguistic theory should not be constrained by generativist assumptions: it should be concerned with a broader range of languages (natural and non-natural) and it should cover a much wider range of data.

Of the six previously published articles which are now being republished in *Essays I*, some have been left more or less unchanged (except for the notes), whilst others have been extensively revised. Two of them, which have been widely quoted in textbooks and monographs and have appeared in whole or in part in readers and anthologies (Chapters 6 and 7), could not be revised, I felt, without causing confusion. I have therefore reprinted them without changing them at all, as far as the text is concerned; but I have provided them with an Epilogue (and with very full notes) which contextualizes them historically and, for what it is worth, gives my own assessment of their content. Whenever I have made significant changes in the text of one of the republished articles, I have then changed its title; and, generally speaking, the degree of difference between the old and the new title reflects the degree of change that I have introduced into the text. In all cases the provenance of each chapter, whether it derives from a previously published article or not, is given in the accompanying notes.

This work has been several years in preparation, its publication having been delayed, initially by the pressures of administrative work and subsequently by recurrent ill-health. Also, the task of bringing together and editing a set of previously published articles has turned out to be more difficult than I had originally envisaged – far more difficult than writing a completely new book from scratch – and this has further delayed publication.

The delay in publication has had several consequences (not all of them detrimental, I think, to the final product). The first is that, in several other publications over the years, I have referred to *Essays in Linguistic Theory* as 'forthcoming', and, on occasion, have even provided it, in references, with a year of publication. For this I apologize.

The second consequence – for which I should perhaps also apologize – is that it has now become a two-volume work and includes several previously unpublished chapters which I had not originally intended to write up for publication, in their present form at least.

The third results from the development, in the intervening years, of a much greater interest on the part of linguists and historians of ideas in the recent history of linguistics and, more particularly, of one or two of the movements with which I happen to have been associated in the 1960s and 1970s. For this reason I have now greatly expanded the notes that I have added to the relevant chapters and have made them rather more personal and autobiographical than I would have done otherwise. For the same reason I have republished, as an Appendix, the text of my 1965 Inaugural Lecture at the University of Edinburgh and have provided it with very full explanatory notes: I trust that my erstwhile colleagues at Edinburgh, now as then, one of the major centres of linguistic theory in Great Britain, will find my personal account of the local history acceptable.

The fact that *Essays I* contains (in addition to the previously unpublished chapters written especially for the purpose) republished articles of varied provenance means that there is a certain amount of stylistic and terminological inconsistency. It would have been impossible to eliminate this entirely, even if I had felt free to make anachronistic and historically irresponsible changes in the text of previously published and widely quoted articles. Whenever it has seemed important or helpful to draw the attention of readers to potentially confusing differences of terminology and notation, I have done so in the notes.

One of the stylistic consequences of my decision not to introduce any changes into the text of previously published and widely quoted articles is that I have not been able to eliminate from such articles in their republished form the use of the pronoun 'he' for sex-neutral (and gender-neutral) indefinite and generic reference, which was of course until recently normal usage. I trust that I shall be forgiven by those of my readers who find this usage stylistically awkward or offensive. I have done my best to avoid it (with the sharp-eyed assistance of my Cambridge University Press sub-editor) in all the newly written or rewritten passages, even though in doing so I have occasionally had to introduce a stylistically or semantically undesirable disjunction or to replace a true generic with a somewhat less precise plural. But even the most pedantic of semanticists must concede that a contextually acceptable degree of imprecision or ambiguity is preferable to what has now become an unacceptable degree of linguistic discourtesy.

It is impossible for me to list here all the colleagues, friends and students who have influenced my views on linguistics, directly or indirectly, over the years. I hope that I have made sufficient acknowledgement of their influence in the notes and references and that they will accept that here I can do no more than thank them collectively for all that they have taught me (sometimes perhaps without realizing it). I must also thank Cambridge University Press for their willingness to publish a very different book from the one that I was expected to produce and for the encouragement and guidance that I have received from the editors with whom I have worked, intermittently, for the last ten years or so: Jeremy Mynott, Penny Carter, Marion Smith, Judith Ayling and Julia Harding. I would also like to thank Maureen Elvin, my secretary, who typed the newly written articles. Finally, I must record my gratitude, once again, to my wife and family for their continued love and support, making particular mention of my grandchildren, Chloë and Edward, who do not yet appreciate how much I have learned from them about language.

Cambridge,   J.L.
November 1990

xiv

Typographical conventions

The following conventions have been used throughout the present volume, except in the case of previously published and widely quoted articles (see Preface).

Italics

1 For forms (as distinct from expressions, including lexemes) in their orthographic representation.
2 For utterances (as distinct from sentences).
3 For certain mathematical and logical symbols, according to standard conventions.

Single quotation-marks

1 For expressions (including lexemes) in their citation-form.
2 For sentences (except when they are displayed: see note 2 below).
3 For titles of articles and chapters.

Double quotation-marks

1 For meanings.
2 For propositions.
3 For quotations.

Notes

1 Single quotation-marks are omitted when a sentence (or other expression) is displayed and set on a different line; but italics and double quotation-marks are still used in such circumstances.
2 In quotations, the original typographical conventions have usually been preserved. Occasional adjustments have been made in order to avoid confusion or ambiguity.

I

Language, speech and writing

What I am concerned with in this chapter is not language in the most general sense of the term 'language' but with what can be described more fully as natural human language.[1] Arguably, this fuller description is redundant in respect of either or both of the two adjectives, 'natural' and 'human'. Indeed, this is the view that most linguists and many philosophers of language would take. But it is worth making the point explicit and concentrating for a moment upon the implications of both of the qualifying adjectives, without prejudice to the question of whether there is any language, properly so called, that is non-natural or non-human.

Without dwelling upon the details let us say that a natural language is one that has not been specially constructed, whether for general or specific purposes, and is acquired by its users without special instruction as a normal part of the process of maturation and socialization. In terms of this rough-and-ready operational definition, there are some thousands of distinct natural human languages used in the world today, including English, Quechua, Dyirbal, Yoruba and Malayalam – to list just a few, each of which is representative, in various ways, of hundreds or thousands of others. But Esperanto, on the one hand, and first-order predicate calculus or computer languages such as ALGOL, FORTRAN and BASIC, on the other, are non-natural. Many non-natural languages are parasitic, to a greater or less extent, upon pre-existing natural languages. This being so, though non-natural, they are not necessarily unnatural; they may be comparable, structurally and perhaps also functionally, with the natural languages from which they derive and upon which, arguably, they are parasitic. I say 'arguably', not only because the point, as I have put it, is debatable, but also because by putting it in this way I am hinting at a deeper and theoretically more interesting sense of 'natural', and of its contrary 'unnatural', than my operational definition of 'natural language' requires.

It has been argued, notably by Chomsky, that languages that meet my operational, and intuitively applicable, definition of 'natural' do so, not simply as a matter of historical contingency, but by virtue of biological necessity: that natural human languages are structurally adapted to the psychological nature of man; and that if they were not so adapted, they could not be acquired, as I have said they are, without special instruction as an integral and normal part of the process of maturation and socialization. The question of whether natural human languages as we know them are also natural in this deeper sense (which I distinguish from other senses of 'natural' in Chapter 4 below) is of course philosophically controversial. I am not concerned with this question as such. It suffices for my present purpose that Chomsky and others inspired by his work, philosophers and psychologists, have provided a serious defence of innatism (or nativism).[2]

Granted that it is appropriate to use the term 'language' to refer to a wide range of communicative and symbolic systems employed by animals and machines, we can proceed to distinguish human from non-human languages. And this distinction can be drawn in various ways: we can define human languages as languages that are actually used by human beings; as languages that could be used by human beings (with what is meant by *could* spelt out); as languages that are normally or naturally (in one or other sense of 'naturally') used by human beings and so on. For present purposes, the following operational definition will suffice: a human language is one that is attested as being used (or as having been used in the past) by human beings; and a non-human language is one that is (or has been) used by any non-human being (either an animal or a machine). This definition leaves open the possibility that the intersection of the two sub-classes of languages thus distinguished is non-empty; i.e., that there are languages which are both human and non-human. It also presupposes, of course, that we have some way of identifying human beings that does not make the possession of language criterial in their identification. It would not do for us to adopt Schleicher's (1863) attitude: "If a pig were to say to me 'I am a pig', it would *ipso facto* cease to be a pig."[3]

As with the distinction between natural and non-natural languages, so too with the distinction between human and non-human languages, as I have just drawn it; it can be argued that human languages share a number of structural properties, or design characteristics, that set them off as a class from the languages of other species, so that it is legitimate to talk not only of human languages, but also of human language in the singular. It is by coupling the two predicates 'natural' and 'human' and giving to each its deeper sense that we arrive of course at the characteristically Chomskyan thesis of innatism. As Chomsky put it in his *Reflections on Language*: "A

2

human language is a system of remarkable complexity. To come to know a human language would be an extraordinary intellectual achievement for a creature not specifically designed to accomplish this task. A normal child acquires this knowledge on relatively slight exposure and without specific training" (1976: 4).

It is an obvious, but none the less important, fact that one cannot possess or use language (henceforth I shall restrict the term 'language' to natural human language) without possessing or using some particular language – English, Quechua, Dyirbal, Yoruba, Malayalam, or whatever. Each of these differs systematically from the others, so that, due allowance being made for the well-known problems of drawing a sharp distinction between languages and dialects, styles or registers, we can usually determine that someone is using one language rather than another on particular occasions.[4] We do this, whether as investigating linguists or as participating interlocutors, by observing and analysing, not the language-behaviour itself, but the products of that behaviour – strings of words and phrases inscribed (in a technical sense of 'inscribe') in some appropriate physical medium. But the language, for the linguist at least, is neither the behaviour nor the products of that behaviour, both of which are subsumed under the ambiguous English word 'utterance'.[5] What the linguist is interested in is the language-system: the underlying, abstract, system of entities and rules by virtue of which particular language-inscriptions can be identified as tokens of the same type or distinguished as tokens of different types;[6] can be parsed (to use the traditional term) or (in Chomskyan terminology) assigned an appropriate structural description; and can be interpreted in terms of the meaning of the constituent expressions, of the grammatical structure of the sentences that have been uttered, and of the relevant contextual factors.

We may distinguish the language-system, then, on the one hand from language-behaviour of a particular kind and on the other from language-inscriptions. The latter, together with native speakers' intuitions of grammaticality and acceptability, of sameness and difference of meaning, and so on, constitute the linguist's data; but they are not the object of linguistic theory or linguistic description. The linguist, I repeat, is interested in language-systems; and this is true not only in microlinguistics but also in the several branches of macrolinguistics (see Chapter 2).

And when linguists come to describe language-systems, whether they subscribe to the aims of generative grammar or not, they do so by drawing a distinction between phonology and syntax and by making reference, in the description of both, as also in the account that they give of the meaning of sentences, to the information that is stored in the lexicon, or dictionary. The

3

term 'grammar' is commonly used nowadays to cover the rules of phonology, syntax and semantics, but not the lexicon. Taking 'grammar' in this sense, we can say that a language-system comprises both a grammar and a lexicon, and that each presupposes the other. The lexicon is a list of expressions, every one of which has one or more forms, belongs to a particular syntactic (or morphosyntactic) category, and has one or more meanings;[7] the rules of the grammar cannot operate otherwise than upon the expressions supplied by the lexicon and the phonological, syntactic and semantic information associated with them in individual lexical entries. (Under a rather broader interpretation of 'grammar', the term may be held to cover not only the phonological, syntactic and semantic rules of a language-system, but also the lexicon. Nothing of consequence hangs upon this particular point of terminology, unless the difference of usage is deliberately associated with a difference of view on the boundary between grammar and lexicon.)

We can now move on to consider Chomsky's distinction between competence and performance in relation to the other terminological and conceptual distinctions that have been drawn so far. Performance can be identified, without difficulty, with what I have called language-behaviour. It can thus be distinguished, in the same way, both from the products of that behaviour, language-inscriptions, and from the underlying language-system. But what is linguistic competence? At one level this question, too, can be answered without difficulty. One's linguistic competence is one's knowledge of a particular language-system: that is to say, one's knowledge of an interdependent grammar and vocabulary.

When it comes to developing this notion of linguistic competence in greater detail and giving it empirical content, the question gets more complicated and correspondingly more interesting. Here I will simply make the point that, although Chomsky recognizes the logical validity of the distinction between a language-system and someone's knowledge of the system (whether that someone is an actual or an ideal user of the system), he maintains that the distinction can, for theoretical purposes, be ignored. He has therefore tended to use the term 'grammar' with what he calls systematic ambiguity: to refer indifferently to both the rules of the language and the ideal user's knowledge of the rules. For Chomsky, it would appear, the only kind of reality that can be ascribed to grammars and to natural human languages is psychological reality. It is for this reason that he takes the view that linguistics is a branch of cognitive psychology. But Chomsky differs from many others who are working towards psychologically real grammars in that he pays relatively little attention to what is otherwise

4

known or hypothesized of psychological processes. He does not believe that performance shapes competence, and his notion of psychological reality is considerably more abstract than that of most psychologists.

I now wish to make explicit the distinction, which has been implicit in everything that I have said so far, between a language and the medium in which that language is manifest. It is in terms of this distinction that I propose to discuss the relation between language and speech. 'Medium' in this sense is connected, on the one hand, with the information-theorist's notion of the channel of communication and, on the other, with the psychologist's notion of input and output modalities (in a sense of 'modality' which has nothing to do with its more usual specialized sense in linguistics and philosophy[8]).

Spoken language is manifest, normally, in what I shall refer to as the phonic medium: that is, the products of speech are signals, actual or potential, inscribed in the physical medium of sound. More precisely, they are inscribed (in this technical sense of 'inscribe') in the range of sound produced by the human voice – hence the term 'phonic'. Written language, on the other hand, is normally inscribed in what may be referred to as a graphic medium: anything that will sustain the requisite distinctions of shape. It is possible for spoken language to be written, and conversely for written language to be spoken. In the present context, we can safely neglect these additional complexities. It is worth noting, however, that by virtue of this possibility the term 'spoken language' is used in various senses, and at times perhaps is used equivocally, in linguistics (see Addendum below).

The main reason why we have to draw the distinction between language and medium is that human languages, as we know them in modern literate societies, are very largely independent of the medium in which they are manifest. As far as their syntactic and lexical structure are concerned, they are, in principle, completely independent: any spoken language-inscription can be converted – transcribed – into a corresponding written language-inscription in the same language, and vice versa. To the extent that written and spoken language-inscriptions are interconvertible in this way, we can say that they have the property of medium-transferability. In practice, medium-transferability is reduced in all the major languages of the world (though less in English than in many others) by virtue of the conservatism of scribal traditions, the greater standardization of the written language and its association with more formal or more official situations, and other such historically and culturally identifiable factors.[9] Although the consequential lack of isomorphism at the syntactic and lexical levels may have important implications for the design of certain psycholinguistic experiments, I will

5

not dwell upon this aspect of medium-transferability. There are other points to which I want to give a more particular emphasis.

The first is that the medium-transferability of language is far from complete, even in principle, in respect of what is handled for spoken language by phonology. Some writing systems, of course, are based on the ideographic or logographic principle, so that for them the question of isomorphism does not even arise at this level.[10] The very existence of such written languages, of which Chinese is the most notable example, demonstrates that language-systems can be isomorphic in syntax and semantics, and yet be quite different as far as their segmental phonological structure is concerned. It demonstrates, therefore, that segmental phonology and syntax are independent of one another, in a way that syntax and semantics are not.[11] Of greater importance for the moment, however, is the fact that there is more to the phonological structure of spoken language-inscriptions than the strings of consonants and vowels of which their constituent word-forms are constructed. My earlier characterization of utterance-inscriptions as strings of forms inscribed in some physical medium was incomplete for spoken language. Superimposed upon the string of word-forms there will be an intonation pattern, which will usually be integrated with the syntactic structure of the language-inscription and will also be relevant to its semantic interpretation. None of the world's writing systems preserves the suprasegmental intonation-contour, in the transcription of speech from the phonic to the graphic medium.[12]

Also, there is more to speech than is covered by segmental or non-segmental phonology; and therefore, according to standard assumptions, by the grammar of the language that one is speaking. In addition to the suprasegmental intonation-contour of any spoken utterance-inscription, there will be a variety of other suprasegmental features commonly described as paralinguistic – such features as significant variations of loudness, rhythm and tempo. The speaker therefore has to superimpose upon the verbal component of his utterance-inscription two analytically distinguishable non-segmental components, one of which, by common consent, is linguistic and the other of which is not.[13]

Where has all this been taking us? My main purpose, in this chapter, is simply to introduce a number of conceptual distinctions that are relevant to issues that arise in current discussions of the psychological mechanisms of language. I shall now apply the distinction between language and medium very briefly to three such issues.

The first has to do with the putative naturalness of the association between language and speech. Now, there is a clear sense in which

6

language is indeed naturally associated with speech. Spoken languages satisfy the operational definition of naturalness that I gave earlier: they are acquired without special instruction as a normal part of the process of maturation and socialization. This is not true of written languages. But is speech natural to man in the deeper sense that we also identified earlier? There is evidence to suggest that children are biologically equipped not merely to vocalize, in the sense in which this term is customarily employed, but to produce and recognize particular classes of speech-sounds (cf. Mehler, 1981; C. J. Darwin, 1987). If we also grant, for the sake of the argument, that the syntactic and semantic structure of human languages is narrowly constrained by a species-specific, innate, language-faculty, as Chomsky has argued, we might seem to be justified in concluding that it is spoken language as such, if not the whole of speech, that is innately determined by the principles of universal grammar.

On present evidence, this would be a hasty conclusion to draw. In my view, it is quite possible that the language-faculty and the predisposition to vocalize are biologically independent and only contingently associated in speech. The graphic medium, though non-natural, is clearly not unnatural with respect to the medium-transferable verbal component. Having learned to read and write, we do so without difficulty and, apparently, without needing to transcribe to or from the phonic medium at the time of reading or writing. Furthermore, there are various reasons for saying that the medium-transferable part of language-inscriptions is more characteristically linguistic than the non-verbal, suprasegmental, part (cf. Lyons, 1977a: 70–94). It is in any case quite clear that the process of speaking, in so far as it involves the integration of the verbal and the non-verbal components of language-utterances, makes use of rather different psychological mechanisms. It has also been suggested that the control of what I have called the more linguistic, medium-transferable, part of speech and of the less linguistic part, which is not so readily transcribed from one medium to another, is localized in different parts of the brain.

I have just drawn attention to the possible biological independence of language and speech; and I have implied that this is not only a logical, but also an empirical, possibility. I should perhaps add that many would say that recent research on the origins of language, on the one hand, and of sign languages of the deaf, on the other, convert what I have here cautiously described as a possibility into a probability (cf. Hewes, 1973; Siple, 1978; Klima & Bellugi, 1979; Marshall, 1980; Deuchar, 1984). Sign languages, such as ASL (American Sign Language) and BSL (British Sign Language), are certainly natural in the sense of the "rough-and-ready operational definition" of 'natural' that I gave earlier (if not in all senses of the term); they are not only not isomorphic with known spoken languages (despite what has frequently been said about them in the past), but they are not parasitic upon, and cannot always be traced back historically to, particular spoken languages; and yet they are comparable, both structurally and functionally, with such languages (cf. Deuchar, 1984: 18–25). But whether they are natural or not in all relevant senses of the term, it would be absurd to deny them the status of languages by metatheoretical fiat, simply because they do not fall into the category of what linguists think of as prototypical, or ordinary, languages. I will return to this question in later chapters of this book. In the present context, I would merely emphasize that, even if our main concern, as theoreticians, is with psycholinguistics (and for me 'psycholinguistics' covers the investigation of both competence and performance in the Chomskyan sense: see Chapter 3), it is important not to assume that the association between language and speech is essential, rather than contingent.

The second issue is that of linearization (cf. Levelt, 1981). The structure of spoken utterance-inscriptions is partly linear and partly non-linear. It is non-linear, as we have just seen, with regard to their non-verbal component. It is linear, however, as far as their verbal component is concerned: the words must be in one sequential order rather than another.[14] Is this linearity a property of language or of speech? Here I would simply point out that languages vary considerably in the grammatical and stylistic use that they make of word-order. This cannot but be of relevance to the construction of models for on-line speech-processing. And it is arguable that the factors that determine the linearization of spoken language-utterances have operated, historically, to fix the word-order of sentences in some, but not all, languages. If this is so, it would be another way in which performance shapes competence (cf. J. D. Fodor, 1981).[15]

Granted that sentences, as distinct from utterance-inscriptions, may have a non-linear structure, at what point in the production of speech are they linearized? Indeed, is it psychologically plausible to suppose that there is some stage in speech-production at which medium-independent sentences are constructed, before their linearization for utterance and the superimposition upon them of an appropriate intonation pattern?[16] These are questions which I raise without even attempting an answer and which, not being a psychologist, I could not begin to answer. I raise them in the present context because I have the impression that scholars from other disciplines frequently take over from linguistics notions such as 'word', 'sentence', etc., and certain assumptions about them, without realizing how unclear these

8

notions sometimes are. It is incumbent upon linguists taking part in interdisciplinary discussion to bring to the attention of their collaborators from other disciplines the fact that many of the technical and semi-technical terms and concepts of linguistics are far from being as well defined as they are commonly thought to be. For what it is worth, my own feeling is that sentences (in the sense of system-sentences: cf. Lyons, 1977a: 29; 1981b; 196) play no role at all in the on-line, real-time production or reception of speech, but are artefacts of the linguists' idealization of their data (see Chapter 3 below).

Finally, at the risk of rushing in where angels fear to tread, let me say something about language and speech in relation to the organization of the mental lexicon. As we have seen, the language-system comprises a grammar and a lexicon. To say that someone knows a language is to say that he or she has internalized both its grammar and its lexicon: that they are stored in long-term memory, so that they can be accessed during the production and reception of language-utterances. Linguists usually take the view that phonology is an integral part of the language-system and that the phonological representation of a lexical item is essential to it in a way that its orthographic representation is not. It follows from this assumption that words and phrases should be more directly accessible in spoken form than they are in written form, during normal language-processing and also in psycholinguistic experiments. At the very least, we should be suspicious of this interpretation of the principle of the priority of spoken language. If the argument that I am developing here is accepted, we should be prepared to consider the possibility that words and phrases are stored in the mental lexicon in a medium-independent form, so that they can be accessed equally well in either their phonological or their orthographic representation. It is, of course, an empirical question – to be resolved not by linguistics but by psychology and neurophysiology – whether this possibility is actualized in any or all of us.[17]

Addendum

In the original version of the paper reprinted (with certain changes of wording) above I noted that "the term 'spoken language' is used in various senses, and at times perhaps is used equivocally, in linguistics". There are, in fact, at least three senses, which must be kept apart, if we are to avoid confusion in theorizing about language. Two of them can be readily distinguished by drawing upon the related, but theoretically distinct, notions of channel and medium. A spoken language, in the first sense, can

9

be defined as a particular language-system which, as far as what is sometimes called its cenematic structure is concerned, results from the imposition of a particular form or structure, upon the phonic (rather than, for example, the graphic) medium: i.e., it is phonologically (rather than, for example, orthographically) structured.[18] A spoken language, thus defined, can of course be transmitted in either speech or writing: i.e., it can be transmitted phonically or graphically (or, indeed, in indefinitely many ways, but we do not need to go into this question in detail in order to establish the main point that is being made here). A spoken language, in the second sense of 'spoken', is the product of speech: i.e., of the transmission of language-signals along the vocal–auditory channel. It follows from what has just been said that Spoken English in the first sense is what Saussure would have called a 'langue' (and in this sense the qualifying adjective 'spoken' merits an initial capital-letter), whereas spoken English in the second sense is what Saussure called 'parole'.

The first two senses of the term 'spoken' are, in principle, easy enough to distinguish, and they are more or less well recognized as distinct.[19] There is, however, yet a third sense of the term 'spoken language' which has recently been introduced into the literature and which threatens to confuse yet further an already confused discussion of the nature of language. This third sense can be glossed, roughly, as "language which is normally/ naturally/primarily manifest as speech". Spoken languages, in this third sense, are contrasted not with, for example, written languages, but rather with gestural sign-languages, such as ASL or BSL (cf. Deuchar, 1987b). It requires but little reflection to see that the term 'spoken' is wholly inappropriate in this usage, since languages of the class to which it applies, as I have insisted above, have (to a considerable degree and as far as their pleerematic structure is concerned) a high degree of isomorphism. When we contrast 'Spoken English', in this third sense, with, let us say, ASL, we are operating at a higher level of abstraction than when we are opposing Spoken English (in the first sense of 'spoken') to, for example, Written English.

The point that has just been made is but one of many that could and should be made in a fuller discussion of the distinction between language and speech, on the one hand, and between written and spoken languages, on the other. I have said nothing at all, for example, about the historical impact of the invention of writing: of its role in the development of particular concepts of literacy and literal meaning; of its effect upon linguistic theory; and so on.[20] My main purpose has been to emphasize the importance for linguistic theory of drawing a distinction between languages as abstract systems and their physical manifestations in speech, writing or whatever. The distinction in question is, of course, familiar enough as Saussure's 'langue' vs. 'parole', Hjelmslev's 'system' vs. 'process', Chomsky's 'competence' vs. 'performance', etc. But none of these terminological dichotomies as it stands will support the weight that it has been called upon to bear in late-twentieth-century linguistic theory; and each of them emphasizes a different aspect of the distinction between language-systems and their physical manifestations. The most striking inadequacy perhaps of all three of the terminological dichotomies that I have just referred to is their failure to give due recognition to the further distinction, within what is called 'parole', process or performance, between language-activity (physical and mental) and the physical products of that activity: between what I have elsewhere called utterance-acts and utterance-inscriptions (or utterance-signals: cf. Lyons, 1977a, 1981b). This latter distinction is obscured by the process/product ambiguity of the English word 'utterance' (see notes 5 and 6 above).

A secondary aim of the chapter has been to challenge the assumption that the association between speech and language is natural (in the fullest or deepest sense of this term: see Chapter 4). This assumption has reigned unchallenged for far too long, not only in linguistics but also in the philosophy of language (not to mention both ancient and modern speculations about the origin of language: see Chapter 5). We need not go all the way with Derrida (1967, 1972) when he criticizes what he calls the phonocentrism (or logocentrism) of Western thought. But, as linguists reflecting upon the history and present state of our discipline, we cannot but be struck by the almost universal acceptance of what might also be called phonocentrism (if not logocentrism) in twentieth-century linguistics: i.e., the identification of language and speech.[21]

2

In defence of (so-called) autonomous linguistics

I will begin, if I may, with a quotation from one of my own works:[1]

One topic that commonly finds a place in discussions of the status of linguistics as a science (or has done until recently) is its 'autonomy', its independence of other disciplines. Linguists have tended to be somewhat insistent on the need for autonomy because they have felt that in the past the study of language was usually subservient to (and distorted by) the standards of other studies such as logic, philosophy and literary criticism. For this reason the editors of Saussure's posthumous *Cours de linguistique générale* (the publication of which is often taken to mark the beginning of 'modern linguistics') added to the text of the master its programmatic concluding sentence, to the effect that linguistics should study language 'for its own sake' or 'as an end in itself' [Saussure, 1916].[2]

The above quotation comes from the editorial Introduction which I wrote for *New Horizons in Linguistics 1* some twenty years ago (Lyons, 1970a: 8). When I came to rewrite this Introduction, more recently, for *New Horizons in Linguistics 2*, I noted that, even when the earlier volume was being written, "there were many linguists who felt that the principle of 'autonomy' had outlived its usefulness"; and that "this feeling is probably more widespread today than it was then" (Lyons, 1987b: 4–5). The fact that nowadays linguists tend to be less inclined to emphasize the *sui generis* nature of language and correspondingly less eager to assert, as a corollary, the independence and hermetic self-sufficiency of linguistics is, on the whole, very much to be welcomed. Apart from anything else, coupled as it is with a reduced insistence on the scientific status of the subject, it is indicative of a greater self-confidence, of a more firmly grounded conviction on the part of linguists of the academic respectability of their subject. And there is little doubt that linguistics is academically more respectable now than it was a generation ago. It has benefited, in this respect, first of all and especially in Europe, from the popularity of structuralism, with both anthropologists and literary critics vying with one another to proclaim their indebtedness to Saussure, and then, throughout the world, from the extraordinary impact that Chomskyan generativism has had on a whole range of disciplines, including philosophy and psychology.

It is also very much to be welcomed that linguists should be working with representatives of other disciplines towards "the incorporation of the theory of language into a more embracing synthesis of science and philosophy" (Lyons, 1970a: 9). There are none the less occasions when it is incumbent upon linguists, especially when they are engaged in these interdisciplinary endeavours, to affirm the continued validity of the Saussurean (or post-Saussurean) principle of 'autonomy', properly interpreted and properly understood.[3] And there have been such occasions when I have found myself defending views on language and linguistics which many of my colleagues might indeed regard as outdated and narrow-minded. They are views that I have held for a long time and have written about in various books and articles, supporting them with a battery of technical distinctions, some generally accepted by my fellow-linguists, others more idiosyncratic. Let me begin then by saying, somewhat provocatively perhaps, that I know of nothing that has happened in linguistics in the last twenty or thirty years to make these views, which I formed, under the influence of my teachers, in the late 1950s, less defensible now than they were then; and I make this statement in full cognizance of the fact that an enormous amount of work has been done, particularly by sociolinguists, which has demonstrated that there is no such thing as a homogeneous, Saussurean, language-system for proponents of (so-called) autonomous linguistics to study.

I, for my part, have never believed that there was. Recent empirical research in sociolinguistics, ethnolinguistics and psycholinguistics has greatly improved our knowledge of the details of synchronic variation in many language-communities throughout the world. But in confirming the fact of synchronic variation, systematic and random, it has done no more than confirm what has long been obvious to most linguists anyway. What is at issue, as I have argued elsewhere, is not the factual question whether there is or is not such a thing as a uniform, or homogeneous, language-system underlying the language-behaviour (or, more precisely, the products of the language-behaviour) of a given (so-called) language-community: we can readily agree that there is not (Lyons, 1977a: 585ff.; 1981a: 24ff.). What is at issue, rather, is the methodological, or meta-theoretical, question whether it is none the less legitimate, at times and for clearly stated purposes, to discount, or abstract from, the variation that undoubtedly exists in any language-community and to postulate the existence of "some kind of [idealized] overall system underlying those utterances which most members of the language-community would accept as being relatively neutral with respect to minor differences of dialect, situation, medium and chronological period" (Lyons, 1977a: 588). And I see no reason to give a different answer to this question from the answer that I have given on other occasions. It might be helpful, however, if I elaborate the answer somewhat differently and make explicit one or two points that have perhaps not been made sufficiently clear in previous publications.

But before proceeding, I should first of all emphasize that (as will, I think, be evident from other publications of mine) my defence of what I have been calling autonomous linguistics in no way implies a lack of interest in what, by contrast, may be referred to as non-autonomous linguistics, of which sociolinguistics and ethnolinguistics (or anthropological linguistics), on the one hand, and psycholinguistics, on the other, are subparts. I would be the last to deny the importance of the contribution that sociolinguistics, ethnolinguistics and psycholinguistics – not to mention stylistics, neuro-linguistics, etc. – can make, and are making, to the construction of a comprehensive theory of the structure and functions of language. And at this point, I should like to invoke the distinction between microlinguistics and macrolinguistics and, having drawn this distinction, to restrict the scope of the principle of autonomy to the former.[4] I would not wish to put myself in the absurd position of defending, or appearing to defend, the view that any of the several branches of macrolinguistics is, or should be, independent of cognate disciplines: I do not believe that psycholinguistics should take no account of the findings of psychology, that sociolinguistics should be similarly independent of sociology, and so on. Nor am I implying that these several branches of macrolinguistics are less important or less worthy of consideration than what I am calling microlinguistics.

A further point to be emphasized in this connection is the importance of not confusing or conflating the distinction between microlinguistics and macrolinguistics with the distinction between theoretical and applied linguistics. What is, or might be, meant by the term 'theoretical linguistics' will be dealt with in Chapter 3. Here it is sufficient to note that, in linguistics as in other disciplines, 'theoretical' enters into two rather different oppositions: (i) 'theoretical' vs. 'experimental/descriptive' and (ii) 'theoret-ical' vs. 'applied'.[5] Both of these oppositions are as relevant to the different branches of macrolinguistics as they are to microlinguistics; and there is, or ought to be, a theoretical sub-branch of ethnolinguistics, sociolinguistics, psycholinguistics, etc., just as there is a theoretical sub-branch of micro-linguistics. Chomskyan generativism, for example, being directed towards an understanding of linguistic competence, is in my view a sub-branch of theoretical psycholinguistics and, as such, is to be distinguished from theoretical microlinguistics as I have defined it. The fact that Chomsky himself does not describe what he is doing as psycholinguistics (and makes little or no reference to current psychological theories) does not invalidate what I have just said.[6] And the fact that many scholars, both linguists and non-linguists alike, nowadays associate the term 'autonomous linguistics' with Chomskyan generativism, rather than with Saussurean (or post-Saussurean) structuralism, should not be allowed to obscure the issues. Chomskyan generativism is, in intent if not in practice, a particular version of autonomous psycholinguistics, which I, for one, have no wish to defend (cf. Lyons, 1981a: 228ff.).

The question whether what I am calling microlinguistics is, or should be, independent of the several branches of macrolinguistics and of other disciplines – whether microlinguistics is, or ought to be, autonomous (in this sense of the term) – immediately gives rise to two further questions:

(1) Why should it be autonomous?
(2) How can it be autonomous?

And the *why*-question, to take this first, splits into, or presupposes the answer to, a variety of sub-questions, two of which are relevant to our present concerns, in that they bring into sharper focus the principal objections that have been made to the point of view that I am defending:

(1a) Is autonomous linguistics possible?
(1b) Is autonomous linguistics desirable?

These two sub-questions are, of course, logically independent of one another. To answer yes or no to either still leaves open the possibility of giving an affirmative or negative reply to the other.

Whether synchronic descriptive microlinguistics is possible – and I take it that this, more precisely formulated, is the question with which we are really concerned – cannot be answered sensibly without first addressing the question of the relative adequacy of alternative, non-equivalent, descriptions of the same language. It was Chomsky, in his earliest work, who first made explicit for theoretical linguistics the full implications of the fact that indefinitely many non-equivalent grammars can be written for any given language. And this, I would emphasize, is indeed a fact. Its truth is unaffected by criticisms that might be rightly made of Chomsky's definition of a language as a set of sentences and of a sentence as a string of forms. If sentences are defined – as any traditionally minded grammarian with sufficient control of the terminology of modern structural linguistics would define them – as structured syntagms, rather than as unstructured strings, the applicability of Chomsky's distinction between what he called weak and strong equivalence to the grammatical analysis of natural languages is much reduced, but the distinction itself loses none of its theoretical validity for all that: two grammars are weakly equivalent if they generate exactly the same set of sentences and they are strongly equivalent if, in addition to generating the same set of sentences, they assign to each sentence the same structural description.[7]

Comparable with this distinction between weak and strong equivalence is the distinction between weak and strong adequacy: a weakly adequate grammar will be one which generates the set of sentences it is intended to generate and a strongly adequate grammar will be one which, in addition to being weakly adequate, assigns to each sentence that it generates the correct (or, less controversially, the best) structural description. Subsequently, in *Aspects of the Theory of Syntax*, Chomsky tackled the question of adequacy in somewhat different terms: in terms of what he referred to as the three levels of observational, descriptive and explanatory adequacy (1965: 24ff.).

The terms in which Chomsky himself fomulated these three levels at which alternative grammars of the same language could be evaluated, at least in principle, were and remain controversial; and I for one do not accept his formulation of the distinction between descriptive and explanatory adequacy. But we need not go into that particular issue here. For present purposes, we can operate with a simpler and cruder formulation of the distinction between descriptive and explanatory adequacy: we can say that a grammar is descriptively adequate if it correctly describes the facts (in so far as they are determinate) and it is explanatorily adequate if it not only describes the facts (how things are) but also explains why they are as they are. This deliberately non-technical formulation of the distinction between descriptive and explanatory adequacy is, admittedly, no less controversial, in its way, than is Chomsky's. What I have done, in effect, is (i) to collapse Chomsky's observational and descriptive adequacy under the single term 'descriptive' (without however committing myself to the view that a descriptively adequate grammar should directly reflect the intuitions of native speakers) and (ii) to provide a quite different (a much more general, and less theory-dependent) definition of 'explanatory'. There is plenty of scope for dispute about what is meant by "correctly" describing the "facts" (especially if correctness implies not only weak, but also strong adequacy). But this is another question that we can leave on one side for the moment. It is answered, indirectly, below.

In defence of (so-called) autonomous linguistics

Before we continue, I should perhaps take this opportunity of stressing the importance of distinguishing between generative grammar and Chomskyan generativism, which I classified earlier as a sub-branch of psycholinguistics (cf. Lyons, 1981a: 228ff.). Generative grammar is a mathematical theory of the structure of what it defines to be languages and, as such, is neutral with respect to the distinction between microlinguistics and macrolinguistics, on the one hand, and between any two of the different branches of macrolinguistics, on the other. Generative grammar is therefore, in principle, no more closely to be associated with psycholinguistics than with, for example, sociolinguistics of ethnolinguistics. This is something which, unfortunately, is all too often not appreciated by non-specialists. And Chomsky himself has done little, in recent years, to maintain the distinction between generative grammar, as such, and what I am calling generativism.

The reason why I have introduced the distinction between descriptive and explanatory adequacy and have formulated it in the way in which I have done is that I wish to make it clear that, in defending a particular version of autonomous linguistics, I am concerned solely with the level of descriptive adequacy. I concede immediately that explanatory adequacy is unattainable to any significant or interesting degree without merging microlinguistics with macrolinguistics of one kind or another. Also, if pressed, I will concede – more readily than others might – that semantics necessarily takes us into a consideration of the link between language and culture even at the level of descriptive adequacy. At the same time, I would still draw a motivated distinction between microlinguistic and macrolinguistic semantics (in terms of the distinction between sentence-meaning and utterance-meaning: cf. Lyons, 1981b; 1987c).

Granted that we are restricting ourselves to the level of descriptive adequacy, as I have defined it, we need not spend much time on the question whether synchronic microlinguistic description is possible. As the old axiom has it, *esse valet posse*: existence is a proof of possibility. The accumulated experience of linguists in the field, working on languages which initially might be completely unfamiliar to them, confirms that synchronic microlinguistic description is indeed possible. Particularly striking, in this connexion, is the fact that modern, theoretically sophisticated, descriptions of both long-familiar and more exotic languages can draw upon, supplement and correct older descriptions, including the unsophisticated, or even naive, descriptions of non-European languages made by linguistically untrained explorers, colonists and missionaries. Obviously, various terminological refinements have to be introduced, and

17

allowances have to be made for the distorting effects of the glossocentric (and ethnocentric) prejudices of traditional grammar and of the attitudes associated with it. The fact remains that *esse valet posse*: the possibility of autonomous linguistic description is validated by its actuality.

The accumulated experience of linguists over the centuries – and we are talking in terms of centuries: much of modern (so-called) autonomous linguistics, it must not be forgotten, is highly traditional – confirms, first of all, that language (in the sense of Saussure's 'parole': a set of utterances) is fairly readily separable, pre-theoretically, from non-language and, second, that a fairly high degree of agreement can be reached about the phonological, grammatical and (to a less degree) semantic structure of the language-system (Saussure's 'langue') underlying the corpus of utterances which constitutes the descriptive linguist's primary data. This is not to say, of course, that there are not certain theoretical and methodological decisions to be taken or that the phonological, grammatical and semantic structure of the language-system being described is fully determinate or immediately determinable. Linguists differ on the question whether natural languages, as distinct from formal, artificial languages are of fully determinate structure. I myself incline to the view that they are not. At the same time, I do not believe that they are wholly or even largely indeterminate. If they were, their use as more or less successful instruments of communication would be inexplicable. So too would be the fact (and it is a fact) that descriptions of what is pre-theoretically identifiable as the same language by different linguists, operating at times within different theoretical frameworks, are to a high degree interconvertible. Because linguists whose interest in particular languages is primarily theoretical spend much of their time, not surprisingly, arguing about more or less controversial, and controvertible, data which can be seen as lending support to one theoretical position rather than another (and which may well be indeterminate), non-linguists frequently get the impression that descriptive linguistics is more divided on all issues than is in fact the case. And this impression is, perhaps, reinforced by confusing and unnecessary differences of terminology. Generally speaking, any two linguists describing what is pre-theoretically taken to be the same language will recognize that some parts of the description are more firmly grounded in fact than are others; and they know which these parts are.

Linguistics, in this respect, may be untypical of the social sciences: I am not at all sure that anthropology, sociology or psychology can so often claim to be dealing with what can be fairly described (*pace* Popper) as theory-neutral facts as often or as confidently as microlinguistics can.[8] But then linguistics, as a whole, is not properly classified among the social sciences, any more than it is properly classified among the natural sciences, the humanities, or such wholly non-empirical disciplines as mathematics and formal logic. But more of that later (see Chapter 3).

Let us turn now to the second sub-question: whether synchronic microlinguistic description is desirable. There are three main reasons, in my view, why this question is to be answered in the affirmative. The first has to do with the complexity of the phenomena involved in what is pre-theoretically identified as language and with the multiplicity of the connexions that they have with other phenomena constituting the data of other disciplines. Such phrases as 'language and society', 'language and mind', 'language and culture', 'language and speech' and 'language and style', which are by now well established as book titles, chapter headings and names of university courses of study, testify to the existence and continued vitality of a variety of recognized areas of research and teaching, more or less distinct from one another and identifiable by their subject matter. And the emergence, over the last generation or so, of such terms as 'sociolinguistics', 'psycholinguistics', 'ethnolinguistics', 'neurolinguistics', etc., to complement longer-established terms such as 'phonetics' and 'philosophy of language', testify in turn to the formation of more or less independent specialized sub-disciplines to deal with the data that fall, pre-theoretically, within the scope of these newer terms (sociolinguistics, etc.). It can be argued that some of the macrolinguistic sub-disciplines to which I have referred are theoretically more advanced than others. No one could reasonably deny, however, that very considerable progress has been made recently in our understanding of the subject matter of macrolinguistics in all areas.

A second reason for saying that synchronic microlinguistic description is desirable is that at present there does not exist, and there may perhaps never exist, a unified theory of all the phenomena that fall within the scope of the term 'language' in its broadest sense (i.e., in the sense of Saussure's 'langage'). The data that the various macrolinguistic sub-disciplines deal with are ontologically and methodologically heterogeneous, as are the data of the neighbouring disciplines with which they severally form their alliances: psychology, anthropology, sociology, acoustics, literary criticism, logic, computer science, etc. But this may well be, in the nature of things, inevitable: only time will tell. Old-style physicalist reductionism, character-istic of the Unity of Science movement (with which Bloomfield, 1939; Carnap, 1939; and Morris, 1938 were associated in their day) is now rightly out of fashion. I see no reason to replace it prematurely with any other kind of reductionism based on different ontological assumptions or metatheoretical preferences. And that is what is involved, it seems to me, in the attempts that are constantly being made to link linguistics more closely with one discipline than with another, with psychology rather than with anthropology, or with logic rather than with literary criticism or aesthetics.

The third and most important reason for asserting the desirability of making microlinguistics autonomous is that language-systems appear to have interesting distinctive properties that are unique to them as semiotic systems. These properties have been intensively researched over the last twenty or thirty years, particularly within the framework of generative grammar. The question whether the apparently unique properties of language-systems are to be explained by their reflection of the structure of the human mind, as Chomsky has maintained, or can be accounted for in some other way falls under the rubric of the search for explanatory adequacy (in his view of explanatory adequacy and also in mine). As such, it is not a question for microlinguistics, but rather for theoretical psycholinguistics. And here I would repeat, and emphasize, the point I made earlier: although Chomskyan generativism sets out in principle to investigate the structure of language-systems as they are represented in the mind, in practice it does so without paying much regard to current psychological theory, so that it is in fact very largely autonomous in the sense in which the term is being used here. It is none the less important to maintain the distinction between theoretical microlinguistics and theoretical generativist, or cognitivist, (psycho-)linguistics. (I will have more to say about this in the following chapter.)

Having disposed of the *why*-question, we may now look briefly at the *how*-question. The short answer to this (which will be elaborated below: see Chapters 3 and 4) is: by a process of deliberate abstraction or idealization, involving what I have elsewhere called regularization (i.e., the elimination of so-called performance-errors), standardization (the discounting of systematic variation) and decontextualization (which, *inter alia*, establishes sentences as units more abstract than, and ontologically distinct from, utterances) cf. Lyons (1977a: 585ff.). Not all proponents of (so-called) autonomous linguistics would develop their answer to the *how*-question in quite the same terms; and some might protest, wrongly I believe, at my employment of the term 'idealization' in respect of their own methodology. But I will not take up that point here. Let me just say, for the moment, that those who proclaim their adherence to the Saussurean and post-Saussurean tradition, as I do, would begin by drawing the distinction that he did (within 'langage') between 'langue' and 'parole': i.e., between the language-system and the utterances that are the products of that system. They would then go on, if they take the same view that I do of the ontological status of language-systems, to acknowledge that there is no single uniform language-system underlying the utterances of all members of what is pre-theoretically identified as the same language-community. They would insist, however, that this does not mean (although critics of the notion of the uniform or homogeneous language-system have often implied that it does) that there is no justification for continuing to subscribe to what I have elsewhere referred to as the fiction of uniformity (Lyons, 1981a: 24–27). On the contrary, provided that we operate with a controlled and properly motivated notion of abstraction, there is every justification for maintaining the fiction of uniformity in the construction of our microlinguistic models of the language-system.

I have just used the term 'model'. It is my contention that what all linguists who are engaged upon the description of languages are doing (whether they express themselves in these terms or not) is constructing a more or less abstract model of what is pre-theoretically identifiable as a language (Saussure's 'langue'). Their model may be microlinguistic (and autonomous) or macrolinguistic (and therefore, in my view, non-autonomous): whether it is the one or the other will depend upon the data that they select and the kind of abstraction that they practise. What we are concerned with at this point is the relation between the data and the model in microlinguistic description.

But let me first say something about the word 'model' itself, which is used in many senses, in linguistics and in other disciplines (cf. Lyons, 1975d). For the mathematician and mathematical logician, a model is a formal system considered from the point of view of its interpretation, or application to some practical problem, rather than abstractly for its own sake. When social scientists or physical scientists employ the term 'model', however, they usually mean some deliberately restricted and abstract representation of the phenomena whose structure or behaviour is being studied, from which hypotheses can be derived for testing. Typical models, in this latter sense of the term, are a physicist's representation of atomic structure or an economist's representation of free-market competition. And this is the sense in which I am employing the term here. Since any model of this kind is necessarily based upon an idealization of the data that it is designed to describe or explain, how one decides which variations in the data are of significance and which variations can be discounted becomes a question of crucial importance; and the answer to this question will depend upon the nature of the correspondence that it is assumed to hold between the data and the model, and upon a fairly precise prior specification of what it is that the model is intended to explain or describe.

Apart from the two technical senses of 'model' that I have mentioned, there are various everyday senses of the term, which can affect our intuitive interpretation of its more technical senses and, at times, cause unnecessary controversy. Sometimes we think of a model as a norm to which actually existent objects or actually occurrent patterns of behaviour merely approximate; at other times, we talk as if the model were but an imperfect and purely derivative representation of independently existing objects. Reflected in these alternative ways of thinking of a model are conflicting attitudes with respect to the age-old philosophical controversy between realism and nominalism or between idealism and phenomenalism. As we shall see later, there are realist and non-realist interpretations of the models that linguists construct when they are describing languages (see Chapter 3). We need not get into that issue for our present purpose: the justification of (so-called) autonomous linguistics. I cannot but feel, however, that much of the opposition to what is called autonomous linguistics derives from the failure to appreciate the nature, not to mention the necessity, of abstraction and the surely by now outmoded assumption that phenomenalism, or materialism, is scientifically more respectable than idealism.

What concerns us now, as I have said, is the nature of the linguist's data and the relation between the data and the model in microlinguistic description. When we say that someone is speaking a particular language, English for example, we imply that he or she is engaged in a certain kind of behaviour, or activity, in the course of which he or she produces language-utterances. Native speakers of English will recognize these utterances as belonging to the language and as being, for the most part at least, grammatically acceptable and meaningful, appropriate to their situation of utterance and interpretable.

So much is a matter of pre-theoretical observation or empirical discovery, and it provides us with our data: a sample of relevant language-utterances, which may be characterized, pre-theoretically, as being utterances in, or of, a particular language; as being similar or different in meaning; as being typical, or diagnostic, of certain social groups; and so on. What linguists do when they describe a language, however, is to construct a model, not of actual language-utterances (and still less of language-behaviour), but of the system of regularities which underly, or are manifest in, utterances which are a product of language-behaviour: a model of what I have been referring to technically as the language-system. And this holds true, it must be stressed, not just of microlinguistic description but also of sociolinguistic, ethnolinguistic and psycholinguistic description.[9] The distinction between language-utterances and the underlying language-system is, of course, the one that was drawn by Saussure (1916) – or rather, as we shall see later, it is one of the distinctions that he drew – in terms of the opposition between 'parole' and 'langue' (both 'parole' and 'langue' being complementary parts of the more comprehensive 'langage'). And it is an essentially Saussurean, or post-Saussurean, viewpoint that I have been adopting in my formulation of the goals and *modus operandi* of autonomous microlinguistics (see Chapter 3).

A very similar distinction to Saussure's has, of course, been drawn by Chomsky in terms of performance and competence (1965: 4). But Chomsky, as I have mentioned already, deliberately adopts a psychological, or cognitive, view of language; and this means that, in principle if not in practice, the Chomskyan language-system (which he locates, as competence, in the mind of the native speaker) is to be distinguished, ontologically, from that of autonomous microlinguistics.

According to Chomsky, when we say that someone can speak English, we imply that he or she has acquired, normally in infancy, the mastery of a system of rules or regularities underlying the behaviour which we refer to as speaking English. And, as Chomsky has rightly emphasized, competence is logically prior to performance: it is by virtue of competence that one is able to perform, and one can have competence without ever exercising it in performance. In this sense, performance presupposes competence, but competence does not presuppose performance: this is a crucial point, which incontrovertibly establishes the logical priority of the language-system over language-utterances, as far as psycholinguistics is concerned. Another no less important point, but one that is less often mentioned, is that, not only for microlinguistics, but also for most branches of macrolinguistics, including much of psycholinguistics, it is not language-behaviour as such, but the products of that behaviour, which supply linguists with their (so-called) primary data. I will come back to this point.

But let me first say something further about variation in the (so-called) language-community, the existence of which is often held to invalidate the Saussurean notion of the language-system and, thus, to undermine the very foundations of autonomous linguistics. I have been not only admitting, but emphasizing, the more or less obvious fact that no two people speak precisely the same language, or even the same dialect; and I have been maintaining that, for certain descriptive purposes (though not of course for all), this fact can be deliberately and responsibly ignored. In any language-community, however small and however narrowly it is defined geographically, socially or stylistically, there will always be differences of vocabulary and there will probably be systematic differences of grammar and pronunciation, which may or may not inhibit communication and of which the persons in question may generally be aware. The reason why communication is not necessarily inhibited by such differences are several. First, conversation and discourse normally proceed on the basis of shared assumptions and expectations, which supplement what is said and forestall many potential ambiguities and misunderstandings. Second, most utterances, in the context in which they occur, contain a good deal of redundancy (i.e., they contain a good deal of information that is predictable from context); and many differences of vocabulary, grammar and pronunciation, as well as slips of the tongue and other (so-called) performance-errors are (like misprints when one is proof-correcting) simply not noticed. Third, it is not generally necessary for the listener to extract from an utterance all the information that the speaker, if interrogated, would say it contains. It follows that people may go through life without discovering that their understanding of even quite common words and expressions differs from the understanding that others have of the same words and expressions. It also follows – and this is a point whose significance is not always appreciated by semanticists – that successful communication, or apparently successful communication, by means of language does not presuppose determinacy of meaning.

Not only do no two people speak exactly the same language or dialect (i.e., have exactly the same language-system stored in their brains), but no single person speaks the same language or dialect on all occasions. Everyone switches from one so-called style or register to another – from the colloquial to the formal, from the hortatory to the expository, from the technical to the non-technical, etc. – according to circumstances. Establishing and explaining the correlations between these circumstances, or situations, and the styles or registers that are associated with them is the business of such overlapping interdisciplinary sub-disciplines as stylistics, sociolinguistics and pragmatics.

The language-system underlying the utterances of any one person (that person's competence) turns out, then, upon analysis, to be made up of several partially disjoint (not wholly determinate) systems of vocabulary, grammar and pronunciation; and each of these could, in principle, be regarded as a separate language. Furthermore, each of these more or less different language-systems that are combined and integrated in a so-called monolingual's competence, first of all, changes over time – dramatically during the period of (so-called) language-acquisition, gradually and less noticeably throughout life – and, secondly, is always at any one time more or less indeterminate.

And yet not only the ordinary person, but also the linguist (the latter at least in full cognizance of the facts of the matter), continues to talk as if there are such things as (so-called) natural languages (English, French, German or whatever: see Chapter 4) and that they are homogeneous, determinate and well-defined systems, common to all members of a particular community (which is thereby identifiable as a language-community) and constant over space, time and situations of utterance: we continue to say, for example, that something is or is not an English word or phrase and has such-and-such a meaning. How can one make sense of this evident mismatch between the facts and the way we describe them – this evident mismatch between the data and the model?

Quite simply, by recognizing that, in both non-technical and technical usage, the word 'language' – and more precisely a phrase such as 'the language' or 'a language' – involves different kinds of hypostatization and can be used to refer to many different kinds of entities. The language-system stored in the individual's brain as what Chomsky calls competence, which is investigated by psycholinguistics, is quite different, ontologically, from the language-system postulated by sociolinguistics as something shared by all members of a given language-community, and both of these differ in turn from the language-system which is described by historical linguistics as an entity which endures through time but passes through a succession of synchronically distinct states. As I have already emphasized, each of these different views of the language-system is metatheoretically and methodologically defensible and each of them involves, whether explicitly or not, the construction of a model which inevitably idealizes what is being described, by discounting, more or less deliberately, a certain amount of indeterminacy and variation in the data. Critics of (so-called) autonomous linguistics frequently talk as if it is both desirable and possible to describe languages more realistically (whatever this means) from some non-autonomous vantage-point which does not involve idealization of what they take to be the primary data. This is not so. Idealization of the kind that I have referred to as regularization (the elimination of performance-errors) is just as necessary, and desirable, in most branches of macrolinguistics, theoretical and descriptive, as it is in microlinguistics. So too, even in sociolinguistics, is some degree of standardization (cf. Lyons, 1977a: 587ff.).

In my view of the matter at least, there is (as I said earlier) little prospect of reconciling the several legitimately different macrolinguistic views of language within a single theoretical framework and accounting for them, descriptively, within a single model. Admittedly, this is a view that is not shared by all of my colleagues.[10] And I may be proved wrong. If and when they can successfully deploy against the view that I have been defending the *esse-valet-posse* argument that I have deployed in favour of (so-called) autonomous linguistics, I would be the first to concede defeat: I shall then be only too happy to endorse (misquoting Ockham) that even more famous (though logically more challengeable) axiom of the philosophy of science, *entia non sunt multiplicanda praeter necessitatem.*

3

Linguistic theory and theoretical linguistics

One of my aims in this chapter, which complements the preceding one, is to motivate a distinction between two terms that are currently employed by most linguists as synonyms and to use this terminological distinction as a peg upon which to hang some comments about the present state of linguistics.[1] The terms in question are 'linguistic theory' and 'theoretical linguistics'. Another aim is to comment further upon the theoretical term 'language-system' in relation to Saussure's terms 'langue' and 'langage'.

The distinction between 'linguistic theory' and 'theoretical linguistics' is by no means the only terminological distinction that I shall be drawing, here and in other chapters of this book. I do not wish to give the impression, however, that my sole (or primary) concern is at any point purely terminological. I am much more interested in the metatheoretical or methodological issues that the use of one term rather than another, or of one term in addition to another, helps us to identify. As far as the terms 'theoretical linguistics' and 'linguistic theory' are concerned, I wish to suggest that, if they are kept distinct, each of them can be usefully employed to refer to what have now emerged, or are in process of emerging, as two rather different, but equally important, sub-branches of linguistics.

When my *Introduction to Theoretical Linguistics* (1968a) was published, more than twenty years ago, it was hailed by Bar-Hillel as "the first [book of its kind] ... to carry the long overdue adjective 'theoretical' in its title" (1969: 449). It is worth noting in this connexion that, although most of the foreign-language editions did not hesitate to use the equivalent of 'theoretical' in the title, the publishers of both the French and German versions seem to have felt that the use of this adjective was not so much overdue as, in this case at least, premature or inapposite. In preference to (the equivalent of) 'theoretical linguistics' the former chose (the equivalent of) 'general linguistics' and the latter (the equivalent of) 'modern linguistics'. The term 'modern linguistics' is of no interest to us in the present context, but 'general linguistics' is; and I will come back to it below. Another review of my book, more critical than Bar-Hillel's and written from a more or less orthodox Chomskyan, or generativist, point of view – more orthodox, incidentally, than I myself have held either then or since – was published in *Language* (Starosta, 1971). It rightly drew attention to my failure to develop, seriously and consistently, the implications of the programmatic opening sentence, "Linguistics may be defined as the scientific study of language" (Lyons, 1968a: 1), and of *obiter dicta* ("statements with theoretical import . . . scattered in odd places throughout the book"; Starosta, 1971: 431) to the effect that one of "the proclaimed aims" of linguistics is "the construction of a scientific theory of human language" (Lyons, 1968a: 45).

This criticism was, I think, well founded. And I would now concede, further, that in the *Introduction* I not only failed to define 'theoretical linguistics' (tacitly identifying it with 'general linguistics' or even with 'linguistics' *tout court*), but I adopted far too narrow a view of its subject matter. In effect, I restricted the scope of theoretical linguistics to what I would now characterize as general, theoretical, synchronic microlinguistics (cf. Lyons, 1981a: 34–37). I still think that this constitutes the central and most distinctive part of theoretical linguistics (for reasons that I have explained in the preceding chapter). But I certainly do not believe that diachronic linguistics is intrinsically less theoretical than synchronic; that such branches of macrolinguistics as sociolinguistics, psycholinguistics, or stylistics are, by virtue of their data and the questions they address, less theoretical than microlinguistics; or even (though I grant that this is more debatable) that descriptive linguistics (i.e., the description of particular language-systems) is necessarily less theoretical than general linguistics (i.e., the study of language in general). I will not labour this point (though it has been much misunderstood by linguists) but shall take it for granted in all that follows.

The view of theoretical linguistics that I put forward in my 1968 textbook was more restricted than I now think it ought to have been in at least one other respect. Having started by defining linguistics, programmatically and perhaps tendentiously, as "the scientific study of language", I confined my attention thereafter to what is arguably but a subclass of languages – a subclass of which English, French, Italian, Chinese, Arabic, etc. are held to be members and exemplars. Such languages may be referred to as N-languages (see Chapter 4). I shall have more to say about the properties of N-languages presently. An initial and provisional indication of the membership of the subclass of languages that I am referring to can be provided, however, by saying that N-languages are what are commonly called natural languages, but are more accurately – or at least more fully – described as natural, human, spoken languages. The letter 'N' is thus mnemonically connected with 'natural', as this term is commonly employed, loosely and without definition, by linguists and philosophers; but it also bears a mnemonic connexion, as we shall see, with 'normal'. N-languages are what are normally thought of, pre-theoretically and prototypically, as languages.

I am of course aware that many linguists, philosophers and semioticians would say that one or other of these adjectives – 'natural', 'human' and 'spoken' – is redundant as a modifier of the noun 'language'; and some would argue that all three of them are. However, I see no reason why either linguistic theory or theoretical linguistics should make this so by definition. Why I take this view will be clear from the approach to theoretical linguistics that I am about to present, albeit briefly and with minimum development of the several points that I shall be making.

Each of the adjectives that I have used to characterize the class of N-languages – 'natural', 'human' and 'spoken' – presents its own problems of definition and application. The term 'natural', as I have come to realize increasingly in recent years, is especially troublesome. It is widely used, in collocation with 'language' and other terms, in several distinguishable senses, which, to the best of my knowledge, have never been properly clarified either by philosophers or linguists. I shall be discussing this question, with particular reference to its implications for linguistic theory and theoretical linguistics, in Chapter 4. Here I must be content with what I have elsewhere referred to as "a rough-and-ready operational definition": a natural language, let us say, is one "that has not been specially constructed, whether for general or specific purposes, and is acquired by its users without special instruction as a normal part of the process of maturation and socialization" (Lyons, 1981c: 2; see also Chapter 1 above). Natural languages, in this sense, are – to quote Carnap (1955: 33) – "historically given" and in this respect contrast with the artificial languages of logicians and computer scientists, on the one hand, or Esperanto, etc., on the other. And of the set of historically given natural languages a relatively small subset are, or have been, attested and described, in greater or less detail, by linguists.

It is pertinent to note, at this point, that the journal that bears the title *Theoretical Linguistics* (founded in 1974) has as its editorial policy the publication of "studies, both of natural and [of] constructed languages, employing formal methods". And the policy statement that I have just quoted (from the inside cover of the journal) continues as follows: "Theoretical linguistics being, historically, the outcome of independent developments in linguistics, logic and the philosophy of language, workers in all of these fields are invited to submit articles to the editor". I have drawn attention to this implicit definition of the field of theoretical linguistics for two reasons. First of all, I wanted to make the point that there is now a well-established field of research and scholarship, as there was not in 1968, which is referred to by those who work in it as 'theoretical linguistics'; that it has close links with logic and the philosophy of language; that its hallmark is formalization (or mathematicization); and that it embraces not only natural languages but at least that (heterogeneous) subclass of non-natural languages whose investigation is held to be revealing in the study of what I am calling N-languages. Second, I wanted to make it clear that, although this is by now a relatively well-established sense of the term 'theoretical linguistics' and was probably the one that Bar-Hillel (1969) had in mind when he commented on the title of my 1968 textbook (cf. also Bar-Hillel *et al.*, 1974), it is a narrower sense than the one with which I was myself operating, most of the time at least, when I wrote the book. It is also somewhat narrower than the sense that I want to give it here.

Interestingly enough, there is another journal (founded in 1983) which uses the term 'linguistic theory' (not to mention the highly ambiguous 'natural language') in its title: *Natural Language & Linguistic Theory*. Its purpose, as formulated on the inside cover, is "to provide a forum for detailed and lively discussion of theoretical research that pays close attention to natural language data", and, thus, "to bridge the gap between descriptive work and work of a highly theoretical, less empirically oriented nature". It is not clear what, if anything, has motivated the choice of 'linguistic theory' in preference to 'theoretical linguistics' in this instance. What is worth noting, however, is the implicit contrast that is drawn between 'theoretical' and 'descriptive' on the one hand, and between 'theoretical' and 'empirical', on the other. Many linguists would no doubt say that these contrasts are indeed legitimate; and I myself would agree that they have some basis in current practice. Much of the day-to-day description of particular languages by linguists is conducted without regard to the theoretical consequences of describing the data in one way rather than another. And some highly theoretical work appears to make little contact with empirically attested or attestable data. But there is obviously no conflict in principle between theorizing about languages (natural or non-natural) and describing them.[2] The term 'theoretical' enters into several different lexical oppositions ('theoretical' vs. 'applied', 'theoretical' vs.

'experimental', etc.). Not all of these are relevant to the distinction between theoretical and non-theoretical linguistics, as this has been developed in recent years.[3] And I have already made the point that there is now, as there was not until the advent of generative grammar, a branch, or sub-branch, of linguistics that is both theoretical and descriptive.

As we have seen in Chapter 1, human languages can be distinguished from non-human languages in various ways: as languages that are actually used by human beings; as languages that could be used by human beings; as languages that are normally or naturally (in one or other sense of 'naturally') used by human beings; and so on. For the limited purpose of characterizing N-languages – a subclass, whether proper or improper, of actual, "historically given", languages (not all of which are, or have been, attested and described) – the operational definition invoked above will continue to serve: a human language is "one that is attested as being used (or as having been used in the past) by human beings". And we can tacitly qualify this with some such phrase as 'under normal conditions'. Whether actual human languages, thus defined, are representative of a wider set of potential human languages that share a number of structural properties, or design-features, which distinguish them from non-human (natural or non-natural) languages is a question that has of course been debated, from many different points of view, by philosophers, semioticians, ethologists, psychologists and linguists. It is a question that I do not propose to discuss here (cf. Lyons, 1972; 1977a: 70–94). As I have made clear in Chapter 2, it is one of the central questions for theoretical psycholinguistics, but not, in my view, for theoretical microlinguistics.

The third adjective that I have used in order to characterize the pre-theoretically identifiable class of N-languages is 'spoken'. This, like 'human' and 'natural', has more than one relevant sense; and it is important to distinguish at least two of them by drawing upon the related, but theoretically distinct, notions of channel and medium (see Chapter 1 above, especially the Addendum). The reason for drawing this distinction is ultimately the same as that which led Hjelmslev (1943b) to split Saussure's (1916) 'substance' into what the English translation of the Danish original, as Eco (1976: 52) points out, misleadingly labels as 'substance' and 'purport'. The medium is the substance, continuum or stuff in which a language-system (Saussure's 'langue') is realized, considered in abstraction from its physical properties; the channel is the physical link between sender and receiver along which, or through which, language-signals travel in the process of communication.

For historically explicable reasons, most twentieth-century schools of linguistics (with the notable exception of the Hjelmslevian, or Glossematic, version of post-Saussurean structuralism) have not only failed to take proper account of the distinction between channel and medium, but have too readily equated language and speech. N-languages, to which descriptive linguistics, both synchronic and diachronic, has until recently given exclusive attention, do of course bear a special relation to speech. Nevertheless, as I have argued elsewhere, there are good reasons for not making the adjective 'spoken' (in either of the two senses that I have distinguished) tautologous or redundant in collocation with 'language'. Even if our main concern, as theoretical linguists, is with psycholinguistics (i.e., with the investigation of either competence or performance in the Chomskyan sense), it is important not to assume that the association between language and speech is essential, rather than contingent (cf. Lyons, 1981c: 6; see also Chapter 1 above).

A fortiori, if our concern is with theoretical microlinguistics, rather than with this or that branch of macrolinguistics, we must be correspondingly more careful not to equate language and speech. For microlinguistics deliberately abstracts from considerations of the neuropsychological basis of language and the possibly genetic determination of the language-faculty.

Before proceeding to say more positively what I, if not most linguists, mean by 'theoretical linguistics', on the basis of the characterization of N-languages that I have just provided, I should like to make a further terminological, or metalinguistic, comment, of general and also of more specific import. This has to do with the role played by the linguist's pre-theoretical, non-technical, metalanguage in the determination of linguistic theory. It is not as widely appreciated as it ought to be that most of our everyday metalanguage – i.e., most of the metalinguistic vocabulary used by the man-in-the-street (which may or may not have been coined or reinterpreted, in the past, for specialized purposes: cf. 'sentence', 'phrase' and even 'word') – is, on the one hand, both language-specific and culture-specific and, on the other, ambiguous or vague. Much of the ambiguity or vagueness carries over, unrecognized as such, into the philosophy of language and theoretical linguistics; and distinctions that seem self-evident (dare I say 'natural'?: see Chapter 4) to native speakers of one language will not seem so to another.

This general comment will be developed and illustrated in greater detail elsewhere. Its particular import has to do with the language-specificity and ambiguity or vagueness of the word 'language'. It would be easy for me to quote passages from the works of eminent theoreticians in which this word, from the everyday metalinguistic vocabulary of English, is used informally, but tendentiously, because of its ambiguity (or vagueness) and its language-specificity, in the explanation or explication of theoretical concepts. But a passage written by me some years ago will serve equally well for the purpose. It is by no means untypical of what most linguists might have written with equanimity at the time. Indeed, many linguists would still find it acceptable today. But I now consider it to be conceptually obscure and unacceptably imprecise in its pre-theoretical, or perhaps I should say semi-theoretical, use of the English word 'language'. The passage in question comes from the Introduction to *New Horizons in Linguistics* 1 (Lyons, 1970a: 11–12). In it I refer to "the assumption that particular languages (English, Chinese, Swahili, Malay, Eskimo, Amharic, Quechua, etc.) are specific instances of something more general than we may appropriately refer to in the singular as 'language'; in other words, that all human languages have something in common, not shared by anything else, other than the fact that we have learned to apply to each of them the word *language* (or its equivalent in other languages)". I then go on to suggest: (i) that in phrases such as 'sign language', 'the language of mathematics', 'the language of bees' and 'the language of flowers', the word 'language' is being employed in a related, but more general sense; (ii) that "in its more general sense, the term 'language' may be defined as 'a system of communication'"; and (iii) that "in the narrower sense in which the linguist uses the term, languages ... are the principal systems of communication used by particular groups of human beings within the particular society ... of which they are members".

There are several points here that are worthy of critical discussion. In particular, the assumption that a language, in either "the most general sense" or "the narrower sense" of the term, may be described as a system of communication is far more controversial these days than it seemed to be twenty years ago. But this is a point that I do not wish to take up here.[4] What I want to do is to concentrate upon my own equivocal use of the word 'language' in the passage to which I have referred and to draw upon the points that arise in order to formulate the distinction between theoretical linguistics and linguistic theory.

In my more recent (more comprehensive, but deliberately more elementary) textbook *Language and Linguistics*, I have in effect rewritten the passage from *New Horizons* 1 to which I am drawing attention, in the opening pages of the book, under the heading 'What is language?' (Lyons, 1981a: 1–3). I have also noted that the question "What is language?" (which uses the word 'language' as a non-count, or mass, noun in the singular without the indefinite article) differs significantly, under one interpretation at least, from the question "What is a language?" (in which 'language' is used, with the indefinite article, as a count noun); and that this grammatical difference within what would generally be taken to be a single lexical item in English correlates "up to a point" with a distinction that is lexicalized (as well as being grammaticalized) as a difference between two semantically non-equivalent words in French and other Romance languages. If the passage from *New Horizons 1* is read carefully in the light of these observations, it will be seen that the word 'language' is used sometimes in one sense and sometimes in the other, without explanation and perhaps also without good reason. For example, granted that languages, in either the "narrower" or the "more general" sense, are systems of communication (I will come back to the implications of the term 'system' presently), it does not follow that language is also a system of communication. A more important point for our present purpose, however, is this: once we see that there is a potentially significant difference between the two grammatically distinct uses of the word 'language', we shall also find it easier to see not only that the ontological status of language is quite different from that of languages, but also that there are different ways in which "particular languages ... are specific instances of something more general than we may refer to in the singular as 'language'".

As I have said, there is a lexical difference in French and other Romance languages which can be correlated, partly but not wholly, with the two grammatically distinct uses of the word 'language' in English. Consequently, a French translator of the passage from *New Horizons 1* would have to switch between 'langue' and 'langage', as an Italian translator would have to switch between 'lingua' and 'linguaggio', a Spanish translator between 'lingua' and 'lenguaje', and a Portuguese translator between 'lingua' and 'linguagem'.[5] It is interesting to note in passing that, although all these four Romance languages draw a distinction within what English subsumes under 'language', it is not exactly the same set of distinctions. (For example, the Italian 'lingua' and the French 'langue' are not intersubstitutable, as translation-equivalents, in all contexts; and the Portuguese 'lingua' is intersubstitutable with neither.) It is also worth adding that grammatical, as well as lexical, differences may be significant in this connexion. For example, the German 'Sprache' and the Russian 'jazyk' are more or less exact translation-equivalents of the English 'language', but differences in the use of the definite article (in generic expressions) in the former and the non-existence of both definite and indefinite articles in the latter make the difference between "What is language?" and "What is a language?" less obvious in what might be conventionally regarded as 'literal' translations of those questions into German and Russian than it is, or ought to be, in the original English.

For historical reasons, it is the difference between the French 'langue' and 'langage' that concerns us here. Saussure, the acknowledged founder of what I shall identify as theoretical linguistics (in contrast with linguistic theory) took one of the distinctions between the everyday metalinguistic words 'langue' and 'langage' and, in the *Cours* (1916), exploited it for theoretical purposes; and this has given his translators problems. In fact, I think it is no exaggeration to say that one of the currently available English versions of the *Cours* is, in places, literally incomprehensible because of the difficulty it has in maintaining consistently the technical and the non-technical, but significant, difference or differences between 'langue' and 'langage'.[6] (This is not to say that it is always clear what distinction, if any, is relevant when Saussure or his successors use 'langue' rather than 'langage', or, conversely, 'langage' rather than 'langue', in non-technical or semi-technical contexts. I have myself experienced considerable difficulties of exegesis, from this point of view, in respect of crucial passages in the works of Benveniste: cf. Lyons, 1984.) I mention Saussure's technical distinction between 'langue' and 'langage' because, rooted as it is in everyday metalinguistic usage in French, it is (together with the 'langue'–'parole' distinction) the very foundation-stone of all modern theoretical linguistics. In saying this I am not suggesting that the distinction as Saussure drew it is absolutely clear; still less that it is sufficient to bear the superstructure that has been built upon it by his successors. Scholars such as Hjelmslev (1943b) and Coseriu (1952) have drawn attention to the necessity of distinguishing at least one other theoretical term in addition to 'langue' and 'parole' – namely 'norme' – in order to handle the whole of what Saussure calls 'langage'. I myself would prefer to say that we need several distinct, but equally valid, interpretations of 'langue' – which in its technical sense I will translate into English as 'language-system' – and that the various branches of theoretical linguistics are to be distinguished, one from another, by the interpretation that they give to this term. This is the central point of my argument. In developing it, I will be simultaneously making a plea for greater tolerance and understanding of alternative points of view than is commonly to be found among theoretically minded linguists. I will also be illustrating, in respect of a historically important instance, the relation that holds between the theoretical and the pre-theoretical meta-language of linguistics.

It will have been noted that, in the reference that I have just made to the

Saussurean concept of the language-system, I have given at least as much emphasis to Saussure's terminological distinction of 'langue' and 'langage' as I have to the much more extensively discussed 'langue' vs. 'parole' distinction. They are of equal importance; and both of them are related to, though not of course fully explained by, semantic distinctions that are lexicalized in the everyday metalinguistic vocabulary of certain N-languages, including French. Saussure himself makes this point, contrasting French, on the one hand, with German and, on the other (less satisfactorily perhaps), with Latin.[7] It so happens that English, like German, fails to draw the "langue" vs. "langage" distinction; like German it does however distinguish "speech" from "language" ('Rede' vs. 'Sprache'), which as we shall see later is only one, and not the most important, of the distinctions associated with the opposition that Saussure establishes between 'langue' and 'parole'.

Of the several more or less readily identifiable semantic distinctions that hold between 'langue' and 'langage' in appropriate contexts in everyday French, there are two that are of concern to us here. The first, as I have said, is captured, "up to a point", by the syntactic distinction that holds, in many contexts, between 'language' used as a count noun and the same word construed as a non-count, or mass, noun. For example, linguistics is commonly defined in English as "the scientific study of language" (as it is, for example, in Lyons, 1968a, 1970a, 1981a); and this would normally be translated into French as "l'étude scientifique du langage" (cf. Italian "lo studio scientifico del linguaggio", Portuguese "o estudo científico da linguagem", Spanish "el estudio científico del lenguaje"). Similarly, the central defining question of linguistics, "What is language?" (cf. Lyons, 1981a: 1–2, 34), would normally be translated into French as "Qu'est-ce que le langage?" (Italian "Che cos'è il linguaggio?", Portuguese "O che e a linguagem?", Spanish "Que es el lenguaje?").[8]

The second semantic distinction that holds, in everyday French, between 'langue' and 'langage' reveals itself in the fact that the former, though not the latter, is normally restricted to what I have earlier referred to as N-languages. For example 'the language of bees', 'the language of music', 'the language of mathematics', would have as their accepted equivalents not 'la langue des abeilles', etc. but 'le langage des abeilles', etc.[9]

Now, these two aspects of the opposition between the French words 'langue' and 'langage' can be brought under the same head by saying that the latter is broader, or more general, than the other; and this is what makes them appropriate for Saussure's purpose. (He does not in fact comment explicitly, in the *Cours*, on either of the two differences between 'langue' and 'langage' to which I have just drawn attention. But his usage of the two words throughout, both technically and non-technically, is consistent, I believe, with what I have said.) These two aspects of the everyday 'langue' vs. 'langage' opposition are, however, logically independent of one another; and it is important, in my view, that they should be clearly distinguished in the construction of the technical metalanguage of linguistics and in the delimitation of its various branches and sub-branches. I have said that I am using the term 'language-system' as the English equivalent of Saussure's 'langue', as he defines it, for technical purposes, in the *Cours*. Saussure never uses the term 'langue', whether technically or non-technically, in respect of languages other than N-languages. It is not clear, however, whether this is because, like most linguists down to the present day, he simply did not seriously consider the status of non-natural, non-human and non-spoken languages in relation to the distinction of 'langue' and 'langage'. However that may be, I have made my own stand on the principle that theoretical linguistics should not restrict its attention to N-languages. This implies that the term 'language-system' should be broadened to include non-natural, non-human and non-spoken languages (some of which would normally be referred to by means of the French word 'langage' rather than 'langue'). It does not imply, however, that theoretical linguistics should jettison either the centrality of N-languages, on the one hand, or what I take to be the essence of the Saussurean and post-Saussurean distinction of 'langue' and 'langage', on the other.

It is its acceptance of the principle of the centrality of N-languages that distinguishes linguistics from a variety of other disciplines, including semiotics and formal logic, which are also concerned with systems of communication (or signification). As to what I have described as the essence of the Saussurean and post-Saussurean distinction of 'langue' and 'langage', this can be expressed in terms (a) of the distinction between the pre-theoretical and the theoretical and (b) of Hjelmslev's (1943a,b) generalization of the Saussurean distinction of 'langue' and 'parole' to a distinction between the system and the process. Actually, if we want to be precise about these matters, we need to draw a further distinction between the process and the products of that process: between language-behaviour (or language-activity) and language-signals (or language-inscriptions); between utterance in the sense of 'énonciation' and utterances in the sense of 'énoncés'. Given the Saussurean equation (implicit rather than explicit in the *Cours*) of "langage = langue + parole", we can say that 'langage' denotes a set of phenomena which (as they manifest themselves to us as 'parole') we recognise as 'langage' and which we describe and explain by

37

postulating as theoretical constructs one or more underlying 'langues' (language-systems).

Theoretical linguistics, like theoretical physics, theoretical chemistry or theoretical biology, is, of itself, non-empirical. It is free to create its own theoretical constructs as it will. But, also like these other theoretical sciences to which I have just referred, it originates with the observation and systematization of identifiable phenomena which appear pre-theoretically to have something in common. In so far as it retains its internal coherence and distinctive identity – in so far as theoretical linguistics is to be distinguished from the theoretical branches of other sciences – it maintains, and must maintain, its connexion with what is pre-theoretically identifiable, across all societies and cultures, as the referent of Saussure's 'langage'.

Theoretical linguistics – more precisely, theoretical general linguistics – is that branch of the subject which sets out to provide a non-trivial, intellectually satisfying, answer to what I referred to earlier as the central defining question of linguistics: "What is language?" (construed, as we shall see below, in a particular way).

Although this question contains the ontological presupposition that there is such a thing as language ("langage"), of itself it says nothing about its ontological status. It does not necessarily imply that language is empirically and pre-theoretically separable from non-language. Both general and descriptive linguistics have always operated, however, with the assumption that this is so. To quote W. S. Allen, on this point: "We presume that there is a particular mode of human behaviour which it is legitimate to isolate and to label as 'language'; we assume also that this behaviour is such that systematic statements may be made about its various manifestations" (1957b: 13). Once again, if we wish to be precise, we need to be clear about the distinction between process and product, and consequently about the different ways in which language "manifests" itself to us in the physical world. Most branches of linguistics draw their data from the products of the process, not from the process itself (various kinds of muscular and neurophysiological activity). This is an important point which has been dealt with above (see Chapter 2): I will not elaborate upon it further. For present purposes, let us simply note that the two assumptions, or postulates, made explicit in the passage just quoted – the postulate of isolability and the postulate of systematicity – have proved their worth over the centuries (the history of linguistics, in some of its branches at least, and of linguistic theory is measured in centuries) and need not be justified in detail here. Nor is there any need to labour the point that the isolability of the "particular mode of human behaviour" that is pre-theoretically identifiable as language

38

('langage') rests, operationally, upon the relatively clear, empirically determinate and theory-neutral, difference between speech and non-speech.

The question "What is language?" can be addressed from several points of view and can be answered in several different, but equally legitimate, ways according to the point of view that is adopted. Theoretical linguistics, founded upon the Saussurean and post-Saussurean trichotomy of 'langage', 'langue' and 'parole', interprets the question as meaning "What is a language?" ("Qu'est-ce qu'une langue?"). The different branches of theoretical linguistics adopt characteristically different points of view and consequently postulate different kinds of theoretical constructs in the answers they give to the question. Theoretical microlinguistics (often called autonomous linguistics: see Chapter 2) adopts the point of view expressed by Saussure, or rather his editors, in the famous final sentence of the *Cours*: "la linguistique a pour unique et véritable objet la langue envisagée en elle-même et pour elle-même" (1916: 317). It is the controversial "en elle-même et pour elle-même", of course, which distinguishes theoretical microlinguistics from the various sub-branches of theoretical macrolinguistics. But they too, as I shall argue, have their own distinctive conceptions of the language-system. It must not be thought that sociolinguistics or psycholinguistics, or the other branches of macrolinguistics, can dispense with the distinction between the system and the process (or its products). I will come back to this point. But first let me make explicit something else which is not immediately obvious.

This is the fact that 'la langue' in the famous passage from the *Cours* that I have just quoted can be interpreted either generically or specifically.[10] Its generic interpretation defines the field of theoretical general linguistics; its specific interpretation, that of theoretical descriptive linguistics. This is the gloss that I would add to Katz's formulation of the goals of what he calls linguistics *tout court* (I would call it theoretical linguistics) in his recent defence of Platonic realism (as an alternative to both American structuralism and Chomskyan cognitivism): "linguistics tries to construct theories to answer the questions, first, 'What is English, Urdu, and other natural languages?' and second, 'What is language in general?'" (Katz, 1981: 21). Two further terminological comments may be made about this passage, by way of exegesis: (i) by "natural languages" Katz, like most philosophers and linguists, clearly means N-languages; (ii) by "language in general" he means, in Saussurean terms, not 'langage', but 'langue' (construed generically). His two questions are in fact post-Chomskyan reformulations of Saussure's "la linguistique a pour ... objet ..." (Chapter 4). Although theoretical general linguistics existed long before Chomsky published his seminal work in the mid-1950s, modern theoretical descriptive linguistics is very much his creation.[11] A generative grammar of any N-language – English, Urdu, etc. – is a theory of that language: more specifically, a theory of the well-formedness of the sentences of the language.

So far, I have been concerned, first of all, to point out that, although until recently there was no need to distinguish between 'general linguistics' and 'theoretical linguistics', nowadays there is; and, second, to prepare the ground for the distinction that I am drawing between theoretical linguistics and linguistic theory and for the necessarily brief presentation of my own approach to the definition of the field of theoretical linguistics, on the basis of alternative, equally legitimate, conceptions of language-systems.

But why, it may now be asked, is it not possible to operate with a single notion of the language-system valid in all branches of linguistics, micro- and macro-, theoretical and non-theoretical? This is a question that has been dealt with in some detail in the preceding chapter. The answer, as we have seen, derives partly from the apparently *sui generis* properties of N-languages and partly from the complexity and heterogeneity of the pre-theoretically isolable phenomena identifiable as 'language' (i.e., as Saussure's 'langage').

The multiplicity and heterogeneity of the connections that can be established between what are pre-theoretically classifiable as language-data ('des données langagières', if I may employ this useful post-Saussurean adjective) and other data, natural and cultural, constituting the subject matter of other disciplines are such that, in my view at least, there is no immediate possibility, perhaps even no ultimate possibility, of constructing a unified theory of the natural and social sciences within which a unitary theory of language (of 'langue' construed generically) would find its place and be descriptively and explanatorily adequate to the data that it systematizes and accounts for. As to the apparently unique, or *sui generis*, character of what are commonly referred to as natural languages, this may well have been exaggerated at times by proponents of so-called autonomous linguistics. The discontinuity between language and non-language, on the one hand, and the determinacy, arbitrariness and closedness of grammatical structure, on the other, have certainly been greatly exaggerated by linguists of various schools, generativist and non-generativist. The fact remains that nothing remotely resembling a comprehensive, intellectually interesting and empirically satisfactory account of the grammatical structure of N-languages in terms of the theoretical concepts and explanatory principles of other disciplines has yet been provided by any of those who have challenged the *sui generis* character of languages. There is every reason therefore to continue to subscribe to a working hypothesis that has proved its heuristic value in the practical description of languages over the centuries and has been, more recently, the foundation-stone of what is so far the most sophisticated branch of theoretical linguistics, both general and descriptive: theoretical (synchronic) microlinguistics. This does not mean, however, that we should, as practitioners of microlinguistics, whether general or descriptive, close our minds to those aspects of language that are not, or do not appear to be, *sui generis* or deny the validity of alternative views of the nature and ontological status of language-systems.

The ontological status of the language-system (Saussure's 'langue') has been controversial ever since the publication of the *Cours*. Saussure's own views are unclear and perhaps contradictory.[12] At one time, he says that they are supra-individual social facts; at another time, that they are stored in the brains of individual members of the language-community (1916: 23–32). And each of these conflicting views is incompatible with the view, recently advocated by Katz (1981), that language-systems are purely abstract, mathematical (so-called Platonic) objects (see Chapter 4). As will be obvious from what has been said earlier, Katz's view (which is close to Hjelmslev's, 1943a), is the one that I accept for microlinguistics, though not for psycholinguistics, sociolinguistics or other branches of macrolinguistics.

Some part of the confusion and controversy that has surrounded the Saussurean distinction of 'langue' and 'parole' over the last half-century or so is to be attributed to the fact that both words are used in the *Cours* non-technically (i.e., pre-theoretically) as well as technically; and, since the theoretical distinction (or, as we shall see, distinctions) that Saussure draws between them correlates with differences of meaning in everyday French, it is not always clear in what sense they are being employed in particular contexts. It must also be admitted that Saussure's own comments (or those of his editors) about the rough equivalence between French 'parole' and German 'Rede' (and Latin 'sermo' in contrast with 'lingua') are less than helpful (1916: 31). They must have encouraged, even for those who have read the *Cours* in French, what has undoubtedly been, over the years, by far the most serious misunderstanding of the technical distinction between 'langue' and 'parole': the view that it relates basically, or primarily, to the distinction between language and speech. It does indeed cover one dimension or one part of the semantic difference between 'language' and 'speech' (between German 'Sprache' and 'Rede', between Russian 'jazyk' and 'recj', etc.): or rather, to be more precise, between 'language' construed as a count noun and 'speech' understood as referring to the product, rather

41

than the process, of speaking. But it does so, as we have seen, only secondarily. The primary distinction is between a language and utterances (spoken, written, or whatever: i.e., products, not processes, inscribed in some appropriate physical substance or medium) which, by virtue of their structure (and independently of their physical manifestation), are identifiable as utterances of the language in question (see Chapter 1). It is unfortunate that the beginnings of theoretical linguistics should have coincided, for historically explicable reasons, with a period of extreme phonocentrism. But no more needs to be said on that score.

Much of the controversy, if not confusion, that still attaches to the Saussurean, or post-Saussurean, distinction between 'langue' and 'parole' (or the Chomskyan distinction of 'competence' and 'performance', which is valid for psycholinguistics but not for microlinguistics) must, however, be attributed to what in this and the previous chapter I have characterized as a false assumption: the assumption that there is only one kind of reality and that so-called natural languages, N-languages, must be either psychological or social entities, or, in terms of an alternative dichotomy, that they must be either physical or non-physical. It is my contention that microlinguistics, on the one hand, and the several branches of macrolinguistics, on the other, start from the same pre-theoretical notion of N-languages and that, according to their own viewpoint and the alliances that they forge with other disciplines (mathematics, psychology, sociology, anthropology, etc), they each practise a particular kind of abstraction and idealization in the construction of the ontologically appropriate model of the underlying language-system.

I have already referred to one common misunderstanding of Saussure's terminological distinction between 'langue' and 'parole': a misunderstanding based on the view that it correlates directly with the distinction between language and speech. Another equally common misunderstanding (for which admittedly there is stronger support in the text of the *Cours* itself) is that it has to do primarily with the difference between what all members of a given language-community share ('la langue') and what varies from one individual to another ('la parole'). Whatever might have been Saussure's own view of the theoretical status of systematic variation, dialectal or stylistic, within the language-community, it is clear that this cannot be attributed to 'parole', just as it cannot be attributed to what Chomsky (1965) calls 'performance'.[13] As we have seen, the primary, or basic, distinction between 'langue' and 'parole' has to do with the difference between a language-system and language-utterances (considered as its products). The individual's idiolect is just as much a language-system, in this sense, as is the language of the whole community. The two kinds of systems differ, of course, ontologically. It is the former, not the latter, that is stored neurophysiologically, as what Chomsky calls competence, in the brain of each and every individual. The ontological status of the latter is much more problematical and has been the subject of a good deal of debate recently. We need not be concerned with that here (see Chapter 4). The important point to emphasize for present purposes is that the concept of the language-system is as relevant and applicable to the study of a single person's idiolect as it is to the study of the language of a whole community.

Nor should it be thought that the idiolect, in contrast with the language of the community, is structurally homogeneous, fully determinate (i.e., well defined in the mathematical sense), or even constant over time. Obviously, there is less systematic variation and less indeterminacy in the idiolect of any one member of a language-community than there is in the totality of the idiolects of all its members: i.e., of all those who are said to know, or be competent in, a particular language. But the idiolect is the product of the individual's membership of many different social groups and of his or her participation in a variety of social activities, each with its more or less characteristic differences of style and register; and what, if anything, is genuinely and irreducibly unique to the individual is rarely of interest to the linguist. The fact that the idiolect differs ontologically from the language of the whole community (just as the individual differs ontologically from the community) is therefore of secondary importance as far as theoretical linguistics is concerned. Usually the individual who supplies the primary data (whether this is the linguist or some other informant) will be thought of generically, rather than as a unique individual, and as being representative of the whole language-community or of some dialectally or stylistically sub-community within it. And it makes no difference to the validity of the concept of the language-system, as such, whether the linguist considers it microlinguistically ("en elle-même et pour elle-même") or macrolinguistically: i.e., from a psychological, sociological, anthropological, social-psychological, or some other point of view, etc. (see Chapter 2).

It also makes no difference to the validity of the language-system as a theoretical construct, in macrolinguistics as also in microlinguistics, whether the linguist adopts what I have elsewhere called the fiction of homogeneity and abstracts from more or less of the systematic variation that is known to exist in the language-system of either the individual or the community (cf. Lyons, 1981a: 24–27). Sociolinguists have tended (for good reasons) to concentrate recently upon variation whereas psycholinguists, for the most part, have tended (for equally good reasons) to neglect it. But in

43

the long term this is a matter of historical contingency. It has little or nothing to do with the co-operative endeavour of linguists working patiently towards the construction of some all-embracing theory of language-structure and language-use and with their prior agreement that it would be advantageous for sociolinguists to work, temporarily, with one concept of the language-system and psycholinguists with another. And it depends as much upon what are perceived to be immediately exploitable and relevant advances in neighbouring disciplines as it does either upon progress in sociolinguistic theory or psycholinguistic theory as such or upon significant increases in the data-base of one or the other branch of macrolinguistics. After all, there is a psychological or cognitive dimension to such sociolinguistic phenomena as code-switching, bilingualism, diglossia, etc., which must eventually be described and accounted for from a psycholinguistic point of view. Similarly, there is much in the structure and use of a language that is determined by, or correlates with, sociocultural characteristics shared by all members of a language-community; and sociolinguistics can quite reasonably study these under the simplifying, but of course counterfactual, assumption of homogeneity.

What has been said in the last few paragraphs reinforces the point that was made earlier in this chapter about the current, and perhaps ultimate, impossibility of operating with a single concept of the language-system, adequate for the description of language and languages from all legitimate points of view. Scholars will of course disagree about this. Many will also challenge the opinion that all theoretical linguistics, and not just theoretical microlinguistics, depends upon the construction of formal (i.e., mathematical) models of language-systems. But in the present state of the subject this is perhaps largely a matter of terminological decision. I have suggested that a distinction can usefully be drawn between linguistic theory and theoretical linguistics. But I have not said that the latter has outmoded or demoted the former, or indeed that it ever will. Even in microlinguistics, linguistic theory is, on its own terms, more comprehensive and both descriptively and explanatorily more adequate than theoretical linguistics. And theoretical microlinguistics is far more advanced than any branch of theoretical macrolinguistics. It may well be that there are aspects of language-structure and language-use that will continue to resist mathematical formalization, not just temporarily, but permanently. This is something about which we can, as yet, do no more than make an act of faith, one way or the other, according to our temperament and philosophical and metascientific preferences. Whatever view one takes on this issue, however, it cannot be denied, I think, that the recent emergence of

44

theoretical linguistics has considerably enriched linguistic theory and, conversely, that theoretical linguistics depends upon linguistic theory – and for the foreseeable future will continue to depend upon it – for its formalizable insights. As the title indicates, I see myself as being concerned, in the present volume, with linguistic theory (and for the most part, more narrowly, with microlinguistic theory), rather than (except occasionally) with theoretical linguistics.

4

Natural, non-natural and unnatural languages: English, Urdu and other abstractions

The immediate and most readily identifiable sources of this chapter are, on the one hand, Katz's (1981) book, *Language and Other Abstract Objects*, which supplies part of the title, and, on the other, Pateman's (1983) article, 'What is a language?'.[1] The ideas that it contains are ideas that I have held, I think, for many years; but I have been greatly assisted in clarifying them, to my own satisfaction at least, by reading and pondering the two works that I have just mentioned and others by the same authors (Katz, 1984; Pateman, 1982, 1985).

My title deliberately echoes the title of Katz (1981): I have, however, substituted the term 'abstraction' for his 'abstract object', and I will explain presently why I have done this. More immediately to the point, it also echoes, and is intended to evoke, his initial formulation of the goals of the philosophy of linguistics:

Whereas linguistics tries to construct theories to answer the questions, first, 'What is English, Urdu, and other natural languages?' and second, 'What is language in general?', the philosophy of linguistics tries to construct philosophical theories to answer the questions, first, 'What are theories of English, Urdu, and other natural languages?', and second, 'What is a theory of language in general?' (Katz, 1981: 21).

There are several points worth noting here. For present purposes, it suffices to mention the following:

(i) English, Urdu, etc. are implicitly classified as natural languages;
(ii) a grammar of a natural language is assumed to be a theory of that language;
(iii) whereas the goal of descriptive linguistics appears to be restricted to the description of natural languages, the goal of general linguistics – unless the omission of the qualifying epithet 'natural' is unintentional and unmotivated – is not.

46

The assumption that grammars are theories – i.e., theories of grammaticality and sentencehood in the languages that they generate – reflects, of course, a point of view which Chomsky introduced into linguistics in the mid-1950s. Chomsky himself has recently modified his view of the relation between grammars and languages (1981, 1986). Katz, however, has not. This may not be evident from the short quotation that has just been given, but it is clear from the rest of his book and from his later article 'An outline of Platonist grammar' (1984) that he still holds to the original Chomskyan view that a grammar of a language is a scientific theory of that language. What has changed is his view of the ontological status of what he, like most people, refers to as natural languages: English, Urdu, and so on. Earlier, like Chomsky, he said that they were psychological entities, located or stored in the minds of their users. Now he believes them to be so-called Platonic entities: i.e., purely abstract mathematical objects without any kind of spatiotemporal location. Is he right to have changed his mind?

I do not intend to address this question immediately. The answer that I will eventually give, as will be evident from Chapters 2 and 3, is a rather extended and highly qualified "yes and no", and will emerge gradually and indirectly in what follows. It is, in fact, already implicit in my use of the term 'abstraction', in preference to Katz's 'abstract object'. The reason why I have used this term is to emphasize that the language-systems postulated by theoretical linguistics are the products of the linguist's more or less conscious and deliberate process of abstraction, or idealization, and have no independent or prior real-world existence. Languages, in so far as they are brought within the scope of theoretical linguistics, are certainly abstract objects in this sense. Whether they have any kind of so-called Platonic existence independently of the process of abstraction, I do not know; and I am not sure that I know what it means to assert that they have or that they have not. Let us grant, however, that they are ontologically on a par with other mathematical systems.

I have said that my view of the ontological status of language-systems, though sharpened and clarified by recent work in what, following Katz (1981) and Pateman (1987b) we may call the philosophy of linguistics, was formed many years ago. It is perhaps appropriate at this point to quote the words of my Cambridge mentor.[2] In his inaugural lecture, W. S. Allen, to the scandal of many of those who heard the lecture or read it in print later, delivered himself of the following opinion:

Linguistics . . . is a creative and not an observational activity: . . . the assumption of [a definite, single system, immanent in the language,] rules out the possibility of alternative analyses. This seems a high price to pay for the satisfaction of presuming to deal in realities (1955: 14–16).

Allen was talking, here, primarily about descriptive linguistics, and more especially about what I would now call descriptive microlinguistics (see Chapter 2). General linguistics, which for him, as for Firth (1951b: 69), and indeed for most contemporary schools of structural linguistics, had as its goal the construction of "a general theory applicable to particular linguistic descriptions", rather than of a general theory of the structure of all languages (cf. W. S. Allen, 1957b: 5), was no doubt to be viewed as being even more creative.[3]

Allen's view of the ontological status of language-systems, which I share, was formulated before Chomskyan generativism had replaced post-Bloomfieldian descriptivism as the dominant paradigm in American linguistics; and long before Chomskyan generativism had split into a variety of schismatic sects, each excommunicating the others for ontological, methodological or metatheoretical heresy. To the best of my knowledge, however, nothing has happened in linguistics in the last thirty years to make it any the less attractive now than when it was first formulated. It may be observed in passing that it is a view that is not readily accommodated within Katz's idiosyncratic and procrustean classification of philosophies of linguistics: nominalist, conceptualist or realist. But all this means, perhaps, is that Katz's rather simplistic classificatory trichotomy, which produces some ill-assorted bed-fellows, is insufficiently refined or comprehensive to do justice to the diversity of distinguishable views.[4]

As we shall see, the fact that languages (in the sense of language-systems, Saussure's 'langages') are legitimately regarded, from one point of view, as natural entities, does not imply that they cannot be regarded, from other points of view and with equal legitimacy, either as supra-individual social entities or as neither natural nor social, but autonomous and *sui generis* (see Chapter 2). Indeed, it is my contention that a good deal of unnecessary controversy among theorists in recent years has resulted from the failure to accept that different branches of linguistics must of necessity practise different kinds of abstraction and that it is pointless to argue that one is right, or more realistic, and another wrong, or less respectful of the facts, without having justified the selection of one set of facts, rather than another, and established their relevance to the purpose in hand. Personally, I would not go so far as to say that "there are no facts in linguistics until the linguist has made them" (W. S. Allen, 1957b: 80). I would, however, very much support the spirit that motivated this forceful assertion of the priority of theory over theory-neutral, undirected, observation and data-collection; and its forcefulness and lack of qualification were perhaps not only justifiable but necessary, if it was to achieve its effect at the time that it was made, when empiricism (though not of course behaviourism) reigned supreme in linguistics, on both sides of the Atlantic.[5]

Before moving on to consider what linguists mean, or ought to mean, when they use the phrase 'natural language', let me first say something briefly and apologetically about the word 'language'. If I feel rather apologetic about making the points that I am about to make, however briefly, it is because I have now made them so often in other publications. In fact, I find it increasingly difficult these days, as did Saussure in his later years, to say anything at all about language or linguistics without feeling defeated in advance by the hopelessness of having to use language to talk about language: by the necessity and the impossibility of using an everyday metalanguage, at least initially and pre-theoretically, to make clear and precise, unqualified, statements about the subject matter of linguistics. On this occasion, however, it is particularly important that I should draw attention to certain properties of the word 'language' as it is commonly used, technically and non-technically, by linguists speaking or writing in English.

It is all too often forgotten that 'language' is an English word which has translation-equivalents in some European languages, but not others (Lyons, 1981a: 1). And English-speaking students of linguistics are not always made as aware as they ought to be that the technical distinction that Saussure draws between 'langue' and 'langage' in the *Cours* is grounded in differences between these two words in everyday French (see Chapter 2 and 3 above; Lyons, 1984). I do not wish to go into this question again here. Let me simply say that the word 'language' (unlike 'langue') can be used either countably or uncountably, and (like 'langue') either generically or non-generically. This means that "What is language?" can be, but is not necessarily, interpretable as equivalent to "What is a language?" As I have explained in Chapter 3, the former question, for me, sets the goal for linguistics as a whole (with 'language' being given the meaning that Saussure gave to 'langage'); the latter sets the goal for the various branches of theoretical linguistics (with 'language' now having assigned to it one or other of the technical senses that derives from the sense that Saussure gave to 'langue'). It will be noted that, unlike Katz, for example, in the title of his book *Language and Other Abstract Objects*, for my own chapter title I have deliberately used 'language' in the plural. This eliminates some of the possible interpretations of the phrase 'natural language' that are of no direct concern to us in the present context, including "the (product of the) natural use of a language" and "the (product of the) natural use of language". By 'languages' I mean language-systems: a class of semiotic systems that includes, but is not exhausted by, the denotata of Saussure's 'langue'.

My starting point will be that of post-Saussurean, and more especially Hjelmslevian, so-called autonomous linguistics (see Chapter 2). This means that I am going to take it for granted that, for the purpose of microlinguistic description, a language-system must be distinguished not only from performance, but also from competence. This is, of course, a controversial view, which, since I have defended it above, I will now simply reiterate, rather than defend or further develop. It will later appear, however, that under another, non-autonomous but equally legitimate, interpretation of 'language' – and one that is especially relevant to the present theme – a language-system is rightly identifiable with Chomskyan competence. What Chomsky calls competence is, in principle, in the terminology I am using here, a language-system of the kind that is postulated by theoretical psycholinguistics. In practice, however, Chomsky has always operated with autonomous (microlinguistic) language-systems (see Chapters 2 and 3). To this extent, therefore, Katz (1981) is right to criticize what he refers to as Chomsky's conceptualism. Where Katz goes wrong, as we shall see, is (i) in supposing that the only kind of language-systems with which linguistics must operate are of the abstract, purely mathematical, kind that he calls Platonic and (ii) in identifying these with natural languages – in an unanalysed sense of 'natural'.

It is my principal purpose to discuss the validity of the epithet 'natural' in collocation with the noun 'language'; and I shall be drawing upon the points I made earlier about the several interpretations of phrases containing the English word 'language' in the singular which are made possible by its grammatical properties. Let me now remark, further, that, although linguists commonly define their subject as "the study of language" (which, as we have seen, is open to several interpretations, some of which are eliminated by applying the Saussurean distinction between 'langue' and 'langage'), in practice they usually confine their attention to so-called natural languages and indeed frequently switch between the two terms, 'language' and 'natural language', without making it clear whether they are to be interpreted as synonymous or not. When linguists do use the term 'natural language' in contrast with 'language' to refer to a proper subclass of the totality of languages, actual and potential, they customarily have in mind as members of its complementary subclass either artificial languages such as Esperanto, on the one hand, or the formal languages of logicians and computer scientists, on the other. Let us grant that, in terms of the pre-theoretical, operational, definition of 'natural' (in one of its senses) that I have used elsewhere, English and Urdu (not to mention Quechua, Dyirbal, Yoruba and Malayalam) are pre-theoretically identifiable as natural languages; they have "not been constructed, whether for general or specific purposes" and they are "acquired by [their] users as a normal part of the process of maturation and socialization" (Lyons, 1981c: 216; see Chapter 1 above).

But the term 'natural language' is usually further restricted by linguists, tacitly rather than explicitly, in two other respects:

(i) by excluding from consideration non-human languages – granted that they are languages – used by animals and machines;

(ii) by excluding such gestural languages as American Sign Language (ASL) or British Sign Language (BSL), which, though they are certainly both human and natural (in terms of the operational definition of 'natural' that I have just given, if not in other senses that I will establish presently), differ from what linguists usually think of as prototypical languages, in that they are not normally – and, in one sense of 'naturally', perhaps not naturally – associated with speech.

One of the terminological problems that confronts us in discussing the relation between gestural languages such as ASL or BSL and what linguists usually think of as natural languages is that the latter are commonly referred to, contrastively, by scholars who have done research on the former as spoken languages (see Chapter 1, Addendum). The problem, trivial enough in itself and easy enough to avoid, once the ambiguity of the term 'spoken language' is pointed out, is that it introduces into any discussion of the linguistic status of ASL, BSL, etc. a confusion between language and speech. But the terminological problem, as we shall see, reflects another much more interesting, substantive, problem.

I have argued elsewhere in several places about the importance of drawing a clear distinction between language and speech, between language-systems and the medium in which they are manifest (Lyons, 1968a, 1977a, 1981a). As far as microlinguistics is concerned, I am of course merely adopting (with certain qualifications and refinements that I need not go into here) Hjelmslev's elaboration of the central tenet of Saussurean structuralism (cf. Hjelmslev, 1943b). But I have also argued more recently that the distinction is also valid for the psycholinguistic and neurolinguistic study of language-acquisition and language-performance:

that "in one sense of 'natural' [the sense that satisfies the operational definition that I have already quoted], language is indeed naturally associated with speech"; but that, nevertheless, "it is possible that the language faculty and the predisposition to vocalize [each of which is natural, both in terms of the operational definition of 'natural' and probably, as present evidence strongly suggests, in another, deeper, sense of 'natural'] are biologically independent and only contingently associated in speech"; and that "the graphic medium, though non-natural, is clearly not unnatural with respect to the medium-transferable verbal component" of what are usually referred to by linguists – and others – as natural languages (Lyons 1981c: 219–20; see also Chapter 1 above).

Now, I do not wish to discuss the naturalness of such languages as ASL and BSL in detail. It will already be evident that they may be natural in one or more senses, but not in others; and I do, in fact, believe this to be the case. (Something further is said on this topic in the following chapter.) I have mentioned them here because they are now being intensively studied by linguists and because much of the discussion that I have seen is bedevilled by the lack of a pre-theoretically applicable term for what linguists and others usually refer to in this context as spoken languages and elsewhere as natural languages. Making use of the term that I introduced for this purpose in Chapter 1, I will henceforth refer to them, pre-theoretically, as N-languages. ASL, BSL, etc. may then be referred to, contrastively but also pre-theoretically, as S-languages. This classifies them, at least pre-theoretically, as languages, but leaves open both the question whether they differ typologically from N-languages and also the question whether they are fully or in all respects natural.

The letter 'N' is mnemonically connected both with 'natural' and with 'normal': N-languages are what are normally thought of, pre-theoretically and prototypically, as languages – as belonging to that subclass of languages for which French, in everyday, non-Saussurean, usage employs 'langue' (in contrast with 'langage': see Chapter 3). The term 'N-language', I must emphasize, is a pre-theoretical term which would lose its usefulness if it were given theoretical status. One of the difficulties with the French word 'langue' is that it is often used by structuralists writing in French both theoretically and, of necessity, also pre-theoretically in the same work. If 'langue' is used as a theoretical term by structuralists writing in English, as it has been, this problem does not of course arise. But it seems preferable to employ for theoretical purposes, instead of 'langue', the by-now familiar technical term 'language-system', as I have been doing in the preceding chapters.

Natural, non-natural and unnatural languages

It is characteristic of N-languages – English, Urdu, etc. – that in all known instances:

(i) unless there are inhibiting factors, physiological or environmental, they are acquired naturally (in our operationally defined sense) in association with speech (even if this association with speech is in itself, in another sense, either not natural or not fully natural);

(ii) they have certain semiotic properties, or design-features, including not only arbitrariness, duality, discreteness, productivity, etc., which have so often been listed and discussed by linguists and semioticians, but also what I have called medium-transferability (cf. Lyons, 1981a: 11).

Some of these design-features have been selected as criterial for the distinction between languages and other semiotic systems, notably in the Saussurean tradition by Hjelmslev (1943a). Hjelmslev's definition or characterization of language-systems in terms of duality of structure and arbitrariness is, no doubt, subtler and more interesting than those of Hockett (1958: 574) and his followers in the American ethological tradition (cf. Lyons, 1977a: 70ff.). But it is, in my view, unnecessarily restrictive.

It also suffers from what I take to be the fundamental and vitiating error at the heart of Glossematics: the postulation of parallelism between the expression-plane and the content-plane (cf. Bazell, 1952). Interestingly enough, Chomskyan generativism had been guilty, independently, of the same error with its equivocal use of the terms 'interpretation' and 'representation' in both phonology and semantics and, in earlier days at least, its commitment to the analysis of both form and meaning in terms of minimal features or components. But that is another story. It is relevant to our present concerns only in so far as it has tended to blur the distinction between speech and language and to lend support to what has rightly been criticized as the phonocentrism of modern linguistics (see Chapter 1, Addendum). And, independently of the question of parallelism between semantics and phonology, how often these days, in introductory textbooks of linguistics, do we come across the proposition, presented as axiomatic, that a language relates sound and meaning? This proposition is philosophically suspect on other grounds. All that needs to be said in the present connexion, however, is that it is unduly restrictive.

It is important in theoretical linguistics not to use the term 'language' too narrowly, restricting it by definition to N-languages and to such other actual or potential semiotic systems as share an arbitrary selection of what may turn out to be contingently associated properties. I agree with

Hjelmslev, then, and perhaps also with Katz, that it is the aim of theoretical, general, linguistics to define the set of possible languages (L) without prejudice to the empirical question whether N-languages (NL), on the one hand, or natural languages (NatL) – so far undefined – or human languages (HumL) on the other, constitute a typologically identifiable subset of L. But what is or ought to be meant by the term 'natural' in the present context? This is the question to which I now turn.

The word 'natural' enters into several lexical oppositions, some of which have a long and complex history in linguistics, philosophy and related disciplines. Among its relevant antonyms (apart from the formally related terms, 'non-natural' and 'unnatural', which I will come back to), we may include:

(i)   in more or less technical usage, 'artificial', 'conventional', 'cultural' and 'acquired' (by experience, learning, environmental conditioning, etc.);

and

(ii) in less technical usage, 'awkward', 'unusual', 'constrained', 'unexpected', 'inexplicable'.

Some of the different senses of 'natural' (though it is perhaps not always clear which) are exemplified in the following quotations from well-known and influential authors:

(i)   The natural condition of language is to preserve one form for one meaning, and one meaning for one form (Bolinger, 1977: x).

(ii)   There is in my opinion no important theoretical difference between natural languages and the artificial languages of logicians: indeed, I consider it possible to comprehend the syntax and semantics of both kinds of languages within a single natural and mathematically precise theory (Montague, 1974: 222).

(iii) [Natural meaning, in contrast with non-natural meaning, can be explicated in terms of] the sense in which what something means is closely related to the idea of what it is a natural sign for (as in 'Black clouds mean rain') (Grice, 1968: 231).

Such quotations could be multiplied almost indefinitely. But these will suffice for the present. They will help us to see the point of certain of the distinctions that I shall be drawing and of their relevance to current linguistic theory and to the philosophy of linguistics.

Grice's use of 'natural' (in contrast with 'conventional') goes back ultimately, of course, to the old Greek opposition of "nature" ('phusis') and "convention" ('nomos'), which has dominated philosophical speculation about the origin of language from the earliest times, has played a crucial role, at various times, in the development of traditional grammar, and is to this day a commonplace of semiotics (cf. Lyons, 1968a: 4, 403). It derives from a view of languages, or more generally of semiotic systems, which sees them as reflecting, in whole or in part, the structure of nature. I will refer to this, for good historical and etymological reasons, as the speculative view of language (Latin 'speculum', "mirror": cf. Lyons, 1968a: 14). The speculative view of language has left its mark terminologically in such traditional phrases as 'natural gender'. Less obviously perhaps, it underpins, on the one hand, the picture theory of Wittgenstein's *Tractatus* (1922) – and other versions of the correspondence theory of truth and therefore, derivatively, a good deal of twentieth-century truth-conditional semantics – and, on the other, many of the principles of what is currently referred to as 'natural syntax' (cf. Haiman, 1985). It is also worth mentioning that 'arbitrary' in Saussure's sense is more or less equatable with 'non-natural' (= 'conventional'); and Saussure's (1916) insistence on arbitrariness as one of the defining principles of N-languages puts him firmly on one side in the age-old controversy to which I have already referred. But Saussure, of course, gave a new twist to the argument when he located the arbitrariness of the linguistic sign ('l'arbitraire du signe') not in the relation between the sign and what it signified, but inside the sign itself, in the bonding of a language-internal signifier ('signifiant') with a language-internal what-is-signified ('signifié').

Bolinger's use of 'natural', on the other hand, is perhaps more suggestive of the evolutionary or Romantic view of languages, which sees them, if only metaphorically, as organisms – either as species or as specimens (i.e., either as natural kinds or as individual members of natural kinds), whose diachronic development is determined by species-specific principles. This organismic view of languages (if I may so refer to it) was implicit in a good deal of eighteenth-century and nineteenth-century linguistic theory and made explicit by Schleicher (1863): it was challenged by his opponents, including Whitney (1872), who was cited with approval in Saussure's *Cours* (see Chapter 5 below). As we shall see presently, Chomsky's theory of universal grammar and language-acquisition implies an organismic view, not of the diachronic development of N-languages, but of the ontogenetic development, or growth, of idiolects; and he has for some years now made this quite clear. But Bolinger's use of 'natural' can also be seen as involving what I identified above as a less technical, more everyday, sense of the term in which it stands in implicit contrast with such words as 'unusual', 'unexpected', etc. It will be evident from the points that I shall be making below that it is not always easy to distinguish the technical or semi-technical senses of 'natural' from its non-technical senses. And this is hardly surprising given that the latter derive historically from the former.

Montague uses the word 'natural' twice in the short passage that I have quoted above. The phrase 'natural language', which is explicitly contrasted with 'artificial language', need not delay us long at this point: it clearly denotes what I am calling, pre-theoretically, N-languages. Whether what Montague has to say about such languages is true is, to say the least, debatable; but it cannot be sensibly debated until we have answered the questions that I am posing here and substituted for 'natural language', used pre-theoretically, the appropriate theoretical term. As it stands, like most of the generalizations about so-called natural languages made by philosophers, logicians and linguists, it is quite simply uninterpretable.

As to Montague's second use of 'natural', to qualify 'theory', this illustrates once again the difficulty of distinguishing the non-technical from the technical or semi-technical. Mathematicians and logicians are perhaps justifiably more confident than linguists can be about what counts as naturalness as a property of theories or formal systems and would no doubt set about defining it in terms of elegance, economy, etc. But what I want to emphasize here is that, in the empirical sciences, prior to the objectivization of naturalness as a property of the theory or of the descriptive models associated with it, in the handling of the empirical data (and also in their selection as data), we first meet its subjective correlate in the expectations and prejudices of the theorist. In short, what is referred to as a more natural theory or description is, first and foremost, one that fulfils the prior expectations of the theorist better than does a less natural one. This certainly seems to be the case as far as what is currently referred to as natural phonology, natural morphology or natural syntax is concerned. In each case, the term 'natural' can be given a more or less satisfactory objective interpretation. But the objective sense of 'natural' differs from case to case. It is only the subjective sense of 'natural', it seems to me, that makes it applicable without equivocation to a property that all these various theories have in common. This might appear, at first sight, to be a somewhat dismissive comment. But, as we shall see later, it is not intended to be. I have the healthiest respect for the pre-theoretical prejudices of experienced practising descriptive linguists.

Also to be noted, before we embark upon a more systematic explication of the phrase 'natural language', is the etymological connexion between 'natural' and 'native', which initially might appear to be of no more than historical, not to say antiquarian, interest. Its present relevance can be made more immediately apparent by drawing attention to the theoretical and methodological status of the concepts of the native language and of the native speaker in modern linguistics. Do we not all assent readily to the proposition that it is only their native language (or languages) that children acquire naturally (other languages being acquired non-naturally, or at least less naturally)? And do we not also assent, no less readily, to the further proposition that the utterances of native speakers of a language are generally more natural than those of non-native speakers? Is 'natural' being used in the same sense in the formulation of both propositions? And can we reasonably subscribe to their truth without first deciding what that sense is? Indeed, what reason is there for descriptive linguistics to be as concerned as it is with native speakers as the source of acceptable (natural?) data if it cannot give a satisfactory answer to such questions?

To the best of my knowledge, there has been no attempt to distinguish carefully the various senses of 'natural' in the collocations in which it is used, technically, semi-technically, or at times quite loosely, in linguistics, and to determine which, if any, of these can be identified with the meaning of 'natural' in any theoretically defensible interpretation of the phrase 'natural language'. I do not propose to engage here in a full-scale treatment of the topic: this would require a whole book, rather than a single chapter. What I will do is to distinguish, briefly and non-philosophically, just four senses of 'natural' and comment upon each of them in a way which demonstrates, I trust, the importance of using the term 'natural language' with due circumspection in theoretical linguistics and, more especially, in any discussion of the ontological status of language and languages. At the very least, I should succeed in preventing anyone from ever using the word 'natural' naturally again! But I hope to do more than that.

Naturalness$_1$

By 'natural' in the first sense – "natural$_1$" – I shall mean "in conformity with nature". I draw attention both to the double quotation-marks and to the subscript numeral: "natural$_1$" is one of the meanings of the English lexeme 'natural', whose citation-form is *natural* (I am here using the typographical conventions explained in Lyons, 1977a, 1981a, b, and summarized on p. xv of the present volume.) And the word 'nature' in this context is being employed in a traditional philosophical sense: one that gave rise to such terms as 'natural philosophy', 'the natural sciences', 'natural law' and 'the laws of nature'. This is also the sense in which I used it above: on the one hand, in the formulation of the realist's (speculative) view of the relation between language and the world (nature) and, on the other, with reference to the 'nature'-vs.-'convention' debate.

Various more particular interpretations of the phrase 'in conformity with nature' would yield various classes of natural$_1$ languages. For example, given a realist theory of the external world, with its associated notion of natural kinds, a grammatically or semantically natural$_1$, language might be defined as one which in its grammatical or semantic structure directly and faithfully reflected the ontological structure of the world (Latin 'rerum natura', "the nature of things"). Whether N-languages are wholly or partly natural, in this sense, is of course one of the long-standing issues in the philosophy of language. Few philosophers or linguists would nowadays take the strongly realist view of either the grammatical or the lexical structure of N-languages: i.e., the view that they are fully determined by the structure of the world and reflect that structure at all points. If they did, they would presumably be committed thereby to a correspondingly strong version of what was traditionally known as universal grammar. And, even in the past, in what we might think of as the formative period of traditional universalism – the period of medieval speculative grammar – the proposition that all N-languages had the same structure needed to be qualified by invoking the Aristotelian and scholastic distinction between essential and accidental properties (cf. Lyons, 1968a:/16; and Chapter 7 below). As far as languages other than N-languages are concerned, it is worth mentioning in passing that some artificial languages, including most notably the predicate calculus, have been held by some of their advocates in the hey-day of logical positivism and logical atomism to reflect more faithfully than N-languages the ontological warp and woof of the world.

Despite the centrality of this issue in the philosophy of linguistics, I do not propose to take any further account of it here. For present purposes, I am going to select another interpretation of 'in conformity with nature': I am going to interpret it as meaning "being constrained by the laws of nature". And, for reasons having to do with the more recent history of linguistics, I am going to interpret this gloss in a rather particular sense: a natural$_1$ language, I will say, is one that could be used by organisms or devices that are subject to the laws of nature. This has the effect of biasing the rest of our discussion towards issues that first assumed prominence in generativist discussions of language: issues having to do with finite storage, real-time processing, etc. N-languages are generally, and no doubt correctly, assumed to be not just a subclass, but a proper subclass, of natural$_1$ languages (Nat$_1$L).

Naturalness$_2$

My second interpretation of the word 'natural' can be glossed as "constrained by the nature – i.e., constrained by the physical, or psychophysical, make-up – of the organism or device using it". For rather obvious reasons, which make clear immediately its contemporary relevance, I will refer to the set of properties denoted by 'natural' under this particular interpretation of the term as species-specific naturalness. And I will let the word 'species' denote classes of artefacts, including computers, as well as biological organisms.

What is at issue here, in addition to species-specific limitations of storage, processing, etc., which vary from species to species (and less significantly from specimen to specimen), is the far trickier and philosophically more interesting question of the possible species-specificity of meaning. It is generally assumed – and I do not wish to challenge this assumption – that semanticity (expressing, or being able to express, meaning) is an essential property of anything that might reasonably count as a language. (I leave on one side the question how one might go on to define or explicate semanticity.) In what sense, then, is 'natural' being used by such philosophers as Grice (1968) or Bennett (1976), who wish to ground the characteristically non-natural, conventional, meaning of N-languages in what is assumed to be a more basic kind of natural meaning, which *ex hypothesi* is not restricted to N-languages? And this brings us back, once again, to one of the central concerns of speculative grammar and the philosophy of language (and linguistics): what degree of congruence is there between ontology and epistemology and between each of these and grammar (in the broadest sense)? The cognitivist, or, at least, Chomskyan, notion of species-specific universal grammar is compatible with several philosophically distinguishable answers to this question. But Chomsky himself has frequently emphasized the role played by what he takes to be the species-specific determinants of human cognition in the acquisition and use of N-languages. And this would seem to imply an anti-realist view of the relation between ontology and epistemology and, consequently, between ontology and grammar.

However that may be, it will be noted that I have deliberately distinguished and defined the first two senses of 'natural' in such a way that

(i) natural$_1$ languages include as a subclass natural$_2$ languages (i.e., $\text{Nat}_1\text{L} \supset \text{Nat}_2\text{L}$).

And on the assumption that Nat_2L splits into species-specific subclasses

59

which are typologically distinct from one another in various ways (including, perhaps, but not necessarily, their particular kind or degree of semanticity):

(ii) actual and potential human languages (HumL = $Nat_{2H}L$) constitute a proper subset of Nat_2L (i.e., $Nat_2L \supset HumL$, but $HumL \not\supset Nat_2L$).

As to N-languages (NL), they too (or their formally well-defined models or analogues) are, like HumL, obviously included in (but presumably do not include) Nat_2L.

The Chomskyan research programme is, of course, based on the assumption that NL, whether or not it is co-extensive with HumL, is a typologically definable subclass, not just of Nat_1L, but also of Nat_2L.

Naturalness₃

The third sense of 'natural' is the one that the earlier operational definition was intended to capture and takes into account not just the natural₂ determinants of linguistic competence, but also constraints relating to acquisition: "acquired [or acquirable] by [their] users as a normal part of the process of maturation and socialization". As it stands, this gloss does not apply directly to computers and other artefacts; and there seems little point in modifying it so that it would. The points to be noted about this property – naturalness₃ – include the following:

(i) Naturalness₃ is perhaps strongly related to naturalness₂ in that, as the Chomskyan research programme assumes, it depends upon a species-specific, genetically transmitted and environmentally triggered blueprint for maturation. But naturalness₃ for any given species is conceptually distinct from naturalness₂; and it is an empirical question whether any given subset of Nat_3L is typologically definable and, if so, whether it is co-extensive with a typologically definable subset of Nat_2L. We can, however, distinguish in principle human-specific natural₃ languages ($Nat_{3H}L$) from human-specific natural₂ languages ($Nat_{2H}L$ = HumL).

(ii) Naturalness₃, more obviously than naturalness₂, is a gradable property. But naturalness₂ may also be gradable, and interestingly so. As we have noted earlier, among actual human languages (a proper subclass of HumL) both N-languages (NL) and such S-languages (SL) as American Sign Language (ASL) and British Sign Language (BSL) are Nat₃-languages, regardless of whether they also constitute a typologically distinct subclass of Nat₂-languages. And, given appropriate environmental circumstances (let us not quibble about the normality of the circumstances), S-languages appear to be Nat_3L to the same degree that NL are. The question whether SL are Nat_2L or, more particularly, human-specific Nat$_2$L to the same degree as NL, is, however, unclear. As I have suggested elsewhere, it is at least possible that the phylogenetic, or evolutionary, naturalization of whatever properties distinguish NL from SL make SL in that respect less natural$_2$ than NL (see Chapter 5).

It is not clear, then, either that Nat$_2$L $\supset$ Nat$_3$L or, conversely, that Nat$_3$L $\supset$ Nat$_2$L. It also follows from the points that have just been made that human languages (HumL), as I previously characterized them, may not be a well-defined class.

Naturalness$_4$

The fourth and final sense of 'natural' that I will distinguish is formulated with deliberate looseness: "conforming to the linguist's expectations about what is normal or typical". Any property (or set of) properties that satisfies the criterion built into this gloss is a natural$_4$ property; any language that satisfies it (i.e., any language characterizable as having natural$_4$ properties) is a natural$_4$ language.

Let me now make a number of more or less self-evident comments about my definition of this fourth sense of 'natural'.

(i)   I have referred to it as a single sense, but it might be preferable to describe it rather as a set or cluster of more or less heterogeneous senses and subsenses. It would be easy enough to distinguish some of these senses and subsenses and to make certain of them more precise. But that is not necessary for present purposes.

(ii) Naturalness$_4$ is obviously gradable, at least intuitively: so that one language can be said to be more natural$_4$ than another, either globally or in some particular respect, and, at least in principle, one language, or class of languages, can be described as being maximally natural$_4$.

(iii) Naturalness$_4$ has been objectified: i.e., it has been characterized as a property of languages. Its identification in particular instances, however, is clearly subjective.

(iv) Naturalness$_4$, or its correlate, can also be seen, not as a property of languages, but as a property of either theories or descriptions: NB, the second use of 'natural' in the quotation from Montague (1970: 222) given above.

(v)   The naturalness$_4$ of the theory or description and the naturalness$_4$ of the language being described are not always clearly distinguishable. Granted the validity of some kind of distinction – not necessarily that of Chomsky (1965) – between descriptive and explanatory adequacy, on the one hand, and between the weak and strong (or relatively strong) equivalence of alternative analyses of the same language, on the other, a language might be held to be more natural$_4$ under one analysis than it is under an alternative non-strongly-equivalent analysis. The linguist will then prefer (naturally!) the analysis which shows the language to be more natural$_4$; and the theory or description which supports this analysis will then in turn, for that reason, count as having a higher explanatory value and as being, to that degree, more natural$_4$. To put it like this, however, might seem to imply the complete theory-neutrality of empirical data: it might seem to imply that the directionality of determination between the naturalness$_4$ of languages and the naturalness$_4$ of theories or descriptions is always the same. Clearly, this is not so. It may not be quite true that "there are no facts in linguistics until the linguist has made them" (see p. 48 above), but it is certainly the case that the selection and arrangement of data, prior to their systematic description, is often strongly influenced, in particular cases, by general linguistic theory.

(vi) There are both formal and non-formal determinants of the naturalness$_4$ of theories in linguistics which are relatively independent of such theory-neutral linguistic facts as there are. The formal determinants, which do not concern us here, include what is perceived as greater simplicity, elegance and consistency. The non-formal determinants include particular linguists' philosophical and metatheoretical convictions about matters as diverse as the unity of science, on the one hand, and, on the other, the relations between language and communication, between language and society, between language and mind, between language and the physical world, and so on. And this complicates in various ways the separation of naturalness$_4$ as a property of theories or descriptions, not only from naturalness$_4$ as a property of languages, but also from the other kinds of naturalness that were identified earlier.

It is no part of my purpose to look at the naturalness$_4$ of particular theories of the structure of N-languages in the light of these comments. As far as modern theoretical linguistics is concerned, the quest for naturalness$_4$, as such, was initiated, indirectly, by Chomsky & Halle (1968) with their employment of a certain version of the Prague School notion of markedness as a constraint on the excessive power of the phonological rules of a transformational-generative grammar (seen as a model of an N-language). But some sense of naturalness$_4$ has been present as a control on Chomskyan generative grammar from its very beginnings. Phrase-structure grammars (whether context-free or context-sensitive) were rejected by Chomsky (1957) as models of N-languages, not because they could not in principle generate all and only (the correlates of) the sentences of N-languages (including English), but because the structural descriptions that they assigned to N-language sentences were, in some sense, less revealing than the structural descriptions assigned to what were taken to be the same sentences by more powerful transformational grammars. And, when we come to the later period, from a sufficiently general point of view both the Chomsky & Halle (1968) theory and theories of so-called natural generative phonology that were developed in opposition to it can be described as being, at least in intent, natural$_4$ theories (of N-languages).

But to say this is simply to draw attention to the heterogeneity of naturalness$_4$ as a property of current theories, not only of phonology, but also of morphology, syntax and lexicology. After all, if we take the view expressed by Chomsky (1968, etc.) that the most distinctive properties of N-languages are natural$_{2H}$, i.e., human-specific (deriving from the biologically unique structure of the human mind), rather than just natural$_1$ ("in conformity with nature"), we shall be inclined to rate more highly (on the relevant dimension of naturalness$_4$) any theory which emphasizes what is (apparently) arbitrary or conventional in the structure of N-languages in contrast with an otherwise comparable theory which emphasizes what is non-arbitrary or non-conventional.

I shall have nothing further to say here, then, about particular more or less natural$_4$ theories of the structure of N-languages. It is clear that linguists' expectations and assumptions about the structure of N-languages have often been promoted to theoretical or quasi-theoretical status, not just recently, but throughout the history of linguistics, in the search for both descriptive and explanatory adequacy. And what is seen, by some linguists at least, as the greater naturalness$_4$ of one theory of the structure of N-languages, rather than another, may be related to any of the different kinds of objective naturalness that have been distinguished above.

This does not mean, however, that we must discount or undervalue naturalness$_4$ in the description of particular N-languages or in the formulation of general theories of the structure of N-languages. As I have argued in Chapter 2 above (in defence of so-called autonomous linguistics), much of the primary observational data of descriptive linguistics is independently identifiable as such and analysable, up to a point, in what we can reasonably call theory-neutral terms. All linguists, in the course of their reading and research develop a sense of what they are likely to find in attested N-languages. And whatever their prior expectations are based on, most of what they do find – in so far as it is objectively determinate or, at least, intersubjectively determinable by linguists of different theoretical persuasions – will prove to be, in the event, in conformity with these expectations.

For example, such questions as whether a language has a distinction between nouns and verbs, whether it has the grammatical category of tense, whether it makes use of word-order for syntactic purposes, whether it has vowel-harmony, these, and many other questions like them, may not be theory-neutral in any absolute sense (and they may not always be answerable with an unqualified yes or no), but they are not theory-dependent to a degree which renders them empirically unanswerable. They are questions of the kind that have been investigated by typologists in relation to a large number of genetically unrelated N-languages across the world (cf. Shopen, 1985a, b, c). And many, if not all, of the typological statements that are made on the basis of such investigations – provided that they are formulated in what is by now the traditional metalanguage of general linguistics – are readily falsifiable. Furthermore, as Bazell (1958) pointed out many years ago, the fact that some of the empirical data in particular N-languages lend themselves to alternative analyses may be indicative of objective structural indeterminacy. If so (as he also pointed out), this will itself be a fact to be taken account of both by the descriptive linguist and by the typologist.

In what follows in this chapter, then, I will take it for granted that the structure of N-languages is sufficiently determinate for many of the typological generalizations made about them, expressible in terms of naturalness$_4$, to be empirically falsifiable. And I shall not be further concerned with the relation between naturalness$_4$ and the other kinds of naturalness.

Before leaving the question of the naturalness$_4$ of languages, however, let me make explicit what may be referred to as the paradox of naturalness$_4$. A maximally natural$_4$ language, for any arbitrary linguist (or group of linguists), may be defined as one which conforms in all respects to that linguist's (or group of linguists') prior expectations about its structure (phonological, morphological, lexical and syntactic). The paradox is that a maximally natural$_4$ language, so defined, will also be, for the same linguist (or group of linguists), highly unnatural$_4$. Not only is no known N-language, considered as a whole, maximally natural$_4$, but we can confidently predict that no such N-language will ever be found. Explaining why this is so may be left as an exercise for the reader! It is a problem upon which certain structuralist theories of language-change have foundered. For such theories would seem to predict that, over time, all N-languages will tend towards the maximization of naturalness$_4$. And this does not happen.

I said earlier that, if we are to establish theoretical linguistics on a broad enough base, we must not restrict it in advance to N-languages and to "such other actual or potential semiotic systems as share an arbitrary selection of what may turn out to be contingently associated properties".

Attested N-languages are but a small and historically contingent subclass of actual N-languages, past and present; and actual N-languages in turn are presumably but a relatively small, historically contingent, subclass of possible N-languages. The definition of L (the class of all languages) cannot but be a matter of arbitrary decision. Though arbitrary, it will not however be unconstrained. Any definition of 'language' with which linguistics would wish to operate will be influenced or conditioned – or, as Hjelmslev (1943a) put it somewhat paradoxically, motivated – by the linguist's sense of the centrality of N-languages, actual and potential, and by the accumulated experience that linguists have had in the analysis of actual N-languages, from which they can then extrapolate, on the basis of naturalness$_4$, to the much larger class of possible N-languages. If we want L to include, in addition to N-languages, what Montague referred to, in the passage quoted above, as "the artificial languages of logicians" without begging the question whether there is or is not any "important theoretical difference" between them (see above), we shall need to adopt a fairly broad definition. The definition will none the less be conditioned or motivated by the linguist's sense of the centrality of N-languages.

This should rule out immediately any definition which converts what is a patently contingent and non-universal property of only some N-languages into an essential defining property of all languages. It should have ruled out under this head, for example, the definition of a language as a set of (well-formed) strings over some vocabulary. This definition, with which most generative grammarians have operated since the publication of Chomsky (1956), is to be rejected because it is biased in favour of that typologically restricted subclass of N-languages whose members are (i) linear and (ii) morphemic. That is to say: (i) it makes linearity an essential property of the grammatical structure of (well-formed) syntagms (phrases, clauses and sentences), rather than allowing it to be just one of the possible exponents of well-formedness and one which may or may not be invested with specific grammatical functions; and (ii) it (implicitly) defines the vocabulary-units of all languages to be minimal forms (i.e., morphemes in the Bloomfieldian sense of this term). Few, if any, actual N-languages are either wholly linear or wholly morphemic; many, including so-called free-word-order languages, are to a greater or less degree non-linear; and many, including so-called fusional or inflecting languages, are non-morphemic.[6]

Given that this is so, it might seem surprising that Chomskyan transformational-generative grammar should have been formalized from the outset within the framework of concatenating rewriting systems (which had been devised initially for the construction and investigation of artificial logical languages). That it was so formalized is to be accounted for, no doubt, partly in terms of the prior existence of a body of what appeared to be applicable work dealing with such systems and partly in terms of its origin, as far as linguistics is concerned, in Bloomfieldian theories of grammatical structure (cf. Lyons, 1968a: 209ff.; 1977b). That it was nevertheless able to satisfy at least the conditions of weak adequacy in the description of non-linear and non-morphemic constructions is to be attributed to what is now acknowledged to be the excessive power of transformational rules and also to some linguists' willingness to turn a deaf ear to the promptings of their inner voice expressing what should have been recognized as a well-founded sense of naturalness$_4$.

Other definitions, or characterizations, of L (and indeed, as we have seen, of several of its subclasses including HumL) that must be rejected are any which include a reference to the phonic medium. This means that, whereas grammatical structure, and more particularly syntactic structure, is clearly essential to a language, phonological structure as such is not. In fact, it is not obvious that we should follow such scholars as Hjelmslev (1943a) or Martinet (1960, 1962) in making duality of structure of defining property of languages. But if we do, we should certainly not associate with it the condition that the elements (or figurae) of what the Glossematicians referred to as the expression-plane must necessarily be segments (in the phonologist's sense of this term). Linearity, or unidimensional segmentability, is not even a universal property of the phonological structure of N-languages (see Chapter 6). And it might be preferable anyway to let duality of structure serve as one of the typological characteristics of a subclass of L.[7] It would then turn out, as a matter of empirical discovery, not that all N-languages have the property of duality in all layers or components of their grammatical and lexical structure, but rather that they all have this property (to a high degree) in their verbal, or non-prosodic, component (cf. Lyons, 1977a: 71ff.).[8]

As with linearity and duality, so also with arbitrariness. It may well be that all N-languages have this property, though (as we have noted above) they also have a good deal of (different kinds of) non-arbitrariness. And there seems to be no good reason for making the arbitrariness of the connexion between form and meaning criterial for any semiotic system that might count as a language (in the broadest sense of this term). If we do, apart from the problem of deciding what degree or what kind of arbitrariness should be criterial, it would be difficult to justify the application of the term 'language' to the semiotic systems constructed by logicians. When it comes to the assignment of an interpretation to the units and well-formed expressions of such systems, the question of arbitrariness simply does not arise explicitly; and there is nothing to prevent us from making the connexion between predicate-symbols and their interpretation iconic or otherwise non-arbitrary. Moreover, there is far from being a non-arbitrary connexion between form and meaning in standard interpretations of, say, the propositional calculus or predicate calculus, as far as syntactic structure is concerned. Of course, it is generally agreed that iconicity and other kinds of non-arbitrariness impose severe constraints upon the expressivity and semiotic versatility of a system. And it may also be the case that the development of N-languages, as we know them, out of different kinds of semiotically less versatile or expressively less powerful languages (or out of what we might prefer to call non-language or pre-language) came about as a consequence of a reduction of arbitrariness (see Chapter 5).

These are questions that cannot even be posed precisely if we begin by restricting unnecessarily and by metatheoretical fiat the membership of L (the class of all languages). At the same time, some restrictions must be imposed in the definition of L. How then do we proceed? So far I have been operating with the principle of the centrality of N-languages (coupled with an unanalysed notion of naturalness$_4$). And in the discussion of non-phonic, non-linear and non-morphemic languages – and perhaps also of languages without the structural properties of arbitrariness and duality – I have interpreted this to imply that we should not include among the defining properties of L anything that is patently a contingent and non-universal property of only some (actual) N-languages. But the notion of patent, or obvious, contingency, though reliable enough, I believe, in the cases to which I have applied it, is hardly one that can be taken for granted more generally. Let me substitute, therefore, for what might be referred to as the non-universalization of the (patently) contingent, the following two working principles:

(A) Any structural property that is found to be present (to whatever degree) in any actual N-language will be allowed (without restriction of degree) as a possible property of the members of what is thereby defined to be a typological subclass of L.

(B) No structural property that is not found (to some degree) in some actual N-language will be allowed (to any degree) as a possible property of any member of L.

These two working principles, it must be emphasized, are not being presented as satisfactorily definitive of L. To define L – to answer the question "What is a language?" – is after all the goal, not the starting point, of theoretical (general) linguistics. We are a long way from having reached the goal; and when do reach it we may well find that there is no clear or interesting distinction to be drawn, in terms of their structural properties, between languages and non-languages. What our working principles do is to ensure that we do not start by unduly restricting the field or skewing it in favour of particular subclasses of languages. These principles are like Hjelmslev's (1943a) definition of a language-system, in that they are (as he put it) arbitrary, but motivated; and although they look very different from his, not only are they motivated by a very similar attitude towards the philosophy of linguistics, but they might well have the effect, in practice, of defining as languages all and only those semiotic systems that satisfy his definition.[9]

Nor is it being suggested that the application of principles (A) and (B) is in all respects unproblematical. But they are readily applicable in a sufficient number of cases for them to be worth formulating. And taken together they turn out to be quite powerful, in that they considerably extend the class L beyond what have so far been seriously investigated in theoretical linguistics, not only as natural languages (in one or other of the senses of 'natural' that we have distinguished), but even as possible N-languages, without at the same time admitting as a member of L any semiotic system whatsoever. They are also of considerable heuristic value in the practical description of actual N-languages, in that they can draw to our attention alternative analyses of the data which we might otherwise miss and they can give us a truer sense of the range of structural variation that is actually to be found across what we as linguists tend to refer to, all too glibly, as 'the languages of the world'. But to pursue either of these two points would take us too far from the present task.

This task is now all but accomplished. It remains only to introduce the distinction between non-natural and unnatural languages which is invoked in the title of this chapter and to make fully explicit – it has been implicit throughout – the fact that English, Urdu and other N-languages (in so far as they are brought within the scope of theoretical linguistics) are, in the particular sense that I will give to this term, non-natural (but not unnatural).

By 'non-natural', in the present context, I will mean something like, but broader than, "artificial" or "constructed". More precisely, I will say of any language-system which is (in whole or in part) the product of human construction that it is a non-natural language. As for 'unnatural', this is to be interpreted as the antonym of 'natural' and will therefore have as many relevant senses as I have associated with 'natural'. It is intuitively clear (and was taken for granted in our earlier discussion of naturalness) that a language could be unnatural$_4$, but natural$_3$; or unnatural$_3$, but natural$_2$; or unnatural$_2$, but natural$_1$; and so on. It also seems clear that a language can be non-natural without being unnatural – in the first three senses of the term at least. What is of particular concern, however, in the context of our present enquiry into the ontological status of N-languages, is the connexion between various subclasses of non-natural languages and unnatural$_4$ languages, some or all of which may also be unnatural$_3$, if not unnatural$_2$.

The most immediately obvious subclass of non-natural languages comprises what are more usually described as artificial (or constructed) languages and, as such, contrasted with what I am referring to as N-languages. It includes two very different subclasses: on the one hand, various kinds of formal languages constructed by mathematicians, logicians and computer scientists (the propositional calculus, predicate calculus, ALGOL, etc.); and on the other, such invented auxiliary languages as Esperanto. The latter are known to be derived from particular N-languages and might seem to be of little interest in the present context. All that needs to be said about them for the moment is that they appear to be as natural (except partly perhaps in respect of naturalness$_4$) as the N-languages from which they are derived. The artificial languages of logicians, etc., in contrast, are clearly unnatural$_3$, but natural$_1$, and they may also be natural$_2$. It is interesting to note that some of the positions defended by philosophers, psychologists and semanticists would imply that a formal language structurally comparable with the propositional calculus and combined with first-order predicate calculus associated with a particular interpretation of the names and predicates (let us call it Mentalese or the language of thought) is indeed natural$_2$, but operates at a neuropsychologically deeper level than that at which particular N-languages are differentiated.[10]

A second subclass of non-natural languages, not sharply distinguishable in principle from languages such as Esperanto, may be referred to collectively as quasi-N-languages (QNL). It has as its members all those (more or less unnatural$_4$) languages which may be constructed from attested N-languages by deliberately changing one or more of their structural properties. There are of course indefinitely many such languages, some of which are theoretically more interesting than others. For example, QNL has as a subclass Quasi-English, one of whose members is like English in all respects except that it is inflectionally regular, all plurals of nouns being formed with the -*s* suffix (*childs, sheeps, gooses,* etc.), all past-tense forms of verbs with -*ed* (*goed, runned, gived, beed,* etc.), and so on. This is a language part of which children construct for themselves (and then in part deconstruct – if I may so express it) at a certain stage in the normal (natural₃) process of acquiring English. It is also the language into which English would presumably have developed under particular environmental conditions which maximized the effect of what is traditionally referred to as analogy. Other members of Quasi-English, theoretically interesting for various reasons, are: the language which is otherwise like English but lacks the deictic category of person (cf. Lyons, 1977a: 641; 1984); English-with-classifiers (cf. Lyons, 1977a: 461); Tenseless English (cf. Lyons, 1977a: 686); English-without-the-category-of-definiteness; English-without-relative-clauses; English-without-syntactic-nominalization (cf. Lyons, 1989a); and so on. Some of these are not obviously less natural₂ or less natural₃ than English and other N-languages, and many of them (including Tenseless English and English-without-the-deictic-category-of-person), in my view, are demonstrably natural₄.

No less interesting, however, from a theoretical point of view is yet a (very heterogeneous) third subclass of non-natural languages (which intersects with QNL): and it is interesting precisely because its members are all highly unnatural₄. The may be defined (loosely) as languages which manifest to an extreme degree any structural property that is found in attested N-languages only as what would be regarded as an irregularity. Once again, there are indefinitely many such languages, and some of them are not obviously less natural₂, or even less natural₃, than actual N-languages. It is important that theoretical linguistics should not so define its terms as to exclude them. Let us take, for example, what might be described as a maximally, or totally, suppletive (inflecting or agglutinating) language in which there is no connexion between its morphological and its syntactic structure. It is easy enough to construct such a language: e.g., by taking the (phonologically unrealized) morphosyntactic words of English and the set of English word-forms and by randomly mapping the one set onto the other (cf. Lyons, 1977a: 378). Another example would be an agglutinating language with fixed word-order, but free morpheme-order within word-forms (cf. Lyons, 1968a: 203).

Examples like the ones I have just given (some of which I have discussed in detail elsewhere) are important and useful for at least three reasons. First, they can be used to demonstrate that many of the assumptions with which linguists customarily operate (and many of the definitions and descriptive procedures to be found in standard textbooks) combine logically separable components and, if we are to develop theoretical linguistics on a sufficiently broad base, must be rejected. Second, the deliberate construction of non-natural languages out of an attested and familiar N-language by changing one or more of its properties and holding the rest constant may serve to demonstrate the possible contingency of much of its structure that we might otherwise be inclined to regard as universal and gives us a better understanding of the properties, universal or non-universal, that it does have. Third, by highlighting the logical independence of particular combinations of properties whose deliberate separation results in unnaturalness$_4$, it encourages us either to revise our sense of naturalness$_4$ or to look for an explanation of what we continue to accept as a well-founded sense of naturalness$_4$ – possibly, but not necessarily, in the species-specific naturalness of N-languages that is hypothesized in the Chomskyan research programme.

The fourth subclass of non-natural languages (and the last one that will be identified here) is, paradoxically perhaps, the class of N-languages itself (NL), in so far as they can be brought within the scope of theoretical linguistics. This qualifying proviso is, of course, crucial. So too is the definition of 'non-natural' with which we have been operating in this final section. The point is that theoretical linguistics deals with N-languages as rule-governed systems (of more or less determinate structure); and language-systems are, inevitably, the product of abstraction (and other kinds of idealization). Ontologically (if not typologically), therefore, they are no different from such non-natural languages as quasi-N-languages (QNL) or, indeed, from the artificial languages of mathematicians, logicians and computer scientists. And, being at least partly the product of human construction, they do of course satisfy the relevant definition of 'non-natural'. Nor should it be thought that it is only the language-systems postulated by synchronic microlinguistics that are non-natural in this sense. As I have emphasized in the previous chapter, abstraction is just as necessary (and no less desirable) in most branches of theoretical macro-linguistics (descriptive or general), which also operate, whether explicitly or not, with their own kind of language-system. The abstract system with which the sociolinguist or the psycholinguist actually operates must be distinguished from the language-system which is postulated as having some kind of real-world existence in the individual or in the community and of which the abstract system is assumed to be a more or less faithful model.

At the very beginning of this chapter, I drew attention to the fact that Katz (1981), having originally taken the view, like Chomsky, that N-languages are psychological entities stored (as competence) in the minds of the members of particular language-communities, now holds them to be so-called Platonic (abstract, mathematical) entities. But these two views are not in fact irreconcilable, if (i) we accept that, as I argued in Chapter 2, N-languages may be considered from several different points of view, each of which practises its own kind of abstraction and makes its own ontological assumptions, and (ii) we respect fully the ontological distinction between the theoretical models of N-languages constructed by linguists and N-languages considered as real-world objects, whether physical or cultural.[11]

5

The origin of language, speech and languages

It is an interesting, and initially surprising, fact that at the very time when what was already coming to be known as Darwinism was being rapidly and enthusiastically adopted as the new scientific paradigm, the Linguistic Society of Paris, the most prestigious such learned society of the day, anathematized all speculation, whether Darwinian or not, about the origin of language.[1] Since then, it has been traditional for philologists and linguists speaking or writing on this topic to begin by referring to this fact, apologetically or defiantly as the case may be, and by quoting the relevant statute of 1866: "The Society does not accept papers on either the origin of language or the invention of a universal language".[2] Why, it may be asked, did the founding fathers adopt such an apparently obscurantist attitude?

What may now be thought of as the standard view of linguists was expressed in typically forthright fashion by Whitney, whose words have frequently been quoted:

no theme in linguistic science is more often and voluminously treated than this, and by scholars of every grade and tendency; nor any, it may be added, with less profitable result in proportion to the labour expended; the greater part of what is said and written upon it is mere windy talk, the assertion of subjective views which commend themselves to no mind save the one that produces them, and which are apt to be offered with a confidence, and defended with a tenacity, that is in inverse ratio to their acceptableness. This has given the whole question a bad repute among sober-minded philologists (1872: 279).

One cannot help adding that this did not prevent Whitney from delivering himself confidently of views on the origin of language that are hardly less speculative or subjective than those he castigated in the famous passage that I have just quoted:

if the first man had not had a power of analytic apprehension, and the mastery over consciousness, very different from those of other beings, neither hearing or imitation

73

would have led him to anything. This power is man's characteristic, and where he received it, at whatever time and in whatever way, he became man. We object entirely to having his conversion into man treated as the result, rather than the cause, of his cultural development as man. When the process of language-making began, man was man *in posse*, ready to have his powers drawn out and educated – just as is every human being nowadays at the commencement of its [*sic*] existence and the specific moving power to the working out of speech was not the monkeyish tendency to imitate but the human tendency to sociality, the desire of communication with one's fellows (1872: 296 [Koerner, 1983: 77]).

It may also be added that "sober-minded" twentieth-century philologists and linguists have not always practised the agnosticism that they have preached about the origin of language. Much of what they have had to say about the relation between language and thought or between language and social organization implies one view or another of language-origins, and frequently a view of the kind that Whitney here makes explicit.[3]

For the moment, let us simply note that Whitney was writing just a year or two after Darwin himself had written in *The Descent of Man*: "I cannot but doubt that language owes its origin to the imitation and modification of various natural sounds, the voices of other animals, and man's own instinctive cries, aided by signs and gestures" (1871). The view of the origin of language to which Darwin here makes reference combines elements of what have been called the bow-wow and the pooh-pooh theories, the former being based on the assumption that the first words were onomatopoeic and imitative of the barking of dogs and other animals, the latter on the assumption that they were derived from instinctive cries of pain and other feelings or emotions. These two theories were not of course of nineteenth-century origin. They had already had quite a long history and had long been in competition with other theories of the ultimate origin of language, some of which have acquired their own distinctive nicknames, such as the ding-dong theory and the yo-he-ho theory (cf. Jespersen, 1922: 412–16; Bloomfield, 1933: 6). I hasten to add, however, that these nicknames are not necessarily to be understood as scornful or dismissive. Nowadays at least, we can treat them as technical terms. The point being made here is simply that the theories to which they refer would have been condemned by Whitney and other "sober-minded philologists" of the period as subjective and unscientific. In fact, Whitney and his colleagues took the view that any enquiry into the ultimate origins of language was inevitably and irredeemably unscientific. Either it was avowedly speculative and non-empirical (i.e., non-inductive); or, if it aspired to be inductive and scientific, it was based on evidence whose relevance or reliability could not be substantiated. The various theories that I have just mentioned fall into the first category: they rested, as Jespersen put it, on the method "of trying to picture oneself a speechless mankind and speculating on the way in which language could then have originated" (1922: 416). The alternative, empirical (or, perhaps one should say, pseudo-empirical) approach to the question was usually based on the assumption that some languages were more highly evolved than others (richer in some sense or more complex) and that these more highly evolved languages had developed out of less highly evolved languages. Granted this undoubtedly plausible assumption, it remained, first of all, to find relevant examples of less highly evolved languages and, second, to show how they might have developed into more highly evolved systems. The problem was that by the late nineteenth century it had become clear that none of the very many languages of so-called primitive people, on the one hand, or languages of an earlier period, on the other, was in any relevant sense simpler, or less highly evolved, than any other.

For reasons that will occupy us presently, there has recently been a certain renewal of interest in the question of the origin (or origins) of language. But so far, I think it is fair to say, this is confined to only a small minority of linguists. The attitude of most linguists to evolutionary theories of the origin of language is probably still one of agnosticism. Those who adopt this point of view are well justified in doing so. Although there is now a certain amount of evidence relating to the origin of language that was not available to our predecessors, much of the new evidence, as we shall see, is, to say the least, difficult to interpret and far from conclusive. It does not follow, however, that it has not been worthwhile reopening the question of the origin of language and trying to answer it, in the light of currently available evidence and present-day linguistic theory. There are certain questions which may be empirically unanswerable, at a particular time if not permanently, but which are none the less well worth formulating as precisely as one can, so that they can be investigated from a scientific point of view and their implications can be explored. This is especially the case if such questions have a philosophical dimension to them. For it is of the nature of a philosophical question that, even if it is answerable, it is not disposed of, once and for all, by the answer that is given to it. This point was well made by J. H. Stam in his treatment of eighteenth- and nineteenth-century theories of the origin of language, who emphasized the philosophical dimensions of the question, as it was formulated and discussed by earlier generations of scholars: "if the philosopher offers an answer to my queries I still have (or should have) a question" (1976: 3). The answer that I

75

will offer to the question of the origin, or origins, of language, though it is intended to be construed as empirically defensible, is motivated as much by personal philosophical commitment, or prejudice, as it is by the empirical findings of linguistics and other disciplines. It would be challenged, on the basis of their philosophical commitment, by many of my colleagues. But more of that later.

At this point, it is appropriate to draw the first of several distinctions that I shall be operating with: the distinction between language and languages. It was papers on the origin of language ("l'origine du langage"), rather than on the origin of languages ("l'origine des langues"), that were proscribed in 1866 by the Linguistic Society of Paris (see note 2). This is an important point. One of the dominant concerns of nineteenth-century linguistics was to determine the origin of particular languages by grouping them into families and showing how the members of these families had developed, or might have developed, from either an attested or a hypothesized proto-language: by showing, for example, how the Romance languages (French, Italian, Portuguese, Romanian, Spanish, etc.) had developed from Latin; how the Germanic languages (English, Dutch, German, Swedish, Danish, Norwegian, etc.) had developed from Proto-Germanic and, going back a stage or two, how Proto-Italic, Proto-Germanic, Proto-Celtic, Proto-Indo-Aryan, etc. developed from Proto-Indo-European. But surely, one might say, this implies an evolutionary theory of the development of language. And, so it does – in one sense. Indeed, it is compatible with, though it does not necessarily imply, a Darwinian theory of the origin of languages: i.e., a theory which takes the existence of a proto-language as given and seeks to explain its 'evolutionary' development into different languages (and perhaps also the 'survival' or 'death' of particular languages) in terms of the linguistic analogue of the principle of natural selection: e.g., communicative efficiency. Many such theories have been propounded by linguists.

The point I want to make, however, is this (and it will be clear how it relates to what I have just been saying about the date of the famous Linguistic Society ban and the reasons why it was imposed): The proto-languages of historical and comparative linguistics, whether attested like Latin or hypothetical, as Proto-Germanic, or at one remove Proto-Indo-European, were assumed to be, by "sober-minded philologists" of the late nineteenth century at least (if not by their predecessors), fully developed languages comparable in structure and function, in all relevant respects, with contemporarily attested languages. Comparative philologists of the early nineteenth century could be forgiven for thinking that, in reconstructing what we now call Proto-Indo-European on the basis of Latin, Greek and more particularly Sanskrit, they were reconstructing a language that was more similar to the so-called Ursprache, or original language, than any of the attested languages upon which the reconstruction was based were to one another. After all, they had no reason to believe that the length of time separating the Sanskrit of the Vedic hymns from the Ursprache was appreciably greater than that which separates Vedic Sanskrit from present-day languages like German, French or English. By the second half of the nineteenth century, however, the scholarly, if not yet the popular, view of the geological time-scale had changed dramatically. There was so far no directly interpretable evidence bearing upon the antiquity of either man or language. But it no longer seemed necessary, or even reasonable, to try to fit everything into a few thousand years.

Furthermore, partly for methodological reasons and partly as a consequence of sound empirical investigation, philologists and linguists of the late nineteenth century were beginning to formulate their own principle of uniformitarianism, comparable with that of contemporary geologists and palaeontologists (cf. Christy, 1983). Interpreted diachronically, this principle implies that, however far back we go in time, in the historical description or reconstruction of languages, we shall find no evidence of any radical or essential difference between one kind of language-system and another. Interpreted synchronically (i.e., at any one point in time), but diatopically (i.e., in different places), it says that all the languages spoken at any one time, past or present, in so far as they are accessible to linguistic science, are very similar, if not identical, in structure and function. The principle of uniformitarianism also implies linguistic egalitarianism: the principle that all languages, in so far as they are of interest to the linguist *qua* linguist, are of equal worth.

The principles of linguistic uniformitarianism and linguistic egalitarianism have frequently been misunderstood by non-linguists. And they cannot be properly understood, I think, without discussing them at considerable length and bringing into that discussion far more of the conceptual apparatus of modern theoretical linguistics than is necessary or appropriate in the present context. Let me just recall that I introduced the principle of uniformitarianism by saying that it was based partly on methodological considerations and partly on the empirical findings of descriptive linguistics. Having reigned more or less unchallenged, within linguistics at least, for much of the twentieth century, it has recently been called into question, on both methodological and empirical grounds. However, I believe I am right in saying that none of the modifications or qualifications that informed opponents of it would wish to make are such that we need to take account of them here.[4]

The relevance of the principle of uniformitarianism in the present context is that it rules out immediately two of the traditional empirical (or pseudo-empirical) approaches to the question of the origin of language: the use of evidence from the historical, or diachronic, investigation of languages, on the one hand, and from the investigation of the languages of so-called primitive peoples, on the other (cf. Jespersen, 1922: 416). A third empirical approach is of more recent origin, but is nevertheless by now well-enough established to be called traditional: that of making use of evidence from the acquisition of language by children.

Mention of this third approach reminds us that there is an alternative interpretation of the phrase 'origin of language' to the one that I have tacitly adopted so far. Instead of asking the so-called phylogenetic question "How and when did language originate in the remote history or pre-history of mankind?", we can ask the ontogenetic question "How and when does language originate in the individual?", and if we subscribe to a linguistic version of Haeckel's famous slogan, "Ontogeny recapitulates phylogeny", we can make legitimate use of ontogenetic evidence in the formulation of phylogenetic hypotheses.[5] But does the ontogeny of language recapitulate its phylogeny? Many researchers have argued or assumed that it does, in general if not in detail; and it is of course possible that the principle holds for language, even if it does not hold in respect of the origin and evolution of biological species. There is, however, no very convincing reason to believe that it does; and this must, at the very least, give us pause for thought.

We shall return presently to the ontogenetic question. But before we do, there is a further distinction to be drawn. This is fairly obvious (once it has been explained), but it is none the less theoretically profound and highly relevant to our present concerns: the distinction between language and speech.

The fact that language is distinguishable from speech, not only in principle, but also in practice, is a matter of everyday experience for anyone who has been brought up in a modern literate society, and it is readily demonstrable (see Chapter 1). But it is, for all that, a fact that is frequently lost sight of in discussions of both the phylogenesis and the ontogenesis of language. All too often, language is identified with speech, and evidence for the origin of the one is taken, uncritically, as evidence for the origin of the other. We must keep in mind at least the logical possibility of their separate and independent origin. And this is not just a logical possibility. One theory of the phylogenesis of language (to a modified version of which, as it happens, I myself incline) is that language – or, to be more precise, the more characteristically linguistic part of language – did not originate in vocalization, but in gesture. This is not a new theory. Condillac, in his famous *Essai* of 1746, probably the most original and the most influential of the many eighteenth-century treatments of the origin of language, argued for it (cf. Robins, 1982; Aarsleff, 1974, 1975). So too, subsequently, did Tylor (1871, 1881), Morgan (1877), Wundt (1912) and many other scholars, representative of several different disciplines (cf. Hewes, 1973, 1976, 1983). And some of its more recent advocates would say that now there is new evidence for the gestural theory which reinforces its plausibility. The evidence comes in part from linguistics, but principally from physical anthropology, palaeontology, psychology, ethology and neurophysiology; and I will summarize it later. I will also give my own reasons for subscribing to the gestural theory, which are only partly dependent upon the newly available evidence.

If we think, for a moment, not about the when and the where of the origin of language, but rather about the whence and the how, we can postulate, in the abstract, two possibilities; and one of these, as we shall see, can be divided into two sub-possibilities. The first major possibility is that language comes from nowhere – or, perhaps I should say, from nothing: that its provenance is *ex nihilo* and *de novo*. (It sounds more respectable in Latin!) And one traditional answer to the *how*-question associated with the thesis of *ex nihilo* provenance, as far as the phylogenesis of language is concerned, is that of the Book of Genesis and of comparable works in other cultures: the hypothesis of divine creation. Now, I do not wish to defend the thesis of *ex nihilo* provenance, still less that of creationism. It is worth pointing out, however, not only that it is logically possible, but that it must not be rejected out of hand as scientifically disreputable. *Ex nihilo* provenance, if not creationism, has in fact been defended recently by scholars whose scientific and secularist credentials are beyond reproach. For example, Chomsky's view that the language-faculty is the result of a specifically human genetic mutation and 'grows', organically, in the mind under the influence of an innate bioprogram seems to imply *ex nihilo* provenance (cf. Chomsky, 1980a: 83, 180). So too, perhaps, do comments such as the following, on Grice's (1981) inferential account of how language might have originated (presented by Grice as a 'myth'): "We will never know how far hominid efforts at conventionalizing inference might have gone towards establishing a fully-fledged human language. The fact is that the development of human languages was made possible by a specialized biological endowment" (Sperber & Wilson, 1986: 53).[6]

The alternative major possibility is that language develops out of something else. And it is this second possibility that splits into my two sub-possibilities, which can be related to the classical geological and biological alternatives of gradualism and catastrophism (cf. Washburn & McCown, 1978: 19ff.). It will be easier to see what is involved, perhaps, if we first restrict our attention to the ontogenesis of language: the acquisition of language by children.

We commonly talk about the acquisition of language by children. In doing so, however, we recognize that, in any normal sense of the word 'language', it is impossible for the child to acquire language without acquiring some particular language (English, French, German, etc.) which is identifiable as such by virtue of its structural differences from other particular languages (Arabic, Chinese, Russian, etc.). It is of course conceivable that there is some 'inner' language of thought, innate or acquired, which is neutral between particular 'external' languages, and that this 'inner' language – let us call it Mentalese – is such that its pre-existence is a condition of the acquisition of any particular 'external' language. This is a traditional rationalist view; and it has been revived, recently, with support from Chomsky's theory of generative grammar (cf. J. A. Fodor, 1975, 1983). It is further conceivable that language-utterances are translated out of and into Mentalese in the course of their production and interpretation. This too is a recognizably traditional view, and one which has recently been brought up to date by psychologists and psycholinguists influenced by Chomskyan generativism. But the arguments in favour of the psychological reality of a universal language of thought which plays the kind of role that is attributed to it in the acquisition and psychological processing of diverse 'external' languages do not appear to me to be very convincing. I concur with one of its critics who has commented that "it has won few hearts and minds among those actively engaged in the study of language acquisition" and "there is an objection, namely, that an ontogenetic mystery has been dispelled by postulating a phylogenetic one" (Campbell, 1986: 30, 44).

A provocatively novel elaboration of the argument that the 'inner' language of mental representations is phylogenetically prior to the 'external' language used for communication is to be found in Sperber & Wilson (1986: 173):

Language is an essential tool for the processing and memorizing of information. As such, it must exist not only in humans but also in a wide variety of animals and machines with information processing abilities ... The great debate about whether humans are the only species to have language is based on a misconception of the nature of language. The debate is not really about whether other species than humans have languages, but about whether they have languages which they use as mediums of communication. Now the fact that humans have developed languages that can be used to communicate is interesting, but it tells us nothing about the essential nature of language. The originality of the human species is precisely to have found this *curious additional use* for something which many other species also possess, as the originality of elephants is to have found that they can use their noses for the curious additional purpose of picking things up. In both cases, the result has been that something widely found in other species has undergone remarkable adaptation and development because of the new uses it has been put to [my italics].

Interestingly enough, although it is based on a very different view of "the essential nature" of language from the one that I adopted in this chapter, this theory of the evolution of human ('external') language from its origin, or origins, to its present form does not seem to be incompatible with more conventional theories – or indeed with the gestural theory outlined below. In what follows, I shall discount the possible existence of this kind of rich and highly structured 'Mentalese' – not, I hasten to add, as having been disproved or as self-evidently absurd, but simply as not proven. I will take it as a valid assumption, then, that only when the child has acquired a particular language can we say that he or she has acquired language.

And what about speech? As we have seen, language is independent of speech and does not presuppose its prior existence. The converse however, ontogenetically at least, is not true. The child cannot be said to have acquired speech until he or she has acquired language by acquiring a particular language; and in the normal course of events this will be what we call the child's native language. With these considerations in mind, we may now look briefly at the acquisition of language which normally, but not necessarily, involves the acquisition of speech.[7]

All (physiologically and psychologically) normal children who acquire their native language in (socially) normal circumstances pass through a relatively constant developmental sequence, regardless of race and culture and regardless of the language that they are acquiring. The first stage, which begins some three months after birth, is that of babbling. The second, which starts towards the end of the first year is that of so-called holophrastic speech, consisting of one-word utterances. This is followed, during the second year of postnatal life, by the third stage, characterized by the production of simple two-word and three-word utterances of a so-called telegraphic character. As children pass through the second and third stage of language-acquisition, they gradually improve their control of the sound-system and may begin to make use of some of the grammatical distinctions of the language that they are acquiring. It will still be some time before we will be inclined to say that they have acquired the language (in fact, it is unclear that there is any definite terminal point for language-acquisition), but we might be prepared to say that they have by now acquired some kind of rudimentary language.

There are several points that I now want to make on the basis of this very brief outline of the first three stages of language acquisition. First, the child, in the normal environmental circumstances that I am invoking, is simultaneously acquiring both speech and language. And his or her progress from one stage to another appears to be relatively smooth and gradual. We can identify various stages, including the first three that I have mentioned, in the child's acquisition of language and speech. But the transition from each stage to its successor, though rapid, is not instantaneous. In fact, the boundary between one stage and another is somewhat indeterminate, so that it is impossible to say, at any particular moment, that the child has just passed from babbling to holophrasis or from holophrasis to so-called telegraphic speech. The child's progress, in short, is gradual, rather than catastrophic.

Second, everything characteristic of an earlier stage, except for babbling, continues to be part of the child's competence and performance, for a while at least, at the next stage. For example, the child does not suddenly, or even gradually, stop producing holophrastic utterances when he or she has reached the stage at which he or she is able to produce two-word and three-word utterances. What the child does at the second stage, if I may so express it, is to produce a mixture of stage-1 and stage-2 utterances, and at the third stage a mixture of stage-2 and stage-3 utterances. And this is so at every subsequent stage in the acquisition of language and speech. Not only is the progress from one stage to the next gradual, rather than catastrophic, but there is a sense in which the earlier stage for some time overlaps with the later or is encapsulated in it. In fact, speaking very generally (and omitting certain qualifications that do not affect the import of the point I am making), we can say, of any stage after the second, that it will encapsulate its predecessor, which in turn will encapsulate *its* predecessor, and so on. And this generalization holds (with certain qualifications) throughout the whole process of language-acquisition.

Third, the acquisition of language and speech is a natural process. In fact, it appears to be natural in at least two relevant senses of this rather troublesome word (see Chapter 4). First of all, it happens naturally in the sense that, unlike learning to read and write, it does not require instruction or training; and this is one reason why the more general term 'acquisition' is nowadays preferred to the term 'learning', which has a more specific sense, both technically and non-technically, and might be held to imply the reciprocal term 'teaching'. One is not taught one's native language and arguably one does not learn it. It is acquired without formal instruction (i.e., naturally, in this first sense of 'naturally') as part and parcel of the process of growing up in normal environmental conditions, which include, of course 'exposure' to spoken utterances.

The second sense of 'natural' can be expressed by the phrase 'as a matter of biological endowment'. It has been argued, notably, in recent times, by Chomsky, that human languages are structurally and functionally adapted to the psychological nature of man: that they are, to use the biologist's term, 'species-specific' (see Chapter 1). His argument that what he calls the language-faculty – the capacity to acquire language – is species-specific and genetically transmitted depends partly, but not wholly, on the fact that they are acquired naturally, in the first sense: without special instruction, as an integral component of the process of maturation and, it may be added (though Chomsky does not give much emphasis to this), socialization. There is much in the way that Chomsky develops this argument which is highly controversial and need not detain us in the present context. In particular, we need not be concerned whether the child's acquisition of language proceeds independently of his or her more general cognitive development and whether there is an innate language-faculty which is as highly determined by the principles of what Chomsky calls universal grammar as he supposes. It is perhaps worth noting, however, that, after a period in the 1970s when psychologists investigating language-acquisition reacted against the possibly excessive concern with grammatical structure characteristic of the 1960s and tended to favour cognitive and social explanations, they are now once again giving recognition to the child's interest in the purely formal patterns of grammar, which seems to be inexplicable from this point of view (cf. Karmiloff-Smith, 1987). Chomsky's hypothesis that the child is born with a language-acquisition device (LAD) of a problem-solving character, if not his notion of universal grammar, has been, to that degree at least, confirmed by recent work. As for the innateness of the child's predisposition to acquire speech (or, more precisely, to produce and recognize the vocal sounds and contours in which language is realized as speech): it has been demonstrated experimentally that from a very early age (long before he or she produces them) the infant is able to recognize speech-sounds, only some of which he or she can have heard in the spoken language to which he or she is 'exposed', and furthermore that, unless the infant's ability to produce and perceive particular distinctions is reinforced by environmental 'exposure' it will, as it were, 'atrophy' (cf. Bullowa, 1979;

Stark, 1986). Let us grant, then (and, although it may not be absolutely conclusive, there is a good deal of evidence for this), that human beings are genetically programmed to acquire both language and speech.

Granted that language and speech are natural in this second sense, the question I now want to raise is whether the link between them is also natural in the second, rather than in the first, or perhaps in some third, looser, sense of 'natural' (see Chapter 4). Most linguists, I think, assume that it is. But, as I have argued elsewhere, the evidence is consistent with the alternative possibility: that the child is genetically programmed (i) to vocalize and to produce and recognize speech-sounds, on the one hand, and (ii) to acquire a complex and flexible communication-system whose grammatical structure in particular is such that we would call it a language, on the other, but that the association of the two is a matter of environmental circumstances (cf. Lyons, 1981c, and Chapter 1 above).

Evidence that the link between language and speech can be severed in abnormal environmental conditions comes primarily from recent work on the structure of gestural sign-languages used by the deaf (cf. Friedman, 1977; Stokoe, 1978; Klima & Bellugi, 1979; Deuchar, 1984, 1987b). Such languages can certainly be acquired naturally in the first of the two senses that I have identified. Moreover, contrary to what used to be widely believed and is still sometimes asserted by non-specialists, there is no reason to deny that they are fully fledged languages or, alternatively, to say that they are parasitic upon or derived from spoken languages used in the same community. In the present state of research and theory, it is important neither to exaggerate nor to minimize the naturalness of gestural language in comparison with speech. It is sufficient for the point that is being made here, however, that the gestural languages of the deaf are natural in the first of the two senses distinguished above. Whether the association of languages and gesture is biologically natural (i.e., genetically and neuro-physiologically) and consequently whether the realization of language in the gestural medium requires more special – less natural, if not wholly unnatural – environmental 'triggering' would seem to be an open question. It is, in any case, possible (and consistent with the evidence cited later in this chapter relating to the localization of functions in the brain) that what might be called the 'naturalization' of language as speech, rather than gesture, should be a matter of degree; and perhaps also, though this is more speculative, that the now less natural realization of language as gesture should be available for activation, residually, whenever its more natural realization as speech is, for physiological or environmental reasons, impossible. However that may be, the relevance of current research on sign languages of the deaf to the gestural theory of the ontogenesis and phylogenesis of language is evident enough. And a good deal has been made of it, as we shall see, in recent discussion.

At the beginning of this chapter, I referred to the recent renewal of interest in the phylogenesis of language; and I said that there was new evidence from a variety of disciplines. As far as linguistics is concerned, the renewal of interest dates from the 1960s and derives, interestingly enough, from two opposing viewpoints. One of these, which I have mentioned already, is Chomskyan generativism, with its bias towards rationalism and its insistence upon the biological uniqueness of man. The other viewpoint is characterized by its attachment to behaviourist psychology and to what one may call the ethological attitude.

A prominent representative of the second viewpoint was Charles Hockett, whose main contribution to our now considerably increased understanding of the issues involved derives from his comparison of human language with animal communication-systems in terms of selected key properties or design-features (Hockett, 1954, 1960a, b; Hockett & Altmann, 1968). I do not propose to go into the details of Hockett's classificatory framework: I have done this elsewhere (Lyons, 1972, 1977a: 70–85). Suffice it to say that it was of historic importance in giving an impetus to modern studies of animal communication-systems and in focussing the attention of investigators on a common set of problems. But it suffers, I believe, from three fundamental flaws: (i) it fails to distinguish language from speech and this relates language more closely to vocal signalling, such as particular kinds of bird-song, than it does to non-vocal signalling, and in particular to gestural signalling, among other primates; (ii) it treats all the properties as being simply present or absent, rather than as being present to different degrees; (iii) it treats as properties of languages as a whole, properties that are characteristic of only the verbal, in contrast with the non-verbal, component of language.

There is no space to develop these criticisms here or to provide an alternative. Let me simply say that, if one takes account of the points that have just been made, one cannot escape the conclusion that human languages have a component that is unique to them, both structurally and functionally, and another component that makes them comparable with the communication-systems of other species (cf. Lyons, 1977a: 70–94).

Let me now refer briefly to the other kinds of evidence that have been brought to bear on the question of the phylogenesis of language in the last twenty years or so (cf. Foster & Brandes, 1980; Grolier, 1983; Harnad *et al.*, 1976; Lieberman, 1975; Lock, 1978; Washburn & McCown, 1978;

85

Westcott, 1974). It is impossible to deal with this in detail, since it is often highly specialized and can be properly evaluated only by someone who is competent in a large number of disciplines: psychology, physical anthropology, neurophysiology, ethology, palaeontology and many others. Furthermore, much of it is controversial.

The relevant new evidence, such as it is, comes from the study of hominid fossils and making inferences about brain-size and the vocal tract; from the study of cerebral dominance and the lateralization of certain aspects of language-storage and language-processing in one hemisphere of the brain rather than the other; from the study of child language, of sign language and of creole and pidgin languages; and from the study of animal communication-systems and of non-communicative behaviour in respect of manual dexterity.

I will now comment, briefly and selectively, on some of the evidence to which I have just referred, in the light of the terminological points made earlier, beginning with what is *prima facie* most directly relevant to the origin or origins of human language: evidence that comes from the study of hominid fossils.

As I mentioned above, two topics are of principal concern here: first, the shape of the vocal tract; and, second, the size of the brain, in so far as this can be assessed accurately from the hominid skull fossils that have been investigated from this point of view. The relevance of the first of these two new research topics derives from: (i) the fact that the human vocal tract (the height of the larynx, the mobility of the tongue, the size and shape of the resonating chambers, the size, shape and disposition of the teeth, etc.) differs significantly from that of other contemporary primates; and (ii) the assumption that the differences can be plausibly accounted for, in evolutionary terms, as the result of the adaptation of bodily organs whose primary biological function has to do with respiration and with the intake and mastication of food to the biologically secondary function of producing articulate sound which, when it serves as the medium for language, we call speech. The relevance of the second topic derives from the assumption that human languages, in the form in which we know them today at least, require a larger brain than is found in other contemporary primates, and perhaps also a brain in which the specifically human, and evolutionary 'new' or enlarged areas, are specialized for the storage and processing of language. Before we proceed, I would like to emphasize the fact that I have deliberately related the first of the two topics to speech – and somewhat indirectly at that – and the second to language. This is not customarily done in general discussions of the origin of language.

It is generally agreed that the development of the human vocal tract (in particular, the lowering of the larynx and the curvature of the supra-laryngeal cavity) must be connected with the adoption of upright posture and bipedalism. This implies that speech could have started to evolve from non-speech or pre-speech (or, to be more precise, from the distinctively human vocalization of the kind that serves as a medium for language in human beings and, when it serves this function, is identified as speech) from less distinctively human, non-linguistic or pre-linguistic, vocalization with Australopithecus (i.e., some four million years ago) or with one of his successors in the line that leads ultimately to modern man: with *Homo habilis* or *Homo erectus* or even *Homo sapiens*. So far there appears to be no positive anatomical evidence that would justify the assignment of even an approximate starting-point for the evolution of the specifically human vocal tract or for the postulation of datable intermediate stages in its assumed evolutionary development.

There is of course the now famous, and controversial, reconstruction of a Neanderthal vocal tract and the computer modelling of the sounds that this would have been capable of producing (cf. Lieberman 1976, 1983; Lieberman & Crelin, 1971; Lieberman *et al.*, 1972). This purports to demonstrate that Neanderthals (despite their brain-size, which might suggest that they had the neural capacity both for the storage and processing of language and for the control of speech-production) were incapable of rapid and fully articulate speech. But two comments are in order here (apart from noting that the reconstruction itself is controversial): first, Neanderthal is commonly, if not universally, believed to be on a collateral line of descent from that of *Homo sapiens*; second, granted that Neanderthals of, say, fifty thousand years ago were incapable of rapid and fully articulate speech of the kind that is found in all known human societies today, it does not follow that they could not produce a subset of what we now identify as speech-sounds and at a slower rate (cf. Lieberman, 1976, 1983; Lieberman & Crelin, 1971; Passingham, 1981).

Whether we opt for one date or period rather than another for the hypothetical starting-point of the evolution of speech or of its relatively rapid development from pre-speech into a more or less modern fully articulate system, making use of a wide range of sounds, depends partly, as we have observed, upon the assumption that speech and language evolved together *pari passu*. It also depends upon the correlation of such sparse and inconclusive evidence relating to the development of the vocal tract as is currently available with other kinds of evidence relating to mainly non-anatomical factors – ecological, climatic, cultural or social – and the association of these, more or less convincingly, with the adoption of bipedalism and with signs of intelligence or of the kind of symbolization that the possession and use of language is held to require, such as tool-making or the production of representational carvings and paintings. Some aspects of this enterprise I must confess to finding less than convincing. For example, I am somewhat sceptical about arguments based on the development of what are taken to be increasingly sophisticated stages of symbolization or of the representation of meaning (cf. Alinei, 1982; Foster & Brandes, 1980; Lock, 1978). I may be wrong. But much of the argument appears to rest, in practice if not in principle, upon rather shaky theoretical foundations as far as the semantic structure of natural human language is concerned.

Another kind of evidence that has been adduced in recent interdisciplinary discussion and about which, I believe, one must be equally sceptical, comes from the investigation of pidgins and creoles. It has been argued, notably by Bickerton (1981), that recently developed creoles (and early child-language) share a number of basic structural properties and that these can be assumed to be the very properties whose maturational development is controlled by a species-specific, innate, bioprogram, which must therefore have been 'naturalized' at a relatively early period in the evolution of human language. This general thesis, like the thesis which relates early child-language to a postulated rudimentary form of phylogenetically early adult language, on the one hand, and to the kind of language acquired by chimpanzees, on the other, has its attractions. But the evidence that is adduced in support of it has been rightly criticized on grounds of selectivity (cf. Aitchison, 1983; Stephany, 1984: 380; Weist, 1986: 364).

The fossil evidence relating to the size and configuration of the brain is also somewhat controversial and of itself equally inconclusive. It is generally, and no doubt plausibly, assumed that an increased brain-size/body-weight ratio is positively correlated, phylogenetically, with increased intelligence and with the evolution of language; and furthermore that the evolution of human intelligence and of human language are causally connected (possibly by means of a feedback relation). If we make these assumptions, we can interpret the evidence relating to brain-size as implying that none of man's ancestors earlier than *Homo erectus* could have had a more or less fully developed language. But, once again, it must be emphasized that the interpretation is based on far from self-evident assumptions, and also that the non-existence of what I am calling a fully developed language (i.e., a language that is comparable with existing natural spoken languages in terms of the quality and degree of its structural complexity and expressive power) at a given period does not necessarily imply the non-existence of a less highly developed language at a considerably earlier period.

It is not just the fact of having a relatively large brain, however, that correlates with having a fully developed language in human beings. It is also the fact of having a brain with a particular cortical structure and with some degree of localization of specifically linguistic functions in certain areas of the neo-cortical tissue of the dominant hemisphere. Unfortunately, we are not yet in a position to interpret "the patterns of the major gyri and sulci of the brain which can sometimes be seen in fossil endocasts" with any degree of confidence (cf. Hill & Most, 1978: 656). If we were, we might also be in a stronger position to decide whether the development, if not the origin, of both language and speech, is temporally and causally connected with 'sapientization' (cf. Krantz, 1980; Wind, 1982, 1983).

Let us now turn to the question of cerebral dominance and lateralization, which has just been mentioned in connexion with the interpretation of the fossil evidence and may now be considered in a more general context. The adult human brain is distinguished from that of other present-day primates, not only by its greater overall size (relative to body-weight), but also by the greater development of the parietal regions, especially in the left hemisphere. Now, the left hemisphere is normally the dominant one as far as man's general cognitive abilities are concerned. Moreover, it contains Broca's Area, which, since its discoverer, Paul Broca, started publishing his findings in 1861, has been popularly regarded as the 'speech centre' or 'language centre' in the brain.[8] Therefore, it is generally, and once again no doubt plausibly, assumed that the development of the left hemisphere is causally connected with either the origin or the evolution of language (cf. Passingham, 1981). Unfortunately, as we have just seen, one cannot infer with certainty from the fossil record anything about the cortical structure of the brains of the ancestors of *Homo sapiens* or about cerebral dominance. What one can do, however, is to note one or two points about the lateralization of speech and language in present-day human beings, which, on certain assumptions, can be seen as relevant to the questions that concern us.

The first point is that we now know that there is no single area of the brain in which language is stored and processed. Nor is it the case that all the processing of speech and language is carried out in the left hemisphere – or, indeed, by exclusively 'new-brain', neo-cortical, tissue: evidence from the study of certain kinds of aphasia suggests that the limbic brain has access to words with highly emotive associations (cf. Hill & Most, 1978:

655). But there is still a very real sense in which the left hemisphere – and, moreover, certain identifiable regions of the left hemisphere, of which Broca's Area is one and Wernicke's Area is another – can be correctly described as having a specifically linguistic function. As far as the reception of speech is concerned, it seems that the segmental phonemes are usually processed by the left hemisphere, but that the non-segmental features of spoken utterances (e.g., stress and intonation) can be handled equally well by either hemisphere. Both hemispheres are involved in the grammatical and semantic processing of language-utterances; but, once again, with some degree of specialization, the right hemisphere being able to interpret expressions referring to concrete objects, the left hemisphere alone being capable of interpreting more abstract expressions. Now, there are quite independent reasons, both structural and functional, for saying that the layers, or strands, in spoken language which are processed normally by the left hemisphere are just those that are uniquely or characteristically linguistic (i.e., unique to, or characteristic of, human speech and language, in contrast with animal communication-systems); but also that they are wholly contained within that part of language which is readily transferable from one medium to another (cf. Lyons, 1977a: 70–85).

The second point that I want to emphasize here is that the localization, or lateralization, of the more characteristically linguistic components of speech and language (under normal circumstances) in the left hemisphere is a maturational process that takes place over a period of the few years during which the child is (under normal circumstances) acquiring his or her native language. If for some reason (e.g., as a result of brain-damage) lateralization is inhibited or one of the relevant areas in the left hemisphere is rendered inoperative, the other hemisphere can take over the characteristically linguistic functions – provided that the trauma or lesion that occasions the transfer of function occurs in early childhood. There is, then, a certain functional plasticity or flexibility as far as lateralization is concerned, but this is lost as the child approaches or passes what is often referred to as the 'critical age' for fully successful language-acquisition. And it is worth adding in this connexion that there is some evidence to indicate that foreign languages learned after childhood may be handled by the non-dominant hemisphere (cf. Albert & Obler, 1978).

Taken together, the two points that I have just made imply first, that not all the layers, or strands, in speech and language, have necessarily evolved at the same time or at the same rate or in the same way; and, second, that the localization of the more specifically linguistic functions in the dominant hemisphere may be a relatively recent development on an evolutionary time-scale. Admittedly, most of what I have been saying is somewhat speculative. Also, the generalizations that I have been making are subject to innumerable qualifications on points of detail; and I have strayed far from my own field of expertise in making them. But they do contain a sufficient amount of what may now be regarded as established fact. At the very least, they should disabuse us of the all too common assumption that speech and language, in their entirety, must have evolved together with cerebral dominance or the development of neo-cortical tissue. So, too, should the discovery that, just as not all the processing of language and speech is carried out by the 'new brain' in human beings, so the communication-systems of other primates may not be located wholly in the limbic brain (cf. Hill & Most, 1978: 655). The neurological evidence, as I understand it, strongly supports the hypothesis that human language is a multi-layered or multi-stranded phenomenon, each of whose layers or strands may be of different antiquity and of different origin.

I will not attempt to summarize the other evidence that has recently been brought to bear on the question of the origin, or origins, of language, some of which has been briefly mentioned above. To the best of my knowledge, none is inconsistent with the hypothesis that I have just propounded, and some of it is positively supportive. For example, it is now known that not all the phonetic distinctions characteristic of human speech are innate and species-specific in the strong sense of not needing to be learned by human beings and being unlearnable by non-humans (cf. Juszczyk, 1981; C. J. Darwin, 1987). Similarly, careful examination of the transition from babbling to speech indicates that, even as far as segmental structure is concerned, no sharp distinction can be drawn between pre-linguistic and linguistic vocalization (Vihman *et al.*, 1985). In fact, much of the recent work on what has come to be called pre-speech in children casts doubt on the possibility of establishing any absolute discontinuities either between one stage and its successor in language-acquisition or between human and non-human vocalization (cf. Stark, 1986; Crystal, 1986). In drawing attention to research in child language-acquisition at this point, I am not of course now adopting the thesis that ontogeny recapitulates phylogeny, which I said must be treated with caution. It suffices for the argument that I am advancing here, not that the findings of recent research in child language-acquisition should be held to give positive support to the hypothesis of continuity in the phylogenetic evolution of language, but rather that they can no longer be cited as readily as they have been in the past in favour of radical and absolute discontinuity. It was to illustrate the difficulty of deciding between catastrophism and gradualism that I referred earlier to the identifiable stages of language-acquisition and to the fact that each stage overlaps with, and is encapsulated in, its successor. We do not have to subscribe to a strong version of the ontogeny-recapitulates-phylogeny thesis to consider that this may also be the case as far as the phylogenetic development of language is concerned. And it is nevertheless worth noting that the vocal tract of the human neonate is more similar to that of the adult non-human primate than it is to that of the adult human being and that some researchers have proposed developmental schedules which correlate identifiable stages in the earliest period of language-acquisition with the maturation of the more distinctively human anatomical and neurophysiological 'hardware' that is involved in the production and reception of spoken language (cf. Jurgens & Von Cramon, 1982; Kent, 1981; Milner, 1976).

Exactly the same conclusions that I have been drawing from the evidence of recent work in child language-acquisition can also be drawn, in my opinion, from the study of animal communication, and more particularly from the now famous chimpanzee experiments (cf. Sebeok & Umiker-Sebeok, 1980). I will not go into these here. But it is worth making the point that they were, in various respects, far more successful than most linguists, if not most psychologists and ethologists, would have anticipated; and they have demonstrated that at least one species of non-human primates has the ability to acquire a communication-system with some degree of syntactic structure and productivity. Whether we say that the chimpanzees' ability differs from the human capacity for language in degree or in kind is, in my view, largely a question of how we define 'language'; and this is the point that I am concerned to establish. None of the various systems that the chimpanzees have learned has the grammatical complexity of the language-systems used by adult human beings. But they do not appear to differ significantly, in terms of formal complexity, from the language-systems of young children (cf. Brown, 1970; Terrace & Bever, 1976). And the fact that parallels can be drawn between the communicative behaviour of children and the communicative behaviour of chimpanzees casts doubt upon the view of those who would say that there is an unbridgeable gap between human and non-human communication.

I should perhaps mention at this point that many linguists, psychologists and philosophers would say that I have exaggerated the similarities between the communicative behaviour of young children and that of the chimpanzees that have been involved in the language-learning experiments. This may be so. In experiments of this kind, it is very difficult to control for the so-called 'clever Hans' effect, without introducing into the context in which the communicative behaviour is learned and exercised such a high degree of artificiality that comparability with the naturally acquired linguistic (and pre-linguistic) behaviour of human infants is seriously impaired (cf. Sebeok & Umiker-Sebeok, 1980: 21–5). But it is also very difficult, it should not be forgotten, to interpret the utterances of very young children in respect of intentionality and motivation.

There is the further problem that scholars working in different academic disciplines are subject to the influence of different professional prejudices. It is perhaps significant, as has been suggested, that "the academic scepticism and even denigration which greeted Washoe's performance [and, subsequently, that of the other famous chimpanzees, Sarah and Lana] ... came principally from scholars working in theoretical linguistics and psycholinguistics – precisely those fields which might be said to have a vested professional interest in maintaining [a particular] concept of a language" (R. Harris, 1980: 182). At the very least, while recognizing that ethologists and animal psychologists might be said to have their own vested professional interest in seeking to establish the thesis of continuity and of the non-uniqueness of man, one has to concede that they have been right to complain, as many of them have done, about the arbitrariness of the linguist's decision that this or that set of design-features is criterial for language (properly so called).

It is for much the same reason that I am inclined to subscribe, on present evidence, to the updated version of the gestural theory of the origin of language to which reference was made earlier: because most linguists, committed as they are by the bias of their training to the primacy of speech, unhesitatingly reject it. The evidence in favour of the gestural theory is, admittedly, not very strong; and it has also been argued that the "normal standards of parsimony" go against it (Hill & Most, 1978: 657). But the evidence, for and against, is so fragmentary and disparate that I am not sure that normal standards of scientific parsimony are applicable. There are times, it seems to me, when one ought to admit, both to oneself and publicly, that one is inevitably going beyond the evidence and opting for or against a hypothesis, personally if not in the name of one's professional discipline, on non-scientific, but none the less intellectually respectable, grounds. For man does not live by scientifically justifiable hypotheses alone, but also by myth and more or less well-motivated prejudice. After all, *Credo quia improbabile* is logically, and even scientifically, more defensible as a profession of faith than *Credo quia impossibile*! And all hypotheses in this area are, if not unprovable, so far unproven. At the very least, whether it is classified as myth or hypothesis, the gestural theory of the origin of language encourages the linguist to be critical of disciplinary orthodoxy and to think of language, independently of speech, in a broader theoretical context. It is for that reason that I have been concerned with the question in the present volume.

For what it is worth, the evidence that has been cited in support of the gestural theory comes not only from the chimpanzee experiments, but also from the study of primates in their natural habitat and from the investigation of sign languages of the deaf; and this has been interpreted in the light of what is known (and has been referred to above) relating to early tool-use and symbolization, on the one hand, and to cerebral dominance in respect of speech and manual dexterity on the other (cf. Hewes, 1973, 1983). As far as the relevance of sign language is concerned, it is worth mentioning that some of the arguments that were advanced against it when the gestural theory was revived, in its modern version, a decade or so ago, have proved to be fallacious. As we have seen, it is now known that the gestural languages of the deaf are neither parasitic upon co-existing spoken languages nor strikingly simpler than, or different from, other natural human languages in grammatical structure and expressive power. Nor, it would appear, are they strikingly different in their degree of iconicity, which is generally regarded as one of the design-features separating non-linguistic, or pre-linguistic, systems of communication from fully fledged languages. But iconicity, more generally defined as non-arbitrariness of the association of form and meaning, is (like the other design-features to which I referred above) not a matter of yes or no, but of more or less; and there is much more iconicity in 'ordinary' natural languages, at all levels of their structure, than the conventional wisdom in linguistics would have us believe (cf. Haiman, 1985).

On the basis of this and other evidence, including the fact that gesture continues to play an important 'paralinguistic' role in the modulation and punctuation of normal spoken utterances (cf. Lyons, 1977a: 63–7), it is argued that languages, as we know them in their fully developed form, may have developed, whether by relatively slow evolution or catastrophically, between 100,000 and 40,000 years ago, not as a direct outgrowth of the expressive, or emotive, use of vocal signals characteristic of non-human primates, but out of a pre-existing system of manual gestures; and that this gestural system may have evolved at a time when man's hominid ancestors were adopting an upright posture, thus freeing the hands for this purpose and for tool-using, and when the brain was both increasing in size and acquiring the potential for the specialization of complex processing in the dominant hemisphere.

I for one find the arguments seductive. However, I would not wish to overplay my commitment to the theory, or myth, of the gestural origin of language. If it is correct, it implies that spoken language in more or less its present form has evolved by integrating structural and functional properties from different sources – some of which link us with other species and others of which, arguably, make us unique. And regardless of the question of origins this is what I believe to be the case. Whether we emphasize our kinship with other primates, and more generally with other species, or our differences from them depends, as I have said, on wholly non-scientific considerations.

The reason why I spent so much time at the start of this chapter on clarifying the difference between 'language' and 'speech' and between 'language' and 'languages' will now be clear. The conclusions to which we have come, tentative and precarious though they may be, are, as I have said, either supported by or, at least, not contradicted by the findings of all the relevant disciplines, including linguistics. And possibly the most valuable contribution that a linguist can make to the discussion is to establish and promulgate the following proposition: the question whether language (i.e., N-languages: see Chapter 4) evolved from some non-verbal communication-system is not formulated precisely enough to be answered positively or negatively. And it must be emphasized that it is not just that we lack the evidence which would enable us to answer it. Although there is perhaps no sharp distinction between human and non-human communication and between language and non-language, there are certain properties of adult language at least, having to do with its grammatical complexity and its descriptive, or propositional, function, which appear to be unique to natural human languages (and of course to different kinds of artificial languages derived from them) and to be associated more particularly with their verbal component. If we decide to make the possession of these properties a defining characteristic of what we will call language, we can then say, correctly, that languages are fundamentally, or qualitatively, different from all other communication systems.[9] We might equally well have framed a definition of 'language', however, according to which we would be inclined to say that the difference between language and non-language is a matter of degree rather than kind. This purely definitional aspect of the question should be borne in mind when we consider whether language is or is not unique to the human species. So too should the fact that, whether we define language in such a way that it turns out to be unique to the human species or not, there is much in the everyday use of language that links it with other kinds of communicative behaviour in both men and animals.[10]

6

Phonemic and non-phonemic phonology: some typological reflections

American linguistics has proudly and more or less consciously adopted the pragmatic position; the philosophy of justification by results, of first getting things done and only then, if at all, asking what in fact has been done.[1] In the preface to his collection of articles by American linguists, Martin Joos brings out this point well. He goes on to remark: 'Altogether there is ample reason why both Americans and (for example) Europeans are likely on each side to consider the other side both irresponsible and arrogant. We may request the Europeans to try to regard the American style as a tradition comme une autre; but the Americans can't be expected to reciprocate: they are having too much fun to be bothered, and few of them are aware that either side has a tradition' (Joos, 1957: vii)[2]. As a representative of one European tradition in the enviable position of having secured a captive American audience for an hour or so, I propose to put before you views that absorption in the fun might otherwise prevent you from considering. To those of you who, having heard these views, might feel inclined to say that they are 'of only theoretical interest' and that the linguist's job is to describe what actually occurs in particular languages without troubling himself about what might occur (for I have heard this said), I would suggest that the history of science is full of examples to support the opinion that the actual cannot be properly described, perhaps not even recognized, except in the framework of what has previously been envisaged as possible. At the same time, of course, the sphere of what is thought of as possible is being constantly revised under the impact of discoveries made in the description of actual languages. Such is the relation between the theoretical and the applied. And, as a consequence of this, linguistic typologies should be built of a judicious mixture of induction and deduction. This view is at least defensible; and it underlies what I have to say here on phonological typologies.

The concept of the phoneme is so widely accepted nowadays, especially in

America, that it may seem perverse to question it.[3] The use of the same terminology, it is true, tends to conceal a number of differences both of theory and of practice among the several schools of phonemicists. These differences, however, important though they are, do not concern us in the present connection. There is a common core of doctrine upon which all phonemicists are agreed and which sets them apart from non-phonemicists: this is expressed in their aim to describe language-utterances, on the phonological level, as a unidimensional sequence of discrete units, every one of which is in opposition with every other of the inventory in at least one pair of distinct utterances of the language.[4]

A radically different kind of phonological analysis has been developed and practised in recent years by what might be called 'the London school' of linguistics headed by J. R. Firth.[5] To this they give the name 'the Prosodic Approach'. Since this type of phonological analysis is less familiar to American linguists than the phonemic, I shall first give a brief exposition of what seem to me to be its main distinguishing characteristics. Though this cannot claim to be either an authoritative or an adequate statement of prosodic theory, it will have served its main purpose if it arouses the interest of readers sufficiently for them to turn up and study the several articles listed in the bibliography.[6] After discussing and illustrating the prosodic approach by comparison with the phonemic, I shall suggest that neither the one nor the other is completely satisfactory as a general theory of phonological structure, but rather that the applicability of the one rather than the other model to the description of a particular language can be used as a means of typological classification along a continuous scale ranging from one extreme point, the cardinally phonemic, to the other, the cardinally prosodic, and that, in fact, there is probably no language that is either cardinally phonemic, or cardinally prosodic.[7] Other independent variables may then be sought for the typological classification of the phonology of different languages. If this approach is pursued we are led to the view that the phonological system of a given language (or its phonological sub-systems) may be thought of as a point (or set of points) in a multidimensional space – the number of selected variables giving the number of dimensions in the hyperspace. Classical phonemic theory would fit perfectly only languages whose phonological systems were placed by this kind of classification at one 'corner' of the hyperspace. That there is probably no such language does not mean that phonemic description is never appropriate: it will be more or less appropriate according as the language being described is more or less close to the phonemic 'corner'; and in no language will each of the phonemes have equal claim to legitimacy.[8]

97

The two main differences between the prosodic approach and the phonemic seem to be these:

1. whereas the phonemicist maps the phonic data onto a unilinear sequence of phonological segments (phonemes), the prosodist describes the data in terms of two fundamentally different kinds of elements, PHONEMATIC UNITS and PROSODIES, the former being ordered with respect to one another in terms of successivity, the latter having as their 'domain' a variable, but determinate, number of phonematic units;

2. the prosodist, unlike the phonemicist, does not set up one overall inventory of phonological units for the language he is describing, but a number of different subsystems, each relevant for different phonological structures or for different places in these structures.[9]

These differences may be summarized by saying that the phonemic model is UNIDIMENSIONAL and MONOSYSTEMIC, and the prosodic TWO-DIMENSIONAL and POLYSYSTEMIC. Though both of these characteristic features of prosodic analysis have been associated with it from the beginning and are insisted upon equally by prosodists, they are clearly independent of one another and may be discussed separately.

The idea of describing the phonology of a language in terms of a two-dimensional model is not new to American linguists. In an early article, Zellig Harris pointed out that 'Two independent breakdowns of the flow of speech into elements are physically and logically possible. One is the division of the flow of speech into successive segments. ... The other is the division of each segment into simultaneous components, (1944: 181 = Joos, 1957: 124). He went on to show that in many languages the 'simultaneous components' recognized in the analysis extended over more than one segmental phoneme and could frequently be associated with the whole of a higher-level structure: *eg*, tongue-retraction in Moroccan Arabic, nasality in Swahili, etc. This point of view, which is essentially that of the prosodist, does not seem to have commended itself to the majority of American linguists; and Harris himself appears unwilling to draw from it its full implications, at least in the practical description of languages.[10]

To illustrate the difference between the phonemic and the prosodic approach to analysis we may briefly consider what is generally called 'vowel harmony' in Turkish. It seems that any phonemically-based analysis of Turkish must recognize eight vowels: *viz*, /i ï u ü e a o ö/. Any one of these vowels may occur in monosyllabic words: in words of more than one syllable, however, there are systematic restrictions on the co-occurrence of the several vowel phonemes. Thus, in words of native Turkish origin, front vowels, /i ü e ö/, and back vowels, /ï u a o/, do not occur together; nor do rounded vowels, /ü ö u o/, and unrounded vowels, /i e ï a/. Moreover, the phoneme /o/ occurs generally only in the first syllable of a word (with the exception of certain verbal forms). A phonemic representation of poly-syllabic words is therefore very highly redundant, since it represents each vowel in the structure as a selection from eight contrasting units, whereas all but two of the eight vowel phonemes are excluded from occurrence by the occurrence of any other given vowel phoneme of the word. The phonemicist may of course take account of the limitations upon the co-occurrence of vowel phonemes in his statement. It is to be noticed, however, that the redundancy is of his own making, and the corrective distributional statement a consequence of the phonemic preconceptions of the analysis in the first place. Redundancy at a particular point in a language can be measured only by reference to the set of 'choices' permitted by the language at that point.[11] By introducing the two binary PROSODIC contrasts of front/back and rounding/non-rounding, and admitting only two contrast-ing segmental PHONEMATIC UNITS, high/low, not only do we secure economy in the inventory of phonological elements, but we produce a much more satisfying description of the language – one based on the patterns actually operative in the language.[12]

The advantages of the prosodic approach in a description of Turkish are especially apparent as soon as one moves from phonology to morphology. The phonemicist must either make use of morphophonemes in his representation of the Turkish suffixes or list the allomorphs of each suffix and append a statement of the rules governing the automatic conditioning in different PHONOLOGICAL environments. C. F. Voegelin and M. E. Elling-hausen (1943), in their account of the structure of Turkish, set up two morphophonemic variables to handle 'vowel harmony' in the suffixes, x^2 and x^4, the former taking the two phonemic 'values' /e/ and /a/, and the latter the 'values' /i ü ï u/. The 'value' taken by the variables is then said to depend on the phonemic shape of the preceding vowel. 'The phonemic shape of the determined vowel may be any of the four high vowels or either of the two unrounded low vowels ... ; the rounded low vowels o and ö are never determined in vowel harmony, but may serve as influencing vowels' (Voegelin & Ellinghausen, 1943: 37). Determination by the preceding vowel is expressed graphically as follows:

(*a*) in vowel harmony of the x^2 type:

```
i   ü       ï   u
↓   ↙       ↓   ↙
e ← ö      a ← o
```

eg, with the plural suffix -lx²r: /kibritler/:/kollar/, etc.

99

(*b*) in vowel harmony of the x^4 type:

i ü ï u
↑ ↑ ↑ ↑
e ö a o

eg, with the possessive suffix -x^4m: /kibritim/:/evim/:/üzümüm/, etc.

For comparison, we may consider a prosodic representation of words containing the same suffixes, using lower case letters for phonematic units and upper case for prosodies. Prosodies will be put before phonematic units: but this, it may be noted, is simply a matter of arbitrary decision – they might just as well be written above or below, at the end of the word, or even in the middle.[13] For the phonematic contrast between the high vowel and the low vowel, I use *i:a*; for the prosodies of front/back and rounding/non-rounding, I use *F:B* and *R:N* respectively. (One might equally well, of course, treat one of each pair of prosodies as the absence of the other and so dispense with two symbols.[14]) With the exception of *R* when it 'combines' with *a*, the domain of these prosodies is the whole word (independently definable in Turkish in terms of stress[15]): in combination with *a* the domain of *R* is the first syllable, in succeeding syllables *N* necessarily occurs (and, therefore, need not be written).[16]

The following table brings together for comparison the morphophonemic, phonemic and prosodic representation of selected words:

gözlx²r	/gözler/	FRgazlar
evlx²r	/evler/	FNavlar
kollx²r	/kollar/	BRkallar
adamlx²r	/adamlar/	BNadamlar
güllx²r	/güller/	FRgillar
kibritlx²r	/kibritler/	FNkibritlar
bulutlx²r	/bulutlar/	BRbilitlar
kïzlx²r	/kïzlar/	BNkizlar
gözx⁴m	/gözüm/	FRgazim
evx⁴m	/evim/	FNavim
kolx⁴m	/kolum/	BRkalim
adamx⁴m	/adamïm/	BNadamim
gülx⁴m	/gülüm/	FRgilim
kibritx⁴m	/kibritim/	FNkibritim
bulutx⁴m	/bulutum/	BRbilitim
kïzx⁴m	/kïzïm/	BNkizim

It will be observed that the prosodic representation here, and elsewhere,

does away with the need for morphophonemics. And t...
(with a few exceptions, which must be treated as exce...
description) however many suffixes occur: thus what is morph...
cally *gözlx²rx⁴mx⁴zdx⁴n* and phonemically /gözlerimizden/, is pro...
FRgazlarimizdan. That is to say, both stems and suffixes have everyw...
the same phonological form. That this gives a 'truer' picture of the langua...
seems impossible to deny. If it is objected that prosodic formulae are difficult
to read, it may be replied that it is worth making the effort, if thereby we
come to see things as they are.[17] If it is objected that the prosodic formulae
are longer than the phonemic, it may be pointed out that even shorter
formulae than the phonemic may be secured by using a syllabic notation.
The only relevant criterion is that of phonological opposition; and if this is
consistently applied in the analysis of Turkish, it will lead us to something
like the statement given here, according to which the prosodies are 'long
components' (not of sequences of phonemes, but of words as structural
units on the phonological level of analysis) and phonematic units are
minimal segmental elements following one another in serial order within
morphemes and words.[18]

What is customarily called 'dissimilation' is no less suggestive of prosodic
treatment than is 'assimilation', of which 'vowel harmony' is one instance.
Suppose, for instance, there was a language in which (phonetically
speaking) the occurrence of a front vowel in any given syllable excluded the
occurrence of a front vowel in contiguous syllables within the same word,
and likewise in the case of back vowels. It would seem to be quite justifiable
to set up a pair of contrasting word-length prosodies whose phonetic
realization would be contrasting frontness and backness in alternate
syllables: that is $P_1 : P_2 = bfbfb \ldots : fbfbf \ldots$, where P_1 and P_2 are the prosodies
in question, = denotes phonetic realization and *f/b* represents a syllable
marked by frontness/backness. And of course we can envisage prosodies
with a far more complex phonetic 'realization'. There is no reason to fight
shy of recognizing phonological units of a quite 'abstract' nature or of great
phonetic complexity.[19]

Enough has been said to make clear the distinction between phonemic
and prosodic analysis. It should be clear also that some languages are more
satisfactorily described by the one than the other. This being so, it may be
suggested that the goodness of fit of one model of analysis rather than the
other should be made a criterion in the typological classification of the
phonology of languages. It will be evident that there will be a continuous
'line' separating the cardinally phonemic from the cardinally prosodic
languages.

ere is not good reason to divide what the
e head of prosodies into two different kinds
ould comprise those features that are called
usage of linguists (namely: tone, quantity
er suprasegmental consonantal and vocalic
ponents'. If this division is made, we may
sody' to the former, and the term 'supra-
of phonological unit. The division itself is
es (the term now and henceforth being used
on syntagmatic contrast, while supraseg-
mentals, like phonemes, depend upon paradigmatic opposition,
being what Jakobson calls 'inherent' features. Indeed, if the matter is
pressed, there seems to be no reason to group together prosodies and
suprasegmentals as against phonematic units. We may therefore use three,
rather than two, cardinal points for the phonological typology, each point
representing the employment of one of the phonological variables to the
exclusion of the others. It is easy to construct at least rudimentary
languages that make exclusive use of only one of the phonological variables
(and this establishes their theoretical independence). It is improbable in fact
that there exists any natural language that is cardinally of any one of the
three types: but this does not invalidate the proposed typology, any more
than the fact that few languages, if any, are purely agglutinating, isolating
or fusional invalidates the particular morphological typology implied by
these terms (cf. Bazell, 1958). The phonological systems or subsystems of
given languages can be represented as points within the triangle formed by
lines joining the cardinal extremities. To the present writer at least, this
appears to be a much more satisfactory system of typological classification
than that of forcing all languages into the same phonemic mould, often at
the price of arbitrariness, and then comparing them as to the number of
phonemes, the ratio of consonants to vowels, etc. That it is always *possible* to
phonemicize a language does not prove that one always *should*
phonemicize.

There are at least two other theoretical questions touching on phonological analysis upon which linguists are divided. The first is the question of
'coexistent phonemic systems' (cf. Fries & Pike, 1949), or, better, coexistent
phonological systems: the second is that of 'grammatical prerequisites' (Pike,
1949, 1952). As has been said above, the view that the phonology of a
language cannot be described satisfactorily in terms of one, overall system,
but should be considered as a set of subsystems, is an integral part of the
London school approach; and it is accepted by linguists of the London

school that the sphere of relevance of a given subsystem may be, though is not necessarily, grammatically, as well as phonologically determined. The 'orthodox' American view seems to be: (*a*) that the phonology of any given language is a uniform system; and (*b*) that phonological analysis can, and should, be carried out independently of grammatical analysis. Neither of these propositions is acceptable.[20] A more reasonable point of view would be that the phonology of a given language may or may not form a uniform system and that, in a given case, it may or not be desirable to do the phonological analysis independently of the grammatical. In Turkish, for example, it would be desirable to set up a different phonological system or different systems to handle those words to which 'vowel harmony' does not apply (in the manner described above), since such words form a minority and, being loan-words, may have other 'non-Turkish' features. Methodological differences among linguists may here again reflect an inherent difference in languages. And, if this is so, the possibility or non-possibility of (*a*) describing the phonology of a language satisfactorily in terms of a uniform system and (*b*) carrying out the phonological analysis independently of the grammatical could be used to provide a further pair of (two-valued) variables in the phonological typology. And of course these variables gould be given more values by quantizing the complexity of the phonological subsystems and of the grammatical correlations.

Further variables may suggest themselves: but the five mentioned above, especially the first three, would seem to have a good claim to inclusion in any reasonably comprehensive phonological typology of languages.

Epilogue[21]

Since the article reprinted here as the main part of this chapter (Lyons 1962a) has been cited frequently in the literature and has been included primarily for its historical interest, I have not wished to introduce any unnecessary confusion by revising or updating the text itself in any way. At the same time, I felt that I ought to take the opportunity of adding to its usefulness for present and future readers, including historians of linguistics, by giving my own account of the context in which it was written and by commenting upon some of the more general points that are raised in the article itself or have been raised by others, explicitly or implicitly, in relation to it. Much of this historical information and commentary is given in the notes, which have been completely revised and considerably expanded.[22]

When Lyons (1962a) was first written in 1961, it was very difficult for anyone who had not been a member of, or in close touch with, the so-called London School, to find out about its characteristically distinct, non-phonemic (not to say anti-phonemic) approach to phonology and to see how this differed from what was still (until Chomsky's trenchant criticisms of it at the Ninth International Congress of Linguists in 1962: cf. Chomsky, 1964a) the dominant American approach. Firth (1948c) was hard to understand without assistance, and Robins (1957b) was almost inaccessible.

The situation has changed dramatically since then. Many of the most important exemplifications of prosodic analysis have been reprinted (several of them in F. R. Palmer, 1970a); other general accounts of London School phonology by several of its principal adherents, in addition to Robins (1957b), have been published (including T. Hill, 1966; F. R. Palmer, 1970b; Robins, 1963); since the mid-1960s, it has benefited from the more or less sympathetic criticisms of proponents of generative phonology, most notably Langendoen (1964a, b, 1968), who have, sometimes anachronistically perhaps, discerned in the pronouncements or practice of the prosodists, prophetic glimmerings of what was subsequently revealed as sound doctrine;[23] and there have been a number of helpful textbook treatments (cf. Sommerstein, 1977: 54–69; Lass, 1984: 238–48; S. R. Anderson, 1985: 169–93). All this has had the effect of making the aims and achievements of prosodic analysis better known and more widely appreciated than it was thirty or so years ago. Several of the works to which I have just referred have pointed out that in many respects the London School phonologists were in advance of their time and have drawn attention to the similarities between prosodic analysis and such present-day theories as autosegmental and metrical phonology. In what follows I will make only occasional reference to current theoretical developments.

Lyons (1962a) has been much quoted and has been widely regarded (mainly by non-Firthians) as an authoritative introduction to prosodic analysis and has been reprinted as such in at least three collections of readings (Fudge, 1973; Jones & Laver, 1973; V. B. Makkai, 1972). It is undoubtedly the most 'Firthian' of my own publications. But it is in certain respects an unorthodox and idiosyncratic presentation of the subject and, in my view, is best seen as an exposition of the work of my London colleagues (and mentors) from a viewpoint that most of them did not share. I was already committed to the principles of post-Saussurean structuralism and Chomskyan generative grammar (and saw them as fully compatible with one another) when I went to London in 1957, to join the staff of what had been Firth's department at the School of Oriental and African Studies. My own understanding of prosodic analysis has therefore always been rather different from that of Firth and his associates, not only because I had not been involved in the earlier seminars and discussions in the so-called London School's formative years, but also, no doubt, because my own interests, both in teaching and research, were at that time very different from theirs and, unlike them, I had no practical experience of the problems of describing spoken languages.[24]

One notable difference between my presentation of prosodic analysis and more orthodox accounts was my failure to give due emphasis to the syntagmatic function of prosodies. And the failure to do so (coupled with my choice of Turkish vowel-harmony for the purpose of illustration) may well have had the effect of making prosodic analysis look more like Harris's (1944) long-component analysis, or even the distinctive-feature analysis of Jakobson & Halle (1956), then it really was. The term 'prosody' was originally chosen for the non-segmental units (or processes) of phonology, not only because such phenomena as quantity, tone and stress, which had traditionally been handled under this heading, could not be readily accommodated within a theoretical framework constrained by the assumptions of linearity and unidimensionality, but also because such phenomena frequently had higher-level units as their domain (syllables, word-forms, phrases, clauses or sentences) and, like Trubetzkoy's 'Grenzsignale', could be seen as having as their primary linguistic function the demarcation, or identification, of such units in the stream of speech (cf. Haas, 1964).

But Firth thought of his prosodies not as being simply demarcative of larger, higher-level, units (i.e., as indicative of the boundaries between them), but rather as constitutive of their very identity and internal cohesion. And, unlike Trubetzkoy, or more explicitly Martinet (1960), he did not accept the validity of the principle of duality of structure as this is normally explained: he did not think of utterances as being structured on two separate levels, a primary level of meaningful units (morphemes, monemes, words or whatever) and a secondary (phonological) level of meaningless units whose sole function it is to distinguish one higher-level, primary, unit from another. For Firth, phonological function, whether phonematic or prosodic, was itself a kind, or rather a part, of meaning (cf. Lyons, 1966a, 1977a: 607–10).[25] It is not possible to give a proper account of Firth's own view of prosodic analysis, and more particularly of the syntagmatic role of prosodies, without setting it within the more general context of his so-called monistic theory of the structure of language.

If we do not follow Firth (as I of course did not) in rejecting the principle of the duality of structure (not to mention the distinction between the language-system and language-utterances), it becomes necessary, at least for typological purposes, to distinguish between the phonological and the non-phonological syntagmatic function of (Firthian) prosodies. For example, the syllable, the consonantal cluster or the so-called phonological phrase is not necessarily co-extensive with any grammatically identifiable form. And I think it will be clear from earlier chapters in the present volume what adjustments and extensions need to be made to my treatment of phonemic and non-phonemic phonology in Lyons (1962a) in order to give fuller effect to the typological implications of the points that I have just made. For the more limited purpose of correcting the imbalance in my presentation of prosodic analysis as such, reference may be made, especially, to F. R. Palmer (1970b).[26]

I will not comment in detail on the typological suggestions made in the 1962 paper. I think it is true to say that the London School linguists were as little interested in typology, at the time, as were the adherents of most other schools of linguistics, apart from Hjelmslev and his followers. Since typology has now become much more popular than it was at the beginning of the 1960s, it may be worth quoting a contemporary comment by an influential American scholar:

[Morphological] typology ... has interested very few modern American linguists ... The reason for this may lie, as Kroeber has suggested in the question 'What do we do with a morphological classification of world languages when we have it?' The question is not easily answered (Hoijer, 1961: 121).[27]

My response, in a review of the volume containing Hoijer's article, published a few months after Lyons (1962a), was as follows:

The question is not difficult to answer; but it is a shocking question to put to anyone engaged in scientific enquiry, suggesting that the classification of phenomena in terms of general principles ... requires some ulterior justification. The linguist studies language because it interests him. Of the generalizations he makes about language some will be definitional and tautological, others empirical and inductive ... Thus the fact (if it is a fact) that all languages have a phonological and a grammatical structure is an interesting empirical fact about languages ... On the other hand, the "fact" that all languages have phonemes and morphemes (in the view of many linguists) is, under the common definition of these units, trivial; since in the last resort allowance is made for arbitrary segmentation. The fact that the distinction between morphology and syntax is profitably made in the analysis of some languages, but not at all – or to a different degree – in the description of others, is again an interesting discovery about languages, and one of great generality. At a lower level of generality we may classify languages into different morphological (or syntactic) types. The answer to the question posed by Kroeber, and echoed by Hoijer, is: when we have a morphological classification of the languages of the world, we shall contemplate it with wonder and satisfaction. We may of course then be impelled to do other things with it: we may try to answer the question why there are more languages of one type than another (cf. Greenberg's discussion of prefixing and suffixing languages); we may investigate the correlation between different morphological 'indices' (assuming that these measure a priori independent variables) or the correlation between phonological and morphological types, etc. The field of further enquiry is inexhaustible. Indeed one might almost say, as do the glossematicians, that linguistics is in aim none other than the establishment, partly a priori by the axioms and definitions of the controlling theory, partly empirically, of the most general and most systematic typology of languages (Lyons, 1962b: 1121–2).

The attitude to typology expressed here, as will be evident, informs much of Lyons (1962a). It is an attitude which, I suspect, would not have found favour with Firth or most of my SOAS colleagues, apart from Bazell, thirty years ago. As will be evident from earlier chapters in the present volume (especially Chapter 4), it is an attitude which I still hold. To the best of my knowledge no one has pursued in detail the typological suggestions made in Lyons (1962a): it is these which constitute, to my mind, its most original part, the part which makes it worth republishing. I would of course formulate them differently now, and I hope more satisfactorily, in the light of the advances that have been made in linguistic theory in general, and in phonological theory in particular, in the intervening years.

Modern readers of Lyons (1962a) will find many echoes of past disputes: especially of the 'God's truth' vs. 'hocus-pocus' and 'item-and-arrangement' vs. 'item-and-process' controversies (cf. Householder, 1952; Hockett, 1954). A superficial reading of the recent history of linguistics might suggest that, because linguists no longer engage, at least overtly, in the disputes that bear these labels or use the same, rather quaint terminology, the underlying issues have been resolved. This I do not believe to be the case. It may well be that linguists will no longer argue against the use of process terminology (or, what amounts to the same thing, against rules that operate upon linguistic entities and change their form) in the same way as they did in the 1950s. In this sense, therefore, the 'item-and-arrangement' vs. 'item-and-process' controversy, in its crudest form, may have been permanently removed from the agenda by the all-but-universal acceptance of the need for some kind of distinction between a language-system and language-utterances, by the rise of generative grammar and the development of a more sophisticated understanding of the notion of a rule. (I am of course aware that some linguists will demur.) There are other aspects of the controversy, however, which are but dormant. As for the 'God's truth' vs. 'hocus-pocus' dispute, this is certainly not resolved. Nor has it been, to my mind, to any significant degree illuminated by the rise of generativism (see Chapter 4).[28]

However that may be, I think it is fair to say that most London School linguists, although they might not have used the terminology itself, were hocus-pocus item-and-arrangers (if I may so express it). They were thus closer to certain of the post-Bloomfieldians, in this respect if not in others, than they were to Chomsky and early proponents of (transformational-) generative grammar. S. R. Anderson seems to me to be entirely right when he says that "Firthian prosodic analysis is entirely a theory of representations" and that "several Firthian papers cite as a virtue of their analysis the fact that it allows them to avoid the rule-related notions of 'assimilation', 'dissimilation', and 'action at a distance'" (1985: 189). My own memory of the reactions of most, if not all, members of the London School to Chomsky's earliest publications confirms the evidence of the written record (which for the most part antedates the rise of generative grammar).

Personally, I have never seen the force of the objections that were directed against process models of description by their critics, either post-Bloomfieldian or Firthian; and in my 'Phonemic and non-phonemic phonology' article I simply assumed that prosodic descriptions could, and should, be reformulated, in item-and-process terms. In fact, I just took it for granted, before the development of generative phonology as such, that the phonological description associated with a generative grammar of certain languages, such as Turkish, could, and should, be cast in the terms of prosodic analysis. (I would therefore have been very responsive to the proposals made a few years later by Fromkin, 1965.)

As to the 'God's truth' vs. 'hocus-pocus' controversy, I make it clear in the article that I subscribed at that time (and still do) to the view that the structure of what are normally called natural languages (i.e., N-languages as these are defined in Chapter 4 of the present volume) are to a very considerable degree, but not wholly, determinate. The linguist's description therefore would aim for what Householder himself, in a later, less well-known, paper on the controversy (1957), called "rough justice", combining (as I myself would put it in terms of the original dichotomy) the quest for God's truth in respect of the determinate with a certain amount of arbitrary, but judiciously motivated, hocus-pocus in respect of the indeterminate. For 'hocus-pocus' – despite its etymology and its employment by Householder (1952) in his criticism of Zellig Harris's (1951) *Methods* for his failure to take account of what would later be called naturalness – can now be taken, in this context, as a stylistically neutral, non-pejorative, term of art, more or less synonymous with 'regularization', 'systematicization' or 'mathematicization'.[29]

7

Towards a 'notional' theory of the 'parts of speech'

The purpose of this article is to initiate a discussion of the 'parts of speech' within the framework of generative grammar.[1] The present writer has long been of the opinion that the traditional, 'notional' theory of the 'parts of speech' merits a rather more sympathetic consideration than it has received from most linguists in recent years and feels, with Chomsky (1965: 118), that 'although modern work has, indeed, shown a great diversity in the surface structures of languages ..., the deep structures for which universality is claimed may be quite distinct from the surface structures of sentences as they actually appear', and that 'the findings of modern linguistics are thus not inconsistent with the hypotheses of universal grammarians'. The distinction that is drawn by Chomsky between 'deep' and 'surface' structure was implicit in traditional grammatical theory and has been reasserted by a number of modern scholars (cf. also Hockett, 1958; Lamb, 1964b; Halliday, 1966c: 57; etc.).[2] This distinction will be taken for granted throughout the paper. It will also be taken for granted that any satisfactory general theory of syntactic structure must be 'transformational' (in the sense of Chomsky, 1957; etc.). Towards the end of the paper, however, it will be suggested, on the basis of the arguments presented below, that current theories of transformational grammar stand in need of radical revision; in particular, that the rules of the base component should operate upon two different kinds of elements, 'constituents' (bracketed categories) and 'features' (for the most part, the traditional 'secondary grammatical categories' – tense, mood, aspect, etc.). It may not be without interest that this view of the nature of 'deep' structure appears to lie somewhere between that adopted by Chomsky (1965) and his followers, on the one hand, and that of Lamb (1964b) and Halliday (1966c), on the other, as well as having something in common with Shaumjan's approach (1965).[3]

We may begin by making the distinction that is commonly drawn between 'formal' and 'notional' grammar. According to Jespersen (1922: 55) 'notional' grammar starts from the assumption that there exist 'extralingual categories which are independent of the more or less accidental facts of existing languages' and are 'universal in so far as they are applicable to all languages, though rarely expressed in them in a clear and unmistakable way'. By contrast, 'formal' grammar (in this particular sense of 'formal') makes no assumptions in advance about the universality of the grammatical 'categories' and claims to describe the structure of every language on its own terms. Further, the 'formal' approach to grammatical analysis is generally taken to imply the rejection of semantic considerations both in the determination of the units of grammatical analysis and in the establishment of rules for their permissible combinations: in this respect 'formal' grammar can be compared with 'formal' logic. For the purpose of the present argument we will take for granted the validity of the distinction between 'formal' grammar and 'notional', and semantically based, grammar; and we will go on to enquire, first, whether the 'notional' approach to the definition of the 'parts of speech' can be followed (subsequently to their 'formal' establishment in particular languages) and, second, what reasons there might be for wishing to do this.[4]

The first point that must be made, and it has often been made before, is this: in their discussion of the 'parts of speech' many traditional grammarians confused, or may have appeared to confuse, two different questions. The first of these may be described as the question of class-membership; and the second as that of labelling the classes (as 'nouns', 'verbs', 'adjectives', etc.). It has often been pointed out, for instance, that, if the class of nouns is defined as the class of units which 'name persons or things', the definition cannot be applied without circularity to determine the membership of a syntactic class which includes such units as *truth, beauty, electricity*, etc. (cf. e.g. R. Hall, 1965; 174). It does not follow, however, that, given the extensional definition of a 'formally' determined syntactic class which includes *boy, cow, table, truth, beauty, electricity*, etc., the same, or a similar, 'notional' definition of the noun cannot be applied to decide whether the class in question is more appropriately labelled as a class of 'nouns' than as a class of 'verbs', etc. It is this second question that we are concerned with here.[5]

Traditional grammatical theory provides us with a set of definitions (not always consistent with one another) of such 'functional' notions as 'subject', 'predicate' and 'object', on the one hand, and of such 'categorial' notions as 'noun', 'verb', 'adjective', etc., on the other (for this opposition of 'functional' and 'categorial', cf. Chomsky, 1965: 64–74), of which it would be impossible to say whether they are primarily logical or syntactic in nature. What we propose to do here (without going into the details of the historical development of the traditional definitions of the 'parts of speech' in western linguistic theory, cf. Robins, 1966) is to recognize and separate three distinct approaches to the question and to assess their validity in general, or 'universal', terms. These three approaches will be referred to, for convenience, as (1) the 'contextual'; (2) the 'logical'; and (3) the syntactic approach. We shall be mainly concerned with what might be called the four MAJOR 'parts of speech' – nouns, verbs, adjectives and adverbs.

Our argument will tend to the conclusion that the primary 'categorial' notions of general grammatical theory are those of 'noun', 'predicator' and 'sentence', and that 'verb', 'adjective' and 'adverb' (unlike 'noun') should not be regarded as substantive universals of grammatical theory, but as complex 'cover-terms' to be employed in the description of particular languages. At this point, therefore, we make contact with, but propose a modification of, the view put forward by Chomsky (1965: 28): that 'certain fixed syntactic categories (Noun, Verb, etc.) can be found in the syntactic representations of the sentences of any language, and that these provide the general underlying syntactic structure of each language'.

We will assume, throughout the first part of the paper, that the syntactic component of our grammar consists of two parts: a constituent-structure section which accounts for the 'deep' structure of sentences in terms of a labelled-bracketing of the sentence-constituents, and a transformational section which assigns to sentences their 'surface syntactic structure'. (Whether or not the grammar also contains a separate inflexional subcomponent as a 'bridge' between syntax and phonology (cf. P. H. Matthews, 1965a), is immaterial for the present purpose.) In this paper we are of course concerned primarily with 'deep' structure; and we will assume that the 'deep' syntactic relationships involved in the definition of the major 'parts of speech' are to be found on the 'surface', as it were, in what were referred to in earlier transformational theory as 'kernel' sentences (Chomsky, 1957; but cf. 1965: 18): that is to say, in simple, non-passive, declarative sentences.

One of the oldest and most persistent features of the traditional theory of the 'parts of speech' is the view that the most fundamental division is between 'noun' and 'verb', and that the distinction between these two is to be drawn in terms of a prior distinction of 'subject' and 'predicate' as 'topic' and 'comment' (for the terms 'topic' and 'comment', cf. Hockett, 1958: 191). A quotation from Sapir will serve as a concise statement of the traditional argument (1921: 119): 'There must be something to talk about and something must be said about this subject of discourse . . . . The subject of discourse is a noun. . . . No language wholly fails to distinguish noun and verb, though in particular cases the nature of the distinction may be an elusive one. It is different with the other parts of speech. Not one of them is imperatively required for the life of language.'[6] It is noteworthy that this argument is to be found not only at the origin of linguistic theory in the West (cf. Robins, 1951: 17), but also in the Indian theory of the 'parts of speech' (Wackernagel, 1920: 13–14; but cf. Thieme, 1956: 2–3). It is the 'topic–comment' approach to the definition of 'subject' and 'predicate' that we are calling 'contextual'. But this term is something of a *lucus a non lucendo*! For one of the most striking features of the argument is that it usually takes no account of the context in which sentences are uttered, although it clearly ought to. For instance, Hockett says (1958: 201): 'the speaker announces a topic and then says something about it. . . . In English and the familiar languages of Europe, topics are usually also subjects, and comments are predicates: so in *John ran away*.' But it is evident that we cannot say what is the 'topic' and what is the 'comment' in a particular sentence (or indeed, whether it can reasonably be divided into 'topic' and 'comment') unless we know what question, explicit or implicit, the sentence is answering.[7] If the statement *John ran away* answers the question, expressed or implied, *Who ran away?*, then by the 'topic–comment' criterion *John* is the 'comment' and *ran away* is the 'topic' (or 'subject of discourse'); only in answer to the question *What did John do?* is *John* the 'topic' and *ran away* the 'comment'. Typically, of course, explicit questions like *Who ran away?* and *What did John do?* would be answered, not with the complete sentence *John ran away*, but with the 'elliptical' or 'derived' sentences *John (did)* and *He ran away*. In English, and possibly in all languages, the 'topic–comment' criterion finds its main application not in the determination of the syntactic structure of sentences, but in the establishment of the conditions of deletability and of pronominal and pro-verbal substitution ('anaphora') in connected discourse. And in many languages (e.g., German, Russian, Chinese, Greek, Latin, etc.), though not normally in English, it is, in addition, an important determinant, together with what is often referred to vaguely as 'emphasis', of word-order in complete sentences. These facts are well known, and have often been discussed by linguists and logicians. And yet, when presented with sentences like *John ran away* or *The horse is white* in isolation from the context in which they might occur, both linguists and logicians, as well as ordinary speakers of the language, seem to agree that something is being said about John or the horse, rather than about running away or whiteness. This agreement can only be explained on the assumption that, in the absence of the contextual information which is required in order to apply seriously the 'topic–comment' criterion, our informants will make an appeal, explicitly or implicitly, to certain other criteria whether logical or syntactical.

The second approach, which we are calling for convenience the 'logical' approach, is the one which underlies the traditional definition of the noun (or 'substantive') as 'the name of a person or thing' – the definition which so many linguists object to on the grounds of circularity. In various systems of formal logic, a distinction is made between 'names' and 'predicates', and 'predicates' are classified as 'one-place', 'two-place', 'three-place', etc., according to the number of 'names' with which they may or must combine in well-formed formulae or propositions. This distinction of 'names' and 'predicates' may be referred to the logical and philosophical distinction of 'particular' (or 'individual') terms and 'universal' (or 'general') terms and the traditional distinction in Aristotelian logic between the 'subject' and 'predicate' of 'propositions': whereas particular terms (the terms which name or denote individual objects, the paradigmatic instance of particular terms being the class of proper names) may occur only as subjects of propositions, universal terms may occur as either subjects or predicates.[8] (Stock examples of propositions constructed out of a particular term and a universal term would be *Socrates is a man*, *Socrates is mortal*; and of a proposition constructed out of two universal terms would be *Men are mortal*.) In general, we might say that the traditional distinction rests on the prior recognition, for the universe of discourse, of a class of individual things (including persons) and a class of general properties (including 'actions') which may be predicated of them. We might doubt whether the distinction of things and properties can be clearly drawn in all cases, or even whether it can be drawn at all within the framework of certain philosophical attitudes to the physical world. However, from the point of view of 'everyday' confrontation with the physical world, it is quite reasonable to say that there is a general human tendency to regard certain relatively constant and discrete 'Gestalten', made up of ('spatiotemporally contiguous': Chomsky, 1965: 29) properties, as 'things'.[9] If this is so, we have a satisfactory explanation of the agreement, noted above, as to what is the 'topic' in sentences isolated from their context. Moreover, if we have a language-neutral and workable notion of 'thing' (and there seems to be no reason to doubt that we have this in a sufficient number of instances), the question whether there is any correlation between the class of elements which denote things in a given language and one or other of the distributionally valid syntactic classes of elements in that language is open to empirical investigation. In other words, we can proceed to ask, and answer, the question whether a particular class is appropriately labelled as nouns. We will not expect to find that all members of the class name things, but we may expect to find that all the lexical items which do denote things fall within a syntactic class, X; and, if this is so, we will call the class X the class of nouns (a distinction being drawn within this class, as traditionally, between 'proper' and 'common' nouns, according to whether the items in question may occur only as 'particular' terms or both as 'particular' and 'universal' terms). By this criterion, it would appear that the class of units in English which includes *truth, beauty, electricity, boy, cow, table, John, Mary*, etc. is the class of nouns; and that the label is not arbitrary. Whether there exists any language in which a syntactically-valid class of nouns cannot be recognized by applying in this way the traditional criterion, whether they denote 'things', is therefore an empirical question, and one that admits of a non-circular answer. (The distinction between 'universals' and 'particulars', as drawn above, has been rather imprecisely formulated. It requires supplementation in terms of a distinction between 'characterizing' and 'sortal' universals: cf. Strawson, 1959: 168.)

In the 'logical' approach, it is to be noted that the definition of the noun takes precedence over the definition of the other major parts of speech: that the primary distinction is between 'nouns' and 'non-nouns' and that the definition of the 'verb' and the 'adjective' (in terms of such notions as 'action' and 'quality', where these notions can be applied non-circularly) is a secondary matter. This fact we will note and return to.

A purely syntactic approach to the definition of the major parts of speech does not figure very prominently in traditional grammatical theory. However, the oppositions 'subject'–'predicate' and 'subject'–'object' are employed in conjunction with the notions of 'noun', 'verb', 'adjective', etc., in certain traditional statements about sentence-structure that can be given an interpretation in terms of 'formal' syntax: every simple sentence is made up of two parts, a SUBJECT and a PREDICATE; the SUBJECT must be a noun (or pronoun, or noun-phrase, etc.), and the PREDICATE must be either (i) a transitive verb with an OBJECT, which must be a noun (or pronoun, or noun-phrase, etc.), or (ii) an intransitive verb, or (iii) a copula with a COMPLEMENT, which must be either (a) an adjective or (b) a noun. From the various propositions contained in this account of the syntactic structure of the three main types of the simple declarative sentence, it follows (if we assume that the classes of elements we wish to recognize as 'nouns', 'transitive verbs', 'intransitive verbs' and 'adjectives' are distributionally-valid classes and that instances of the three types of sentence exist in the language) that both the 'subject' and 'predicate' of each sentence and the 'nouns', the 'intransitive verbs', the 'transitive verbs' and the 'adjectives' can be determined from the constituent-structure. This point may be illustrated with reference to the following instances of the three main types of sentences we wish to consider ('intransitive', 'transitive' and 'copulative'):

(1) *Mary dances (beautifully).*
(2) *Mary cooks fish (beautifully).*
(3a) *Mary is beautiful.*
(3b) *Mary is a child.*

The constituent-structure grammar and associated lexicon which together generate these and similar sentences we will take to be (provisionally at least, and omitting details of tense, mood, aspect and number, and of countability and definiteness):

Grammar A

(i) $\Sigma \rightarrow X + Y$

(ii) $Y \rightarrow \begin{cases} Z(Q) \\ S + T \end{cases}$

(iii) $Z \rightarrow \begin{cases} P \\ R + X \end{cases}$

(iv) $T \rightarrow \begin{cases} X \\ V \end{cases}$

Lexicon A

$X = \{Mary, fish, child, \ldots\}$

$P = \{dance, \ldots\}$

$Q = \{beautifully, \ldots\}$

$R = \{cook, \ldots\}$

$S = \{be\}$

$V = \{beautiful, \ldots\}$

All the symbols with the exception of the initial symbol Σ ('sentence') are arbitrary and deliberately non-mnemonic; for the purpose of the argument we are adopting a purely 'formal' approach. We will return later to the questions whether Q and V are to be distinguished lexically (whether 'adjectives' and 'adverbs', of this class at least, are distinct 'parts of speech') and whether S (the 'copula' verb) is to be regarded as a lexical category at all. In addition to the lexical classification (in terms of X, P, Q, R, S, V), we have of course assumed a particular bracketing of our model sentences by means of three auxiliary symbols to label the 'nodes' (Y, Z, T).

All the sentences are bipartite at the highest level of constituent-structure $(X + Y)$: X must be the subject (and therefore must be a noun) because it is the one constituent at this level which (i) all sentences have in common and which (ii) is not distinguished in any of the sentences at the next level lower: in (1) P must be the class of intransitive verbs, since this class alone combines directly with nouns to form sentences; in (2) X must be the object (since it is the same class as the subject) and therefore R is the class of transitive verbs; in (3a) and (3b) S must be the 'copula verb' since it combines with another class (V) as well as with nouns (X) to form the predicate; and in (3a) V must be the class of adjectives. This argument would appear to be flawless (though a little devious); but it does rest upon very specific traditional assumptions about constituent-structure: we shall see later that these assumptions are far too specific to be promoted to the status of universality. It is interesting to observe, however, that this formulation of traditional statements about the structure of the three sentence types agrees with the logical approach in that it takes the distinction between nouns and 'non-nouns' as syntactically primary and draws the distinction between different kinds of 'non-nouns' at a lower level of 'predicate' structure. This being so, it may be suggested that, if any one of the traditional 'parts of speech' is to be regarded as a 'substantive universal' of general syntactic theory it is the noun.

At this point we must anticipate, and suggest an answer to two possible objections, each of which might appear to gain support from the traditional theory of the 'parts of speech'. The first has to do with the relationship between the noun and the adjective in the Indo-European languages; the second concerns the status of the verb.

It is well known that although the position we are defending with respect to the definition of the noun and the verb is in accord with the earliest Greek tradition (in Plato and Aristotle), from Alexandrian times it has been customary to group the noun and the adjective together (the distinction of 'nomen substantivum' and 'nomen adjectivum' as separate 'parts of speech' being a medieval development: cf. Brøndal, 1948: 25; Wackernagel, 1920: 22–3) and to distinguish them sharply from the verb. The reasons for this treatment are twofold. First, the adjective, like the noun, is inflected in Greek and Latin for case and number; and, second, the adjective may be used without an accompanying noun as the subject of a sentence. But neither of these reasons is valid in the framework of a transformational theory of syntax which distinguishes between 'surface' structure and 'deep' structure. In the first place, when the adjective is used 'attributively' it bears the same relationship to the noun which it 'modifies' as it does when it occurs 'predicatively' with the same noun as subject, and in both 'functions' it derives its characteristics of gender, number and case from the noun. It may be assumed that (apart from a small number of attributive adjectives which may have a different source) the occurrence of the adjective as the modifier of a noun in a nominal phrase is a matter of transformational development from its occurrence in predicative position: from this point of view the status of the adjective in Latin, Greek, Russian, etc. does not appear to be any different from its status in English, where it is not inflected for gender, number or case. Nor does the fact that the adjective can be used freely in Latin, Greek, etc. as the subject of a sentence have any bearing on the question, since, when an adjective is so used, the phrase in which it occurs is equivalent to a relative clause embedded upon either a contextually determinate noun or an indefinite nominal 'dummy': in either case, the gender, number and case of the adjective is determined by the 'antecedent' nominal element present in the 'deep' structure.

Our suggestion that the noun is primary in constituent-structure follows the logical tradition initiated by Plato and Aristotle. Against it there might be urged the view that 'dependency grammar', an alternative theory of constituent-structure to the one we have followed above, makes the verb the principal element of sentence-structure (cf. Tesnière, 1959) and that, since the two theories of constituent-structure are at least weakly equivalent (cf. Hays, 1964), we have made an arbitrary decision between them. This is not so. Although there is a strong tendency to take the verb as primary in relatively recent discussions of the 'parts of speech' (cf. Meillet, 1921: 177; etc.), this tendency can be attributed to factors which must be discounted in a theory of the 'parts of speech' that is based solely upon considerations of relationships in 'deep' structure.

First of all, it may be pointed out that the traditional theory of the 'parts of speech' has been much confused by the ambiguity of the original Greek term, which, as it was employed by Plato and Aristotle, is to be interpreted as 'constituents of the sentence' (or 'proposition': λόγος), but which was later understood as 'word-classes', the classification being carried out in Dionysius Thrax's codification of the Stoic and Alexandrian grammatical analysis of Greek (and even more consistently, and irrelevantly, in Varro's proposal for the recognition of just four 'parts of speech' for Latin: cf. Robins, 1951:54) in terms of the inflexional characteristics of words. (What is here referred to as the 'inflexional' approach is often described, anachronistically and misleadingly, as the 'morphological' approach. Not only is the term 'morphology' itself of comparatively recent origin – it dates from the nineteenth century – but, what is more important, the notion of a morphological level of analysis, including 'derivation', is foreign to classical grammar. The traditional opposition is between inflexion and syntax, each complementary to the other.) Instances of definitions of 'word-classes' couched in inflexional terms are: 'a noun is a part of speech inflected for case and number'; 'a verb is a part of speech inflected for person, number, tense and mood'; etc. Any general theory of sentence-constituents must reject such definitions, because they are clearly not interpretable with reference to other than 'synthetic' languages and because such 'secondary grammatical categories' as 'case', 'number', 'tense', etc. are not manifest in all languages. Moreover, the 'secondary grammatical categories' they invoke are derived from different levels of constituent-structure. In general syntactic theory, 'tense' and 'mood' are features of the sentence (although in many languages they are 'localized' in the verb in 'surface' structure); whereas 'case' (in the languages in which this category is to be found) is not present in 'deep' structure at all, but is merely the inflexional 'realization' of particular syntactic relationships (since 'case' is defined in terms of a prior notion of 'noun', this fact would vitiate any attempt to define the 'noun' in terms of 'case'). The most that one can say of the traditional inflexional definitions of word-classes is that they may be diagnostically valid with respect to particular languages, provided that the sentence-constituents have first been indentified, explicitly or implicitly, in other more general terms and provided that, in addition, the inflexional characteristics chosen as criterial are demonstrably relevant to the determination of 'deep' structure. (*A fortiori*, we must reject, from the point of view of our present concern, such statements as are frequently found in general treatments of the 'parts of speech' to the effect that certain languages have only two word-classes, inflected and non-inflected words: in no case known to the present writer has the relevancy of such statements been justified by the further assurance that all inflected words fall into one distributional class and all uninflected words into another.)

If we adopt the generative approach to grammatical description, and in particular the distinction between 'deep' and 'surface' structure, there would seem to be no reason to promote the verb to the status it is given in 'dependency grammar'. With the possible exception of the small class of impersonal sentences such as *pluit, ninguit*, etc. ('it is raining', 'it is snowing', etc.), even the 'one-word sentences' of inflected languages are of bipartite, subject–predicate structure with the nominal element controlling the selection of the verb. It is only with respect to 'surface' structure that one can say "la grammaire est toute entière dans le verbe" (Bally, 1932: 49). It is of course an important fact that the verb, or more generally the 'predicator', is (in certain languages at least) the 'focal point' of 'dependencies' in the surface structure of sentences. We will suggest what appears to be a plausible explanation for this fact below; at the same time we will take up the question of the status of pronouns, which for the present we neglect.

Having established the fact that, in many languages at least, the noun or nominal is the primary element of 'deep' constituent-structure (a fact which is supported by the 'logical' approach to the definition of 'subject' and 'predicate') let us now look at the other distributional classes which were invoked in the analysis of our model sentences: V ('adjective'), Q ('adverb'), S ('copula'), P ('intransitive verb') and R ('transitive verb').

The first point to be made is that there appears to be no reason to regard S (the 'copula') as a lexical class in English (or in the Indo-European languages generally). The 'verb *to be*', in sentences of the kind we are considering, (3a) and (3b) – though not necessarily in all cases where the 'verb *to be*' is said to occur in traditional descriptions of English – may be regarded as a 'dummy carrier' of tense, mood, aspect and number in 'surface' structure (roughly comparable with the '*do*-auxiliary' in negative, interrogative and emphatic sentences. The advantage of this analysis from a syntactic point of view is that embedding transformations no longer need to delete the element *be* (in accounting for the occurrence of the adjective in 'attributive' position, for various 'appositional' constructions, etc.), since *be* can be introduced, where necessary, by the transformational rules which convert sentences from 'deep' structure to 'surface' structure and which, *inter alia*, handle the features of number-concord, tense, aspect, etc. It is evident, however, that the removal of the 'copula' from the underlying constituent-structure of sentences implies a somewhat different attitude towards the 'secondary grammatical categories' than that which has been generally adopted, so far, in transformational grammar. We shall return to this point. Here let us simply note that our proposed treatment of the copula is in agreement with various 'non-Aristotelian' systems of logic; and that it is clearly more satisfactory for the so-called 'nominal sentences' in various Indo-European languages, which, when they are 'unmarked' for tense, mood and aspect, either do not normally have (e.g., in Russian) or may not have (e.g., in Greek and Latin) any 'surface' representation of the 'copula'.

It is well known that the traditional class of 'adverbs' includes many different subclasses, many of which are not distributionally identical at even the most general level of sentence analysis; and it is very doubtful whether any 'notional' account of 'adverbs' can be given which would bring together all the forms traditionally regarded as 'adverbs' in descriptions of English and other languages. For the purpose of this paper, we shall confine our attention to 'adverbs' which 'modify' the 'predicate' and more particularly (since 'predicate-modifying adverbs' may not constitute a unified class of sentence-constituents) to the subclass of 'adverbs' exemplified by *beautifully* in *Mary cooks (fish) beautifully* and *Mary dances beautifully*. First of all, it should be noticed that there appears to be no possibility of contrast in English between the 'adjective' and the 'adverb' (sentences containing 'verbs of sensation', like *She smells nice* and *She smells nicely* (!), are of course to be distinguished in 'deep' structure). Moreover, most of the 'adverbs' that here concern us are transformationally related to 'adjectives' (cf. *is a beautiful dancer: dances beautifully; is a good worker: works well;* etc.). The obvious solution is to say that the 'adverbs' are positional variants of the corresponding 'adjectives' (the allotment of the 'derivational' suffix *-ly* being a matter of low-level transformational rules). Expressed in terms of Jespersen's notion of 'rank' (1929: 97) the 'adjective' may be either a 'secondary' or a 'tertiary' category in the underlying constituent structure of sentences; it may be employed as a predicate (a 'function') or as the 'modifier' of a 'predicate' (a 'function of a function'). This does not mean that all 'adjectives' must have both 'secondary' and 'tertiary' function; this is clearly not so in English, where for instance the colour-adjectives (*red, green,* etc.) would not normally occur as 'tertiaries' (**The light shone greenly,* etc.) and certain 'adjectives' appear in 'secondary' position only after the application of a transformational rule (cf. *a rapid movement ← move rapidly:* it is assumed that *be rapid in his movements,* etc., is also derived transformationally from the base-structure underlying *move rapidly*). However, the fact that many classes of 'adjectives' may occur both as 'secondaries' and as 'tertiaries' in 'deep' structure (a fact which, in part, accounts for the syntactic ambiguity of *a beautiful dancer*) means that, in terms of the grammatical and lexical rules given above, the element Q is generally to be interpreted as an auxiliary symbol dominating V, or a constituent containing V (where V is the lexical class which includes *beautiful,* etc.) This being so, one is tempted to treat Q always as an auxiliary symbol; to say that it never denotes a lexical category.

At this point, it may be observed that an analysis of our element Q has already been proposed by Katz & Postal (1964: 125–48) which would justify us in saying that it is never a terminal symbol. Moreover, their analysis is supported by a much wider range of facts of English syntax than we are considering here. Briefly, it involves the derivation of 'adverbials' from phrases composed of a preposition and a 'dummy' nominal (in particular positions, the nominal element may be realized 'lexically' as *way, manner, degree,* etc.).[10] If this proposal is accepted (and it fits in with the historical development of many of the Indo-European languages: cf. Gray, 1939: 170), we can eliminate 'adverbs' from the lexicon and introduce them into sentences as 'adjectives' modifying a set of 'dummy' nominals. And once we do this, we cannot but be tempted to go farther!

Given the facts (i) that the 'adjective' and the 'adverb' are never in contrast in 'deep' structure, (ii) that the 'adverb' modifies both 'verbs' and 'adjectives' and (iii) that modification of the noun by an 'adjective' appears to be essentially the same as the modification of a 'verb' or an 'adjective' by an 'adverb', we can 'promote' the element Q (which we now assume contains a 'dummy' nominal and an adjectival 'position') to a 'higher' level of constituent-structure, allowing it to combine optionally with all 'predicates'. We will now revise our phrase-structure grammar (keeping the same lexical classification as before, except for the classes S and Q which we have abolished as terminal symbols):

Grammar B

(i) $\Sigma \rightarrow X + Y$

(ii) $Y \rightarrow \begin{Bmatrix} P \\ R+X \\ V \\ X \end{Bmatrix} (Q)$

Lexicon B

$X = \{Mary, fish, child, \ldots\}$

$P = \{dance, \ldots\}$

$R = \{cook, \ldots\}$

$V = \{beautiful, extraordinary, \ldots\}$

We have now eliminated from this portion of the phrase-structure grammar all auxiliary symbols except Y ('predicate') and the complex, optional element Q, and we are in a position to take up the most important question of all, that of distinguishing between the 'verb' and the 'adjective', both in general terms and with particular reference to English: in the course of the discussion we shall have occasion to refer back to certain points made in the last paragraph. In general treatments of the 'parts of speech', 'adjectives' are frequently said to denote 'qualities', and 'verbs' are classified (independently of their classification as transitive, intransitive, etc.) as either 'stative' or 'action' (according to whether they denote a 'state' or an 'action'). From this point of view, it is clear that 'adjectives' and 'stative verbs' are more similar than are 'stative' and 'action verbs'; indeed, the difference between a 'state' and a 'quality', even if it is not completely illusory, is certainly one that cannot be established (independently of grammatical considerations) in a good many cases. (Do *happy, know, exist, young,* etc. denote 'states' or 'qualities'? And cf. the Russian use of the instrumental for adjectives in 'stative' function, the Georgian adverbial case, the Finnish and Hungarian translative, the Spanish use of *estár,* etc.) This being so, it is hardly surprising that there should be languages in which there is said to be no 'adjective'–'verb' distinction, but rather a 'stative verb'–'action verb' distinction. And there are said to be many languages in which there is no distinction to be drawn between 'verb' and 'adjective' at all (cf. e.g., Gray, 1939: 169–70). These facts would seem to suggest that (unlike the noun) the 'adjective' and the 'verb' are syntactically complex categories and that the particular complexes of syntactic features covered by the terms 'adjective' and 'verb' are not, and cannot be expected to be, constant from language to language. What MAY be constant and universal in language is a distinction between nouns, on the one hand, and 'predicators' (which combine with one or more nouns), on the other. If this is so, and if it is also true that languages are more similar in their 'deep' constituent-structure than they are in their 'surface'-structure ('grammatica una et eadem est secundum substantiam in omnibus linguis, licet accidentaliter varietur', Roger Bacon: cf. Robins, 1951: 77; Jakobson, 1963: 209), then we should not seek to establish such categories as 'verb' and 'adjective', but 'predicators', as substantive universals of syntactic theory. Following the earliest classical tradition, we will use the term 'verb' to refer to all sentence-constituents which function solely as 'predicators'. This terminological decision (which is formally unmotivated, since 'verb', in this sense, is negatively defined in the system by opposition to the one designated category of noun) has the advantage that it is in agreement with the general practice of linguists who, when they are dealing with languages in which only two major 'parts of speech' are recognized, tend to refer to them as 'nouns' and 'verbs' (cf. Bloomfield, 1933: 20, 198-9; etc.).

Let us now develop the implication of the hypothesis that there is no distinction in 'deep' constituent-structure between what are traditionally called 'verbs' and 'adjectives' in English. If Grammar A is compared with Grammar B, it will be seen that, whereas the former allows for the distinction of 'verbal predicates' (dominated by Z) and 'nominal or adjectival predicates' (dominated by T), the latter does not. Grammar B recognizes three classes of singulary 'predicators' ('intransitive verbs', 'adjectives' and nouns) and one type of binary 'predicators' ('transitive verbs') and in this respect, imposes upon simple, declarative, non-passive sentences of English a constituent-structure analysis similar to their analysis in certain systems of formal logic. Let us now say, therefore, that all simple sentences are composed of a Noun and a Predicate; and that the Predicate may be either 'singulary' (in which case it is composed of a Noun or a one-place Verb, 'Verb$_1$') or 'binary' (in which case it is composed of a two-place Verb, 'Verb$_2$', and a Noun). We will introduce further refinements later, but this simplified statement will serve for the analysis of our model sentences and for the general theoretical points we wish to make here. The phrase-structure grammar and lexical classification suggested by our revised treatment of the model sentences is as follows (where Q is to be interpreted as suggested above):

Grammar C		Lexicon C
(i) $\Sigma \rightarrow$ Noun + Predicate		Noun + {*Mary, fish, child,* . . .}
Noun		Verb$_1$ + {*dance, beautiful,* . . .}
(ii) Predicate $\rightarrow$ Verb$_1$	(Q)	Verb$_2$ + {*cook,* . . .}
Verb$_2$ + Noun		

The principal difference between Grammars B and C is that the former distinguishes and the latter identifies the 'deep' constituent-structure of (1) *Mary dances (beautifully)* and (3a) *Mary is (extraordinarily) beautiful*: in other words, Grammar C identifies what are traditionally distinguished as 'verbs' and 'adjectives'. We have justified this above on the general grounds that there are many languages in which no syntactic distinction can be drawn between 'verbs' and 'adjectives'. In fact, the distinction of 'verbs' and 'adjectives' is complicated in English also by a number of factors. In the first place, the 'notional' categories of 'action' and 'state' are relevant to the classification of both 'verbs' and 'adjectives' for the purpose of generating well-formed sentences. Unlike most 'verbs' (which we will call 'verbs of action'), 'stative verbs', such as *know, believe, exist,* etc., cannot normally be used in answer to questions containing *do* as the 'predicator' (e.g. *What did he do?* It is important to distinguish the two different 'dummy' functions of *do*, both exemplified in this sentence. The *do* which 'carries' tense under certain transformations is not restricted to 'verbs of action'.) Moreover, predicates containing 'stative verbs' would seem to have the same limited range of aspectual possibilities as predicates containing 'adjectives'. On the other hand, there are certain 'adjectives' which may be used 'actively' with 'progressive' aspect: cf. *He is being silly (stupid, clever,* . . .) *now*. These facts are not being cited as evidence for the view that there is no syntactic distinction to be drawn at all in English between 'adjectives' and 'verbs', but merely to bring out the connexion between the 'notional' categories of 'state' and 'action' and the category of aspect.

Aspect is one of the 'secondary grammatical categories', which we have mentioned so far only to say that they cannot be used as criteria for the establishment of syntactic 'universals'. This does not mean that we must not take account of at least some of the traditional 'inflexional' categories in the analysis of the 'deep' structure of sentences, but only that they are not to be regarded as CONSTITUENTS of sentences in the same sense as the major 'lexical' categories. What is being proposed here, for the syntactic description of English and for general syntactic theory, is that we should distinguish sharply between 'lexical' and 'grammatical' categories (cf. Chomsky, 1965: 65, 74) and also that we should distinguish between the rules which introduce the two kinds of categories into the deep structure of sentences. It is only 'lexical' categories (and a certain number of 'complex variables', like Q) that will be introduced by constituent-structure rules of the type exemplified in Grammar C (rules of 'concatenation', in the sense of Chomsky, 1965: 124–5). In contrast to nouns, 'predicators' (or verbs, in the widest sense of this term) and 'complex variables', all of which may be true substantive universals of syntactic theory, the 'grammatical' categories (tense, mood, aspect, number, definiteness, etc.) form a very heterogeneous set of elements. Not only do languages vary in respect of the 'selection' they make from the total set of such categories; they vary also in respect of the number and nature of the 'paradigmatic' oppositions they recognize within each 'grammatical category'. Furthermore, the way in which the 'grammatical' oppositions are realized varies from language to language.

If we wish to preserve the traditional sense of the term 'sentence' (as the maximally independent distributional unit of language), it is clear that we need another term for the bracketed strings generated by the constituent-structure rules of the base-component. For this purpose, we shall borrow the convenient term 'theme' (cf. Katz & Postal, 1964: 115, 154; Halliday, 1966c: 61) and re-define it in such a way that it refers to structures of the kind generated by Grammar C.[11] 'Grammatical' categories relevant for the analysis of the 'deep' structure of simple, non-passive, declarative sentences of English include, we will assume, Negative, Tense (past vs. non-past), Modal (*will, may*, etc.), Perfect Aspect, Progressive Aspect, Number and Definiteness. Of these it would appear the Negative, and perhaps also Tense and Modal, are associated directly with the Theme, that Perfect and Progressive Aspect are categories of the Predicate and that Number and Definiteness are categories of the Noun.

Since our purpose in this paper is purely speculative (in the medieval sense of this term!), we will not attempt to formulate the rules whereby the 'grammatical' categories are associated with the Theme and its constituents. This is a very complex question. We have already seen, for instance, that Progressive Aspect is connected, in a general way at least, with the distinction of 'adjectives', and 'verbs' in English; that most verbs are 'active' and most adjectives are 'stative'. This fact suggests that Progressive Aspect is to be introduced into sentences at a lower level than Perfective Aspect. One obvious possibility which suggests itself (although it would require considerably more study than the present writer has yet been able to devote to it) is to use the same low-level transformational rule for the insertion of *be* in surface-structure with 'adjectives' and 'active verb' + Progressive Aspect (also with 'active verb' + *en*, resulting from the Passive transformation). There is some degree of syntactic justification for this: *the good boys* stands in the same relationship to *the boys are good* as *the flying planes* does to *the planes are flying*. (It is to be noticed, however, that the prenominal 'participial' form in *-ing* is not only more restricted than the prenominal 'attributive adjective', but also neutralizes the distinction between the presence and absence of Progressive Aspect with 'active' verbs: *flying planes* is derivable from both *planes fly* and *planes (are) flying*. The same neutralization is to be found in the 'gerundival' use of the '*ing*-form' of 'active' verbs: cf. *living, as I did, in Manchester*: *living, as I was, in Manchester*.) These, and other arguments could be adduced to substantiate the view that the distinction between 'adjectives' and 'verbs', from a syntactic point of view, in English, as in other languages where a similar distinction is drawn in the 'predicators', is not a matter of their CATEGORIAL function (the manner in which they combine with nouns in deep structure to form the underlying bracketed strings of constituents), but of relatively low-level features of 'inflexion' and position. Certain transformations involving 'verbs' and 'adjectives' can be specified without reference to the distinction between them (the derivation of prenominal and postnominal 'modifiers', including 'relative clauses'; nominalizations such as those underlying *Mary's beauty, Mary's dancing*; etc.); others (involving the selection of Progressive Aspect; the insertion of *be*; restrictions upon the occurrence of 'verbs' as prenominal 'modifiers'; etc.) would come later. This distinction between higher-level and lower-level transformations has the advantage that it clearly reflects the identity of the bracketing, 'predicative', relationship between the subject and the 'adjective' and between the subject and the 'intransitive verb' in deep structure.

It is conceivable, of course, although this may be regarded as doubtful, that the constituent-structure rules and the rules introducing 'grammatical' elements would operate to produce underlying phrase-markers of the kind presupposed in current transformational work on English and other languages. Even if this were so, it would not affect the general point we are making here with respect to the 'parts of speech'. For the phrase-markers would not be language-neutral in the way that the constituent-structure of 'lexical' categories and 'complex variables' might be. On the other hand, what may be universal is the FORMAL structure of the constituent-structure rules and of the rules which introduce into sentences of a given language 'grammatical' categories which are specific to that language. This is a weaker, though perhaps empirically sounder, claim than that which is made with respect to 'substantive universals' in such works as Katz & Postal (1964) and Chomsky (1965).

As we have seen, our approach to the question of underlying constituent-structure takes account of a good deal of traditional logical and linguistic discussion of the 'parts of speech'. It has brought us to a point where the constituent-structure base presupposed as universal imposes bracketing upon nouns and 'predicators'. Now, the reader will observe that, although Grammar C has been cast in the form of a 'rewrite' phrase-structure system, it is almost directly convertible into a constituent-structure grammar of the type referred to as 'categorial' (cf. Bar-Hillel, 1964: Chapters 5, 7, 14).[12] A characteristic feature of such grammars is that they have no rules specific to the languages they generate, but only what might be described as a 'metarule' operating directly upon the categorial classification of nouns and 'predicators' in the lexicon (and, with the proposed extension for elements such as Q, upon a further set of 'complex variables', which will have a 'categorial' classification, but will be transformationally interpreted in each language-specific system). If it were the case that all the 'deep' relationships between the lexical elements in languages could be formulated within a 'categorial' system of a fixed type, this would be a very interesting fact about the structure of human language – a fact which would delight, though it might not surprise, logicians, philosophers and 'notional' grammarians. Whether or not the suggestion that the base-component of a transformational grammar should include a truly universal 'categorial' section is empirically plausible is a question that can only be decided after a large and representative sample of the languages of the world have been studied from a transformational point of view – and studied far more thoroughly than any language so far. The suggestion is put forward by the present writer in full recognition of his own inadequacy for its substantiation, but with the hope that it will be taken up by those more competent than he is in these questions – if only to refute it.

Granted that the proposal that has just been made is extremely tentative and has been based on insufficient empirical evidence, there are none the less a number of points which may be briefly mentioned. First of all, since 'categorial' grammars are weakly equivalent to context-free phrase-structure grammars (cf. Bar-Hillel, 1964: 104–6), it might be asked why one should be preferred to the other. The answer to this question lies in the fact that a 'categorial' grammar formalizes certain general syntactic notions more neatly, and perhaps more economically, than does a rewrite-system of the type proposed by Chomsky for the formalization of constituent-structure. This point may be made clear by constructing a 'categorial' grammar and lexical classification for our model sentences. (We will leave out of consideration for the present the sentence with a nominal predicate, *Mary is a child*, and also the question of the 'adverbials'.) The grammar will be 'bi-directional' in the sense that it will permit concatenation ('cancellation') to the left and to the right: whether direction is necessary and what is implied by it we will discuss presently. The symbols used in the system will be 'T' (Theme) and 'n' (Noun), and 'fractional' combinations of these. The direction of concatenation will be indicated by means of a small arrow printed above the 'denominator', the 'fractions' being represented (for typographical simplicity) as an ordered pair of symbols in which the 'numerator' precedes the 'denominator'.[13] Thus one-place 'predicators' (*beautiful*, *dance*, etc.) are represented in the lexical classification as 'Tñ': to be read as 'elements which when they combine with a Noun to their left form a Theme'. For more complex 'predicators' brackets are used. Thus two-place 'predicators' (*cook*, etc.) are represented as '(Tñ)ñ': to be read as 'elements which when they combine with a Noun to their right form an element which when it combines with a Noun to its left forms a Theme'. That this lexical classification, interpreted by the 'metarules' of concatenation to the left and to the right, yields the same constituent-structure analysis of the model sentences

(1) *Mary dances,*
(2) *Mary cooks fish,*
(3a) *Mary is beautiful,*

as Grammar C will be obvious from the tree-diagrams below. From this point of view, therefore, the 'categorial' and the phrase-structure grammar are equivalent. It is also clear that the 'functional' notions of 'subject', 'predicate' and 'object' are definable in terms of this system in the same way as they are in a phrase-structure system: thus, using Chomsky's 'configurational' notation (1965: 71), 'subject-of': [n, T], 'predicate-of': [Tñ, T] 'object-of': [n,(Tñ) ñ]. (There is, of course, no equivalent of 'main verb-of' under our analysis: this is not assumed to be a 'deep-structure' relationship.) The principal difference between the above 'categorial' system and an otherwise equivalent phrase structure systems with rewrite-rules lies in the fact that the latter treats nouns and verbs ('predicators') as being on the same level (i.e., both as unanalysed notions); the former makes clear in the notation the fundamental difference in the syntactic function of the two classes – the verbs are defined by virtue of their combination with nouns to form the underlying themes of sentences. Furthermore, the notation makes it clear that the verb (in the widest sense) is the 'focal point' of the dependencies in the theme. No supplementary generalizations are required to state that the verb is the head of the predicate, and no reference need be made to particular rewriting rules for language-dependent systems in order to establish the relationship between the 'categorial' and the 'functional' notions.

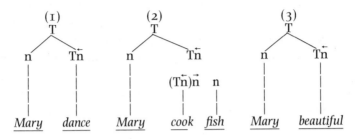

We may now ask what is the significance of 'direction' in the 'categorial' system. The most obvious answer is to say that it represents 'the abstract underlying order of elements' in the deep structure of sentences (cf. Chomsky, 1965: 125). But what does 'order' mean in this context? Chomsky appears to interpret the 'order' in which grammatical elements occur relative to one another in the underlying strings as a direct reflection of their relative 'sequence' in surface structure (allowance being made for 'stylistic inversion' up to the point of ambiguity: 1965: 126–7). We would prefer to interpret grammatical 'order' in terms of 'dependency' ('rection', 'government') and leave open for empirical investigation the question of the relationship between ORDER, in this sense, and the SEQUENCE of elements in the sentences of various languages (cf. W. S. Allen, 1956: 161; F. R. Palmer, 1964; etc.). If it turns out to be the case that 'sequence' always or even frequently, reflects 'order', this will be an interesting 'inductive generalization' (Bloomfield, 1933: 20) about the relationship between 'form' and 'substance'. 'Direction' was introduced into the 'categorial' analysis of the model sentences above on the (traditional) assumption that the subject governs the verb and the verb governs its object. (If this assumption is not made, then there is no need for a specification of 'direction' in the 'categorial' classification of 'predicators'. Instead, one might for instance impose a general convention, according to which the object stands between the subject and the verb (the relative order of subject and verb being immaterial): in this case, the underlying structure of *Mary cooks fish* would be n(*Mary*)+n(*fish*)+(Tn)n(*cook*)=(Tn)n(*cook*) +n(*fish*)+n(*Mary*). By introducing 'direction' into the system, we also allow for the possibility that in certain languages the object might in fact govern the verb.

The 'categorial' classification of 'adverbials' (such as Q: see above) is '(Tñ) (Tñ)': to be read as 'an element which, when it combines to its left with an element combining to the left with a Noun to form a Theme, forms an element combining to the left with a Noun to form a Theme'. This classification of the 'adverbials' brings out another rather pleasing feature of the 'categorial' notation: namely, its direct reflection of the distinction between endocentric and exocentric constructions – the 'modifier' in an endocentric construction will always be of the abstract form '(x)(x)', where 'x' stands for any category. Thus, 'adjectives' which are restricted to 'attributive' position (and all the numerals) can be marked as 'nn' in the lexicon; 'adjectives' which are transformed to this position will be given the derived classification 'nn'.

The one type of sentence that we have not so far considered from a 'categorial' point of view (of the four model sentences with which we started) is that exemplified by (3b) *Mary is a girl*. Sentences of this kind – sentences with a nominal predicate – have been much discussed by linguists and logicians. In order to handle them in a 'categorial' system, we need a rule which recategorizes 'n' as 'Tn'. This might appear to be an inelegance in the system. But the status of 'nominal' sentences is, in any case, unique: in that the nouns which occur as predicates form a proper subset of those which may occur in other positions (as subject, objects, etc.) and do not take the full range of nominal 'features' (in particular, they are not normally definite). More important, from the point of view of general syntactic theory, is the fact that the 'nominal' sentences fall into various logical types (statements of identity, inclusion, temporal or professional 'state', etc.). For instance, any syntactic treatment of English should account for the distinction that is reflected in surface structure as an opposition between *be* and *become*; and in terms of this account, and a subcategorization of nouns in the lexicon, it must be possible to distinguish, for the purpose of semantic interpretation, between meaningful sentences such as *Mary is (has become) a woman*, *John is (has become) a policeman*, etc., and 'tautologous' sentences such as *This rose is (*has become) a flower*, *Yellow is (*has become) a colour*. It may also be observed that the analysis proposed above for a sentence like *Mary is a beautiful child* is plausible for only two of the three possible interpretations of the sentence (i.e., for the 'restricting' and 'non-restricting' interpretations; 'Mary is a child, who is beautiful' and 'Mary is a child and she is beautiful'). The third interpretation is that in which *child* is semantically redundant (cf. *Lions are ferocious animals*). 'Nominal' sentences pose particular problems for general syntactic and logical theory. To the present writer it seems quite probable that nominal predicates should be introduced into underlying themes by means of not just one, but a set of 'selectional rules' (cf. Chomsky, 1965: 113–20), operating upon the subcategorial features of nouns in the lexicon.

The reference made in the previous paragraph to the relationship that exists between the (surface-structure) elements *be* and *become* raises a whole host of potential candidates for 'demotion' from 'lexical' to 'grammatical' status. We will do little more than list some of them here.

(1) The opposition between *be* and *become* (*get*) with 'adjectival' and certain nominal predicates is clearly aspectual (and is 'inflexionally' represented in many languages); it is comparable, and perhaps identical, with the 'mutative' aspect of passive verbs (cf. Strang, 1962: 146).

(2) With locative predicates (*in London*, etc.) *be*, on the one hand, neutralizes the opposition between various 'lexical' verbs of 'location' (*live, reside*, etc.; *stand, lie*; etc.) and, on the other hand, is in a one-to-many relationship of opposition with 'the verbs of motion' (*come, go*, etc.). It is conceivable that all sentences involving 'complementation' of 'direction' and 'place' (cf. Chomsky, 1965: 102, rules (52 iii, iv)) should be derived by embedding an optional 'verb of location' or 'motion' in a string of the form Noun + Locative (where 'Locative' is a 'complex syntactic variable', transformationally interpreted, with the 'categorial classification' 'Tñ'). Many languages have distinct 'locative' and 'predicative' copulas; and some do not require a 'verb *to be*' in either case. However we generate all these sentences, it is counter-intuitive to distinguish at the highest-level between *He is in London* and *He comes to London*.

(3) The relationship between simple predication and what might be called the 'modalities of sensory perception' comes up for consideration. It is interesting that there is in English a 'modal verb' corresponding to each of the five principal 'verbs of perception' (cf. *looks good* (*see*), *sounds nice* (*hear*), *smells superb* (*smell*), *feels smooth* (*touch*), *tastes delicious* (*taste: eat/drink*). Rather than set up a special sentence-type for these verbs it perhaps is worthwhile investigating the possibility of accounting for them by means of secondary modulations of the basic 'modally-unmarked' subject + predicate: e.g., *the soup* (*be*) *delicious*. Contrast *He tasted the soup, and it was* (= *tasted*) *delicious* with **He tasted the soup, and it looked delicious*. The secondary, transformational, derivation of 'predicates' such as *smells delicious* is, in any case, suggested by the necessity to relate systematically (i) *it is delicious; it smells delicious*, (ii) *it is petrol; it smells like petrol*, (iii) *it is burning: it smells as if it is burning*, etc.

(4) The 'verb *have*' in English may be regarded as a purely 'surface-structure' element. In many languages, what is customarily referred to (rather too narrowly) as 'possession' is expressed 'inflectionally', and this notion of 'possession' is frequently associated with aspect or 'transitivity' in the 'verb' (cf. W. S. Allen, 1964). One advantage of treating *have* as a 'grammatical formative' (of multiple origin) in English is that the lower-level transformational rule for inversion, tag-questions, etc. can then be formulated to apply to the first 'non-lexical' element in the verb-phrase (without the addition of special conditions to enable it to apply to *have*, and *be*, as 'verbs').

This very incomplete list of 'candidates for demotion' (it could be considerably extended) will perhaps be sufficient to convince many linguists that discussions of 'universal grammar' are as vague or as empty as ever they were! It must be insisted, however, that the proposals hinted at, rather than justified, in this article are, in principle, empirically testable. The objection made to 'universal grammar' in the past was that it distorted the descriptions of particular languages by trying to fit them into the framework of very specific traditional categories derived from the description of Greek and Latin. This objection loses its force in the face of an explicit and well-motivated distinction between deep structure and surface structure for particular languages (including Greek and Latin). Provided that the claims of 'observational' and 'descriptive' adequacy are not disregarded, there is nothing to lose, and much to be gained, in the search for 'explanatory' adequacy (cf. Chomsky, 1965: 18–27).

The general argument of this paper has been that the noun is the one substantive universal of syntactic theory (the 'predicators' being negatively defined with reference to their concatenation with nouns). What we must now do is to account for the fact that in very many languages the 'verbal complex' may stand as a 'one-word sentence', independently of the occurrence of previous utterances from which nouns may be 'understood' to function as the subject or object of the sentence in question. Here we must distinguish two senses of 'primacy' in sentence-structure. Nouns are primary, in the sense that they are linked referentially with 'things' (in the 'nuclear' instances); and perhaps also in that sense that, whether as subject or object, they determine the selection of verbs (cf. Chomsky, 1965: 115). But the verb is primary in a quite different sense – it is primary with respect to the normal functioning of language in particular situations. Since the 'things' referred to in utterances are often physically present in the situations in which the utterances are spoken, there need be merely a 'pronominal' indication, or no overt indication at all, of the 'things' referred to. Even where there is no 'pronominal' marker of subject or object in the utterance, it is still true to say (except in the case of 'impersonal sentences' that the underlying sentence 'contains' a subject (and, in the case of sentences with a 'transitive verb', an object) which determines the selection of the verb. For instance, 'one-word sentences' are common in Turkish: *Geliyor*, '(He/She) is coming', like all third-person (singular) sentences, has no 'pronominal' indication of the subject (cf. *Geliyorum*, 'I am coming'). It might therefore be suggested that one should derive a sentence with an overt subject, e.g., *Babam geliyor*, 'My father is coming', by expansion of the obligatory verb-phrase with an optional noun-phrase. But *Geliyor* is in contrast with sentences like *Geliyorum*, etc., which are overtly marked for the subject; and, though it need not refer to any previously mentioned person, it will certainly be understood as asserting that somebody is coming and a linguistic specification of that 'somebody' could be supplied by the hearer. The same is true, *a fortiori*, of languages (like Swahili, Abaza, Twi, Hausa, etc.) which have obligatory markers of subject (and object) in the 'verbal complex' and optional 'expansions' of these by means of nouns.

And yet there is some reason to say that nouns may 'stand for' pronouns in certain languages, and indeed in all languages (cf. W. S. Allen, 1956: 134). The traditional term 'pronoun' is misleading in that it captures only one of the two functions of pronouns: 'anaphora' ('standing for', 'reference back to') and 'deixis' (cf. Hjelmslev, 1959: 192–8). Of these two functions, it is 'deixis' which is the more important; in fact, 'anaphora' can be regarded as a special case of 'deixis', but not the converse. Language is normally learned and used in particular spatio-temporal situations at the 'centre' of which are the speaker and the hearer. The 'orientational' or 'deictic' systems of languages (tense, person, pronouns, etc.) are all related to an 'egocentric' spatio-temporal situation. From this point of view, it is not to be suggested that pronouns are 'substituted for' definite nouns any more than, for instance, *now* is 'substituted for' *at 10.15p.m. on 25 November 1965*. Pronouns and nouns (or noun-phrases) are alternative derivations of quite abstract grammatical symbols subcategorized (in terms of gender, animacy, etc.) only to the degree required for the correct selection of verbs.

The fact that the verb is primary from the point of view of communication (it is 'indispensable' and PRESUPPOSES the nominal elements which determine its selection: cf. Bazell, 1949a, for the distinction of 'subordination' and 'presupposition.') explains why it tends to be the 'focal point' of the sentence in surface structure – the point around which the deictic elements 'cluster'. And this same fact (which can, to a certain degree, be interpreted in terms of 'topic' and 'comment') explains why the verb had bestowed upon it by Plato a term (ῥῆμα, 'something said') which could also mean 'utterance' (cf. Robins, 1966: 7).

Since the nineteenth century there has been a good deal of discussion about the relative priority of nouns and verbs from an historical (or prehistorical) point of view (cf., e.g., Schuchardt, 1928: 268; Bally, 1932: 80); and many scholars (doubtless under the influence of the Sanskrit grammatical tradition: cf. Belvalkar, 1915; 8; Emeneau, 1955; 147) put forward the view, or reconstructed 'Indo-European' on the assumption, that all nouns were of verbal origin. The historical implications of this question do not concern us here. However, it is perhaps worth while considering briefly the logical possibility of a language without nouns.[14] This possibility is also raised by Quine's (1953a) 'nominalistic' proposal to eliminate singular terms in favour of existentially quantified, uniquely referring descriptions. Roughly, this proposal involves the replacement of propositions such as 'P has the property q' by 'There is just one x, such that x has the property p, and x has the property q'. Whatever the advantages of this proposal might be in a logical system, it is quite clear, as we shall see, that it has no application to natural languages.

Let us grant that all the nouns in a particular language (including the proper nouns) are in fact demonstrably derivable from verbs by a productive rule of formation. They may, of course, fall into a large number of subclasses (with, for example, 'agentive', 'instrumental', etc., affixes). For simplicity, we will take the limiting case of just one class of nouns, with 'zero-affixation' marking their derivation from verbs, and we will assume that the language is semantically isomorphic with English: *fair* will mean 'fair-haired' and will also denote John (a particular person); *dark* will mean 'dark-haired' and will also denote Mary; *bark* will mean 'bark' and 'dog'; *white* will mean 'white' and 'milk'; *eat* will mean 'eat' and 'table'; and so on. Now, it is quite conceivable that every noun might be recognizably derived from a verb in this way, and moreover by means of a MOTIVATED association between 'things' and 'properties' (if we may use the term 'property' somewhat loosely); and it is also conceivable that new nouns might be created *ad hoc* for 'things' in the situation of utterance (and for each baby at birth). What is not conceivable is that the language in question could function, outside a rather limited range of situations, without the association between 'things' and the nouns used to denote them becoming, not merely motivated, but CONVENTIONAL. Assuming now that somewhat the same selectional restrictions hold between subject and predicate as hold in English, we would wish to account for the acceptability of a class of sentences such as *white white* ('the milk is white'), *white eat* ('the milk is on the table'), *eat white* ('the table is white') *bark eat* ('the dog is eating'), etc. and the unacceptability of **white eat* ('the milk is eating' – structurally distinguished, we will assume, from the 'locative' sentence *white eat*), **white fair* ('The milk is John'), etc. Provided that there are systematizable distributional limitations of this kind (and it is hard to imagine that there could not be), the language recognizes a syntactic distinction between nouns and verbs; even though each noun is identical in form with a verb from which it is derived. This would still be true, even if every form could occur both as a subject position and as a predicate. The distinction between noun and verb would break down only in the, so far unattested, case of a language in the description of which no rules could be given for distributional limitations upon the free concatenation of all the 'major' lexical items.

This concludes the main argument of this paper. There are, however, a number of points arising out of the general proposal that has been made about the nature of 'lexical' and 'grammatical' categories. Most important of all is the question of language-acquisition. Chomsky has argued (1965: 25): 'As a precondition for language learning, [the child] must possess, first, a linguistic theory that specifies the form of the grammar of a possible human language, and, second, a strategy for selecting a grammar of the appropriate form that is compatible with the primary linguistic data'. He has further suggested (1965: 46) that 'we are very far from being able to present a system of formal and substantive linguistic universals that will be sufficiently rich and detailed to account for the facts of language learning'. It may be doubted, however, whether there is any need to postulate a 'rich and detailed', innate 'faculté de langage' in order to explain the fact of language-acquisition. The distinction between nouns and verbs ('predicators') drawn in this paper rests in the 'nuclear' instances (due allowance being made for the subsequent extension of the two major lexical classes: see above on the difference between criteria for 'labelling' and criteria for 'membership') upon the distinction between 'things' and 'properties' in the perceptual world. By the time that the child arrives at the age at which he begins to use language, it may be assumed that he is already in possession of the ability to 'reidentify particulars' and to distinguish between 'sortal' and 'characterizing particulars' (cf. Strawson 1959: 31–8, 168–72). And this ability is sufficient for the learning of the principal 'deep structure' relationship between lexical items – the subject–predicate relationship – provided that the child is presented with a sufficient amount of 'primary linguistic data' containing lexical items referring to 'things' and 'properties' in the 'situation' (cf. Chomsky, 1965: 33). This is of course a very traditional account of the referential component in language-learning. There seems to be no reason to doubt that, within certain limits, it is valid. One must be careful to stress, however, that the establishment of referential associations between lexical items and their denotata cannot be based on a theory of piecemeal 'ostension' (cf. Lyons, 1963a: 54). As for the 'grammatical' features, which vary considerably from language to language: the acquisition of these would seem to depend (as grammarians have long recognized) upon such general notions as 'inherent' vs. 'contingent', 'change of state', 'number', 'sex', 'animacy', 'position', 'motion', 'direction', etc., and, more particularly, upon the 'deictic', or 'orientational', features of the spatiotemporal situations of utterances. The development of notions such as these would not seem to presuppose their genetic transmission as part of a set of 'innate ideas' specific to language. So much, then, for the 'substantive universals' of syntax. The question of 'formal universals' is somewhat different; and we will not go into it here.

The discussion of the 'parts of speech' (and, more generally, of grammatical and semantic structure) from a 'notional' point of view is also relevant to the vexed problem of 'linguistic relativity' ('Whorfianism'). To the present writer it seems evident that neither extreme nominalism nor extreme realism is an acceptable approach to this question. If there were no correspondence at all between the structure of language and the structure of the perceptual world, there could be no sense in the suggestion that language imposes a particular categorization upon the world. To use a standard philosophical example: it is only because the 'nuclear' members of the class of verbs do in fact denote 'properties' which may be predicated of 'things', that *Lions exist* may be misleadingly construed as logically isomorphic with *Lions growl*. There must be some point at which the categories of logic, epistemology and syntax are in correspondence with one another. Recognition of this fact, which does not imply that they are necessarily in correspondence in any particular instance (as traditional, realist grammarians maintained) is implicit in the distinction drawn earlier between the extensional definition of syntactic classes in terms of 'formal' (distributional) criteria and the subsequent intensional definition of 'nuclear' members of these classes by reference to 'notional' categories. 'Il est chose vaine de vouloir prétendre que la linguistique puisse se passer de toute notion épistémologique. La forme du langage est une forme catégorielle' (Hjelmslev, 1935: 49).

Epilogue: so-called 'notionalism' updated

The purpose of my (1966b) parts-of-speech article was to stimulate discussion, within an overtly generative (and transformational) framework, of issues which seemed to me to have been unsatisfactorily treated in recent mainstream linguistics, both structuralist and generativist. It did not, in fact, succeed in this, its immediate, purpose.[15] Nor did it have any discernible effect upon the development of Chomskyan generative grammar. But it has been quite widely referred to in typological studies, partly for its formulation of a particular methodological principle (which will be restated and reformulated below), but also for its content. Since it is still being cited, either directly or indirectly (via the sections that were absorbed into the relevant chapters of Lyons, 1968a: see note 1 above), a few explanatory comments may be in order. The issues themselves have not lost their topicality.

'Notionalism'

In retrospect, I can see that I ought to have chosen a different term, partly because 'notional' has now been employed in a variety of different senses, technical and non-technical (including the sense it has recently acquired in applied linguistics: cf. Wilkins, 1976) and partly because it highlights the psychological rather than the ontological basis for the traditional theory of the parts of speech. As was made clear in the text itself, I took both the term 'notional' and its interpretation from Jespersen (1922) and contrasted it explicitly, in two respects, with 'formal'. (This was another ill-chosen term, perhaps, but it was one that was commonly used in this way at the time: cf. Lyons, 1968a: 135–7.) Notional grammar, in contrast with formal grammar, was held to be (i) semantically determined and (ii) universal. As for (i), I would now prefer to use 'ontologically determined', which captures more precisely than does 'semantically determined' the particular aspect of the traditional theory of the parts of speech that I was anxious to defend: the assumption that the meaning and distribution of the major grammatical categories was basically, or prototypically, dependent upon and determined by the structure of the external world.[16]

Universality

The context in which Lyons (1966b) was written was one in which theoretical linguistics had not yet been influenced by Chomsky's then but recent introduction of the principles of universal grammar into the theory and methodology of transformational-generative grammar. There were, and are, in any case considerable differences between Chomsky's conception of universal grammar and the one which I put forward in Lyons (1966b) – and which, with certain qualifications, I still hold.

There was of course no trace of universalism in Chomsky (1957) or such works as Lees (1960). Transformational grammar in its earliest, pre-*Aspects*, phase seemed to be fully compatible with the relativism that was characteristic of both American and European structuralism. It was also compatible, methodologically, with post-Bloomfieldian distributionalism, once this was stripped of its commitment to corpus-based discovery-procedures. Hence my adoption of this point of view in the parts-of-speech article.

Contrary to what seems to be the majority view among linguists at the present time, it is my belief that, although a considerable part of the categorial structure of (so-called) natural languages (see Chapter 4 above) is ontologically (and psychologically) determined, much of their semantically relevant syntactic structure – and more particularly much of their categorial structure – is non-universal. But I also hold (as I did in 1966) that much of the grammatical and lexical structure of (so-called) natural languages is non-universal and indeterminate and that they differ considerably from one another in the way that they grammaticalize or lexicalize the ontologically indeterminate. It is my view that mainstream linguistic theory moved too swiftly in the 1960s from the excessive relativism of the pre-War and the immediately post-War period to the present-day equally excessive, and often uncritical, universalism.

One point should be emphasized in connexion with universalism and the substitution of the term 'ontologically determined' for 'semantically determined'. This is that semantically determined grammar might well be non-universal. Many structural linguists have, of course, held that the semantic structure of each (so-called) natural language is unique and that natural languages are not necessarily intertranslatable: I share this view (see Lyons, 1980a). Ontologically determined grammar, on the other hand, must indeed be universal – at any rate, in the sense and to the degree that universality was attributed to ontologically determined grammar in Lyons (1966b).

'Parts of speech'

The term 'parts of speech' is used ambiguously throughout the article, as it was in traditional grammar, to denote, on the one hand, classes of lexemes and, on the other, classes of (word-)forms of various kinds. There are many reasons why it is important to use the term 'part of speech' with care and perhaps to restrict its applicability, distinguishing it, as I have done elsewhere, from 'form-class' (cf. Lyons, 1977a: 423ff.). But one good reason for doing so in the present context is that it makes it possible to say, for example, that different forms of the same lexeme, which would all be described traditionally as nouns, verbs, etc., belong to different syntactic classes: it makes it possible to identify some of the oblique cases of nouns with, say, adverbs or adjectives, rather than to treat them as featurized members of the same syntactic category. At least one theory of generative grammar contemporary with that of *Aspects* (to which reference was made in the article) did take this line (cf. Shaumjan, 1965); and it is of course highly defensible.

Terminology and notation

There are other more or less important terminological and notational changes that I would make if I were writing Lyons (1966b) today. Most of them are such that the failure to make them in the original article does not affect the substance of the argument. It is worth mentioning here, however, that I would now distinguish forms from expressions, reference from denotation, sentences from utterances, and acceptability from grammaticality (as in Lyons, 1977a). And having drawn the relevant distinctions, I would be careful to point out that sameness and difference of distribution, to which a considerable appeal is made in the course of argument, can only be sensibly discussed relative to more or less well-acknowledged ontological assumptions. Apart from anything else, some of the asterisks assigned to certain of the sample hypothetical utterances (or sentences?) in Lyons (1966b) would need to be removed. Linguists are more careful with asterisks nowadays than they used to be and more sophisticated about the difference between grammaticality, meaningfulness and various kinds of acceptability (cf. Householder, 1973).

Chomskyan and non-Chomskyan grammar

Although Lyons (1966b) was written within the framework of contemporary transformational-generative grammar it was in certain respects avowedly non-Chomskyan. I argued that theories of transformational grammar then current needed to be radically revised in various ways. In particular, I suggested that the rules of the base component should operate upon two different kinds of elements: (i) categories (or constituents) and (ii) features, the former being classified as nouns, verbs, adjectives, etc. (i.e., as major lexical or phrasal categories) and the latter as what I referred to as secondary grammatical categories (tense, mood, aspect, etc.). I also noted that the view of the nature of 'deep' structure that I was arguing for appeared "to lie somewhere between that adopted by Chomsky (1965) and his followers, on the one hand, and that of Lamb (1964b) and Halliday (1966), on the other, as well as having something in common with Shaumjan's (1965) approach". Towards the end of the article, I further suggested, somewhat tentatively, that the base component of a transformational grammar should be formalized in terms of categorial grammar rather than phrase-structure grammar. I do not wish to go into these various details here. Syntactic theory, both Chomskyan and non-Chomskyan, has moved on since 1966. But some of the points that I made at the time are still valid.

Categorial grammar

It is no accident that categorial grammar should have attracted increasing attention in recent years and that it should have been especially attractive to logicians and formal semanticists such as Montague (1974), D. Lewis (1972), etc. It formalizes in a particularly elegant way the inherent combinatorial properties of the major syntactic categories; and these inherent combinatorial properties may be held to be ontologically determined, as I sought to demonstrate in Lyons (1966b), and indeed as they were assumed to be by Husserl (1900/1), Leśniewski (1930) and Ajdukiewicz (1935), the originators of categorial grammar (cf. Bar-Hillel, 1950: Lejewski, 1958, 1975, 1979). In short, categorial grammar formalizes that part of what is pre-theoretically identifiable as acceptability which I have more recently called (using the traditional terms 'categorial' and 'congruity' in a partly traditional and partly untraditional way) categorial congruity (cf. Lyons, 1981b: 154ff.).

Nouns and nominals (noun-phrases)

One of the most serious defects of Lyons (1966b) was the failure to draw a distinction between nouns and what I later called nominals – between Ns and NPs in the most widely used Chomskyan notation (between N and N-bar, in X-bar notation). Failure to draw this distinction does not invalidate entirely the main points in the argument. But it does obscure the fact that the question of the universality of such lexical categories as N, V, A, etc. is a quite different question from that of the universality of such phrasal categories as NP, VP, AP, etc. This defect is remedied in Lyons (1977a: 423ff.). In the later work it is argued, I think convincingly, that nominals (NPs) are more universal than nouns (Ns). It was always clear, for example, that Nootka (and related languages) had a category of NPs, even if they lacked a distinct lexical category of Ns (cf. Lyons, 1977a: 433). It is worth noting, however, that, although the weight of modern descriptive evidence seems to suggest, contrary to what I had assumed on the basis of earlier statements by Sapir, Swadesh and others, that Nootka does have a distinction between nouns and verbs (or non-nouns) at the level of lexical categories (cf. Schachter, 1985: 11–13; Anderson, 1985b: 155–7), it is still in principle possible for a language to have nominals (NPs) and non-nominals without having lexically distinct categories of nouns and non-nouns. Much confusion has been caused in traditional grammar and in traditional logic by the fact that Latin does not have as clear a syntactic distinction between nouns and nominals as do many other languages (including English). However, when it comes to the integration of grammar and semantics, on the one hand, and of semantics and pragmatics (to use the modern term), on the other, it is just as important to draw this distinction in Latin as it is in other languages. Nouns, as a lexical category, have denotation, but cannot in principle have reference, whereas nominals (NPs) may, and characteristically do, operate as referring expressions in utterances. As I have already mentioned, reference and denotation are not distinguished as such in my (1966b) paper. But it should be clear when either the one or the other is relevant to the argument and, correspondingly, when nouns or nominals are being defined.

Verbs and adjectives

Contrary to what I took to be the case in Lyons (1966b), Japanese is nowadays usually said to have a distinction between verbs and adjectives. Granted that this is the correct view of the matter, granted even that the distinction between adjectives and verbs is descriptively more soundly based in the languages of the world than I (and many other linguists) assumed at the time (cf. Dixon, 1977), it does not follow that it is as important as the distinction between nouns and non-nouns. In any event, it is important to emphasize that the question is not simply one of the presence or absence of a particular categorial distinction in a particular language, but also of the relative importance of the distinction in question (measured by the number of criteria that are satisfied or the linguist's ease or difficulty in applying them: cf. Bazell, 1958). The distinction between verbs and adjectives (and more generally between any two categories) is drawn in terms of several criteria which may or may not apply independently and which may even be in conflict. There is little doubt that the distinction between verbs and adjectives is less important in the structure of Japanese than it is in, say, Latin or even English. But independently of such considerations, the very fact that the question whether a language has or has not a distinction between verbs and adjectives (or between nouns and verbs) can be raised, discussed and answered in the way it has been in recent typological work is proof of the applicability of the methodological principle which I was defending in Lyons (1966b) and which is reformulated below. In fact, I would claim that the principle that I made explicit was one that many traditional grammarians have tacitly applied in the past, so that the descriptions of particular languages that they produced were by no means as badly vitiated as the definitions that they officially, as it were, used would suggest.

Entities and places: adverbs and prepositional phrases; localism

Another serious defect of Lyons (1966b) was the failure to draw a distinction between entity-referring and place-referring expressions. It is obvious that there is an ontological distinction to be drawn between entities and places. It is also arguable that places (as distinct from spaces) are ontologically secondary, being identifiable as such by virtue of the entities that are located in or near them. Be that as it may, there is no question but that locative expressions in many languages are to be distinguished syntactically from nominal expressions and, more generally, that there is no justification for making the denotation of places criterial in the definition of nouns as a part of speech in universal grammar.

It is also worth noting, in this connexion, that, looked at from an ontological point of view, locative expressions are demonstrably the prototypical or nuclear members of Chomsky's fourth major lexical category: adpositions, which he defines in terms of the features [-N] and [-V], the absence of both nominality and verbality (1986: 68). Adpositional phrases are a subclass of what are traditionally classified as either adverbs or adverbial phrases (with some adverbial phrases, in certain languages, being subclassified as prepositional phrases, by virtue of the typologically restricted criterion of having a preposition as their head) or as case-marked nominals.

Now, it is a fact of considerable typological significance that in some languages place-referring expressions overlap more or less with entity-referring expressions. This is the situation, to a limited extent, in English. Conversely, in other languages case-marked entity-referring expressions are morphologically or lexically identical with place-referring expressions. This is of course the whole basis of localism, which is not mentioned in Lyons (1966b) though it is in subsequent publications, including Lyons (1977a). Localism was not part of my thinking in 1966 (though I had some familiarity with it): it became so to some degree, as it became part of the thinking of other scholars in Edinburgh in the late 1960s and early 1970s: cf. J. M. Anderson (1971, 1977, etc.) and J. Miller (1985, etc). The degree to which languages encourage the hypostatization of places by assimilating the expressions that denote or refer to them to entity-denoting or entity-referring expressions is an interesting typological (and psycholinguistic) question (see Chapter 8). The only point to be made in the present context, however, is that there can be no language-independent ontological justification for grouping places with persons, animals and things as the prototypical denotata of nouns. Traditional definitions of the noun which do this (if they are intended as definitions of universal grammar, rather than as definitions valid for some languages but not others) are therefore to be rejected.

Entities and substances: countable and uncountable nouns

The distinction between entities and substances is yet another distinction which I failed to draw clearly in Lyons (1966b).[17] Quine, to whom reference was made in the original version of Lyons (1966b), is one of the very few major logicians and philosophers of languages, until recently, to have paid sufficient attention to the implications of the fact that attested natural languages distinguish entity-referring and substance-referring expressions to different degrees and in different ways (by means of "a provincial apparatus of articles, copulas and plurals", 1960: 60). The whole tenor of my argument in Lyons (1966b) was that, although a syntactic distinction between count nouns and mass nouns is by no means universal, in any language that has this distinction, it is the former, rather than the latter, which constitute the nuclear, or prototypical, members of the class of nouns. Here, I part company with Quine (1960), who (though he does not express himself in quite this way) takes the denotata (or, as he would say, referents) of mass nouns to be ontologically more basic than those of count nouns and to function, logically, as proper names.

Membership and definition of the parts of speech

We come now to the restatement of the methodological principle, the justification of which was the main point of Lyons (1966b) and which has been widely accepted in recent typological studies. My original formulation of the principle in question was couched in the metalanguage of the purely descriptive, not to say taxonomic, linguistics of the time. This being so, it may appear to have been made to depend for its success upon the validity of the rigid separation of what were presented as two quite different, and chonologically distinct, operations, the first being carried out independently of, and prior to, the second: (i) that of establishing the membership of the major grammatical categories within each language, and independently for that language, on so-called formal (i.e., distributional) grounds; (ii) that of naming, or labelling, the categories across languages on so-called notional grounds. It is, of course, doubtful whether it is possible, even in principle, to operate with distributional discovery-procedures. But the principle can be formulated in wholly non-procedural terms and without regard to the comparison of one language with another.

The crucial question, from a methodological point of view, is simply that of avoiding circularity in the completed description of the language, in which morphology (if relevant), syntax and semantics are all integrated. Circularity is easily avoided (and was no doubt often avoided in practice) if the following crucial theoretical point is understood: that, because the grammatical categories of natural languages are partly, but only partly, determined by the language-independent structure of the world (i.e., ontologically), the ontological definitions of these categories are applicable only to their nuclear, or prototypical, members.

As far as nouns are concerned, the prototypical denotata are persons, animals and other discrete physical entities (but not places): these are what may be called first-order (extensional) entities. Nouns which denote first-order (extensional) entities are what are traditionally referred to as concrete count nouns. Non-concrete nouns, on the one hand, and non-count nouns, on the other, are by definition non-prototypical, or non-nuclear, subclasses of nouns (in any languages that have such subclasses). Languages may or may not grammaticalize the ontological distinction between concrete and abstract, the distinction between entities and places, the distinction between entities and substances, etc., but if they do, the various subclasses of nouns whose prototypical members denote something other than physical entities will be various kinds of non-prototypical, or non-nuclear, nouns, It follows that a particular noun, in a particular language, may be non-nuclear in at least two distinguishable ways: (i) it may be a non-nuclear member of the nuclear class of (concrete) nouns, such as 'cloud' in English: (ii) it may be a nuclear member of a non-nuclear subclass (i.e., satisfying the ontological definition for nuclear members of that subclass), such as the mass noun 'water' or the abstract nouns 'battle' or 'virtue' in English.[18]

Granted this distinction between nuclearity and the two kinds of non-nuclearity, we can now make explicit a principle which has probably guided the practice of grammarians throughout the ages without having been formulated in these terms. This is that, with respect to any ontologically defined grammatical category, X, no (so-called) natural language will have only non-nuclear members of X. For example (to take first the case of non-nuclear members of the nuclear subclass of nouns), no natural language will have a class of concrete nouns all of which are like 'cloud' or 'river' in English, in that they denote substances: 'cloud' and 'river' are, of course, rightly classified as concrete nouns in English, because they are assimilated grammatically to the class of nouns which includes 'boy', 'tiger' and 'table'. Similarly (to take the other kind of non–nuclearity), no language will have a class of nouns, all of whose members denote places, rather than entities (or a class of nouns, all of whose members denote abstract, rather than concrete, entities). A natural language might very well have a grammatically distinct class of place-denoting expressions, but if they are not assimilated grammatically to a class of entity-denoting expressions, they simply will not be called nouns.

In conclusion, I should perhaps emphasize that the methodological principle which I have formulated here is intended for the description and typological comparison of (so-called) natural languages (i.e., N-languages: see Chapters 2 and 4 above). It would be quite possible to construct a whole set of non-natural languages which run counter, in one way or another, to the justifiable expectations and prejudices of descriptive linguistics upon which this methodological principle is based (see Chapter 4). It is easy enough, for example, to construct a non-natural language with a distinct lexical category all of whose members denote abstract, rather than concrete, entities or denote substances, rather than entities (provided that the language in question has the syntactic resources for referring to concrete, first-order, entities). Whether we would call the members of such a category nouns or not is a moot question. As for the binary part-of-speech distinction (if it may be so described) between names and predicates (in the post-Fregean sense of 'predicate') which is found in standard logical languages, such as the predicate calculus, it will be evident that this does not correspond at all closely with the lexico-syntactic distinction between nouns and non-nouns that is characteristic of natural languages. This fact does not emerge as clearly as it should have done in my (1966b) treatment of the question.

8

Deixis as the source of reference

In this paper I shall be concerned with what Quine (1960: 108) describes as the first two phases in the ontogenesis of reference.[1] Like Quine, I shall venture no psychological details as to the actual order in which "the child of our culture" masters the "provincial apparatus of articles, copulas, and plurals" as he "scrambles up an intellectual chimney, supporting himself against each side by pressure against the others" (1960: 102, 80, 93). What I have to say about the child's acquisition of the grammar of referring expressions is not incompatible, as far as I am aware, with any of the data that has been collected and discussed in the psycholinguistic literature: but I am not claiming that all children "of our culture", and still less children of all cultures, must go through the same stages in the acquisition of their native language and that these stages must succeed one another in a fixed order. My purpose, rather, is to show how the grammatical structure and interpretation of referring expressions (other than proper names) can be accounted for in principle on the basis of a prior understanding of the deictic function of demonstrative pronouns and adverbs in what might be loosely described as concrete or practical situations. I will argue that the definite article and the personal pronouns, in English and other languages, are (in a sense of 'weak' to be explained below) weak demonstratives (see Sommerstein, 1972; Thorne, 1973), and that their anaphoric use is derived from deixis. I will also argue, as part of this thesis, that the presuppositions of existence and uniqueness which logicians commonly associate with the use of the definite article derive from general conditions governing singular definite reference – more especially deictic reference – and do not distinguish that definite article in English from the demonstratives *this* and *that*, but that they are grammaticalized as separable components in the underlying structure of demonstrative and definite noun-phrases in English.

In this paper I will construct a language-system which is simple, but rich enough, I believe, to characterize the grammatical and semantic structure of children's early sentences in many languages and also to serve as a basis for the development, differently in different languages, of the more complex sentences of adults. I will call this simple language-system Quasi-English.[2]

There are three grammatically distinct classes of singular definite referring expressions in English: proper names, pronouns, and definite noun phrases. In many languages, however, common nouns may also be used without a determiner as singular definite referring expressions; and they frequently occur with this function in the earliest utterances of English-speaking children. We will therefore build this feature into the grammar of Quasi-English; but we will assume that the semantic distinction between names and common nouns, in certain cases at least, is already established. Our main problem is to show how phrases like *this man, that man*, and *the man* can be derived within the grammar, in a syntactically and semantically revealing way, from underlying structures which contain neither a demonstrative adjective nor a definite article. In doing so, we shall make use of two transformational processes, adjectivalization and apposition, both of which, I am inclined to believe, are universal.

We will operate with just four terminal syntactic categories: names (Nm), common nouns (N), verbs (V), and deictics (D). For reasons of convenience and familiarity, we will also make use of the standard auxiliary symbols NP and VP, and present the rules of the base in terms of phrase-structure grammar. The rules of the base component of Quasi-English at a very early stage are as follows:

PS rules:	(1) S→NP NP
	(2) S→NP VP
	(3) NP→{Nm, N, D}
	(4) VP→{N, V, D}
Lexicon:	(i) Nm: {*John, Daddy,* . . .}
	(ii) N: {*dog, house, table,* . . .}
	(iii) V: {*big, bark, swim,* . . .}
	(iv) D: {*there*}

As they stand, these rules will generate a set of binary syntagms, which we may think of as kernel sentences, in Z. S. Harris's (1957) rather than Chomsky's (1957) sense of this term: each of these sentences, when uttered, will be associated with a particular intonational and stress contour which will, in part, serve to determine the interpretation of the utterance as an exclamation, statement, question, wish, etc. If we wanted the system to generate all the sentential constructions that a child is capable of producing at the age at which the mean length of his utterances (measured in terms of the number of forms in each utterance) is about 1.5 (see Bowerman, 1973), we should need to introduce two-place verbs and we might also have to allow for the deletion of either the subject or the verb, and even the object. One further deficiency in the system, considered as a grammar for the generation of the sentences underlying the utterances of children at an early stage of their linguistic development, is its failure to account for locative and possessive structures, which appear to be well established in children's speech soon after they pass the holophrastic stage. I will say something about these structures later.

Before we introduce the transformational rules and extend the system in a particular direction, some comments on the rules and categories of the base-component of Quasi-English are in order. Rules (1) and (2) distinguish two subtypes of kernel sentences: equative and predicative. I assume, without evidence, that this distinction is grammaticalized in all languages, though differently in different languages: by case, by the use of one copula rather than another, by the use of determiners, etc. In English, the distinction is grammaticalized, partly in terms of the permutability of noun-phrases in equative sentences and their non-permutability in predicative sentences and partly in terms of the restrictions governing the internal structure of predicative nominals (i.e. nouns and noun-phrases derived by rules corresponding to VP→N in the grammar of Quasi-English).[3] Whether or not the distinction between equative and predicative sentences is justifiable on purely syntactic grounds in all languages, the semantic distinction between equative and predicative statements is surely funda-mental. Russell's sentence *Scott is the author of Waverley* is not only ambiguous (out of context) as an utterance; it is also syntactically ambiguous as a sentence of English. *The Morning Star is the Evening Star*, on the other hand, is not a syntactically ambiguous sentence of English: nor is any utterance of this sentence, I assume, ambiguous with respect to the semantic distinction drawn between equative and predicative statements.

I have introduced into the grammar of Quasi-English the principle that the subject precedes the predicate. It has been argued recently that the traditional grammatical distinction of subject and predicate is purely a matter of surface structure (Fillmore, 1968; J. M. Anderson, 1971); and there is some force in the argument. It should not be forgotten, however, that the grammatical distinction was traditionally associated, on the one hand, with the logical distinction of particular and universal terms in the proposition expressed by a sentence and, on the other, with the semiotic distinction of topic and comment in utterance (Lyons, 1968a: 343). In twentieth-century linguistic theory, it has also been associated with the semantic distinction between the actor, or agent, and the action; and subdivisions within topic and comment have also been recognized (Halliday, 1970a). Granted that some or all of these distinctions need to be drawn in the grammatical and semantic analysis of any fully developed adult language, it is perhaps reasonable to assume that they tend to coincide in child language. It has, in fact, been suggested in the literature that the topic–comment construction is "attributable to the innate capabilities of the child" and that the grammatical distinction of subject and predicate develops out of this in languages like English (Gruber, 1967: 39). The topic–comment distinction correlates highly of course with the logical distinction of particular and universal terms, as it does with the semantic distinction (where it is independently determinable) of actor and action. The principle that the topic precedes the comment is one that is widespread in languages. In traditional discussions of the subject–predicate distinction, this was commonly explained in terms of the naturalness of first mentioning, or identifying, what you are going to talk about and then saying what you have to say about it (Sandmann, 1954).[4] I do not wish to make too much of the subject–predicate distinction. But it can hardly be dismissed as a superficial feature of the grammatical structure of certain languages.

Little need be said about the recognition of names, common nouns, and verbs as distinct categories in a very early stage of language-acquisition. Most logicians in modern times have, I suppose, grouped common nouns with predicates, and have distinguished them from names and pronouns; more recently, some linguists have taken a similar view (e.g. Bach, 1968). But there are very few languages, if any, in which grammarians have found it difficult to distinguish nouns and verbs in terms of their syntactic distribution; and the distinction seems to be well established in the child-language data that I have seen. It will be observed that in Quasi-English nouns may be used as either referring or predicative expressions; but that names may be employed only as referring expressions and verbs as predicative expressions. We will not discuss here the distinctions between noun subtypes (e.g., mass/count, concrete/abstract).

Quasi-English has a single deictic particle which is neutral with respect to any distinctions of gender or proximity. Its function is to draw attention to some feature of the situation or some entity in the situation, and it will be normally accompanied by some paralinguistic movement of the head or hands indicating the direction to which the addressee should turn in order to identify the feature or entity in question. We may think of the deictic as meaning something like '*Look!*' or '*There!*'.[5] The child's utterances, whether they contain a recognizably deictic form or not, will often be purely expressive, rather than communicative in the full sense: they will be indicative of his or her own interest in some feature of the environment. It is also important to realize that, even at a stage when we feel entitled to say that the child is drawing the attention of an addressee to some feature or entity, it will not always be clear that part of his utterance identifies a referent and part of it says something about the referent. Utterances such as *Book there* or *There book* might be intended and understood to mean '*I want that book*', '*Give me that book*', '*There's the book!*', '*Look, a book!*', '*That's a book*', and so on.[6] We are not concerned here with the way in which the child's developing control of a language enables him to differentiate and make explicit various semiotic functions. From now on, we will concentrate primarily upon those binary syntagms analysable grammatically as being of [D + VP] or [NP + D] structure and interpretable, as utterances, as being composed of a referring expression (the topic) and a predicative expression (the comment); and we will say nothing about any selection restrictions that hold between particular subjects and particular predicates.

Quasi-English does not distinguish the pronominal and the adverbial function of the deictic. Any theory of deixis must surely take account of the fact (much discussed in philosophical treatments of ostensive definition) that the gesture of pointing of itself will never be able to make clear whether it is some entity, some property of an entity, or some location that the addressee's attention is being directed to. Identification by pointing, if I may use the term 'pointing' in a very general sense, is deixis at its purest; and it is only when deixis operates within at least a rudimentary language-system that ostensive definition, as such, becomes feasible. The single deictic particle of Quasi-English is intended to be the linguistic counterpart of pointing; more precisely, as we shall see later, of non-directional pointing. There is perhaps no language with a single deictic particle which operates exactly in this way, being neutral with respect to pronominal and adverbial (or prolocative) function, on the one hand, and with respect to distinctions of spatial proximity, gender, etc., on the other. We will presently introduce some of these distinctions, although it is not clear that any particular one of them must be grammaticalized in all languages.

However that may be, we will now move on to extend the grammar (and lexicon) of Quasi-English by introducing into the language a syntactic (and lexical) distinction between a deictic pronoun (D_1) and a deictic adverb (D_2). As far as language-acquisition is concerned, this distinction may be thought of as partly reflecting and partly supporting the child's recognition of the difference between referring to an entity and referring to a place. It is my assumption that, even if the adult language did not draw a distinction between deictic pronouns and adverbs, by virtue of the universal and extralinguistic principle that deictics with pronominal function (like proper names) cannot be used as predicative expressions, a deictic which derives from VP in the grammar would necessarily be interpreted as having an adverbial function. When I say that the distinction between pronouns and adverbs, once it is acquired, not only reflects, but also supports, the child's recognition of the difference between referring to an entity and referring to a place, I have in mind the fact that, on the basis of the grammatical distinction, he will come in time to see a parallel difference of meaning between such sentences as *Thát's the park* and *Thère's the park*, on the one hand, and *Thát's John* and *Thère's John*, on the other.[7]

There are various ways in which we can extend the grammar and lexicon of Quasi-English to incorporate the distinction between deictic pronouns and adverbials. Let us do so here by simply replacing rule (4) with

(4′) $VP \rightarrow \{N, V, D_2\}$;

by adding

(5) $D \rightarrow \{D_1, D_2\}$;

and by substituting for (iv) the following two rules in the lexicon:

(iv′) $D_1 \rightarrow \{that\}$
(v) $D_2 \rightarrow \{there\}$.

These rules allow a deictic adverb to occur as the subject of a predicative sentence and as either the topic or comment in an equative sentence. Briefly, there are two reasons for this decision. First of all, by deriving both D_1 and D_2 from D in these positions, and D_2 directly from VP in predicate position, we make explicit what was earlier said to be a universal principle governing the interpretation and distribution of deictics. Secondly, there are positive reasons for wanting to derive D_2 from NP. Sentences like *It's cold there* create problems for any theory of predication which operates solely with entities and properties (or classes); and, as has often been pointed out, we can make statements about places, just as we can make statements about things. Russian, for example, would translate *It is cold there* as *Tam xolodno* literally 'There (is) cold'); and I see no reason why the semantically equivalent English sentence should not be derived from an underlying structure in which *there* is the subject and *cold* the predicate. This analysis is broadly equivalent to that which has been proposed, in terms of case-grammar, by Fillmore (1968) and J. M. Anderson (1971).

The semantic justification for generating sentential structures with a deictic adverbial subject and a nominal predicate is perhaps more dubious. English allows us to say either *This place is cold* or *It is cold here*. But it forces us to say *This(place) is a city* rather than *It is a city here*.[8] In principle, however, there seems to be no reason why a language should not permit reference to a place or region by means of a deictic adverbial in order to predicate of that place or region that it belongs to a certain class. There would of course be selection restrictions holding between the adverbial subject and the predicative noun. But there are similar selection restrictions holding between a nominal or pronominal subject and a predicative noun. We will not, therefore, exclude the possibility of a deictic adverb occurring as the subject of either a verbal or a nominal predicate.[9]

Let us now turn our attention to what are traditionally regarded as noun-phrases composed of a demonstrative adjective and a noun: e.g., *that dog*. The most obvious way of generating such phrases, and one which would formalize the traditional conception of their structure, is by means of an adjectivalization transformation, identical with that which derives attributive adjectives from predicative adjectives (in such phrases as *good dog*) and attributive nouns from predicative nouns (in such phrases as *girl student*). Up to a point this is semantically satisfactory. For there does seem to be a semantic similarity between the following pairs: ⟨*The dog is good, the good dog*⟩; ⟨*The student is a girl, the girl student*⟩; ⟨*The book is on the table, the book on the table*⟩; ⟨*The dog is (over) there, the dog over there* = *that dog*⟩ (see Thorne, 1972). Notice, however, that this parallelism also suggests that the demonstrative adjective in English encapsulates in some way both the definite article (which we have not yet accounted for) and the adjectivalized adverb: *that dog* is interpretable, under one interpretation at least, as *the dog (over) there*. Moreover, there are both syntactic and semantic problems attaching to the derivation of demonstrative adjectives in English from predicative deictic adverbs. Transformations of this kind should produce semantically endocentric complex predicative expressions (*good dog, girl student, book on table*). It is arguable that *that dog* is, in certain instances at least, semantically endocentric (when it is used in explicit or implicit contrast with *this dog*), but it cannot be employed as a predicative expression. Furthermore, when it is used as a referring expression, it cannot be regarded as being syntactically endocentric and having *dog* as its head, since in adult English (in contrast with Latin, Russian, Chinese, Malay, Turkish, etc.) singular countable nouns cannot be used as referring expressions without having some kind of determiner or quantifier adjoined and preposed to them. Quasi-English, as we have so far presented it, is more like Turkish, Latin and Russian in this respect; but even in these languages, it should be noted, demonstrative noun-phrases cannot be used as predicative expressions.

What then are the alternatives? There would seem to be two. We could take *that* as a pronominal head deriving *dog* by means of an adjectivalizing transformation from a predicative nominal. This would be syntactically satisfactory, since it would make phrases like *that dog* endocentric with respect to *that* (i.e., it would account for the fact that demonstrative noun-phrases have the same distribution as demonstrative pronouns); it would also account for the more general fact that, not only in English, but also in Turkish, Latin, Russian, etc., demonstrative noun-phrases are excluded from predicate position in predicative sentences. Analysed in this way, *that dog* would mean 'that entity which is a dog' ('which is a dog' being construed restrictively). However, it requires but little reflection to see that this interpretation, though perhaps not absolutely excluded, is very unusual.

The second alternative is to take *dog* as being in apposition with *that* in such phrases as *that dog*; and this is undoubtedly more attractive. There are many languages in which nouns or noun-phrases seem to operate as optional appositional adjuncts of obligatory personal or demonstrative pronouns (Keenan, 1972: 446–50). But there are two kinds of apposition relevant to the present problem, and each of them is naturally handled in current versions of generative grammar by means of non-restrictive clause-formation (Motsch, 1965). Consider *That man, John Smith, is very rich*; and *That man, an oil magnate, is very rich*. The appositional phrase *John Smith* is most appropriately derived from the comment position of an underlying equative structure [*That man* [*that man be John Smith*] *be very rich*].[10] Now *that dog* in English is in fact interpretable as a referring expression, it seems to me, in either of the two ways suggested by these two types of apposition: (i) 'that entity – the dog'; (ii) 'that entity – a dog'. The first interpretation, however, is perhaps the more normal, both *that* and *dog* having reference and being co-referential: the individual in question is identified simultaneously, as it were, by deixis and description. Since demonstrative pronouns, common nouns, and proper names all occur as referring expressions at a very early stage in the utterances of English-speaking children, if we are forced into adopting a single ontogenetic source for demonstrative noun-phrases, it is perhaps preferable to opt for the grammaticalization of an equative appositional link between the demonstrative pronoun and the associated noun.

But do we need to opt for one of the appositional processes to the exclusion of the other, or indeed for apposition to the exclusion of adjectivalization, even in a synchronic grammar of adult English? The predicative appositional link is what seems to be required for the semantic interpretation of such utterances as *That fool won't do it* and in general for the analysis of demonstrative noun-phrases with what Donnellan (1966) calls an attributive function. And we have already seen that there are some reasons for deriving at least one component of the demonstrative adjectives from predicative deictic adverbs. Since adjectivalization and both kinds of apposition are required anyway in English, my proposal is that we incorporate all three ways of deriving demonstrative noun-phrases within the grammar.

A further question now arises: can any two, or all three, of the three transformations operate in the derivation of the same demonstrative noun-phrase? And if so, how are they ordered? To discuss this question in detail would take up too much space; and a decision one way or the other would seem to be irrelevant to the further points I wish to make in this paper. Let me simply say that the two types of apposition appear to be mutually exclusive on semantic grounds, but that either could be combined, in principle, with adjectivalization. Now it is a language-particular fact about English that countable nouns cannot be used as singular definite referring expressions without a demonstrative or other determiner; and that the demonstrative always precedes the noun with which it is associated, as it also precedes any adjectival modifiers of that noun. These facts are most naturally accounted for if we incorporate in the grammar of English (though not necessarily of all languages) the principle that adjectivalization presupposes apposition, but that apposition may take place without adjectivalization, in the derivation of demonstrative noun-phrases. Every such noun-phrase, e.g., *that dog*, will be four-ways ambiguous in terms of its grammatical structure: (i) '*that entity* $(D_1) - a\ dog$ (N)'; (ii) '*that entity* $(D_1) -$ *the dog*' (N); (iii) '*that entity* $(D_1) - a\ dog$ (N) *which is there* (D_2)'; (iv) '*that entity* $(D_1) -$ *the dog* (N) *which is there* (D_2)'. These structures can be distinguished symbolically (without introducing the definite article as an underlying category) as follows: (i) $(D_1 - N)$; (ii) $(D_1 = N)$; (iii) $(D_1 - (D_2N))$; (iv) $(D_1 = (D_2N))$. In these formulae, '=' symbolizes equative apposition and '–' symbolizes predicative apposition; these are different types of paratactic constructions, each of which resists classification in terms of a simple dichotomy of endocentricity and exocentricity (see Nida, 1966: 17). '(D_2N)' symbolizes an endocentric construction composed of an adjectivalized deictic adverbial and a noun. It should be clear that the grammar of Quasi-English also generates a number of other constructions in which D_2 is in predicative apposition with either D_1, N, (D_1-N), or $(D_1 = N)$. All of these are in fact interpretable; and we shall return to a subclass of them later.[11]

Let us now concentrate on the equative-appositional interpretations (which I have assumed to be more normal). The derivation of *that dog* by means of both equative apposition and adjectivalization might proceed as follows: [*that* [*that* = *dog* [*dog there*]]]⇒[*that* [*dog there*]]⇒[*that* [*there dog*]]⇒[*that-there dog*]⇒[*that dog*]. The hyphenization of *that-there* at the penultimate stage is intended to represent informally a process of amalgamation which has the effect of uniting the two underlying forms in a single surface form.[12] However this process of amalgamation is formalized, its effect would be to incorporate both a pronominal and an adjectival component in the resultant form *that*; and this, as we have seen, is what is required under the interpretation of phrases like *that dog* when they are in contrast, explicit or implicit, with *this dog*.[13] Let us assume, however, that in Quasi-English amalgamation does not take place, so that *that dog* is derived without adjectivalization of a predicative deictic adverb (and contrasts semantically with such phrases as *this dog*, once we introduce the distinction of deictic proximity), whereas *that there dog* is derived as a grammatical phrase, syntactically equivalent to *that good dog*.

How does Quasi-English compare with Standard English (apart from its lack of the amalgamation process)? So far it does not distinguish syntactically or semantically between the definite article, the demonstratives, and the so-called third-person pronouns. It is well known that these three (or four) categories are related diachronically. Postal (1967) has argued, correctly I believe, that they are also synchronically relatable in the grammar of English; and he has suggested that they should all be derived, synchronically, from underlying structures containing the definite article. Sommerstein (1972) and Thorne (1973), on the other hand, have taken the view that the third-person pronouns and the definite article are to be regarded as being basically demonstratives. This latter hypothesis is to be preferred on several grounds. First of all, there are many languages that have demonstratives, but lack a definite article or formally distinct third-person pronouns. Secondly, in all the Indo-European languages which distinguish between either the article and the demonstratives or the third-person pronouns and the demonstratives, the demonstratives are diachronically prior. Finally, and most importantly, the function and distribution of the article and the third-person pronouns, and the grammaticalization of definiteness as it is in fact grammaticalized in English, are explicable by means of the hypothesis that they derive synchronically (and perhaps also ontogenetically) from demonstratives. Since the main lines of the argument in favour of this hypothesis are to be found in Sommerstein (1972) and Thorne (1973), I can be relatively brief at this point.[14]

The English third-person pronouns (*he/she/it*) are distinguished for gender, but not for the deictic distinction of proximity; the demonstratives (*this/that; here/there*) are distinguished for proximity, but not for gender; the definite article is distinguished for neither gender nor proximity, and (unlike the demonstrative and third-person pronouns) cannot be used as a referring expression. In English it is not possible to refer to an individual deictically (other than by using a proper name) without incorporating within the referring expression some information about the location of the referent or about one or more of its properties. The phrase *this man*, used deictically, informs the addressee that the referent is in or near the place where the speaker is and that it is a male, adult, human being; *he* informs the addressee that it is male, but says nothing about its location in relation to the speaker; *this* gives the information that it is located near the speaker, but implies or presupposes nothing about any of the properties of the referent, except (in predicative utterances) that it is non-personal. This last proviso is required, because the use of the demonstrative and personal pronouns in English is governed by the further, and more specific, principle, that *that* and *this* cannot be used as referring expressions, in predicative utterances, to refer to persons (and animals): *That is good* cannot mean '*That person is good.*'[15]

Now, it is important to realize that in the deictic distinction of proximity, as it operates in English, *this* and *here* are semantically marked in relation to *that* and *there*: the opposition is proximal vs. non-proximal, not proximal vs. distal (or distal vs. non-distal). It is only when there is an explicit or implicit contrast with the proximal term in the opposition that the non-proximal demonstratives imply or presuppose remoteness from the speaker. As *bitch* is to *dog* with respect to the lexicalized opposition of sex, so *this/here* is to *that/there* with respect to the opposition of deictic proximity. To say that *dog* has two meanings because it is the unmarked term in this lexical opposition would be to misunderstand the nature of semantic marking as it operates in the grammatical and lexical structure of languages. Similarly for *that* and *there*; and it is, incidentally, the failure to appreciate the significance of this point that vitiates Allan's (1971, 1972) arguments against my proposals relating to existential sentences (Lyons, 1967a, 1968b).[16] Let us, however, purely for convenience of exposition, distinguish weak and strong forms of the non-proximal demonstratives (as Allan does) by means of subscripts – *that*$_1$ and *there*$_1$ being weak, and *that*$_2$ and *there*$_2$ being strong. The use of the strong forms of the demonstratives will always imply a contrast with the marked terms *this* and *here*; but the use of the weak forms of the unmarked demonstratives correlates, to some degree, with the distribution of strong and weak stress (see Sommerstein, 1972; Thorne, 1973); the correlation, however, is quite complex, since strong stress serves a number of different semantic functions in English.

Let us now build into the grammar of Quasi-English this deictic distinction of proximity. We will do this initially by simply amending rules (iv') and (v) of the lexicon:

(iv'') $D_1 \rightarrow \{that_1, that_2, this\}$

(v') $D_2 \rightarrow \{there_1, there_2, here\}$

The grammar will now generate such kernel sentences as *That$_1$ big, That$_2$ big, This big, Dog there$_1$, Dog there$_2$, Dog here.* It will also generate by means of apposition *That$_1$ dog big, That$_2$ dog big, This dog big*; and by means of both apposition and adjectivalization *That$_1$ there$_1$ dog big, That$_1$ there$_2$ dog big, . . . , That$_2$ there$_1$ dog big, . . . , This here dog big,* as well as *That$_1$ good dog big,* etc.[17] The amalgamation rule (if we introduce it into the grammar at this point) will operate according to the principle that a marked or strong demonstrative absorbs a weak form. (This is obviously more neatly formalizable in componential terms; and I will presently reanalyse the deictics in a componential framework.) Thus: *this there$_1$* ⇒ *this; that$_1$ here* ⇒ *this; that$_1$ there$_1$* ⇒ *that$_1$; that$_1$ there$_2$* ⇒ *that$_2$; that$_2$ there$_1$* ⇒ *that$_2$.*

All that is required in order to generate a definite article in Quasi-English is a rule (whose historical counterpart in the development of English was presumably a purely phonological rule based on stress):

that$_1$ ⇒ *the.*

We now have such phrases in Quasi-English as *the dog, the big dog, this dog, that dog,* etc. We also have such sentences as *The big* (i.e., 'He/she/it is big'). The next step is to incorporate in the grammar of Quasi-English rules which will exclude such structures. But before we do so, it is worth noting that, if English had such sentences as these, it would have a demonstrative pronoun (as Classical Greek had in certain environments: Sommerstein, 1972) which was neutral with respect to distinctions of proximity with respect to the location of the speaker: and this pronoun would be the linguistic equivalent, when used to refer to an entity in the situation, of non-directional pointing. It would be an entity-referring expression without sense.

There are various ways in which we can go about incorporating in Quasi-English gender distinctions in the demonstratives comparable with the distinctions found in the set {*he, she, it/that*} in English. What we want to say, it seems to me, is that the speaker of English, when he wants to refer to a person by means of a demonstrative pronoun (in the utterance of a predicative sentence), is forced by the structure of English (as he is not so forced by the structure of certain other languages: e.g., Turkish) to give the addressee the information that the referent is a person and the further information that the referent is male or female; and that he cannot give any information (linguistically) about the deictic location of a personal referent (within a phrasal referring expression)[18] without introducing into the referring expression an appositional noun (or the nominal dummy *one*); but that, when he refers to a non-personal entity, he can locate it deictically, by using the marked or the strong demonstrative, or choose not to locate it deictically, by using the weak demonstrative. We also want to relate *this* to *here* and *that* to *there* rather more satisfactorily than we have done so far. Without entering upon a wholesale reinterpretation of the syntactic categories in terms of features (see Chomsky, 1970a), we can perhaps formalize these facts about English well enough for the present purpose by making a more restricted use of complex symbols, as follows:

Base rules:

(1) S→NP NP

(2) S→NP VP

(3) NP→{Nm, N, D}

(4) VP→{N, V, D_2}

(5) D_2→[+D, −entity]

(6) D→[+D, ±entity]

(7) [+entity]→[±person]

(8) [+person]→[±female]

(9) $\left\{ \begin{array}{l} [-\text{person}] \\ [-\text{entity}] \end{array} \right\}$ →[±proximate]

(10) [−proximate]→[±distal]

Lexicon:

(i) Nm: {*John, Daddy, . . .*}

(ii) N: {*dog, house, table, . . .*}

(iii) V: {*big, bark, swim, . . .*}

(iv) $\begin{bmatrix} +\text{D} \\ -\text{entity} \\ +\text{proximate} \end{bmatrix}$: *here*

(v) $\begin{bmatrix} +\text{D} \\ -\text{entity} \\ +\text{proximate} \\ +\text{distal} \end{bmatrix}$: *there*$_2$

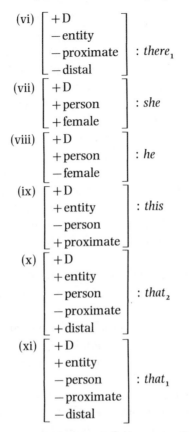

(vi) $\begin{bmatrix} +D \\ -\text{entity} \\ -\text{proximate} \\ -\text{distal} \end{bmatrix}$: *there*$_1$

(vii) $\begin{bmatrix} +D \\ +\text{person} \\ +\text{female} \end{bmatrix}$: *she*

(viii) $\begin{bmatrix} +D \\ +\text{person} \\ -\text{female} \end{bmatrix}$: *he*

(ix) $\begin{bmatrix} +D \\ +\text{entity} \\ -\text{person} \\ +\text{proximate} \end{bmatrix}$: *this*

(x) $\begin{bmatrix} +D \\ +\text{entity} \\ -\text{person} \\ -\text{proximate} \\ +\text{distal} \end{bmatrix}$: *that*$_2$

(xi) $\begin{bmatrix} +D \\ +\text{entity} \\ -\text{person} \\ -\text{proximate} \\ -\text{distal} \end{bmatrix}$: *that*$_1$

This grammar is not entirely satisfactory: apart from anything else, the usual problems with binary features in relation to Boolean conditions have led me to introduce [± distal] into the deictic system. Using [− entity] rather than [+ locative] might also be regarded as unsatisfactory. As part of the grammar of adult English, it has certain other inadequacies which we need not go into here.

One point, however, should be mentioned. There is an obvious redundancy in the grammar of Quasi-English as it stands. The demonstrative noun-phrases, *this dog, that dog,* and *the dog,* are all structurally ambiguous, not only with respect to the nature of the link between the demonstrative and the noun (and this seems to me semantically justifiable), but also with respect to the internal structure of *this, that,* and *the.* For example, *this* in *this dog* is either a purely pronominal deictic (with the feature [+ proximate]) or an amalgam of a pronominal and an adjectivalized deictic (i.e., *that*$_1$ *here, this there*$_1$, *this here* = *this*). But *this* and *that* in what we have taken to be their purely pronominal function are also generated within the system from *that₁ here* and *that₁ there* (*here* and *there* being taken restrictively or non-restrictively according to whether the transformation rule is one of adjectivalization or predicative apposition: (D_2D_1) vs. (D_1-D_2)). I have assumed, perhaps wrongly, that the child might learn and use the demonstratives in their purely pronominal usage before he has mastered the syntactic relation between *this* and *here* and between *that* and *there*. However, it is perhaps plausible to suppose that there will come a time when the child internalizes the relevant transformational relationships and restructures his grammar accordingly. Whatever the psychological validity of this hypothesis, descriptive economy in writing the grammar of English would be served by the elimination of the redundancy referred to, since no distinction of meaning seems to be associated with the alternative derivations. All we need to do by way of restructuring the grammar is to delete [−person] from the disjunction of features on the left-hand side of rule (9).

Given the componential analysis embodied in the above set of grammatical rules and the associated lexicon, we can not only reformulate our amalgamation rule (prior to lexicalization) in terms of strings of deictic complex symbols, but we can also prohibit the application of either the adjectivalizing or appositional transformation to instances of D_1 (i.e., [+entity] deictics) that contain the feature [+person].[19] The substitution of *the* for *that₁* will operate as before, except that it will need to be made conditional upon the association with *that₁* within the same NP of a transformationally derived predicative or equative N. A further rule may then be added, to rewrite *that₁* as *it*, on condition that it has no appositional adjunct within the same NP.[20]

We need not go further with construction of Quasi-English. It now reflects, though perhaps not in the most satisfactory way, what I take to be the central grammatical distinctions of English in so far as they apply to the structure, function, and semantic interpretation of singular definite referring expressions. I would remind the reader, at this point, that I am not assuming that a 'child of our culture' learning English will necessarily proceed, as we have done, in the construction of the grammar of the language, first distinguishing between a pronominal and an adverbial deictic, then mastering the deictic distinction of proximity, and finally distinguishing the personal pronouns *he* and *she* from the demonstratives *this* and *that*. What I have tried to show is that it is possible to see the language-specific features of English developing, ontogenetically, from a possibly universal base.

Philosophers have devoted a lot of attention to the question of uniquely referring expressions; and they have emphasized the logical similarity, from this point of view, between proper names and definite descriptions. Many of them have claimed that the use of the definite article implies or presupposes that there is one and only one entity that satisfies the description contained in the noun-phrase. There is, however, no reason to associate any implication or presupposition with the definite article as such. When the speaker refers to a specific individual, by whatever means, he tacitly accepts the convention that he will provide any information (not given in the context) that is necessary for the addressee to identify the individual in question (see Thorne, 1973: 564). Uniqueness of reference is always, in principle, context-dependent in this sense; and it applies just as much to the use of the personal pronouns and the demonstratives (and indeed to the use of proper names) as it does to the use of the definite article. It is therefore no argument against our analysis of the definite article as a demonstrative pronoun (*that*$_1$) or an amalgam of a demonstrative pronoun and a demonstrative adverb (*that*$_1$ *there* $\Rightarrow$ *that*$_1$ $\Rightarrow$ *the*), that it is functionally different from the marked and the strong forms of the demonstratives (*that*$_2$ and *this*) with respect to its presupposition of uniqueness. The pronominal component in the definite article, *that*$_1$, has exactly the same function as has the same component in the other forms of the demonstrative adjectives: that of informing the addressee that a specific individual (or group of individuals) is being referred to which satisfies the description. The difference is that *that*$_2$ and *this* encode as part of the description offered to the addressee information about the deictic location of the referent. In context, *this dog* and *the dog* will both be construed as uniquely referring expressions; but the former will be descriptively more informative (by virtue of the grammaticalization of [+proximate] in the adjectivalized deictic adverb amalgamated with the pronoun).

Philosophers in their discussions of the logical structure of definite descriptions have also made much of their presupposition or implication of existence; and this is particularly interesting from the point of view of the analysis of the demonstrative adjectives and the definite article that has been proposed here. As we have seen, the demonstratives *that*$_2$ and *this* (when they are used deictically) serve to inform the addressee that some specific individual (or group of individuals) is being referred to and also to locate the referent in relation to the here-and-now of utterance. If something has a spatiotemporal location, it must exist; and it is arguable that any notion of 'existence' that we can operate with is based upon our intuitive understanding of physical existence as spatiotemporal location. I have suggested elsewhere that existential sentences, in English and many languages, are derivable from structures in which the underlying subject is, typically, an indefinite noun-phrase and the underlying predicate a locative (Lyons, 1967a, 1968b). I now want to relate this suggestion, very briefly, to the proposals made in this paper about the ontogenesis of referring expressions in English.

We begin by introducing the notion of deictic existence: location in a physical space, whose coordinates are established by the utterance of sentences of a given language-system. The deictic coordinates vary somewhat from one language to another; but the zero-point, presumably, will always be the moment and place of utterance. The English demonstratives *this/here* and *that/there*, when they are used as deictic referring expressions (or within deictic referring expressions), can be interpreted as instructing, or inviting, the addressee to direct his attention to a particular region of the deictic space in order to find the referent. *There is a boy here* (which I take to be derived from the underlying predicate structure *Boy (be) here*) means, roughly, '*A boy is (to be found) in the place where I (as I am now speaking) am (to be found)*'. In terms of the analysis of demonstrative noun-phrases proposed above *this boy* derives from *that₁ here boy* (*here* being taken either restrictively or non-restrictively, and *boy* being associated with *that₁* in one of several ways): it therefore presupposes or implies that the referent is located in the deictic space. So too does *that man* (derived from *that₁ there₂ man*). But what about *the man*? This is derived either from *that₁ man* or *that₁ there₁ man*. That it should have a double derivation is perhaps inelegant. Let us, however, not stop to consider the possibility of either eliminating this apparent redundancy or motivating it by reasons other than those of formal simplicity in the grammar. Let us ask, instead, what interpretation we can assign to the weak deictic adverbial *there₁* in the underlying string *that₁ there₁*.

Despite what certain philosophers have said about the non-predicability of existence, it seems to me that existential sentences, with a definite or an indefinite noun-phrase as subject, are meaningful. Normally, in everyday discourse, we are not concerned to assert or deny the existence of entities in any absolute sense of 'existence'. It is much more common to say that such-and-such an individual is (or is not) in a particular place (*John Smith is in London, John Smith is here*, etc.) or that an individual (or class of individuals) satisfying a certain description is (or is not) in a particular place (*There is a girl in my soup, There are some unicorns here*). Granted that *John Smith is here* and *There are some unicorns here* are derivable from underlying structures in which the proximal deictic adverbial occurs as the predicate and that we interpret these sentences in terms of the notion of deictic existence, it is my proposal that what might be called absolute existential sentences such as *John Smith exists* and *These are unicorns* (or *Unicorns exist*) are derived syntactically from the same underlying structures, except that it is *there₁* which occurs as the predicate. Just as the meaning of the weak demonstrative pronoun *that₁* is derived by abstraction from the gesture of pointing, so the weak demonstrative *there₁* is derived by abstraction from the notion of location in the deictic context. If the underlying structure of *the man* is taken to be *that₁ there₁ man* (derivable in various ways as we can see), this can be said to separate and segmentalize the components of context-dependent uniqueness of reference (*that₁*) and existential presupposition or implication (*there₁*).

Furthermore, the structural ambiguity of *that₁ there₁ man* – $(D_1 = (D_2N))$, $(D_1-(D_2N))$, $(D_1 = (N-D_2))$, $(D_1-(N-D_2))$ – may account, in part at least, for the enduring controversy as to whether existence is presupposed, implied or asserted in definite noun-phrases. If adjectivalization (restrictive relative-clause formation in current versions of transformational grammar) is associated with presupposition and apposition (i.e., non-restrictive relative-clause formation), not necessarily with assertion, but with an independent illocutionary act (Thorne, 1973), the distinction between (D_2N) and $(N-D_2)$ can be held to represent the difference between the presupposition and the assertion of existence. It is not difficult, I believe, to contextualize the phrase *the man* (as well as *that man* and *this man*) in such a way that the other structural ambiguities are seen to be relevant.

Another point should be made about existential sentences. The standard predicate calculus analysis of sentences with what appears to be a singular definite referring expression as subject, runs into trouble because it makes them assert (or, still worse, deny) what is either asserted or presupposed by the referring expression. *God exists* (and its contrary) is analysable satisfactorily enough (under one interpretation) as $(\exists x)$ (*x be omnipotent* & *x be eternal* & ...). But this analysis will clearly not do for utterances which refer, by name, to individuals (unless one pushes the descriptive-backing theory of proper names to its extreme: see Searle, 1969: 162); and I would argue that *God* should be interpretable in *God exists* as a proper name. In the grammar of Quasi-English, we can generate sentences like *God (be) there₂* and *God (be) here* (cf. *John Smith is there, John Smith is here*) which are surely meaningful with *there₂* and *here* taken as deictic predicative expressions. We can also generate *God (be) there₁*. It is my contention that our understanding of *God exists*, under one interpretation, is based upon our abstraction from the notion of deictic existence of more or less of the spatiotemporal implications of the weak form of the deictic adverb. Whether we are willing or able to carry out this psychological process of abstraction, and how far we go with it, depends of course upon our metaphysical or theological preconceptions or decisions. But that is another question entirely. The point is that the linguistic analysis of absolute existence in terms of an abstraction from deixis enables us, should we so wish, to assign an analysis to existential sentences with a singular definite referring expression as subject which is free from the at times counterintuitive analysis imposed upon them by the use of the existential quantifier.[21]

It should also be stressed that what we may now call the existential adverb *there*$_1$ (i.e., the weak form of the [−proximal] deictic adverb) can be interpreted within the same underlying structure in two or more different ways. One way is to take it as anaphoric, rather than as absolutely existential. For example, *That man does not exist* can be interpreted as meaning (discounting all but one of the analyses of *that man*) 'The entity (*that*$_1$) – a man which is *there*$_1$ – is not there'. If *there*$_1$ in the noun-phrase is construed as anaphoric (i.e., as locating the referent in the universe of discourse) and the second predicative *there*$_1$ as being absolutely existential, the sentence does not necessarily deny what it presupposes, any more than does the sentence *That man is not there* (which contains two occurrences of *there*$_2$ in its underlying structure).

Finally, consider the relationship between anaphora and deixis. It is my assumption that the anaphoric use of pronouns and adverbs is secondary to their basic function as deictics (Lyons (1968a: 275ff.)). Anaphora involves the transference of what are basically deictic, and more specifically spatial, notions to the temporal dimension of the context of utterance and the reinterpretation of deictic existence in terms of what might be called textual existence.[22] The referent of course does not exist in the text. But it is located in the universe of discourse (which derives its temporal structure from the text) by means of an antecedent expression which either introduces or identifies a referent. Subsequent reference to this referent by means of an anaphoric expression identifies the referent in terms of the textual location of the antecedent. If there is no other referent in the universe of discourse which satisfies the description incorporated in the predicative noun *man*, it will be sufficient to use *the man* (i.e., *that*$_1$-(*there*$_1$ *man*)) in order to re-identify the person in question. He is the one such referent that has textual existence: i.e., he is there, in the weak sense of *there*. It is in this sense that I interpret Thorne's (1973: 564) analysis of the anaphoric meaning of *there*. There are of course complexities attaching to the analysis of the function and distribution of anaphoric distinctions in English and other languages. It suffices for my present purpose that anaphora should be seen as, in principle, derivable from deixis.

It is also my assumption – and this will surely not be challenged – that reference to entities outside the situation of utterance, indefinite and opaque reference, reference to hypothetical entities (treated as hypothetical in the utterance), and various other kinds of reference that have puzzled philosophers and linguists are at least ontogenetically secondary. The fact that the referring expressions used in such cases are comparable in terms of their grammatical structure with deictically referring expressions suggests that their use and function is derivative, and depends upon the prior existence of the mechanisms for deictic reference by means of language. It is because I make this assumption that I hold the view that deixis is, in general, the source of reference. Although I have said nothing in this paper about locative expressions other than deictic adverbs, it should be clear that my proposals can be construed as offering support for at least a modified version of the localist hypothesis (J. M. Anderson, 1971).

9

Deixis and anaphora

The topic that I have chosen to talk about – the relationship between deixis and anaphora – turns out to be even more appropriate than I had hoped.[1] Dr Bullowa, Dr Widdowson and Professor Halliday have all touched upon either deixis or anaphora, or both, in their contributions to the Symposium; and they have all made points to which I can refer in the development of the thesis that I am presenting.

I will argue that deixis is both ontogenetically and logically prior to anaphora. By this I mean that the deictic use of pronouns and other such expressions precedes their anaphoric use in the earliest stages of language-acquisition and, furthermore, that anaphora, as a grammatical and semantic process, is inexplicable except in terms of its having originated in deixis. That deixis precedes, and is in some sense more basic than anaphora, is something that the previous speakers would probably concede immediately. But it is not at all uncommon for linguists to describe the meaning of pronouns, as far as possible, in terms of anaphora and to treat that part of the use of pronouns which is irreducibly deictic as a theoretical embarrassment that is best forgotten. It is certainly the case that generative grammarians have been inclined, until recently at least, to underestimate the role played by deixis in the interpretation of utterances; and the very term 'pronominalization', which figures so prominently in works on generative grammar, is loaded in favour of the view that pronouns are, first and foremost, substitutes for nouns (or nominals).

The primacy of deixis is a principle that can be related very directly to what Dr Bullowa and Professor Halliday had to say about the primacy of gesture, attention and interaction in the acquisition of language. The term 'deixis' is revealing in this connexion: it means no more than "pointing" in its original Greek sense; and, as used nowadays by linguists, it means "identification by pointing". Drawing upon work by Bateson and Gruber, Dr Bullowa suggested in her paper that there are two kinds of performatives that can be distinguished among the child's earliest two-word utterances, designations and requests, and that non-performative (i.e., constative) utterances come later. She went on to demonstrate that pointing is developmentally indistinguishable from reaching and that, in so far as the child designates what he is requesting by looking at it, reaching and looking tend to coincide, as do designation and requesting; and that they too are originally indistinguishable. Professor Halliday, for his part, emphasized, as others have done, that the child's earliest semiotic acts are gestural, rather than vocal, and that the earliest exophoric (i.e., deictic) expressions tend to be accompanied with a gesture indicative of attention. I need not remind you that there is some similarity between this way of analysing the protosemantic system of the child and the famous tripartite analysis of the functions of language by Bühler (1934), which was taken over by Roman Jakobson and other linguists of the Prague School. It was Bühler, too, you will recall, who popularized, if he did not actually coin, the term 'deixis' in the sense in which it is employed these days (not to mention the terms 'cataphora' and 'exophora'): and my views on deixis and anaphora have been strongly influenced by his. They have also been influenced by the now classic articles by Benveniste (1956) and Hjelmslev (1935) on the nature of pronouns; by the work of Antinucci (1974) and Bates (1976); and, even more directly, by the ideas of my colleagues who worked on the SSRC-sponsored language-acquisition project in Edinburgh (cf. Huxley, 1970; Atkinson and Griffiths, 1973; Lyons, *et al.* 1975).

The general point that I draw from the papers by Dr Bullowa and Professor Halliday is that the child's earliest semiotic behaviour is very largely gestural (in the broadest sense of 'gestural') and is, in any case, so closely integrated with other kinds of attentive, conative, manipulative and desiderative behaviour as to be indistinguishable from it. But I also draw the more specific point that there are very many semiotic acts, whether gestural or vocal, of which it is impossible to say that their function is primarily that of designating, of requesting or of reporting. It is only when you get a more or less fully developed adult language-system that these three kinds of speech-acts can be clearly and confidently distinguished. Now, Dr Bullowa talked of proto-conversations and Professor Halliday of proto-sentences (and proto-semantics). Not wishing to be outdone by these two protagonists, I will now introduce the term 'proto-reference'. Elsewhere, I have used the term 'quasi-reference' (cf. Lyons, 1975a); but 'proto-reference' is perhaps better. Proto-reference is to be identified with what we have just been calling 'designation'.

The main point that I want to make – and I have made it before (Lyons 1975a) – is that proto-reference, which rests crucially upon the psychological notion of attention, might equally well be called 'proto-predication'. When linguists and logicians analyse the propositional content of utterances, and more particularly of constative utterances, within the framework of formal semantics, they commonly begin by distinguishing two components: the referential component, which identifies the entity (or entities) about which something is being said, and the predicative component, which says whatever it is that is said about the referent (or referents). The underlying notion of the bipartite structure of propositions goes back a long way, of course; and it has given rise to the familiar and related distinctions of subject vs. predicate and topic vs. comment (or theme vs. rheme). I do not wish to go into this question. What I want to do here is to stress that, as far as the early utterances of children are concerned, it is very often impossible to distinguish reference from predication: one cannot say that the child is referring to something in the situation and leaving implicit what he wants to say about it or, alternatively, that he is leaving implicit his reference to some entity in the situation and making explicit what he wants to say about it. It is only later that reference and predication can be distinguished; and they may be thought of as developing ontogenetically from something, proto-reference or proto-predication, that is originally not clearly the one or the other. The constative function of language, important though it is, must not be assumed, by virtue of the philosopher's very natural concern with truth and factuality, to be either basic or ubiquitous, as it all too often is assumed to be.

There are two more preliminary points that I must make – both of them terminological – before I move on to my main theme. The first has to do with the notion of anaphoric reference. It is traditional to say that a pronoun refers to its antecedent. There is, however, an alternative formulation, based on a quite different sense of the term 'refer', according to which we can say that an anaphoric pronoun is co-referential with its antecedent: that is, that an anaphoric pronoun refers to what its antecedent refers to. It is this second formulation of the notion of anaphoric reference that we will adopt: it has the advantage of bringing anaphoric reference within the scope of the current philosophical concept of reference: and, what is far more important for our present purpose, it enables us to relate anaphora and deixis in terms of a single univocal notion of pronominal reference.

The second terminological point has to do with the implications of the term 'pronoun'. According to the traditional conception of the syntactic and semantic function of pronouns, the pronoun is essentially a noun-substitute; and the term 'pronoun' itself reflects this conception of their function. However, to say that pronouns deputize, as it were, for nouns – that the pronomen deputized for the nomen rather as the proconsuls deputized abroad for the consuls – and that this is their primary, or basic, syntactic and semantic function, is misleading in two respects. First of all, it implies that the anaphoric function of pronouns is more basic than their deictic function: we need say no more about this. Second, it fails to draw the distinction between nouns and nominals – between Ns and NPs, to use the now more or less well-established symbols of Chomskyan generative grammar. This distinction, as it happens, is less obvious (as is the distinction between names and nouns) in Latin than it is in many other languages, including English, where countable nouns in the singular do not normally occur in referring expressions unless they are accompanied by a determiner or quantifier. But from a theoretical point of view the distinction is crucial. Nominals (e.g., *John* or *that boy*), unlike nouns (e.g., *boy*), have as their most characteristic function that of referring to, or otherwise identifying (e.g., by summoning or listing), particular entities or groups of entities: nouns, on the other hand, are characteristically predicative in function; and the most typical nouns are sortal, rather than characterizing, predicates (in the logician's sense of 'predicate': cf. Strawson, 1975). The term 'pronoun', unhyphenated, is now so well entrenched in the everyday vocabulary that nothing but confusion would result from any attempt to dislodge it or narrow its application. What we can do, however, is to introduce, as many linguists have done, a set of hyphenated technical terms: 'pro-noun', 'pro-nominal', 'pro-verb', 'pro-verbal', 'pro-adjective', etc.

All of these terms, and others, have been employed by scholars working in the Bloomfieldian tradition (cf. Crymes, 1968); and they have the advantage that they make transparent the defining syntactic relation that holds between nouns and pro-nouns (cf. *book* and *one* in *the red book and the blue one*); between nominals and pro-nominals (cf. *John* and *he* in *When John came in, he was grinning all over his face*, on the assumption that *he* and *his*, refer to what *John* refers to); between adjectives and pro-adjectives (cf. *beautiful* and *so* in *Mary is beautiful and so is Penelope*); etc. Armed with these distinctions, we may note that of the text-forming devices mentioned by Professor Halliday, in his paper, the pro-nominals (*that*, *it*, etc.) were characteristically exophoric, or deictic, whereas the pro-noun, *one*, was anaphoric. There is reason to believe that the notion of anaphora applies rather differently to pro-nouns than it does to pro-nominals; and that pro-adjectives and pro-verbs (e.g., *do* in some uses) are like pro-nouns, whereas pro-locatives (*here* and *there*) and pro-temporals (*now* and *then*), are like pro-nominals. I will restrict my attention, in what follows, to pro-nominals: that is, to what are traditionally described as demonstrative and personal pronouns. But I would also emphasize that there is a very close semantic connexion between pro-nominals and pro-locatives, on the one hand, and between pro-locatives and pro-temporals, on the other.

As nominals and pro-nominals are, characteristically, entity-referring expressions, so locatives and pro-locatives are, characteristically, place-referring expressions. Entities are not places and places are not entities. However, as I have emphasized elsewhere (cf. Lyons, 1975a), it is very difficult to draw a sharp distinction between entity-referring and place-referring expressions in the earliest utterances of children; and this fact is of considerable importance for the proper understanding of deixis, of the transition from deixis to anaphora, and also of the emergent distinction of reference and predication. I cannot go into all this here (cf. Lyons, 1977a). Let me simply say that gestures obviously do not make it clear whether the attention of the addressee is being directed to a region of the environment in which something is happening or to some entity that is located in the environment: and this is one of the reasons why purely ostensive definition necessarily fails of its purpose, unless it is supplemented in some other way. English is a language in which there is a fairly clear distinction, in most instances, between entity-referring and place-referring expressions, But this distinction depends in turn upon the clear distinction that there is in English between the demonstrative pronouns (i.e., pro-nominals) *this* and *that*, on the one hand, and the demonstrative adverbs (i.e., pro-locatives) *here* and *there*, on the other. The proto-referential *Bird*! ("Look! A bird!") has a certain ambivalence as between one interpretation, expressed in the adult language by means of *That's a bird*, and another, expressed by means of *There's a bird*. Until the distinction between entity-referring and place-referring deictics has become established, it cannot really be said to mean the one thing rather than the other. If I mention these questions here, it is merely to indicate that, in the necessarily brief account of the relationship between deixis and anaphora that I am giving in my contribution to the Symposium, there is a good deal of more or less metaphysical underpinning that I am taking for granted.

As we have just seen, we can refer, in principle, either to entities or to places by means of deictic expressions. What counts as an entity I take to be at least partly determined independently of the lexical and grammatical structure of the languages that we happen to speak. In particular, I assume that there are what I will refer to as first-order entities (persons, animals and discrete physical objects); that, in so far as the child refers to entities, rather than places, in the earliest stages of language-acquisition, it is to such first-order entities that he refers; that all languages will provide the means for referring to first-order entities; and that reference to first-order entities is a more basic kind of reference than is reference to various kinds of higher-order entities. All these assumptions are, as far as I know, reasonable in the light of what we know of language-acquisition and of the structure of various languages. Apart from first-order entities, there are also second-order and third-order entities to be reckoned with, though it may well be the case that not all languages provide the means for reference to them as entities. By second-order entities I mean events, situations and states-of-affairs occurring or existing in the physical world; and by third-order entities, in so far as we are concerned with them here, I mean such intensional objects as propositions, individual concepts and the like. The importance of third-order entities, for our present purposes, is that, regardless of whether we have the means of referring to them as entities or not, they are the stuff of which the universe-of-discourse is made; and anaphora, as we shall see, depends crucially upon the universe-of-discourse. It may be observed in passing that the traditional distinction of concrete and abstract nouns in terms of their occurrence in expressions referring to concrete and abstract entities tends to obscure the distinction between second-order and third-order entities. There is a sense in which events are more abstract than persons; but there is nothing non-physical about events, as there is about propositions. It is the tripartite ontological distinction that we have just drawn, rather than the traditional bipartite distinction of concrete and abstract, that is important for semantic analysis.

Distinctions of proximity are lexicalized or grammaticalized in the pro-nominal (and pro-locative) system of many languages; and they are commonly combined with other distinctions, based, as far as reference to first-order entities is concerned, on status, sex, shape, size, etc. It is the function of pro-nominals, when they are used deictically with reference to first-order and second-order entities, to draw the attention of the addressee to referents that are actually present in the situation, identifying these referents for the addressee in terms of their proximity or remoteness relative to the spatiotemporal zero-point of the deictic space. Since third-order entities have no spatiotemporal location, they cannot be referred to deictically in the way that first-order and second-order entities can. It is important to realize, however, that, although third-order entities are not present either in the situation of utterance or in the text, they are, or may be, present in the universe-of-discourse. Furthermore, they are ordered hierar-chically in the universe-of-discourse in terms of salience. By this I mean that, at any one time and for any one person, certain entities are more probable candidates for reference than others are; and the intensional objects in correspondence with these entities in the universe-of-discourse are correspondingly more salient. The intensional correlates of first-order entities in the universe-of-discourse I take to be individual concepts (cf. Carnap, 1956: 41): the intensional correlates of second-order entities I take to be propositions. Our problem is to account for the transition from deixis to anaphora, given that the basic deictic distinction, in many languages at least, is one of proximity vs. remoteness. In doing so, we will draw upon the notion of salience in the universe-of-discourse; and we will relate this to the notion of previous mention, which is more commonly invoked in standard treatments of anaphora.

The link between the deictic and the anaphoric use of pro-nominals can be seen in what I will call textual deixis. Demonstrative pronouns and other deictic expressions may be employed to refer to linguistic entities of various kinds in the co-text of an utterance. Consider the following text, for example:

(*A* says) *That's a ptarmigan, isn't it?*
(*B* says) *A what? Spell it for me.*

The referent of *it* in *B*'s utterance is obviously not the same as the referent of *it* (and of *that*) in *A*'s utterance. The referent of *it* in *B*'s utterance is the form *ptarmigan*: only forms may be spelled (or pronounced). Now the function of *it* in *B*'s utterance is not anaphoric, although at first sight it might appear to be: it is not co-referential with, but actually refers to, an antecedent form. (For simplicity of exposition, I am disregarding at this point the distinction between forms and expressions, which a more careful treatment of reference would need to take account of: cf. Lyons, 1977a). Textual deixis is frequently confused with anaphora, by virtue of the traditional formulation of the notion of pronominal reference, according to which the pronoun is said to refer to its antecedent, and the failure to distinguish clearly between linguistic and non-linguistic entities.

At one remove from pure textual deixis, though not as clearly distinct from it as anaphora, is the relationship that holds between a referring expression and such third-order entities as propositions. This may be exemplified by means of the following text:

(*A* says) *Harold Wilson has just resigned.*
(*B* says) *Who told you that?*

It is clear that *that* in *B*'s utterance does not refer to the sentence uttered by *A*, but rather to the proposition expressed by *A* in the utterance of the sentence. The proposition does not occur in the text, in any literal sense of 'occur'; it cannot therefore be referred to deictically. At the same time, by virtue of the peculiarly intimate and almost symbiotic relation that holds between sentences and propositions, one can refer to propositions by referring, apparently, to the sentences used in expressing them. The function of *that* in *B*'s utterance would seem to fall somewhere between anaphora and deixis; and it partakes of the characteristics of both: its function, I will say, is that of impure textual deixis. It is not always easy to draw the distinction between pure and impure textual deixis in particular instances; and textual deixis, of which there are many other kinds that I have not exemplified, provides us, I would suggest, with the sort of transitional referential mechanism that we are looking for to take us from ordinary deixis to anaphora.

The demonstratives *this* and *that* in English may be used deictically, not only to refer to first-order entities in the situational context and to linguistic entities of various kinds (whose ontological status we need not here go into) in the text or co-text, but also to refer to events (i.e., second-order entities) that have already occurred, are occurring or are going to occur in the future. The conditions that govern the selection of *this* and *that* with reference to events immediately preceding and immediately following the utterance, or the part of the utterance in which *this* and *that* occur, are quite complex. They include a variety of subjective factors (such as the speaker's dissociation of himself from the event that he is referring to), which are intuitively relatable to the deictic notion of proximity vs. remoteness, but are difficult to specify precisely. What does seem clear, however, is that the use of the demonstratives in both temporal and textual deixis, and also in anaphora, is connected with their use in spatial deixis. This is more obviously so in many languages other than English. For example, in Latin the pronoun (or adjective) *ille* ("that") is used anaphorically to refer to the referent of the more remote of two potential antecedents and *hic* ("this") is used to refer to the referent of the nearer of two potential antecedents: and they can be translated (into somewhat stilted English) as "the former" and "the latter", respectively. The same is true of the German *jener: dieser* (though *jener* is perhaps also rather stilted in present-day German), the Spanish *ese* (or *aquel*): *este*, the French *celui-là: celui-çi*, the Turkish *o: bu*, and so on. It is the notion of relative proximity in time to the zero-point of utterance that connects anaphora and textual deixis with deictic temporal-reference. Proximity in space is reinterpreted as proximity in time: and proximity in the text or co-text is based upon proximity in time.

So much is clear enough, in a general sort of way. The basically deictic component in an anaphoric expression directs the attention of the addressee to a certain region of the text or co-text and tells him, as it were, that he will find the referent there. But it is not of course the referent itself that he will find in the text or co-text. What he will find is some appropriate antecedent, which will identify the referent for him, typically by naming or describing it.

It is when we come to spell out the details of what is involved in anaphora that it is revealed as something that is both more complex and theoretically more interesting than it appears to be at first sight. For anaphora, as I mentioned earlier, depends for its operation, not only upon the existence of text and co-text, but also upon the existence of an intersubjective universe-of-discourse. Many French structuralists, like Kristeva (1969) and Barthes (1970), have insisted that what is commonly referred to as intersubjectivity should be more properly described as intertextuality, on the grounds that the shared knowledge that is applied to the interpretation of text is itself the product of other texts (cf. Ducrot & Todorov, 1972; Culler, 1975: 139). Up to a point this is true; and especially in so far as the intersubjective knowledge that is required for the interpretation of literary texts is concerned. But not all the intersubjective knowledge that is exploited in the construction and interpretation of texts derives from what has been previously mentioned in other texts. Furthermore, it seems clear from what we know of the way that our beliefs and assumptions are stored in long-term memory that they are not stored as text. They may of course be stored, as propositions, in some kind of quasi-linguistic form. But the sets and subsets of propositions that comprise our beliefs and knowledge will not have the property of cohesion (as distinct from what Dr Widdowson calls coherence). Since a very considerable part of the intersubjective universe-of-discourse is stored, presumably, in the long-term memory of the participants (speaker and addressee, or writer and reader), it follows that the universe-of-discourse is not stored as a text. At the same time, it must be recognised that much of the information that is contained in the universe-of-discourse is derived from texts. What is more important for our present purposes, it must also be acknowledged that, over the short term at least, the universe-of-discourse has some kind of temporal structure, which is created by the text and continuously modified by the text. Anaphora depends upon this fact.

The entities in the universe-of-discourse, it will be recalled, are third-order entities: they are the intensional correlates of the referents of linguistic expressions. More specifically, individual concepts are the intensional correlates of first-order entities and propositions are the intensional correlates of second-order entities. I am aware, of course, that the ontological status of propositions, and still more of individual concepts, is highly controversial. But we need not be concerned here with this question: we can treat individual concepts and propositions as theoretical constructs whose psychological correlates, if they have any, are for our present purposes irrelevant. One way of thinking of individual concepts is as addresses in some computer-file that is serving as a model of the universe-of-discourse. For simplicity of exposition, if for no other reason, we will adopt this point of view. Furthermore, we will assume (i) that the accessibility of the addresses reflects the degree of salience that each address (i.e., each individual concept) currently has in the universe-of-discourse; and (ii) that there is stored at each address a set of propositions of which the individual concept whose address it is is a constituent. For example, given that there is, in the intersubjective universe-of-discourse, an individual concept, which we may symbolize (with double quotation-marks) as "Napoleon", there will be stored at the appropriate address such propositions as "Napoleon was a Corsican", "Napoleon invaded Russia", "Napoleon was victorious at Austerlitz", "Napoleon was defeated at Waterloo", and so on. In this case, as in the case of very many of the first-order entities, and especially persons, that we have occasion to identify frequently, there is a well-known and widely-used proper name, *Napoleon*, which, though it is not a uniquely referring expression (and very few names are), will, by virtue of the salience of "Napoleon", generally be taken to refer to Napoleon Bonaparte, unless the salience of the individual concept correlated with some other first-order entity whose name is *Napoleon* has been boosted by reference to him in the text or co-text.

Let us now look at the question of anaphoric reference from this point of view; and let us, for the purpose of illustration, make the counterfactual assumption that the English demonstratives *this* and *that*, when used anaphorically, whether as pronouns or adjectives (cf. Lyons, 1975a), do no more than encode the distinction of temporal proximity in relation to the moment of utterance. Thus, *this animal*, used as an anaphoric expression, would (under our counterfactual assumption) direct the attention of the addressee to the most accessible individual concept in the universe-of-discourse satisfying the propositional function "x be an animal"; *that animal* would refer to an entity whose intensional correlate is less accessible; and *the animal* would refer to some entity whose intensional correlate satisfies the function "x be an animal", but it would give the addressee no information about the location (i.e., accessibility) of the individual concept correlated with the referent. No such information would be required, of course, if the referent of *the animal* were the only animal that had been previously mentioned or, alternatively, if there were a generally accepted convention that, in default of any information about the location of the appropriate individual concept in the universe-of-discourse, it was to be taken to be the most recently mentioned entity whose correlated individual concept satisfies the descriptive content of the anaphoric expression.

Things are not quite as simple as this illustration might suggest. The anaphoric use of *this* and *that* in English involves other considerations besides the relative proximity of an appropriate antecedent expression to the moment of utterance; and the considerations that determine the anaphoric use of the definite article are also rather more complex than our counterfactual assumptions have made them. The point that is being illustrated, however, is not affected by these deliberate oversimplifications: it is that, independently of whether particular languages make anaphoric use of demonstratives or not, anaphora rests upon the notion of accessibility in the universe-of-discourse; and accessibility, which reflects salience, is in part determined by recency of mention. In so far as recency of mention is itself, as we have seen, a deictically based notion and is encoded, in one way or another, in the anaphoric pronouns used in particular languages, anaphora rests ultimately upon deixis. *Quod erat demonstrandum*!

However, it requires but little reflection to see that potential referents cannot be indexed solely, or even primarily, in terms of recency of mention or relative order of previous mention. Quite apart from any other factors that might be operative, the limitations of human memory are such that, without having immediate access to a transcript of all that has been said previously (or, alternatively, to some continuously updated computer-file), we could not operate with a system of anaphoric reference which was dependent upon our knowledge of the order of mention of all the entities referred to previously in the text and co-text. The temporal structure that is imposed upon the universe-of-discourse by the succession of referring expressions in texts (which we have assumed to be transformed directly into accessibility) is, therefore, of very limited duration; and the anaphoric use of the basically deictic distinction of proximity to the zero-point of the context of utterance is determined by this fact.

As we have seen, salience in the universe-of-discourse is not determined solely by recency of mention of the correlated non-intensional entity. Indeed, there need not have been any previous mention in any determinate part of the text or co-text. This is obviously so as far as reference by means of proper names, titles or definite descriptions which uniquely identify well-known persons like Napoleon is concerned. But even pronouns can be used to refer to previously unmentioned entities that are not present in the situation of utterance, provided that the individual concept associated with the entity in question is sufficiently salient in the universe-of-discourse. For example, I might offer my condolences to a friend, whose wife has just been killed in a car crash, by saying: *I was terribly upset to hear the news: I only saw her last week.* On the assumption that my friend and I had not previously discussed the accident and that I had heard the news from someone else, there has been no previous mention of her in the co-text (i.e., in some text or set of texts to which both my friend and I have had access). And yet, in these circumstances, there is absolutely no need for me to specify what news I am referring to or who the referent of *her* is. Many scholars, including Bühler (1934), would say that the reference of pronouns in examples like this is deictic, not anaphoric, on the grounds that there is no antecedent and that, although it does not point to anything in the external situational context, it does point to something in the intersubjective experience or common memory of speaker and addressee (cf. Crymes, 1968: 62–3). It is obvious, however, that the notion of intersubjective experience or common memory – formalizable as part of the universe-of-discourse – is the more general notion, without which anaphoric reference, as it is traditionally conceived, cannot be explained. In the last resort, there seems to be no reason to deny that the reference of *her* in the example that has just been given is anaphoric.

It is not possible, on the present occasion, to develop the thesis that anaphora depends ultimately upon deixis in any greater detail than this. Both deixis and anaphora are far more complex, of course, than the somewhat schematic account of them that I have given here. What has been said will be sufficient, it is hoped, to give some indication of the way in which a satisfying explanation of the ontogenesis of anaphora might be constructed. As we have seen, anaphora presupposes that the intensional correlate of the referent should already have its place in the universe-of-discourse. Deixis does not: indeed deixis is one of the principal means open to us of putting the intensional correlates of entities into the universe-of-discourse (cf. Isard, 1975); and this fact alone would make deixis logically, if not ontogenetically, prior to anaphora.

What has been no more than adumbrated in this paper, however, is the ontogenetic relationship between deixis and anaphora. I have suggested that textual deixis, pure and impure, may serve as the link between the two. But I can hardly claim to have demonstrated that this is so; and I do not yet know whether the data that has now been collected by the various research teams working on child-language-acquisition would support the hypothesis that textual deixis is the precursor of anaphora, as I am suggesting that it is. It may be pointed out, however, that this hypothesis would be compatible (to put it no more strongly than this) with the more general hypothesis, of a broadly Piagetian character, which informs a good deal of the more recent psycholinguistic research: the hypothesis that cognitive structures result from the internalization of sensori-motor action-schemata (cf. Bruner, 1974/5). Much of my own understanding of the implications of this hypothesis comes from reading the work of Elizabeth Bates and her collaborators (cf. Bates, 1976); and it seems to me that she has made a good case for the view that what she calls metapragmatics (including talking about talking and referring back to what one has said) plays a crucial role in the child's reconstruction of his sensori-motor knowledge of the world at the level of internal, symbolic representation. However that may be, it seems to me that any account of the ontogenesis of anaphoric reference has got to address itself to the problem of explaining how intensional objects in the universe-of-discourse come to be indexed, at least partly and over the short term, in terms of the relative order of the associated linguistic expressions occurring in the text (and co-text). As far as I know, the stages of the process whereby this comes about have yet to be identified.

Appendix: The scientific study of language. Inaugural Lecture, Edinburgh, 1965

It would seem to be appropriate for the occupant of a new Chair in an ancient and major university to present in his Inaugural Lecture, before an audience representative of many different subjects taught and studied in the university, a justification of the subject he is called upon to profess – an *apologia pro disciplina sua*: to discuss its relation to other disciplines and the contribution it is capable of making to the accepted aims of the university in teaching and research.[1] In my lecture this evening, I will claim a place for linguistics at all levels and in many areas of university activity: as a field of research for scholars confident that they are making a significant contribution to the sum of what we call "science" – that they are, as the currently-fashionable phrase puts it, "advancing the frontiers of knowledge" – and also as a subject with important practical, or "technological" applications; and, at the same time, as a discipline which can be combined with many different courses of university instruction, as a valuable part of a general education.

This then is the task I have set myself in my lecture, and I am conscious of all the difficulties that stand in the way of its successful accomplishment.

Since I have chosen to talk about so many aspects of linguistics, and in doing so to stress both its links with other subjects and at the same time its status as a relatively unified and autonomous science, I shall be obliged to deal very summarily with many questions, to pass over certain controversial points of theory and practice and to omit various qualifications and reservations which I would make in a fuller discussion of these topics. Moreover, I will avoid as far as possible the technical vocabulary of linguistics. Much of what I have to say will therefore seem insufficiently precise to my colleagues who are present. I trust that they will pardon this imprecision in a lecture that is not addressed primarily to them and that will contain nothing with which they are not already familiar.

179

If the task is difficult, I take courage from some words that Plato puts in the mouth of Socrates at a critical point in the *Cratylus*. The *Cratylus* might perhaps be regarded as the first work on general linguistics ever published.[2] The philosophical questions discussed by Plato and the Sophists gave rise to the famous controversy between the Analogists and the Anomalists which raged throughout antiquity and the middle ages and exerted a profound influence upon the development of traditional grammar. These questions are not without interest today, as recent discussions of the origins of Western linguistic theory have shown.[3] If I refer to the *Cratylus* and other ancient works on language in these terms at the beginning of my lecture, it is because I wish to suggest that, although from one point of view linguistics is a relatively new discipline, from another, it is indeed a very old one. The relationship between ancient and modern theories of language will be a *leitmotiv* of my lecture. But the passage in the *Cratylus* that I have in mind and to which I referred earlier has a more particular relevance to the present occasion. It is this (411a):

ἐπειδήπερ τὴν λεοντῆν ἐνδέδυκα, οὐκ ἀποδειλιατέον.[4]

It is with these words that Socrates girds himself, as it were, to face the objections of his critics and proceeds to his exposition of current views on language. His words might be translated as follows: "Since I have myself chosen to appear before you in this guise, I must not now be faint of heart."

But before I move on to my main theme I must make it quite clear that in taking up the Chair of General Linguistics here I do not claim to be bringing linguistics to Edinburgh. To make any such claim would be as absurd as it would be ungracious. As the holder of the Forbes Chair in English Language and General Linguistics since 1948 Professor Angus McIntosh has been responsible for the introduction of courses in linguistics at the undergraduate and postgraduate level and, with his colleagues in other departments, for the promotion of such interdisciplinary contacts as now exist between linguistics and other subjects and for the institution and administration of a number of important research projects. Professor McIntosh was one of the strongest advocates of the creation of an independent Department of General Linguistics, and has prepared the ground for it. It is my responsibility to continue and develop, as best I can, such part of the work initiated by him as now falls to me, and so free him for his more particular interests in the already broad field of English language studies.[5]

Edinburgh is also an important centre for the study of phonetics. Under Professor Abercrombie, the Department of Phonetics has carried out much fundamental research, especially in the field of the acoustic analysis and synthesis of speech, and provides instruction in the theory and practice of all branches of phonetics of a quality which is probably not surpassed anywhere else in the world.[6] The existence of two separate departments in the same university, a Department of Phonetics and a Department of General Linguistics, inevitably raises the question of the relationship between them. It is my view, and I know it is Professor Abercrombie's, that phonetics is a part, though a highly-specialised part, of general linguistics. Whether there are two departments in the university or only one is a question of secondary importance.[7] Under the existing regulations, candidates for diplomas and degrees in General Linguistics and in Phonetics are required to take courses and pass an examination both in phonetics and in other branches of general linguistics. It is very desirable that students should have this opportunity for specialisation; it is also desirable that they should know something at least of the whole field.

There is yet another department which will necessarily have close contacts with the new Department of General Linguistics: I refer, of course, to the Department of Applied Linguistics. However, I shall postpone my discussion of the relationship between these two departments until later in my lecture, when I have said something about the distinction between "theoretical" and "applied" linguistics.[8]

Here I am concerned to emphasise the fact that even before the creation of the Department of General Linguistics there was in Edinburgh both a greater concentration of linguists of various specialisations and a greater interest in linguistics than in any other British university with the possible exception of London. Among the linguists at Edinburgh are to be counted not only the members of the departments I have mentioned but many others, teaching in other departments of the university, or working on research projects. The University of Edinburgh is already recognised then as an important centre of linguistics: it is known particularly for Celtic studies; for Russian; for the Linguistic Survey of Scotland, the *Dictionary of the Older Scottish Tongue* and the *Scottish National Dictionary*; for work on Middle English dialects; for French and Romance Linguistics; for a more serious interest than is found in most universities in stylistics (which combines linguistic analysis with literary criticism); more recently, for research in the analysis of language with computers; and, as I have already mentioned, for phonetics.[9]

At this point, I may be permitted to say something about what has come to be known (though quite recently) as "Edinburgh linguistics".[10] This is a particular approach to linguistic theory which, though it was very largely developed here, probably never was, and certainly no longer is, accepted by all linguists in Edinburgh. However, a number of recent publications have used the term "Edinburgh linguistics" in a way which might suggest that this particular approach to the subject is not only dominant in Edinburgh, but is more strongly represented throughout Great Britain than is in fact the case. It has even been referred to as "the modern British outlook on linguistics" (Strevens, 1966a: 5). It seems to me, therefore, that the Professor of General Linguistics in Edinburgh should state publicly at this time, since many non-linguists may have been misled by the implications of these terms, that what has recently been referred to as "Edinburgh linguistics", or even "British linguistics", is accepted by only a minority of professional linguists in Great Britain and by few, if any, elsewhere. This is a simple statement of fact. And it is all that I have to say here on the subject. We ourselves have no difficulty in distinguishing between "linguistics in Edinburgh", which is the wider term and includes all the different aspects of the subject which I have mentioned in referring to the already flourishing state of linguistics here, and the narrower, and potentially misleading, term "Edinburgh linguistics" which denotes a particular point of view on certain theoretical questions – a point of view which some of us profess, and others do not. And, I am happy to say, we disagree about many other things too! My *ex cathedra* remarks will not be misunderstood by my colleagues here. I hope they will not be misunderstood by those in other universities of Great Britain and abroad who are watching the development of linguistics in Edinburgh. There is no doubt great value in the formation of what are called "schools of thought" in linguistics, as in other subjects. But the Department of General Linguistics recognises as its first obligation that of instructing students in the more generally-accepted principles of the subject and, where there are different points of view maintained by responsible scholars, as there are in linguistics at the present time, of putting these differences as fairly as possible. *Urbi et orbi diximus* – or rather, *orbi potius quam urbi diximus: anathema sit orthodoxia* (if that is a permissible collocation)!

The title of my Inaugural Lecture, "The Scientific Study of Language", is no more than a short and generally-accepted definition of general linguistics.[11] I shall have occasion presently to draw in greater detail some of the more particular implications contained in the term "scientific". For the moment, however, it will be sufficient to say that by the *scientific* study of language is meant its investigation by means of empirically verifiable observations and with reference to some general theory of language-structure.

Although no-one denies the importance of studying language, it must be admitted that the methods and principles of modern linguistics have aroused, and continue to arouse, a good deal of hostility. And it would appear to be the linguist's insistence that he is being "scientific" – at least in aspiration – which provokes this hostility. It is a common assumption, encouraged by our educational system and the traditional attitudes this system reflects, that the study of language belongs wholly and properly to the "arts". It is, of course, for purely historical reasons that the study of language has traditionally been associated with, and made subsidiary to, literary criticism and other branches of the "arts". Many disciplines suffer, and linguistics perhaps more than most, from the assumption that the division of scholarship into "arts" and "sciences", or into "arts", "sciences" and "social sciences", represents something more fundamental than administrative convenience. Whether or not language is properly made the subject of scientific investigation is surely best answered after examining the results so far achieved by those attempting to treat it as such. We should certainly not close our minds in advance to the possibility of establishing the study of language on sound empirical principles. As H. J. Uldall has said, in discussing this very question: "Progress in knowledge has been made only when men were willing to criticise preconceived notions so strongly held that they had never been tested" (1957: 2–3).[12]

A more particular reason for the opposition to linguistics lies in the challenge it presents to many current notions about language. Such has been the success of the established "natural" sciences since the 17th century that their practitioner no longer feels the obligation to justify himself to his fellows. It may be pointed out, however, that the main reason why many of us are prepared to accept that the work done by the natural scientist is valuable is not so much that we really understand what he is doing as the fact that we admire and appreciate the practical results of science. We feel, if I may put it like this, that our faith is justified by his works! This is a point I shall come back to, since linguistics also, as it has now been recognised, has important practical, or "technological", applications. But I wish to stress particularly the importance of theoretical linguistics. And from this point of view the linguist is not in the same happy position as his colleagues in other sciences. The positive side of linguistics, the theories and hypotheses in terms of which the linguist tries to account systematically for what the layman regards as a set of random and unconnected facts, if he considers them at all, is not yet common knowledge. Moreover, the linguist, "is exposed to a hazard from which many other scientists are shielded: a lay public with relatively easy access to observational data concerning which it has a stock of ready opinion" (Lisker *et al.*, 1962: 83). So often the linguist first appears before his audience, as did Socrates, as a person who perversely questions this "ready opinion" and then goes on to demonstrate (if he is allowed to have his say) that many assertions commonly made about language are in need of clarification; that some of them are false, and others tautological or meaningless. No-one likes to be told that he is talking nonsense or platitudes and there are few people who are prepared sincerely to suspend judgment until they have seen and understood the positive content of new doctrine. The linguist may not be forced to drink hemlock or banished from his native city; his books may be ignored or ridiculed rather than banned or publicly burned. Opposition from the academic "establishment" takes a milder though often no less effective form nowadays! All that the linguist can do to combat it and secure a hearing is to remind his audience that every new science appears first in the role of a destroyer of accepted opinions and attitudes; it is only later that it is seen as something liberating, constructive and enlightening. The linguist must insist, however, that both parts of his science – the destructive, or "Socratic", part, as well as the constructive part which depends upon it – both parts of linguistics are essential to it, and are educationally valuable.

Although linguistics is not a recognised school-subject, there is a very real sense in which one can say that everyone who comes on from school to university has inevitably done a certain amount of linguistics already by virtue of his having received formal instruction in reading, writing and composition and, what is perhaps more important, by virtue of his belonging to a community in which certain beliefs about language are passed on without question from one generation to the next. Since these beliefs are often erroneous, they should be corrected; and it is the function of linguistics, in what I have called its "Socratic" mode, to correct them and replace them with what now seem truer, or at least more reasonable, beliefs and attitudes about language. And it is mainly upon this "Socratic" aspect of linguistics that I would base its claim for inclusion as a non-specialised Ordinary Course in the university curriculum: that is to say, as part of a general education.[13]

Nothing is more helpful in acquiring an understanding of the principles of modern linguistics than some knowledge of the history of the subject. Many of the ideas about language which the linguist will question, if he does not abandon them entirely, will seem less obviously self-evident if one knows something of their historical origin. This is true not only of a good deal that is taught formally at school, but also of much that at first sight might appear to be a matter of downright common sense; for, as Bloomfield has remarked of the common-sense way of dealing with linguistic matters, "like much else that masquerades as common sense it is in fact highly sophisticated, and derives, at no great distance, from the speculations of ancient and medieval philosophers" (1933: 3)[14]. As instances of "common-sense" attitudes to language which derive from what Bloomfield refers to as "the speculations of ancient and medieval philosophers" one may cite the commonly-held belief that all languages manifest the same "parts of speech" (in the form in which this belief is usually held and expressed). The traditional theory of "the parts of speech", and the standard definitions of classical grammar, reflect ancient and medieval attempts to force together the categories of grammar, logic and metaphysics. Other commonly-held views about language derive not so much from philosophical speculation as from the subordination of grammar to the task of interpreting written texts and especially to that of interpreting works written in Greek and Latin by the classical authors. To this cause may be attributed the view that the written language is in some sense more "correct", "nobler" or "purer", than the spoken language; in particular what might be called "the classical fallacy" – the idea that languages have a golden period to which they evolve and from which in the course of time they degenerate, unless grammarians, the custodians of correct speech and writing, are successful in arresting this development. This assumption was made by the great Alexandrian grammarians of the Hellenistic period to whom we are mainly indebted for the codification of what we now call traditional grammar. It was taken over by the Romans, together with the framework of grammatical categories developed initially for the description of Greek, and it was embodied in the works of Priscian and Donatus which were used as teaching grammars of Latin throughout the middle ages. With the Renaissance – heralded in this respect by Dante's *De vulgari eloquentia* – interest in the vernacular languages developed enormously, and grammars were written in great numbers. But in all cases it was taken for granted that the grammatical categories established for Greek and Latin were universally valid. In fact the whole classical conception was extended to the modern languages. Language still meant the language of literature; and literature, when it became the object of academic study in our schools and universities, continued to mean the work of "the best authors" writing in the accepted genres.

It is true that a more satisfactory academic approach to literature has developed nowadays, and authors are no longer classified by the normative canons of Alexandria and the Renaissance. But the study of grammar in many of the language departments of our schools and universities still tends to be dominated by what I have called the "classical fallacy". This fallacy, I should like to think, is less strongly entrenched at Edinburgh than in some other universities of my acquaintance.

I do not wish to give the impression, however, that the history of linguistics is of interest only in so far as it enables us to free ourselves of certain commonly-held misconceptions about language. As an aid to the understanding of the principles and assumptions governing modern linguistics a knowledge of the history of the subject has a positive, as well as a negative contribution to make. Some linguists, including Bloomfield, impressed with the great advances made in the scientific investigation of language in recent years have tended to be unduly iconoclastic in their discussions of the past. If we can see this more clearly now than could Bloomfield and other linguists of his generation, it may only be that linguistics, like other branches of knowledge, advances, partly at least, according to the Hegelian pattern of thesis, antithesis and synthesis.

It is certainly the case that many of the attitudes and ideas of linguists today seem to result from a synthesis of certain traditional ideas with ideas directly opposed to them, their antitheses, expressed by linguists of a previous generation. Many examples could be given to support this point. I shall confine myself to one or two which seem to me particularly important.

I have already said that modern linguistics challenges the "classical fallacy" that the spoken language is inferior to and in some sense derived from the standard written language. This challenge has frequently been expressed in strong antithetical form, most notably by Bloomfield: "Writing is not language, but merely a way of recording language by means of visible marks" (1933: 21). Very few linguists nowadays would accept this point of view. They would still maintain, in opposition to the classical view, that there is a sense in which the spoken language is prior to the written;[15] but at the same time they would grant that the written language may have its own grammatical and lexical structure; in short, that the written language has every right to be studied on its own terms. Professor McIntosh expressed this more moderate, "synthetic", view of the relationship between the written and the spoken language in his article on "The analysis of written Middle English" published in 1956: it is a view that is now very generally accepted.[16] Moreover, linguists now tend to recognise not only a difference between written and spoken languages, and the legitimacy of studying each, but also a difference between various "styles" and "registers" in both spoken and written languages. The late Professor J. R. Firth used to express this fact by saying that we all speak "many languages" and switch automatically from one to another according to the situation we are in and the social role we are playing at the time. Firth himself put forward this notion in conscious opposition to the thesis of de Saussure, that all members of a given speech-community speak "une langue une". In my view, neither de Saussure's thesis nor Firth's antithesis is acceptable as it stands. What is now required is the synthesis which will interpret Firth's "many languages" as varieties of de Saussure's "une langue une". I do not think that this synthesis has yet emerged in any precise form, though much illuminating discussion of the question has taken place in the last few years, particularly among followers of Firth in Britain. Meanwhile, it can be said that linguists are now agreed that the literary language may have its own structure which is to some degree independent of that of the spoken language. The path is now open, and some linguists are making tentative steps along it, to a more fruitful discussion of the use of language in literature, of good and bad style relative to the aims of the author and the effect he is trying to achieve. And it may be mentioned in passing that the current renewal of interest in literature among linguists is only one effect of the reappraisal of the attitude of relativism, or *laissez-faire*, characteristic of so many linguists but a few years ago. *Leave your language alone!* was the title of a popular book on linguistics published in 1950 (R. A. Hall, 1950); it is no longer a rallying-cry of linguists in the mid-sixties. In the last year or so a number of books and articles have been published by linguists which express a much more positive attitude towards the question of standardising languages. However – and let me stress this point – this does not mean that linguists have now abandoned the distinction between descriptive and prescriptive grammar which they fought to establish a generation ago. This distinction is maintained. But it is now accepted that there might be valid social or political reasons for promoting the wider acceptance of some particular language or dialect in a given community; and also that it is possible and legitimate to evaluate different languages or dialects (*after* they have been described) in terms of such criteria as efficiency and even expressiveness.[17]

A far more important synthesis of traditional and more recent ideas about language is taking place currently in the field of grammatical theory. Undoubtedly, the most significant advance in linguistics in recent years is the development of the principles of generative grammar. Generative grammar takes as its starting-point the fact that the native speaker of any language is able to produce and understand an indefinitely large number of sentences in the language most of which he will never have heard before, and sets out to describe this indefinitely large set of sentences by means of a set of rules which specify precisely what combinations of elements constitute sentences of the language, assigning to each sentence a unique structural description. It is Chomsky who has been principally responsible for the development of this notion of "generative" grammar. Those of you who heard Professor Chomsky lecture in Edinburgh last November will recall that one of the points he especially emphasised was the similarity between the aims of traditional grammarians and those of present-day generative grammarians;[18] and that he criticised Bloomfield and his followers for misguidedly departing from these traditional aims and restricting the scope of grammatical description to the task of classifying the elements and combinations of elements occurring in particular texts. Chomsky was not of course suggesting that his formulation of the aims of grammatical description is simply a restatement of traditional notions. Although traditional grammar was generative, and to some degree even transformational, in spirit, it was only implicitly so. If we define a generative grammar, in Chomsky's own words, as "a device (or procedure) which assigns structural descriptions to sentences in a perfectly explicit manner, formulated independently of any particular language" (1964a: 995), then no traditional grammar came anywhere near satisfying the definition. And the reason is that traditional grammar never set itself the ideal of explicitness, as we now understand this requirement. The ideal of explicitness was introduced only recently into linguistics and was developed, as much by Bloomfield and his followers as by any other group, or "school', of linguists. Of course, Chomsky's view of what constitutes explicitness in this context has been strongly influenced by work done in the field of symbolic logic and the foundations of mathematics. But this influence is also discernible in the work of certain followers of Bloomfield.[19] In saying this I am not of course trying to diminish either the originality or the magnitude of Chomsky's contribution to linguistics. What I wish to stress is the historical fact that modern generative grammar has not developed, and perhaps could never have developed, directly from traditional grammar. If modern grammatical theory has returned to and revitalised some traditional ideas on language, this is not simply as a result of quietly developing them and drawing out their implications over the years. A period of violent antithesis was necessary and, as I have suggested, has contributed essentially to the present synthesis.[20] If I appear to have emphasised this point unduly, it is because there is a tendency, I think, for those outside the subject to simplify the issues. If linguists now appear to be holding views which they have spent the last thirty years or so condemning – if, for instance, they now say, as many of them will, that there might be such a thing as "universal grammar" after all – you may be certain that this is not so much a matter of *plus ça change, plus c'est la même chose*, if you just sit tight and wait long enough, but rather *plus cela paraît la même chose, plus cela a en fait changé!*[21] (The present "encapsulates" the past, to use Collingwood's expression, it does not repeat it.) It is my conviction that any formal instruction in linguistics given in the university should include courses in the history of the subject. I would reject the stultifying proposal that modern linguistics must be "uninfluenced by previous linguistics insofar as is possible" (Dixon, 1963: 79; cf. Lyons, 1963c: 440), and would echo instead an aphorism of the great George Saintsbury, Regius Professor of Rhetoric and English Literature in Edinburgh from 1895 to 1915: "Ancient without Modern is a stumbling block. Modern without Ancient is foolishness utter and irremediable" (cf. Curtius, 1953: ix). The relationship between ancient and modern I would interpret in the changing, "dialectical" way I have suggested.

The time has now come for me to say something about the different branches of general linguistics and the present state of their development; about their relationship to one another and to disciplines outside linguistics. These questions can be dealt with in terms of three dichotomies: (1) descriptive vs. historical and comparative linguistics; (2) "microlinguistics" vs. "macrolinguistics"; and (3) theoretical vs. "applied" linguistics.

The first of these dichotomies need not occupy us long. Since the publication of de Saussure's *Cours de linguistique générale* in 1915 it has been customary to distinguish between synchronic, or descriptive, linguistics and diachronic, or historical, linguistics; that is to say, between describing languages at particular periods (*états de langue*), without reference to their previous or subsequent development, and giving an account of their attested or postulated historical development from one state to another through time. Since historical linguistics is based upon the comparison of different language-states, it is in a sense part of the wider discipline of comparative linguistics (cf. W. S. Allen, 1957b: 9).

It was the principal achievement of nineteenth-century linguistics to demonstrate the fact of linguistic "evolution" and to group languages into "families" and "sub-families" by means of what is referred to as "the comparative method". We now give a rather different interpretation to the term "evolution" from that given to it by certain nineteenth-century scholars; we may understand the terms "sound-law", "reconstruction" and "analogy" somewhat differently; we may recognise more clearly than our predecessors that language-change is not simply a function of time, but also of social and geographical conditions; and we may admit that languages can, under certain conditions, "converge" as well as "diverge" in the course of time. Most important of all, we now hold that the comparative study of languages is methodologically dependent upon their prior synchronic description. However, none of these modifications is sufficient to invalidate completely either the methods or the earlier conclusions of comparative linguistics.

Comparative linguistics is an explanatory science. It sets out to explain the evident fact that languages change and that different languages are related to one another in different degrees. The changes that languages undergo and the different degrees of relationship between languages are accounted for in terms of hypotheses which, like any other scientific hypotheses, are subject to revision as a result of the discovery of new evidence or of the adoption of a new way of looking at, and systematising, the evidence. The "Indo-European" hypothesis has been continually modified for both of these reasons. These modifications are to be expected and welcomed. They derive from the fact that comparative linguistics is hypothetical and explanatory; and they do not constitute a reason for denying to comparative linguistics its due place as part of general linguistics, the scientific study of language. Having insisted that the comparative study of languages is a branch of general linguistics I can go on to say that it is, however, a less fundamental part of the subject than the descriptive analysis of languages. Comparative linguistics is less funda-mental than descriptive linguistics, since, at least as I understand the relationship between them and have explained it here, comparison presupposes description, but description does not presuppose comparison. Since this is so, it is descriptive linguistics, rather than historical and comparative linguistics, to which we should give the greater emphasis in our teaching of linguistics.

Before passing on to my second dichotomy, I should perhaps mention that I have been employing the term "comparative linguistics" in the conventional sense in which it is restricted to the comparison of languages with a view to establishing their "evolutionary" or "genetic" relationship; that is, the kind of relationship holding between them which is to be explained in terms of their historical development from some common "ancestral" language. The reason for this restriction in the application of the term "comparative" is simply that it was the "evolutionary" study of language which more or less monopolised the interest and energies of linguists in the nineteenth century when the term first became current. Nowadays, the comparison of different languages is undertaken by linguists for other purposes as well. The point I have made about the more fundamental status of descriptive linguistics *vis-à-vis* comparative still holds true under a wider interpretation of the term "comparative". Not everything I have said about "genetic" or "evolutionary" comparative linguistics is, of course, relevant to other kinds of comparison. Nor am I suggesting that "evolutionary" comparison takes precedence over the others.

My second and major dichotomy is between "microlinguistics" and "macrolinguistics". I do not very much like these terms, and I may be employing them in a somewhat different sense from that in which they have been used by other linguists.[22] Roughly, the distinction I am making is between a narrower and wider conception of what constitutes the subject-matter of linguistics. By the narrower conception I am referring to the view that linguistics is an autonomous science which has as its aim the construction of a general theory for the description of languages – in particular for their synchronic description – without reference to such questions as the learning of languages, the role of language in society, the psychological and neurological aspects of language, the influence of language upon thought and the development of logical and philosophical systems. By "macrolinguistics" I mean here the study of language in relation to the questions I have just mentioned, as well as to many others. It was de Saussure himself who first insisted upon the restriction of linguistics to the narrower sphere of what I am calling "microlinguistics"; "la linguistique a pour unique et véritable objet la langue envisagée en elle-même et pour elle-même". By "la langue" de Saussure means, of course, the descriptive system, of elements ("sounds", "words", etc.) and the relations between them, which the linguist establishes in order to account for the utterances (what de Saussure called "la parole") of those who are said to "speak the same language". We can perhaps best translate the term "la langue" as the *language-system*.[23] "Microlinguistics" then, or linguistics proper as understood by most linguists since de Saussure, is the study of language-systems as such.

One may specify the aims of "microlinguistics" by first invoking the notion of "acceptability". "Acceptable" is a primitive, or prescientific term, which is neutral with respect to a number of different distinctions that are made by linguists, including, for instance, the distinction that is tradition-ally drawn between "grammatical" and "meaningful": it is a more primitive term than either "grammatical" or "meaningful" in the sense that, unlike these terms, it does not depend upon any technical definitions or theoretical concepts of linguistics. An acceptable utterance is one that has been, or might be, produced by a native speaker in some appropriate context and is, or would be, accepted by other native speakers as belonging to the language in question.[24] "Microlinguistics" sets itself the task of specifying for the languages being described what utterances are acceptable.

Since, as I said earlier, the native speaker of a language is able to produce and understand an indefinitely large, and perhaps infinite, number of different utterances, most of which he will never have heard before, it follows that any body of recorded material in a given language, however large that body of material, is but a sample of the language in question. It is one of the tasks of the linguist in collecting the material, his data, to make the sample as representative as possible and, in describing the language to do so by projecting, or "extrapolating", from the data a very large number of sentences which have not been recorded and yet which would be regarded as acceptable by native speakers.[25] In other words, the description of the language will take the form of a finite set of elements and rules which, on the basis of a finite number of sentences, will account for a much larger, and perhaps infinite, number of sentences, which, in the ideal, are "all and only the sentences of the language". Any description of a language which has these properties is a generative description. And I shall take it for granted that the construction of generative descriptions is a necessary aim of modern "microlinguistics". Not all linguists would agree with me here perhaps, but one can't be neutral all the time! I shall also take it for granted that the construction of formally different generative systems for the description of different languages is, at least *prima facie*, undesirable; and that it is the construction of a general, generative theory of language-structure in terms of which all languages can be described which is the principal concern of "microlinguistics". This assumption is, if you like, the linguist's παράδειγμα ἐν οὐρανῷ:[26] an ideal which haunts and guides him, which provides grounds for his dissatisfaction with particular descriptions and spurs him on to improve and standardise them. It is an assumption that linguists will hold as long as seems reasonable. And it is in the light of this assumption that they are again, and perhaps always have been really, concerned with "universal grammar".

Linguists customarily recognise three levels in a language-system and in terms of these account for different kinds or "layers" of acceptability: the phonological, the grammatical and the semantic level. A certain amount of acceptability (including much of what is popularly referred to as "accent") can be accounted for at the phonological or even the phonetic level. That is to say, in terms of the "sounds" which occur in the language and their possible combinations. (I am using the non-technical, though ambiguous term "sounds" for simplicity.) At the grammatical level of description we recognise units of a "higher" order than "sounds" (let us say "words" for simplicity, although they are not always words) and group them into classes: nouns, verbs, adjectives, etc. Grammar accounts for as much of the acceptability of utterances as can be accounted for in terms of rules which specify the permissible combinations of these word-classes. Modern grammarians, both in their theory and in their practice, differ from traditional grammarians at this point, apart from being more explicit, in at least two ways: first, they set up the word-classes, or "parts of speech", solely with reference to their general combinatory properties and take no account of the meaning of particular words; second, they make a much finer subclassification of the "parts of speech" in terms of their combinatory possibilities than was achieved or thought possible in the past. However, no matter how far the grammatical analysis is taken – and the limits are far from having been reached in the description of any language, although contemporary partial grammars of English have recognised some hundreds of grammatical sub-classes – it will never succeed in accounting for the whole of acceptability. It is at the third level of description, the semantic level, that one accounts for such acceptable and unacceptable combinations of words as can be specified in terms of the meaning of the particular words in question. This view of the matter, it may be pointed out, does not necessarily involve acceptance of the equation: "synchronic linguistic description minus grammar equals semantics" (Katz & Fodor, 1963: 172).[27]

It is with respect to the levels of phonology and grammar that the "microlinguistic" view has been most strongly, and most successfully, maintained by linguists. Current phonological and grammatical descriptions of languages are undoubtedly freer of vagueness and inconsistencies, and in parts at least are more comprehensive, than those of the past. There is considerable disagreement among linguists about particular theoretical points: I will say nothing about these here. There is also a good deal of controversy about the more general "goals of linguistic theory"; but I think it is fair to say that this controversy is more about widening the scope of phonological and grammatical description than about changing this entirely.

In the more particular approach to linguistic description which, as I said, I am taking for granted – the generative approach – the descriptions of language-systems account for grammatical and phonological acceptability by means of a set of rules which operate in sequence upon certain theoretical intermediate elements introduced for the purpose and "produce", ultimately, "strings" of "words" and "sounds" together with an associated "structural analysis" of each "string". Looked at from this point of view, the grammar of a language – and let me from now on use the term in a wider sense to include phonology – is a formalised, deductive system which "generates" sentences as valid "theorems" of the particular language-system; and the general grammatical theory in terms of which the grammars of particular languages are written determines the form of the rules, the nature of the elements occurring in them, and the conditions for the application of the rules. This conception of the nature of grammatical descriptions and of grammatical theory, for which, as I said earlier, we are of course principally indebted to Chomsky, draws heavily upon formal logic and the foundations of mathematics (cf. Chomsky & Miller, 1963; Chomsky, 1963). Formally different generative systems can be constructed; that is to say, systems which differ as to the nature of the rules or elements that they permit or the more particular constraints that they impose upon the ordering or the application of the rules. Much important work has already been done on the investigation of the relative power and empirical adequacy of systems with different formal properties. This work is very technical; for at this point theoretical grammar, like for instance the theoretical parts of other sciences, merges into applied mathematics. One cannot expect all linguists, still less students of the subject, to become thoroughly conversant with this branch of linguistics; but one can expect, I think, that they should appreciate the general implications of the work being done here and the results so far achieved. Among these results should be mentioned the proof that certain systems with different formal properties which can be set up for a given language may be equivalent in the sense that they will generate the same set of sentences, but non-equivalent in the sense that they will generate these sentences with different associated structural analyses (cf. Chomsky, 1963: 410–15). It thus becomes a question of some interest to decide whether one grammatical description is better than another as the basis for semantic description, in relation to certain wider aims of linguistic theory, or for some particular purpose.

I will not go further into the details of modern grammatical theory. I have deliberately made my stand on what many might consider to be the most arid, "formalistic" and even "inhumane" aspect of the subject. I wish therefore to refer briefly to this criticism which is sometimes made of modern grammatical theory.[28]

It is not only laymen, but also certain linguists, who find what they consider to be the excessive "formalism" of much modern linguistics a stumbling-block. From time to time, books and articles appear which contain pleas for less "formalism" and more "realism" in linguistics (cf. Martinet, 1962: 1–38; Leroy, 1963: 98–9, 102–3, 163). To many the word "realism" has a nice, reassuring sound. To the scientist and the

194

philosopher the word has, of course, quite other connotations. You will recall what Eddington says on this subject in the Gifford Lectures which he delivered in Edinburgh in 1927, on *The Nature of the Physical World*: that "the word 'reality' is generally used *with the intention of evoking sentiment*" and "loud cheers"; that science has no place for this conception of "reality" – it has its own "domestic definition of existence", which "follows the principle now adopted for all other definitions in science, namely, that a thing must be defined according to the way it is in practice recognised and not according to some ulterior significance that we imagine it to possess" (1935: 273, 276; cf. Carnap, 1956: 206–8). The fact is that objections to the "formalism" and "abstractness" of modern linguistics are usually appealing implicitly to some other ontological framework, which though it may be more vaguely described or different is no less abstract. There is of course legitimate disagreement among linguists about the particular theoretical framework to be used in the description of language. All I wish to suggest is that what is sometimes represented as an argument between "formalists" and "realists" – the implication being that the "realists" have a healthy respect for "facts", whereas the "formalists" do not and are moved only by their perverse delight in "mathematical manipulation" – is an argument in favour of one abstract framework rather than another (cf. Z. S. Harris, 1954: 146).

Linguistics is – or perhaps one should say more modestly and more truthfully, sets out to be – a body of scientific theory set up to account for certain data. These data, language-utterances, either result from or are verified by observation. The general theory of language-structure is not, of course, derived simply by induction from the data; it embodies certain assumptions and criteria of relevance taken for granted at the outset (the data, it has been well said – though I cannot now recall by whom – are not "given" but "taken"); the theory also embodies such principles as internal consistency and elegance. The data are the evidence for the theory; and the attempt to apply the theory to account for the data may lead to its confirmation, modification or abandonment. Ultimately the gap must be bridged between the system of elements, rules and relationships which enter into the theory set up to describe language-systems ("langues") and the observed or observable utterances (instances of "parole") which are the linguist's data. This, I take it, is assumed by all linguists – by those working at the most general level upon the theoretical foundations of linguistics, as well as by those engaged upon the description of particular languages.

The "realists" do not deserve the "loud cheers" that the label they have given themselves tends to evoke. If modern linguistics is an abstract subject, this is because it is deliberately and perhaps at times (as in the present lecture) rather too assertively, scientific; if it is striving towards formatisation, this is because mathematical formalisation is the goal of all science. And, if I may quote Eddington again, "we must follow the path [of science] whether it leads to the hill of vision or the tunnel of obscurity". It may be that all aspects of language cannot be brought within the scope of one science. But then linguists are not claiming to deal with "all aspects of language" – at least, not yet!

If the aims of "microlinguistics" are circumscribed in the way I have outlined, the place of semantics immediately comes up for discussion. We are surely interested not merely in the question whether sentences are semantically acceptable, meaningful, but also in *what* meaning they have. And whereas it might be reasonable to adopt the view that a phonological and grammatical description need do no more than identify elements and specify their combinatory possibilities directly, it would seem to be the case that the meaningfulness, or significance, of at least some combinations of words is a function of what meaning each of them has independently;[29] and also that something of what we call their meaning has to do with their relations with things in the world outside the language-system and with the situations in which particular words and utterances are used.[30] The distinction between "microlinguistics" and "macrolinguistics" becomes particularly difficult, and perhaps ultimately impossible, to draw consistently in the case of semantics: and this is no doubt one reason why some linguists have in the past been inclined to exclude the whole of semantics from linguistics proper.

I do not think that linguists have yet produced a satisfactory theory of semantics; nor do I believe that linguistics will ever provide a satisfactory theory of semantics so long as the subject is restricted to the narrower aims of what I have been calling "microlinguistics".[31] Semantics is a field where progress depends necessarily upon the collaboration of linguistics and such other disciplines as philosophy, anthropology and sociology. And it is perhaps philosophy that can give the greatest assistance to linguistics in the study of meaning. Philosophers have always been concerned with language and more particularly with meaning, since this is necessarily involved in such questions as the problem of truth and knowledge. And in recent years the dominant "schools" of philosophy in Britain and elsewhere have been almost exclusively concerned with these questions. As Ryle has said: "Preoccupation with the theory of meaning could be described as the occupational disease of twentieth-century Anglo-Saxon and Austrian philosophy" (1957: 239 [= 1963: 128]). Despite this fact there has been distressingly little collaboration so far between linguists and philosophers, in this country at least, in the discussion of semantic theory.[32]

We have been discussing languages in the deliberately-restricted sense of "language-systems". One can of course take a wider view. Everyone agrees that it is by virtue of his possession of language that man differs most strikingly from other animals and is able to engage in discursive reasoning: it is often said that "homo loquens" would be a more satisfactory classificatory term for man than the traditional label of "homo sapiens". Moreover, language is the foundation, or keystone, of social organisation; it is an integral part of a community's culture and the principal means whereby the norms of conduct and judgment are maintained and transmitted from generation to generation. It is through our mastery of other languages that we are able, either directly or at second-hand, to enter into and appreciate the experience of individuals living in other ages and other cultures, and so enrich our own life. So much will be readily admitted. One might go further, as some have done, and maintain that language is a conditioning factor in all adult human experience, such that the way in which we think or even perceive the external world is to a considerable degree influenced by the particular native language we happen to speak. This is a controversial question which has been much discussed in recent years. A certain amount of experimental evidence has been cited – though so far, it must be admitted, very little – which would tend to support the hypothesis (cf. Lenneberg & Roberts, 1953; Diebold, 1964).[33] It is in any case a widely-held view, and one that has been frequently expressed by those who habitually use more than one language in their normal, everyday life, that the language one is speaking affects not only what one will say in certain situations but even one's moods and emotional reactions; in other words that language affects personality, the "kind of person" one is. All these questions, and many others, one may refer to "macrolinguistics" in the sense in which I am using the term. And it is here that one recognises the links, actual or potential, that linguistics has with such other disciplines as philosophy, psychology, anthropology, sociology, literary criticism, "the history of ideas", and even with neurophysiology, animal and human ecology and the study of animal communication-systems.

In recent years a whole host of rather barbarous neologisms have emerged to refer to the work that is being done in the borderline areas between linguistics and other disciplines: "psycholinguistics", "ethnolinguistics", "sociolinguistics", "neurolinguistics", "paralinguistics" and so on. I obviously have not the time, and am in any case not competent, to review the work that is being carried out in all these various fields. Much of this research is undoubtedly very tentative; and many of the boundaries will almost certainly have to be redrawn. It must be insisted, however, that what are recognised, at least at present, as borderline areas between linguistics and other disciplines are legitimate fields of scientific investigation. In many cases the results achieved even now are encouraging. And where they are not yet encouraging we should not be too ready with the maxim: *Wovon man nicht sprechen kann, darüber muss man schweigen* (Wittgenstein, 1922: 188).

In some instances "macrolinguistic" research has been inspired directly by the achievements of linguistics in pursuit of its narrower goal of describing language-systems. This is perhaps most notably so in the case of current "psycholinguistic" work. Let me quote a recent comment of George Miller in this connexion: "I now believe that mind is something more than a four-letter Anglo-Saxon word – human minds exist and it is our job as psychologists to study them. Moreover, I believe that one of the best ways to study a human mind is by studying the verbal system that it uses" (1962: 761).[34] It is obvious that generative grammar, and in particular transformational grammar, although set up by linguists for the description of language-systems without reference to the psychological aspects of language, has important and suggestive implications for psychological theories of speech-perception and of the learning and use of language. These implications have been drawn in recent theoretical and experimental work.

Many of the topics dealt with by modern linguistics, as I have stressed in the earlier part of this lecture, have been treated by grammarians and philosophers for centuries. Other questions treated by modern linguistics and such other disciplines as I have mentioned here have arisen from a new way of looking at language, or from attempts to relate it to its cultural "matrix" and to the psychological and neurological "mechanism" which the use of language presupposes. It is surely one of the most exciting aspects of science that it advances not only by solving the problems with which it starts, but by creating new problems, by charting and annexing to itself new regions of enquiry, on the way. And we may rejoice that there is at least one sphere of human activity where "Parkinson's law" operates to our entire satisfaction: the field of science expands to occupy fully the time and energies of scholars engaged in it!

It is impossible for any one person to keep abreast of developments in all the fields that I have referred to here under the term "macrolinguistics". But then it is impossible for anyone to be familiar with more than a few languages or to control all the evidence that has to be handled, for instance, in the comparative study of the Indo-European languages. Linguistics has always relied upon the collaborative work of many scholars. Exhaustive descriptions of particular languages are required, as well as work on the general theory, its logical basis and axiomatization. It is by virtue of the development of the general theory by a variety of linguists with different, but overlapping, specializations that progress has been made so far. It is not inconceivable that we shall in time modify our view of what has seemed to be a desirable restriction of the field of linguistics proper, to the study of language-systems. And I have already suggested that in the case of semantics this restriction cannot even now be maintained. We should obviously be more satisfied with a theory of language-structure common to those approaching language from many different points of view – from the point of view of its acquisition, its pathology, its role in culture, and so on. But no such unified theory yet exists, and one may be falling victim to the temptations of "reductionism" in thinking that it ever will.

I therefore believe that, for the present at least, a department of General Linguistics should concentrate particularly upon the field of "microlinguistics" in both teaching and research. However, the Department of General Linguistics here will co-operate, to the best of its ability and competence, and so far as its resources will allow, with any other departments that are interested in those aspects of language which the linguist must for the present consider peripheral. Courses in linguistics already exist for students of social anthropology. One might also consider the institution of courses in linguistics for students of psychology, philosophy, and sociology, as well as for students of different languages.

I turn finally to the distinction I have made between theoretical and "applied" linguistics. Nowadays the universities are heavily supported, both directly and indirectly, by governments and by the great philanthropic and research foundations; and, as our Principal has stressed in the B.B.C. Reith Lectures for 1956 and elsewhere, they are rightly expected to make a substantial return on the capital invested in them by producing men and women trained to apply their scientific knowledge to the solution of socially-important problems (Appleton, 1956).[35] In recent years, it has been increasingly realised that linguistics has a considerable contribution to make in the resolution of many urgent practical problems. Indeed, it seems to be the case that the current expansion of linguistics, both in Great Britain and abroad, is to be attributed in large measure to the expectations which exist in respect of its actual or potential "technological" applications. Nowhere have these "technological" applications been stressed more forcefully than in the Soviet Union; and it is interesting to observe that the official acceptance there about ten years ago of what was previously condemned as "western structuralism" can be directly referred to an appreciation of its applications, particularly in language-teaching and in machine-translation and information-retrieval (cf. Sebeok, 1965: 36, 94–102, 113–25; Akhmanova *et al.*, 1961).[36]

I have referred to two branches of what I am calling "applied linguistics" – language-teaching, and machine-translation and information-retrieval. Other branches which might be mentioned are a variety of medical and remedial applications, including speech-therapy, aphasics and the teaching of the deaf; automatic type-setting; and the many different aspects of "language-planning". With the creation of so many new and independent states in Africa and Asia since the war, the question of "language-planning" (which includes, amongst other things, the standardisation of languages for political and educational reasons) has become particularly urgent. English-speaking linguists, and especially British linguists, have a special responsibility here, since English is now the major international language, and in many of the former British colonies, protectorates and dominions is, and will be for some time to come, the principal medium of communication between citizens from different parts of the same state. The problems of "language-planning" are complex, since there are political, social and historical factors to be taken into account. Recently, a number of conferences have been held, to which linguists have contributed – and books and articles have been written by linguists – devoted wholly or partly to the subject of "language-planning" (cf. Haugen, 1964; Le Page, 1964; Spencer, 1963; Tauli, 1964).

I will not attempt to review the vast field of "applied linguistics". Let me simply assure you that linguists recognise and have accepted their social obligations in different branches of this field. What must be stressed is this: in all parts of what I have, for convenience, called "applied linguistics" it is not linguistics alone that is involved, and certainly not just "micro-linguistics". And in many cases the term "applied linguistics" is perhaps inappropriate in that it seems to overemphasise linguistics at the expense of other disciplines – the computer sciences, psychology, pedagogy, etc. (cf. Halliday *et al.*, 1964: 164).

It must also be stressed that there is no necessary coincidence between the aims of theoretical linguistics, the scientific study of language for its own sake, and the more practical tasks of "applied linguistics". For instance, the grammatical descriptions of a particular language which are devised for such practical purposes as teaching the language or machine-translation might legitimately differ from grammatical descriptions of the same language set up solely with reference to the general theory of language-structure which theoretical linguistics tries to establish. It is important to emphasise this point, since, as I have already said, much of the present expansion of linguistics is due to the deliberate policy of governments and other bodies whose concern is chiefly with the "practical", or "technological", aspects of the subject. And there is a danger that the overconcentration of resources on "applied linguistics", if this overconcentration takes place, will not only distort the true aims of theoretical linguistics, but also, as in other fields of "applied science", will turn out to be a short-sighted policy even for the development of the applications themselves. I hope that I shall not be thought too much of an "ivory-tower academic" if I now proclaim both my personal attachment to the ideals of theoretical linguistics and also my intention of interpreting the mandate of the new Department of General Linguistics in the light of these ideals. If one can draw a general distinction between "science" and "technology" in terms of *understanding* and *control*, I would say that the technological control of man and his environment, granted the social desirability of this, presupposes their understanding. Moreover, the achievement of a better understanding of man and his physical and social environment, and the wider dissemination of this in education, is a no less urgent "practical" matter than what I have referred to, loosely, as technology.

There is all the more reason to interpret the term "general linguistics" in this sense in Edinburgh, since there is here a Department of Applied Linguistics, founded as the School of Applied Linguistics in 1957 and charged with the particular task of promoting and improving the teaching of English overseas, and granted the status of an independent department of the University in 1964, when Mr S. Pit Corder was appointed as Head.[37]

I have now come to the end of my lecture. In the course of it, and in the limited time available, I have tried to show what contribution linguistics, the scientific study of language, can make to the work of the University. I have also tried to convey to you something of the aims and scope of modern linguistics, and of the spirit in which the subject is practised and the results achieved so far. Measured by what was achieved in earlier ages these results are impressive; by comparison with what remains to be done they are almost insignificant. But this is true of the achievements of science in general; and in a new university department it is cause for rejoicing rather than despair. As I promised at the beginning of my lecture, I have made very wide, but I hope not exaggerated claims for my subject, as one to be pursued at all levels of university activity. And if, at the end of it, any of you now feel, as Cratylus did, slightly exhausted by the ordeal and yet convinced that I have not justified the claims I have made, my reply must once again be that of Socrates: "We haven't time to pursue the matter any further now, my friend. And next time you can lecture me!" *Eìs αὖθις τοίνυν ...* (Plato, *Cratylus* 440e).[38]

Notes

1 Language, speech and writing

1 This is a revised and expanded version of a paper with a slightly different title (Lyons, 1981c), which I wrote for the two-day Symposium on 'the psychological mechanisms of language' organized for the Royal Society and the British Academy by H. C. Longuet-Higgins, D. E. Broadbent and myself in March 1981 (cf. Longuet-Higgins *et al.*, 1981). The Symposium was open to the public and there was a capacity audience of more than four hundred, many of whom took an active part in the discussion.

My role in the Meeting was rather different from that of the others delivering papers. The topic that I chose and the way I handled it reflected this difference. Instead of addressing myself to some identifiable narrower or more technical aspect of the general theme, I set out to establish a number of terminological and conceptual distinctions that I thought would be relevant to issues raised in the papers given by other speakers. My paper was intended to serve as an introduction both to the first session, on the nature of language and linguistic knowledge (cf. Chomsky, 1981; Cohen, 1981; Kenny, 1981), and to the Meeting as a whole. It had been the expressed wish of the Officers of the Royal Society and the British Academy that there should be an introductory paper of this kind at the beginning of the Meeting, for the benefit of those attending who had no specialized background in philosophy, linguistics or psychology.

In preparing the present version for publication I have been concerned to remove from the text everything that referred specifically to the organization of the Symposium and I have made numerous small additions, excisions and alterations throughout in order to relate the content of the article to that of the chapters immediately following it in the present volume. I have also introduced three extra paragraphs in the body of the text and an Addendum at the end and have added notes giving bibliographical references to past and present works that deal with the same topic. I am publishing it as the first chapter of the present volume because it introduces in a relatively simple form several of the issues dealt with in later chapters.

2 For a non-technical account of Chomsky's views on this issue and of the context in which it was developed, cf. Lyons (1981a: 242–248). Slightly more technical are Lyons (1977a: Chapters 9–10), Greene (1972), Smith & Wilson (1979). The earliest, now classic, statement by Chomsky himself (1965) excited and informed a considerable amount of philosophical discussion in the late 1960s (cf. Hook, 1969) and was probably the most important factor in the revitalization of cognitive psychology. Chomsky's more recent views – on universal grammar, the modularity of mind, the organic nature of the language-faculty, etc. (1980a) – set the agenda for the first session of the Symposium referred to in note 1 (cf. Chomsky, 1981; Cohen, 1981; Kenny, 1981) and were taken to be more or less directly relevant to work reported in several of the papers delivered at the later sessions. For Chomsky's present position see Chomsky (1986).

3 I am indebted to John C. Marshall for this quotation.

4 In the discussion that followed the delivery of the original version of this paper, Professor R. B. Le Page took exception to this statement (which in the original had "readily" instead of "usually"). He drew attention to the difficulties that linguists have in establishing boundaries between one language and another in many parts of the world, where there exists a continuum of variation between what may be regarded, both by their users and by linguists, either as dialects of the same language or, alternatively and with equal justification, as different languages. His principal example was the continuum that holds between acrolectal and basilectal Guyanese, but he also referred to the similarly "uncertain boundaries of the Punjabi–Hindi–Gujerati–Bhojpuri continuum". He pointed out that the existence of such continua and the descriptive problems that they give rise to have "important implications for one's view of what constitutes a language" (Le Page, 1981; see also Le Page, 1980; Alleyne, 1980; Sankoff, 1980).

My response was: "I do not dispute the facts that Professor Le Page brings to our attention. Nor would I wish to minimize the importance of studying synchronic variation in language communities and such phenomena as the continuum of variation that exists between higher-class (acrolectal) and lower-class (basilectal) dialects of Guyanese Creole. I also agree with him that there are interesting psychological questions that can be raised in relation to a speaker's competence in one or other variety in this continuum and the speaker's own sense of linguistic identity. However, I do not believe that the simple point that I was making in my paper is affected by the existence of phenomena of this kind. Confronted with, say, two people speaking Standard English and two people speaking Standard French, we can readily decide which of the two languages each of the four is speaking. My point is no more subtle, I am afraid, than this. But I would now take the opportunity of emphasizing, as I have done elsewhere (e.g., Lyons, 1977a: 585–588), the fact that a linguist's description of any language-system necessarily involves a considerable measure of idealization" (Lyons, 1981c: 222). This reply was perhaps adequate in the context in which it was given, but the point made about idealization in the final sentence clearly requires the kind of further development that it receives in Lyons (1977a).

5 My use of the term 'behaviour' at this point was perhaps dated and misleading. It would have been preferable to say 'activity' and to make it clear that language-activity is both mental and physical. For the ambiguity of 'utterance', which can refer to either language-behaviour or products of that behaviour, and for other distinctions that can, and at times must, be drawn among subsenses of the two principal senses alluded to here, see Lyons (1977a, 1981b).

6 For 'inscription', which has been used in this sense by Carnap and other logicians and formal semanticists, but is here being generalized to cover both written and spoken language, see Lyons (1981b: 25–26). For the terminological distinction of 'type' and 'token' as it is being applied here see Lyons (1977a: 13–18). This distinction, which originates with Charles Sanders Peirce, though commonly drawn nowadays by semioticians and philosophers of language, is all too often confused with other distinctions.

7 I am here drawing a distinction (between expressions and forms) which is not commonly drawn in these terms. The distinction itself, however, is traditional enough; and it was formalized, for lexically simple expressions, in the standard theory of generative grammar in the definition of (what I would call) the lexeme, as a triple comprising three strings or sets of phonological, syntactic and semantic features (Chomsky, 1965). But the notion of 'expression', as it is being used here, is intended to be more general, in that it allows for the possibility that an expression may have several unrelated forms (no one of which is necessarily to be taken as basic): see Lyons (1977a: 24).

8 For the other sense of 'modality', see Lyons (1977a), F. R. Palmer (1986).

9 There has been a good deal of discussion recently of the importance of literacy in the codification and objectivization of thought, in the development of science and logic and in the promotion of the notion of literal meaning: cf. Goody (1968, 1983, 1986), Coulmas & Ehlich (1983). I have much sympathy for the view that most linguists (with some very notable exceptions: e.g., Vachek, 1945/9, 1973; McIntosh, 1956, 1961a; Haas, 1970, 1976b) have tended until recently to underrate the significance of writing; and it is good to see that a more balanced view is now emerging, though it is still far from being shared by all or even the majority (cf. R. Harris, 1983b). There are several dimensions of the relation between speech and writing that are neglected in the present chapter (see Addendum).

10 For a recent account of various writing systems, from a genuinely linguistic point of view, see Sampson (1985).

11 For an experimental demonstration of this truism see Householder (1962b).

12 After the Meeting at which the original version of this paper was delivered, Professor E. A. Ullendorff drew my attention to the Masoretic Hebrew writing system, which provided its users with the means of accurately representing or transcribing the prosodic features of utterances. This is well described, from a

point of view that is very similar to the one motivating the present article, by Aronoff (1985). Reference might also be made to the Sanscrit tradition (cf. Selkirk, 1980), and perhaps also to the notation used for Gregorian chant and its original connexion with the representation of the prosodic features of spoken language. Although the existence of such specialized notation systems leads to some qualification of the statement made in the text, it does not invalidate the general point that is being made there. It is perhaps worth adding that the universality of the distinction between the segmental and the non-segmental, as it is drawn here, is questionable on both phonetic and phonological grounds. The so-called London School of phonologists and phoneticians has been making this point for at least forty years, and it is now coming to be more widely accepted (see Chapter 6). For simplicity, I have here adopted what has been until recently the conventional wisdom.

13 Actually the consensus among linguists is by no means as complete as I here imply. On the one hand, there are those who, in practice if not always in principle, exclude the prosodic from the language itself; on the other, there are scholars who would argue that not only the prosodic, but much of what is here referred to as paralinguistic, is part of the language-system (for some discussion of the relevant considerations, cf. Lyons, 1977a: 63ff.).

14 Once again, qualification is required. First of all, it must be made clear in what sense 'word' is being used here: 'word-form' or 'lexeme'. If the latter, the statement in the text is either false or meaningless. If the former, it must be pointed out that the distinction between words and non-words (in this sense) is not always clear-cut and that, in many languages, there are examples of what used to be called discontinuous constituents.

15 It has often been suggested that the grammaticalization of word-order, in those languages in which it is grammaticalized, results from the conventionalization of pragmatic or rhetorical principles having to do with what Prague School linguists call functional sentence perspective (FSP). It may also be the case that relatively fixed word-order in particular languages has developed as a consequence of literacy and the greater use of the written language. It has been fashionable for some time now in linguistics to play down the influence of the written language upon the spoken, but there seems no reason to deny this, at least as a possibility.

16 'Sentence' is being used here in the sense of 'system-sentence', not 'text-sentence' (cf. Lyons, 1977a: 29; 1981b: 196). Text-sentences are of course one class of utterance-inscriptions and, as such, are the product of linearization.

17 There was some discussion of this question at the Meeting at which the original version of this paper was delivered (Allport & Funnell, 1981; see also D. A. Allport, 1983). For a general, non-technical, introduction to relevant recent psycholinguistic and neurolinguistic research see Aitchison (1987).

18 The term 'cenematic' is typically Glossematic (cf. Hjelmslev, 1943a; H. J. Uldall, 1957), and contrasts with 'plerematic'; but the same terminology was used in

roughly the same sense by Hockett (1958: 575). The opposition between the cenematic ("[semantically] empty") and the plethematic ("[semantically] full") levels corresponds with Martinet's opposition between the secondary and the primary articulation of language (cf. 1960: 16–17 = 1964: 22–24).

19 Sampson comments, rightly, that spoken language is "paradoxically ... not necessarily spoken" (1985: 27). Otto (1983), in similar vein, draws attention to the need to distinguish between 'writing', 'written speech' and (various senses of) 'written language': in one of its senses, as it is currently used by linguists, 'written language' may be taken to mean "the language that is appropriate for written utterances".

20 Some of the issues that come up under these several heads are discussed, from various points of view, in Coulmas & Ehlich (1983).

21 It cannot be emphasized too strongly, however, that despite its overt commitment to a phonocentric view of language, twentieth-century linguistics has also been strongly influenced, both in theory and in practice, by other attitudes towards language which derive from traditional grammar's almost exclusive concern with written (and, moreover, literary) languages (cf. Aronoff, 1985).

2 In defence of (so-called) autonomous linguistics

1 This chapter is based on an unpublished paper with the same title that I gave to the joint Linguistics and Anthropology Seminar at the University of Sussex on 24 November 1982. I am grateful to the participants for the comments that they made on that occasion (and at other meetings of the Seminar, of which we were all, as colleagues, more or less regular attenders for, in my case, over two years): I am especially conscious of my indebtedness in this respect to Richard Coates, Margaret Deuchar, Ralph Grillo, James McGivney, Ulrike Meinhof, Trevor Pateman, Carol Sanders and Brian Street. I had been asked to lead a discussion on this topic because at previous meetings of the Seminar I had frequently found myself defending a point of view about language and linguistics which was rejected by most other participants (especially but not only the anthropologists). As I noted in my opening remarks (not reprinted in the present version), it was something of a new experience for me to find myself defending what most of my audience judged to be an excessively narrow view of linguistics. Some idea of points of view expressed by others of the participants which I was challenging may be obtained from Deuchar (1987a, b), Grillo et al. (1987), Pateman (1987b), though none of their articles, unlike the present work, derives directly from one of the Seminar presentations. The present chapter can also be seen as an expansion of the brief comments made in Lyons (1987b: 4–5).

2 This is a common, but misleading, translation of the French original, in that it uses the word 'language' as a mass noun for the Saussurean phrase 'la langue' (see Chapter 3). In the 1987 revision I substituted the more technical phrase 'the

language-system'. The importance of this point will be made clear in the present chapter (and also in Chapters 3 and 4).

3 I say "post-Saussurean" because the cluster of ideas that are to be found in the *Cours* were taken up and developed in different ways by the various schools of European structuralism in the post-Saussurean period (during, let us say, the quarter-century following the First International Congress of Linguists, in 1928). As will be evident from Lyons (1968a) and other publications, my own version of structuralism is rather eclectic, but, in its interpretation of what it takes to be the central tenets of (post-)Saussurean structuralism, it owes much to Hjelmslev (1943a, 1959), moderated, however, by the criticisms of Bazell (1952, 1953). Bazell's work is not always easy to read without a very considerable background in linguistics and, regrettably, has never been as well known to the generality of linguists as it ought to have been. But I have also been greatly influenced by other schools of structuralism, both European and American.

4 The terms 'microlinguistics' and 'macrolinguistics' have been used in various senses, and they are not widely used at all these days. They derive ultimately from Trager (1949), who was, at the time, one of the most influential proponents of a (now outdated) version of non-Saussurean, American, structuralism, which also saw itself as autonomous. In my usage, microlinguistics takes a narrower view of language and macrolinguistics a broader view:

> at its narrowest microlinguistics is concerned solely with the structure of language-systems, without regard to the way in which languages are acquired, stored in the brain or used in their various functions; without regard to the interdependence of language and culture; without regard to the physiological and psychological mechanisms that are involved in language-behaviour; in short, without regard to anything other than the language-system, considered (as Saussure, or rather his editors, put it) in itself and for itself. At its broadest, macrolinguistics is concerned with everything that pertains in any way at all to language and languages. Since many disciplines other than linguistics are concerned with language, it is not surprising that several interdisciplinary areas should have been identified within macro-linguistics and given a distinctive name: sociolinguistics, psycholinguistics, ethnolinguistics, stylistics, etc. (Lyons, 1981a: 36).

5 It is also possible to think of descriptive linguistics (i.e., the description of particular languages) as first-degree applied linguistics and of some parts of what is normally called applied linguistics as second-degree applied linguistics. This is the point of view I adopted in Lyons (1965a): see the Appendix.

6 It is because Chomsky is concerned directly with (idealized) native speaker–hearers' knowledge of their language (as reflected in their intuitions about it) that I have said that he is engaged in psycholinguistics rather than

microlinguistics. At the same time it must be recognized, as I mention below, that, since Chomsky does not pay much attention to current psychological theories or to what psychologists would normally regard as primary psychological data, Chomsky's theoretical psycholinguistics is not very different, in practice, from theoretical microlinguistics.

7 Much of the earlier discussion of such famous examples of so-called ambiguous sentences (or rather, ambiguous so-called sentences) as *Flying planes can be dangerous* (which supported the introduction of transformational rules, more powerful than, and formally more heterogeneous and less constrained than, phrase-structure rules) was confused, if not vitiated, by the definition of the sentence as a string of forms, (i.e., as having, necessarily, the property of linearity: cf. Lyons, 1968a: 209). It should have been more obvious than it was to Chomsky and his expositors (including, at the time, Lyons, 1968a: 249ff.): first, that the utterance-inscription *Flying planes can be dangerous* (considered as a type or set of tokens) could, and should, be derived from, or put into correspondence with, two (or more) distinct sentences of quite different structure; and, second, that, even on Chomsky's definition of the sentence, the ambiguity in question can be formalized, without difficulty and using traditional categories, within the framework of (context-free) phrase-structure grammar. But none of this, I repeat, affects the points at issue here. (For further, more technical, comments on linearity and duality of structure see Chapter 4, especially note 7, below.)

8 I accept that Popper's by now well-known criticisms of the empiricist's distinction between observational and theoretical terms are well founded (Popper, 1963). I also accept that, in a very loose sense of 'theory', all observation can be described as theory-laden. I do not accept, however, that, in a stricter sense of 'theory', there is no useful distinction to be drawn between baby and bathwater: between the pre-theoretical and the theoretical vocabulary of science. The pre-theoretical vocabulary of linguistics is not, of course, solely or even primarily observational: it includes many metalinguistic terms ('word', 'sentence', 'meaning', etc.) whose everyday use and interpretation are governed by more or less untutored and unreflecting intuition; and many of these may well be explicable by relating them, historically, to past theories of language in which they operated as theoretical, rather than pre-theoretical, terms. All this is true enough. But it does not affect the point being made here (see Lyons, 1990a).

9 Traditional descriptions of languages that we find in conventional reference grammars and dictionaries can also be seen as models – albeit unformalized, selective and often internally inconsistent and self-contradictory – of the necessarily idealized language-systems underlying the utterances, written or spoken, of particular language-communities. But the main point that I am making here, which will be further developed in Chapter 3, is that it is not only (so-called) autonomous linguistics that operates with a concept of the language-system.

10 Pateman (1983) argues the contrary view; and he does so, unusually, on the basis of a proper understanding both of linguistics and of the philosophy of science.

3 Linguistic theory and theoretical linguistics

1 This chapter is based on Lyons (1988). In order to adapt it to its present purpose and to relate it more satisfactorily to the preceding and immediately following chapters, I have, however, made numerous small changes throughout; I have also excised the final section (on the relation between theoretical linguistics and theoretical semiotics), and I have substituted for it several additional paragraphs on 'langue' and 'parole'.

2 Mention may be usefully be made, at this point, of the recently published four-volume *Cambridge Survey* of linguistics (Newmeyer, 1988). Two of the volumes bear the title *Linguistic Theory* and are subtitled, respectively, *Foundations* and *Extensions and Implications*; the other two are entitled *Language* and are subtitled, respectively, *Psychological and Biological Aspects* and *The Socio-Cultural Context*. In effect, the term 'linguistic theory' is restricted to what I am calling microlinguistics (except that phonetic theory is also seen as foundational to linguistic theory). I cannot see any good reason for this restriction, but it undoubtedly reflects the way many linguists think of the subject.

3 I have said nothing in this chapter about the distinction between theoretical and applied linguistics: for some comments which take as their starting point the account that I have given here of theoretical linguistics and linguistic theory, see Lyons, 1990a.

4 For example, Chomsky has argued strongly – and, within the limits of the argument, it has to be admitted cogently – against the view that what I am calling N-languages are primarily or essentially communicative (1975b: 61). The question is partly definitional. Let us grant that N-languages are a proper subclass of languages and that languages are a subclass (whether proper or improper) of semiotic systems (see Chapter 4). This leaves open the much-debated question whether semiotics is more appropriately defined as the science of communication or the science of signs. (It also leaves open the question whether communication, in contrast with signalling, involves intention: see Lyons, 1977a: 32ff.) It must now be conceded (i) that N-languages are currently and commonly used not only for communication (however we define it), but also for all sorts of non-communicative purposes and (ii) that communication of propositional information (and perhaps also of some kinds of non-propositional information) presupposes signification (or symbolic representation), but not conversely. It is none the less reasonable to take the view (as most linguists have done until recently) that N-languages (if not all languages, and in particular the non-natural languages of logicians and computer scientists: see Chapter 4) are, of their essence, systems of communication. This does not necessarily imply (and

has not generally been taken to imply) either (i) that every N-language-utterance is communicative (or even that most N-language-utterances are) or (ii) that the whole (or even most) of their phonological, grammatical and lexical structure is determined by their use for communication. What it implies, as I at least understand the issues, is that N-languages have been formed (i.e., have acquired the structural properties that they have), over the millennia of their existence and differentiation, and are continually transformed or maintained (as language-systems), by their use, typically, in face-to-face communicative situations. Much of the deictic and modal structure of most N-languages is otherwise inexplicable. So too is the intimate association of social or interpersonal (socio-expressive and instrumental) meaning with propositional (or representational) meaning in both grammar and vocabulary. It may be added that even soliloquy, vocal and subvocal, is typically dialogic. It is for such reasons that I have maintained elsewhere that, "if there is one sense in which certain aspects of the structure of N-languages depends upon communication, there is another in which communication ... presupposes signification (or representation)"; and that "it is for theoretical semiotics to define the two notions, without generalizing either of them to the point of vacuity and without particularizing them to the point that the term 'semiotic system' is made to be synonymous with 'language-system' (Lyons, 1988). Much recent discussion of the relation between language and communication by linguists, philosophers and semioticians has been vitiated, in my view, by the failure to define clearly both 'language' and 'communication'.

5 This point and related points made below are readily verified by consulting some of the published translations of Lyons (1970a). For example, the Italian version has: "che lingue particolari ... sono esempi specifici di qualche cosa di più generale, che si può propriamente definire, al singolare, 'linguaggio'". And the Spanish translators of the passage comment explicitly, and in the context of the present discussion relevantly, on the problem resulting from my use of the English word 'language' in what (in terms of Spanish) seem to be (at least) two different senses (cf. Lyons, (1975b).

6 I am thinking particularly of Wade Baskin's (1960) translation. But, from this point of view, there are also problems at times with Roy Harris's (1972) translation; and his comments on the distinction between 'langue' and 'langage' in everyday, non-technical, French and in the text of the *Cours* do not seem to me to do full justice to the issue. Rey-Debove (1979: 87) distinguishes (1) a stricter, or narrower, and (2) a broader, metaphorical, sense of 'langage', and says of 'langage' in sense (2) that "sa legitimité est controversée", because some systems to which it is applied ("systèmes d'expression et de communication ... dont l'étude relève de la sémiotique") lack the two defining properties of duality of structure and arbitrariness ("une double articulation et l'arbitraire du signe"). This strikes me as being very much a theoretical (post-Saussurean) reinterpretation of the word 'langage', and one which, despite its obvious origins in Saussurean structuralism, blurs the historic Saussurean distinction between

'langage' and 'langue'. Whether the use of 'langage' in sense (2) in such phrases as 'le langage des abeilles' is, from a synchronic point of view, metaphorical or not is debatable. Benveniste, a leading figure in the so-called French School of post-Saussurean structuralism, restricts not only 'langue' but 'langage' to human languages, saying that it is an "abus de termes" to apply 'langage' to "le monde animal" (1966: 87). In ordinary everyday French it is very common (cf. Lyons, 1984: 57). What is not sufficiently appreciated is that there are several different dimensions of the difference between 'langue' and 'langage', which I have associated with the global difference between a more specific and a more general meaning. There is no doubt of course that our understanding of 'langage' is, in any case, determined by our understanding of 'langue'. This is reflected in the theoretical use that I have made of the distinction in my explicit adoption of the principle of the centrality of N-languages (see Chapter 4).

7 Saussure himself comments on the fact that 'Sprache' means both "langue" and "langage", with 'Rede' being roughly equivalent to 'parole'; and says that the Latin 'sermo' means both "parole" and "langage" and that Latin 'lingua' means "langue", but goes on to note that "Aucun mot ne correspond exactement à l'une des notions precisées plus haut" (1916: 31). Actually, Saussure's comments at this point have probably obscured, rather than clarified, the theoretically exploitable differences between the words in question: see below.

8 Roy Harris is quite right to warn us that "'What is a language?' is not quite the impartial, culture-neutral question that it might be taken for at first sight" (1980:21). He might have added that it depends for its formulation upon the grammaticalization or lexicalization of particular semantic distinctions in the language in which it is formulated. And our appreciation that this is so is sharpened by the demonstrable fact that the obvious difference (at a pre-theoretical level of understanding) between "What is language?" and "What is a language?" is not so readily expressed in some quite familiar languages. But the fact that our everyday metalinguistic vocabulary is to some degree culture-dependent does not mean that it cannot be explicated and refined for scientific purposes, as have such terms as 'force' or 'energy'. And he is wrong, in my view, to suggest that "the question 'What is a language?' must take precedence over the question 'What is language?'" (1980: 29). Everything turns, of course, on the one hand, on what is meant by 'precedence' and, on the other, on what is being referred to by the indefinite noun-phrase 'language'. There are several different ways of interpreting 'What is a language?'

9 It is in this respect, if I may judge from the published translations of Lyons (1970a), that Italian and Portuguese differ from French: they can use 'lingua' not only for N-languages, but also for both non-natural and non-human languages in the case of Italian, e.g., 'lingue artificiali' and 'la lingua delle api', or for non-natural languages in the case of Portuguese, e.g., 'linguas artificiais', but 'a lenguagem das abelhas'. Spanish, on the other hand, seems to be like French: 'lenguajes artificiales' and 'el lenguaje de las abejas'.

10 This point is made by Nencioni (1983: 11). But, having defined linguistics as "lo

studio scientifica della lingua" (rather than "del linguaggio"), he then glosses the generic interpretation as "la facoltà di linguaggio, il linguaggio": this is surely to confuse the issue. It is his third "singolare-pro-plurali" interpretation ("le lingue, tutte del globo, morte et viventi") which, in my view, comes closer to the true generic interpretation (but a true generic can never be explicated in terms of universal quantification, and, as I argue in Chapter 4, linguistics should in any case cast its net wider than actual and attested N-languages).

11 This is not to say that theoretical general linguistics (in contrast with general linguistic theory) was anything like as sophisticated as it has now become.

12 Baker & Hacker (1984: 268) refer unsympathetically, but with perhaps some justification, to what they call Saussure's "wild confusions" on the langue–parole issue. But I am not sure that their own account of the matter is especially helpful. There is by now, of course, an enormous body of criticism and exegesis. My own views, as I have emphasized at several points, in this chapter and elsewhere, have been strongly influenced by Hjelmslev.

13 Post-Saussurean structuralists writing in French, following Benveniste (1966, 1974), nowadays tend to use 'énonciation' and 'énoncé' instead of 'parole'. These are best translated by the English word 'utterance', but have the advantage over their English equivalent that they distinguish between process and product. (The Chomskyan term 'performance', like the Bloomfieldian and post-Bloomfieldian term 'behaviour', has the disadvantage that it denotes the process, not the product.)

4 Natural, non-natural and unnatural languages: English, Urdu and other abstractions

1 This chapter is based on a previously unpublished paper that was first read, with a slightly different title and in a much shorter form, at the School of Epistemics in the University of Edinburgh on 26 May 1983, and subsequently, later in the same year, at the Graduate Linguistics Seminar at the University of Sussex, and, on 16 May 1985, at the Linguistic Society in the University of Cambridge. I am grateful to all those – too numerous to mention here individually – whose contribution to the discussion of the paper on these three occasions has influenced the final version.

2 At the time, I had recently started my Ph.D. research (in semantics: cf. Lyons, 1960) with Professor Allen as my supervisor: I had a degree in classics and an undergraduate training in conventional comparative philology, but little knowledge of modern linguistics except for some areas of semantics, on the one hand, and post-Bloomfieldian distributionalism (cf. Z. S. Harris, 1951, 1954), on the other, which (*mirabile dictu*) I was trying to synthesize with what I had so far read of the ideas of J. R. Firth and his followers. It was very shortly afterwards in the summer of 1957, that Allen passed on to me a copy of Chomsky (1957). The immediate effect was that I abandoned the distributional discovery procedures

with which I had been operating and adapted to my purpose the (early) Chomskyan notion of kernel strings (or syntagms) and transformations, but otherwise saw no reason to change what I was doing or to modify my essentially Saussurean view of the (microlinguistic) language-system.

3 For Allen's own retrospective comments, see his (1965) Note and (1971) Foreword in the reprinted versions of (1957b) which appear in Strevens (1966b) and Allen & Corder (1973) respectively.

4 Katz (1985) makes very odd use of the traditional terms 'nominalism', 'conceptualism' and 'realism' in his classification of the various approaches to what he calls the ontological issue. It is perhaps reasonable to group Zellig Harris and Quine together as nominalists, but Bloomfield, though a physicalist or anti-idealist, is surely a realist. So too, though in Katz's terminology a conceptualist, is Chomsky. The editorial Introduction and the chronological-cum-thematic ordering of the eleven papers (all but one of which, Hjelmslev's, are American) strongly suggest that Chomskyan conceptualism, which replaced Bloomfieldian so-called nominalism in the 1960s, is now to be ousted by Katzian realism. It is good to see Hjelmslev's (1947) paper included in the selection (though nothing is said about its content, and there is a very unfortunate misprint on p. 171, where content and expression are said to be "bound up with each other through communication", rather than "through commutation"), but, to the best of my knowledge, Glossematic theory had no discernible influence on the historical development of what Katz calls "Platonist grammar". What is required is a multidimensional classificatory-scheme in which, at the very least, nominalism can be distinguished from physicalism, and realism from idealism. A much better idea of the range of options, coupled with references to a wider and more representative range of relevant work both in linguistics and in the philosophy of linguistics, may be obtained from Pateman (1987a, b).

5 Now that Popper's point about the impossibility of absolutely impartial and theoretically unprejudiced observation has been generally accepted, it no longer needs to be exaggerated. It makes good sense to draw a distinction between a pre-theoretical and a theoretical account of the phenomena; and 'pre-theoretical' is not necessarily synonymous with 'observational' as this term was understood by empiricist philosophers of science.

6 I am here using the term 'morpheme' in its earlier Bloomfieldian sense (to refer to what some linguists later distinguished as morphs, rather than morphemes, cf. Lyons, 1968a: 183ff.). If the morpheme is defined as the minimal unit of grammatical analysis without reference to word-forms or segmentability, it cannot be usefully employed, as I am employing it here, to define a typological subclass of languages.

7 It is in any case important to define duality independently of whether the minimal units of the expression plane are correlated with a particular meaning or not. (This means of couse that the Glossematic definition of a language is too restrictive, in that it makes it a defining condition that the cenemes should

themselves have no content and should be components of higher-level units that do have content.) Incidentally, it is incorrect to say of N-languages that the substitution of one phoneme for another has the effect of changing meaning in the word or utterance in which the substitution is carried out. The substitution of one phoneme for another has the effect (generally) of changing one form into another, and the forms in question may, always in principle and not infrequently in practice, either have no meaning at all (in some contexts) or be synonymous. There has been a good deal of confusion on this point in the phonological literature.

8 The term 'non-prosodic' (vs. 'prosodic') is here being employed in a different sense from the sense in which it is employed in Lyons (1962a; see Chapter 6 below): it covers such phenomena as intonation and stress, which (arguably) are non-segmental even in phonemic N-languages and are less readily characterizable in terms of the properties of arbitrariness, duality and medium-transferability. For these and other reasons (including the fact that their meaning is different from the meaning of words), the prosodic component of N-language-utterances may be regarded as being less typical and distinctive of N-languages than is their verbal component.

9 I am not sure about this, however, because: (i) as we shall see, my principles (A) and (B) can be construed as allowing the construction of (non-natural) languages which would not satisfy Hjelmslev's criteria in respect of duality and arbitrariness; and (ii) Hjelmslev's views on what he calls commutation and the analysability of units of the content-plane (the meanings of words) into pleremes are, to say the least, controversial.

10 This may well have been the view, at one time, of philosophers such as Russell and Carnap, as it quite clearly was that of the so-called generative semanticists of the 1970s. J. A. Fodor's (1975, 1981) view may also be mentioned at this point (without however associating what he calls the language of thought with a first-order logical language structurally comparable with simple predicate-calculus).

11 Chomsky (1980a, 1981, 1986) now takes the view that what I am calling N-languages (English, Urdu, etc.) are ill-defined (and undefinable) social and political constructs and that it is grammars, rather than languages, that are the proper concern of linguistics. Granted the validity of the substantive point that he is making (which has long been familiar to sociolinguists and dialectologists), I see no reason why one should not continue, none the less, to identify the individual's linguistic competence with knowledge of a particular language (for example, English rather than Urdu or Turkish). No two idiolects are structurally identical (and cannot even be assumed to be of determinate structure and constant over time); it is impossible to define a dialect, on purely (micro-) linguistic criteria, as a set of (intersecting) idiolects or a language as a set of (intersecting) dialects; and what counts as the same language or the same dialect in ordinary everyday life is indeed determined, as Chomsky says, primarily by social, cultural and political considerations. All this is true enough.

But to my mind it merely supports the argument that I have been advancing for the validity of different definitions of the language-system for different purposes.

5 The origin of language, speech and languages

1 This chapter is a considerably revised and modified version of Lyons (1987a), based on one of the Darwin Lectures for 1986 (on the general theme of 'Origins'), sponsored by Darwin College Cambridge. This accounts for the initial and subsequent references to Darwin and Darwinism (though I have removed many of these from the present version, as I have removed much that was more appropriate to an oral presentation to a large audience of non-linguists). As will be evident from the text itself, my principal concern, especially in this version of the paper, is to discuss the question of the origin of speech and language from the point of view of general linguistic theory, rather than as an issue for immediate empirical determination.

2 "La Société n'admet aucune communication concernant, soit l'origine du langage, soit la création d'une langue universelle." Speculation about the origin of language, on the one hand, and the elaboration of schemes for the establishment of a universal language, on the other, had dominated philosophical discussion in the eighteenth and early nineteenth centuries (cf. Robins, 1979: 149–153, 121).

3 Facsimile editions of the English translations of two of the works that attracted Whitney's scornful attention, Schleicher (1863) and Bleek (1867), together with Whitney's review of the latter (under the title 'Dr. Bleek and the simious theory of language'), have recently been published with a sympathetic editorial Introduction and a useful selective bibliography on linguistics and evolution theory (Koerner, 1983). Whitney is blamed therein, perhaps rightly, for propagating the now standard, but erroneous, view that Schleicher's evolutionism was from the outset specifically Darwinian.

4 For some comments on this issue, see Lyons 1989a.

5 Haeckel was one of Darwin's earliest and most influential supporters in Germany. His dictum, expressing what he saw as a fundamental biogenetic law operating in association with Darwin's principle of natural selection, was first formulated at almost exactly the same time as the Linguistic Society ban (cf. Haeckel, 1867); and it is worth noting that he was closely connected with both Schleicher and Bleek, introducing both of them to the *Origin of Species* (1859) and contributing a preface to the latter's (1867) pamphlet (see note 3).

6 In the present state of research, it is, I think premature to describe this as a fact, rather than a hypothesis. I am not denying, however, that it is a perfectly respectable scientific hypothesis.

7 Much of what follows is based on Lyons (1977a: 85–94), but it has been restructured, updated and, in parts, abbreviated or expanded, as its present

context requires. For recent work on the acquisition of language and speech, see Fletcher & Garman (1986), Ingram (1989).

8 Broca was an idle admirer of Darwin's *Origin of Species* (cf. Koerner, 1983: xii).

9 Striking confirmation of the validity of the point being made here is provided by the conclusions that Sperber & Wilson (1986: 173–174) draw from their definition of a language, in "the broadest sense", as "a set of well-formed formulas, a set of permissible combinations of items from a vocabulary, generated by a grammar" and, in "a narrower sense", as "a set of semantically interpreted well-formed formulas ... a grammar-governed representational system". Actually, it is doubtful whether natural languages (as distinct from linguists', logicians' and cognitive scientists' models of them) satisfy either the broader or the narrower definition: it is arguable that, unlike the formal languages of logicians and computer scientists, they are not fully determinate, as far as their grammatical structure is concerned, and that the meaning they encode is not wholly representational. This is a point that I have been emphasizing in several of the preceding chapters. But what is interesting in the present context is the role that one arbitrarily adopted definition, rather than another, plays in the argument.

10 This last point would have commended itself to Darwin, as would perhaps also my emphasis on the multi-strandedness of language and on the integration of the expressive and non-expressive, and of the non-verbal and the verbal. This is something to which he himself drew attention, though he did not develop the point in the detail in which it is now possible to develop it, in his *The Expression of the Emotions in Man and Animals* (1872: 354). What he said about the origin or origins of expressive behaviour might also be held to apply, *a fortiori*, to the more distinctively linguistic, non-expressive, part of language: "it is a curious, though perhaps an idle speculation, how early in the long line of our progenitors the various expressive movements, now exhibited by man, were successively acquired" (1872: 368). Incidentally, it was Darwin's view that there were four factors critical for the evolution of hominids: (i) increasing brain-size, (ii) bipedalism, (iii) tool-use, (iv) canine reduction; and that it was the first of these, increased brain-size, that was responsible for the development of more complex social behaviour and language (cf. Wolpoff, 1980). It is interesting to note that current speculation about the evolution of language and speech invokes all four factors, including (though less commonly and without attributing to it the same importance) changes of dentition; and, as we have seen, more emphasis nowadays is put on the structure, rather than simply the size, of the brain.

6 Phonemic and non-phonemic phonology: some typological reflections

1 The present version of this paper is identical with the original upon which it is based (Lyons, 1962a), except for most of the notes and the Epilogue: see note 22. Apart from three or four reviews, it was my first publication. It is the only article

that I have ever written on phonology. And I would never have thought of publishing it, if I had not been encouraged to do so by Professor C. F. Voegelin, editor of the *International Journal of American Linguistics* and, with Professor F. W. Householder, organizer of the series of Ethnolinguistics Seminars, at Indiana University, at which it was presented (to a largely bemused audience) in March 1961. I had been surprised to discover, during the academic year that I spent at Indiana (1960–1961), that the well-founded criticisms of standard post-Bloomfieldian phonemics by representatives of the so-called London School (as it came to be called) were almost unknown and were ignored in teaching. My presentation of the original paper was therefore very much an act of contrition: I had thought that the kind of phonology that I had heard attacked so often by my London colleagues had been by then thoroughly discredited; and, having learned that it was still being taught and practised, I felt obliged to make amends and to do my missionary duty by making their views better known *in partibus infidelium*. (For further comments on the historical context see the Epilogue and later notes).

2 Joos's (1957) *Readings* is still the most comprehensive and the most representative anthology of (post-)Bloomfieldian writings. His editorial comments were characteristically forthright, but they did express an attitude that was widespread among adherents of what is generally, and rightly, regarded as the dominant school of American linguistics in the immediately preceding period.

3 Oral tradition has it that, when Bernard Bloch was told by Firth, in the 1950s, that the phoneme was dead, he replied: "Well, it's got a pretty lively ghost." The story is perhaps apocryphal, but it was certainly my impression when I first went to the United States in 1960 (and, having by then spent three years at the School of Oriental and African Studies, I was surprised to find that this was the case) that what Chomsky was shortly thereafter to call the taxonomic, post-Bloomfieldian, phoneme was indeed alive and still flourishing.

4 It is perhaps worth emphasizing that the term 'phoneme' is used throughout this paper to refer exclusively to segmental, in contrast with suprasegmental, phonemes; and moreover to phonemes defined as they were in what we have learned to call post-Bloomfieldian linguistics. In footnote 3 of the original version of this paper, I commented (Lyons, 1962a: 230): "It is in any case doubtful whether the extension of the term 'phoneme' to include phonologically distinct degrees of stress, tone and quantity is justifiable: for it tends to obscure the important distinction between paradigmatic opposition and syntagmatic contrast"; and I referred to Jakobson & Halle (1956: 25–26) for the terminological, and theoretical, contrast that they drew (in the Prague School tradition) between inherent (segmental) and prosodic (suprasegmental) features. This use of 'prosodic' is of course related to, though not identical with, that of the London School; and what Jakobson & Halle (1956) called prosodic phenomena would normally be handled by London School prosodies in the description of particular languages. There are, in fact, many points of similarity between Prague School

phonology (and generative phonology which developed out of it) and London School phonology. They are not mentioned in the present article (see the Epilogue). The major difference, as far as the analysis of consonantal and vocalic phenomena is concerned, is that what prosodic analysis treats as a single suprasegmental feature, distinctive-feature analysis, whether generative or non-generative, treats as a succession of segmental features, comparable in this respect with Z. S. Harris's (1944) long components (see below).

5 Most of the linguists practising this kind of analysis were at one time colleagues of J. R. Firth in the Department of Phonetics and Linguistics at the School of Oriental and African Studies (SOAS) in London (see F. R. Palmer, 1970b: ix; note 1 above). Hence the more or less equivalent terms 'Firthian linguistics' and 'the London School'. It is generally recognized that prosodic analysis, together with a particular view of meaning (with which for Firth at least it was integrated, in a comprehensive theory of language-structure, by means of his notion of function in context: see Epilogue), was one of the most distinctive and most original components of London School linguistics. And it is perhaps only fair to add that, although Firth's 'Sounds and prosodies' (1948c) is usually cited as the primary source of prosodic analysis, not only most of the exemplification, but also much of the theory is to be found in the works of his pupils and associates, published for the most part in *Transactions of the Philological Society*, the *Bulletin of the School of Oriental and African Studies* and *Studies in Linguistic Analysis* (1957): see note 6. In his chapter entitled 'J. R. Firth and the London School of prosodic analysis', Stephen Anderson remarks, in respect of Firth's seminal 'Sounds and prosodies', "it would perhaps be difficult for the modern reader to see how this could be regarded as establishing a coherent program of research without the benefit of subsequent exegesis" (1985, 185). This is a fair comment. Indeed, it can be seen as applying to most of Firth's work.

6 The bibliography referred to here, which was appended to the original version of this paper, has been omitted (as it was also omitted from the versions reprinted in Fudge, 1973, and Jones & Laver, 1973). The works in question have been included instead in the Bibliography at the end of this volume: W. S. Allen (1950, 1951a, b, 1953, 1954, 1956, 1957a); Carnochan (1951, 1952, 1957); Firth (1948a, c, 1951b, 1957b); Henderson (1949, 1951, 1952); Mitchell (1953, 1957a); F. R. Palmer (1955a, b, 1957a, b); Robins (1952a, 1953a, b, 1957a); Scott (1956); Sharp (1954); Sprigg (1954, 1955, 1957); Waterson (1956). Several of these have now been republished, as have other works of the period exemplifying prosodic analysis, in F. R. Palmer (1970a). Presumably, Robins (1957b) was either not known to me or simply inaccessible when I wrote the original version of this paper: there can have been no other reason for not referring to it; and if I had had it in front of me at the time, my presentation of prosodic analysis might have been less idiosyncratic. F. R. Palmer (1970b) was not published, of course, until several years later, by which time the London School had lost much of its earlier homogeneity, and post-Bloomfieldian

phonemics was under siege in its own homeland. The most important of Firth's own earlier articles are to be found in Firth (1957a). A further, posthumously published collection, which includes the 'Synopsis' (1957b), one of the main primary sources for my own understanding of Firth's general theory at the time that the present paper was written, is Firth (1968a).

7 This approach to the typological classification of languages owed much to Bazell (1958), which was interestingly different on the one hand from Hjelmslev's (1943a) and on the other from Joseph H. Greenberg's (1954). C. E. Bazell was Firth's successor as Professor of General Linguistics (and for a time Head of Department) at SOAS (cf. Kempson, 1985). He would nevertheless not have regarded himself, or have been regarded, as a member of the London School. He was very different in personality from Firth; and his views on linguistics were very different from Firth's, being much closer to those of European post-Saussurean structuralism. It was from Bazell, by attendance at his lectures and in discussion with him, that I learned something of Prague School thinking, on the one hand, and of Glossematics, on the other. (I was already familiar with Saussure.) Bazell was also one of the first linguists in Britain to grasp the significance of Chomsky's *Syntactic Structures* (1957) – which I had read, in the summer of 1957, and which he invited me to review for the journal he edited (cf. Lyons, 1958) – and was already, in the autumn of 1957, engaged in correspondence with Chomsky about it. It is regrettable that Bazell did not publish more or, it must be admitted, in what he did write (often in relatively inaccessible journals), make more concessions to his readers, few of whom had as comprehensive a knowledge of all branches of linguistics, traditional and modern, or as good a mastery, practical and theoretical, of languages as he had. (Several of Bazell's otherwise more or less inaccessible articles can be found in Hamp *et al.*, 1966.)

8 In the original version I commented (footnote 7): "The practical advantages of phonemic description for typing and printing should not of course be allowed to influence the theory of phonological structure" (Lyons, 1962a: 230). And I referred to Firth's argument that phoneme theory had been built on the "hypostatization" of the letters of the Roman alphabet (Firth, 1948c: 134 = F. R. Palmer, 1970a: 8). Firth's argument would be more widely accepted nowadays.

9 For this terminological distinction between 'structure' and 'system', see, e.g., Robins (1953b: 109); W. S. Allen (1954: 556); Firth (1957b: 30 = 1968a: 200). In this usage, a system is a set of commutable terms in paradigmatic opposition; a structure is a complex of syntagmatically related elements which operates as a unit at some higher level of analysis. Victoria Fromkin actually uses the term 'structure-system phonology' in preference to 'prosodic analysis' in the title of the article in which she argues for "the incorporation of certain principles of the British system-structure or prosodic approach into the phonological component of a transformational grammar of Twi" (1965: 601); and it is arguable that it is a better term. However that may be, the terminological distinction of 'system' and

'structure' was of central importance for the so-called neo-Firthians in the formulation of what has come to be known, in recent years, as systemic linguistics (cf. Berry, 1973; Halliday, 1976).

10 Harris's reason is interesting:

> The components are merely generalizations of the phonemes extending the very development which gives us phonemes out of sounds ... Analysis into components completes what phonemics can only do in part: the transfer of the limitations of sounds from distributional restriction to positional variation. This is not an argument for the use of components: phonemics is undoubtedly the more convenient stopping point in this development *because it fits alphabetic writing*; but we must recognize the fact that it is possible to go beyond it (Joos, 1957: 137, my italics).

The prosodist would of course deny that the recognition of so-called long components (prosodies) is an extension of phonemic analysis and subsequent to it.

11 In the original version, at this point (footnote 11), I noted that many of the generalizations made about the degree of redundancy in languages were vitiated by the failure to allow for redundancy artificially introduced into the description by the choice of descriptive model and referred to what I regarded, for this reason, as a fallacious argument to the effect that "the phonetic efficiency of languages is distributed around the 50% point" (James H. Greenberg *et al.*, 1961). Linguistic theory, especially in the United States, was much influenced in the late 1950s by information-theory principles. Independently of the validity of these principles themselves, it should have been clear that the statistics cited in support of the above-mentioned generalization (and others that found their way into the handbooks and became, for a while, part of the conventional wisdom) were almost meaningless.

12 For a more complete account of Turkish phonology in terms of prosodic analysis (one which, apart from anything else, also deals with restrictions on rounding in combination with back vowels – something that is left out of account in the present analysis), see Waterson (1956).

13 This is my own *ad hoc* notation. Prosodists usually write the prosodies above or below the phonematic units and make their domain explicit in the symbolization. As to the arbitrariness of deciding where to place the symbols for the prosodies, the statement made in the text requires some qualification. There is good reason for saying that vowel-harmony is progressive in Turkish and that, normally, its focus is the first syllable of the word (so that my notation is, in this respect, non-arbitrary and well motivated) and its domain the whole word.

14 Had this article been written a few years later, I could hardly have inserted this parenthesis without raising the question of markedness and naturalness (cf. S. R. Anderson, 1985a: 342–347). Indeed, it is not difficult now to see, with the benefit of hindsight, that much of my discussion at this point falls within the scope of Chomsky & Halle's self-criticism in the famous opening sentences of

their 'Epilogue and prologue': "The entire discussion ... suffers from a fundamental theoretical inadequacy ... The problem is that our approach to features, to rules and to evaluation has been overly formal" (1968: 400). But if the question of so-called naturalness (see Chapter 4 above) had been raised with universalist assumptions of the kind that motivated Chomsky & Halle (1968), Postal (1968), etc., and most generative phonology to the present day, I would have had to face the metatheoretically interesting problem that on Turkish-internal grounds, and in contradiction of standard universalist assumptions, the combination of backness with non-rounding (to use the terminology of the present article) would seem to be incontrovertibly less marked than with rounding. It is also worth noting, in this connexion, that the distinction of primary and secondary cardinal vowels, together with the conventions associated with the use of the International Phonetic Alphabet (IPA), rests upon the assumption that front vowels combine with non-rounding more naturally, or more frequently, in the languages of the world, and back vowels with rounding. This assumption, like many other such assumptions which underpin the interpretation of the IPA letters and diacritics, has often been criticized of course by modern phoneticians with greater experience of non-European languages than the inventors of the IPA.

15 More important, perhaps, though it is not mentioned specifically in the article, is the fact that the word (in the Bloomfieldian sense of minimal free-form) is also independently definable as a grammatical unit in Turkish and, generally speaking, the phonological word coincides with the grammatical word. (As is well known, this is not the case in all languages.) This fact is relevant to the point made later about the typological significance of grammatical prerequisites (or correlations). Vowel harmony and stress in Turkish are what Trubetzkoy called 'Grenzsignale': see Epilogue.

16 See notes 13 and 14 above, and for details Waterson (1956: 580 = F. R. Palmer, 1970a: 176), where the domains of these prosodies are described, together with the additional fact that *R* may occur with *i* in a syllable following one in which *N* occurs with *a*, provided that there is labiality before the *i* in question. (Thus – using my notation: BNkarRpiz, /karpuz/, etc. This fact requires a slight, though general and systematic, modification of the statement made in the text, where it was omitted for the sake of simplicity.)

17 In the original version I commented (1962a: 233, footnote 16) that prosodists seemed generally to prefer what, in those days, was commonly called the 'hocus-pocus', rather than the 'God's truth', philosophy of language (cf. Householder, 1952) and I proclaimed my own adherence, following Bazell (1953; etc.), to an intermediate ('rough justice') position: for further comments see Epilogue. The phrase 'rough justice' comes from Householder (1957), but it was through Bazell that I first became familiar with it.

18 In a full prosodic analysis of Turkish phonology further consonantal and junctural prosodies are required: cf. Waterson (1956).

19 The question of so-called abstractness subsequently became notoriously con-

troversial among generative phonologists. The London School attitude (at an earlier period of course) seems to have been somewhat ambivalent. On the one hand, many of its leading members explicitly declared themselves in favour of abstractness (whenever this could be justified in terms of systematicity); on the other, their analyses were often far more highly motivated from a phonetic point of view than those of the phonemicists (and they tended to pride themselves on 'hugging the phonetic ground"). Most of them were of course consummate practical phoneticians.

20 Hockett's (1949: 40) argument that the use of grammatical criteria in phonological analysis necessarily involves circularity I dismissed as "not convincing".

21 This Epilogue was written in April 1987.

22 Several of the original notes which no longer seem relevant have been deleted and a number of sometimes quite lengthy new notes have been added throughout. A few of the original notes, renumbered for the most part, have been kept for purely historical reasons: for their value in contextualizing the points made in the article in relation to theoretical controversies of the time.

23 In this review of the Firth memorial volume, Langendoen (1969) was noticeably more sympathetic to London School linguistics in general and to prosodic analysis in particular than he had been in his earlier works (1964a, b), crediting the proponents of prosodic phonology with the anticipatory discovery of many principles that were to be subsequently "rediscovered" by the generative phonologists. It is worth noting, however, that some of the criticisms in the later, much more sympathetic, work are now outdated, as were several of the earlier criticisms, viewed from the changing standpoint of current orthodoxy. For example, the London School phonologists are criticized in the later work for their failure to respect the criterion of so-called naturalness, which had not of course been mentioned in the earlier publications. The wheel has turned again, and naturalness is no longer an unquestioned part of the orthodoxy of generative phonology. (The whole concept of naturalness is, in any case, confused and theoretically suspect: see Chapter 4.) For a generous and informed, and highly informative, response to Langendoen's earlier criticisms, see Robins (1969). Granted that Langendoen's earlier account of London School linguistics was in many respects unsatisfactory, it must none the less be recognized that he did make a more serious attempt than most American linguists had done until then to understand the general principles of Firthianism; and neither Firth nor most of his followers made things easy for outsiders. (And despite Langendoen's classification of me as a Firthian in the revised and expanded, 1968, version of his, 1964b, MIT doctoral dissertation, I too was, to some considerable degree, an outsider, especially as far as prosodic phonology was concerned: see note 24.)

24 Firth retired from his Chair at the School of Oriental and African Studies (SOAS) in 1957 and was succeeded by C. E. Bazell in October of the same year (see note 7), when I too joined the Department of Phonetics and Linguistics as a very

junior member. Apart from Bazell, I was the only member of staff who had not been first a pupil and then a colleague of Firth's under what was by all accounts, in Firth's time, a rather autocratic (though reasonably benevolent) regime; and the department still had, in 1957 and for a few years thereafter, a strong sense of identity and cohesion. My appointment at SOAS was in Comparative Linguistics and my research interests were in semantics (from a point of view crucially different from, though influenced indirectly by, Firth's: see note 25). I had no knowledge of any kind of modern phonology (and no systematic training in synchronic linguistics as such). What I knew of prosodic phonology when I wrote Lyons (1962a) came from my attendance at lectures and departmental seminars at SOAS between 1957 and 1960 and, subsequently, whilst writing the paper, from reading (and in a few cases re-reading) the works listed in the references (see note 6), by which time I had also learned what I knew of orthodox, post-Bloomfieldian, phonology, partly by teaching an introductory course in linguistics at Indiana University, based on standard American textbooks of the time, and partly from attendance at seminars (see note 1).

25 Sommerstein (1977: 27) rightly emphasizes the fact that it is the notion of context (i.e., meaningfulness in Firth's terms) which gives prosodic analysis its theoretical coherence.

26 Robins makes the point that "it is cardinal for the abstraction of a prosody that the feature or features assigned to it as its exponent(s) should either characterize or demarcate a definite structure [and] the structures to which prosodies are referred may be grammatical (word, affix, etc.) as well as purely phonological" (1969: 113). It is important, however, on more general grounds, to draw a distinction between phonological and grammatical structures. N-Languages vary considerably in the degree to which phonology and grammar (morphology and syntax) are interdependent or congruent (see Chapter 4): this point is mentioned, with reference to prosodic analysis in F. R. Palmer (1970b). For a particularly forceful statement of the London School's commitment to the syntagmatic dimensions of analysis – and of its hostility to monosystemicism – see Mitchell (1958). It is perhaps worth adding, for the historical record, that when Mitchell's paper was read at a meeting of the Philological Society on 28 November 1958, I was bold enough to criticize it, citing both Saussure and Chomsky, for its excessive concern with fixed expressions and a multiplicity of unconnected detail ("les locutions toutes faites" and "les petits faits vrais") and its failure to deal with what could and should be generated by rule. Firth himself, who was in the Chair, made the comment "There speaks a classicist!", effectively, if unintentionally, ruling my question out of order; and that was the end of the matter. There was no discussion of the substantive point (which was, I think, valid). This was, incidentally, the closest I ever came to having any personal contact with Firth.

27 The quotation from Hoijer also illustrates what I referred to, in the opening sentence of this paper, as the "pragmatic" stance adopted by the majority of

American linguists of the time. And Hoijer, as an anthropological linguist, had a broader view of language – and a greater interest in issues that had been of particular concern to Sapir – than many of his colleagues. Post-Bloomfieldian linguistics was frequently criticized by members of the London School for its exclusive concern with descriptive procedures and its neglect of theory. (Since writing this Epilogue I have dealt further with Hoijer's "pragmatic" stance: cf. Lyons, 1990a.)

28 A distinction must be drawn between generative grammar and generativism (see Lyons, 1981a: 228–235). Generative grammar as such is neutral between alternative views of the ontological status of languages; generativism, on the other hand, has always been associated with the God's truth approach.

29 Generally speaking, the reaction was one of hostility. But there were exceptions. W. S. Allen and R. H. Robins, whilst being fully involved in the development of what by then was coming to be known as London School linguistics, had a broader range of interests and, at that time at least, were more receptive to the ideas of other schools of linguistics, American and European, than were most of Firth's followers. I had the good fortune to have them both, successively, as supervisors of my Ph.D. research, the former in Cambridge, 1956–57, the latter in London, 1957–60. (Allen had read *Syntactic Structures* even before it had been published in the United States and had recognized its importance immediately. See Chapter 4, note 2. Robins, too, was soon to have read it, if he had not done so already, and was introducing students to it, at an early date, in the lectures upon which his textbook (1946b) was based.)

7 Towards a 'notional' theory of the 'parts of speech'

1 This article (Lyons, 1966b) was first published in the 'Notes and discussion' section of Volume 2 of the *Journal of Linguistics* (which I edited, at the time, on behalf of the Linguistics Association of Great Britain). It was based, in part, on a lecture which I delivered at Indiana University in the summer of 1963. It was written up for publication during my first year as Professor of General Linguistics in Edinburgh, as was much of my *Introduction to Theoretical Linguistics* (1968a), into which certain parts of it were absorbed; and the *Introduction* was the basis for the lectures that I gave to graduate students in linguistics in the middle and late 1960s (see Appendix 1).

Much of its content derived, directly or indirectly, from a series of seminars on linguistics and logic at the School of Oriental and African Studies in 1959–60, organized by J. Frits Staal and me. Other regular participants in the seminars (whose influence will be discernible) were Charles E. Bazell, John Brough, Frank R. Palmer and Robert H. Robins: cf. Bazell, 1953, 1958; Brough, 1951; F. R. Palmer, 1964; Robins, 1952b). The published version was further influenced by comments from friends (with widely divergent views on linguistic theory) to whom I circulated a pre-final draft: W. Sidney Allen, E. Keith Brown, Noam

Chomsky, Neville E. Collinge, Robert M. W. Dixon, William Haas, Michael A. K. Halliday, David G. Hays, Vincent M. Hope, Fred W. Householder, Donald Macaulay, Peter H. Matthews and Paul M. Postal.

It should be noted that, although the article in its final form makes reference to *Aspects* (Chomsky, 1965), it was very much the product of the pre-*Aspects* period of transformational grammar, as was my treatment of generative grammar in Lyons (1968a). When Chomsky (1965) was published, I was pleased by its reaffirmation of some of the universalist aims of traditional grammar, but I was disappointed by its (to my mind) uncritical acceptance of the traditional parts of speech as substantive universals and by its failure to address some of the criticisms that had been quite rightly directed against traditional grammar in the past) (cf. Lyons, 1966d). I have not changed my view in this respect (see Epilogue).

If I were writing this paper today, there is much of the detail that I would change; in particular, I would not use the term 'notional' (see note 4 below); and I would be more careful with much of the terminology. Because the 1966 version has been widely quoted (and was the basis for several sections in Lyons, 1968a), I am republishing it here without change in the text of the article itself. But, as with Chapter 6, I have furnished it with new notes and an Epilogue, whose purpose is either to clarify or to contextualize points which might be obscure to readers who are not familiar with linguistic theory of the 1950s and early 1960s.

2 Chomsky has frequently protested, in recent years, that he never associated his deep/surface distinction with the distinction between what is universal and what is non-universal in the structure of languages. But many readers of *Aspects* certainly took Chomsky to be making this association, and I still think it is fair to say that what Chomsky has to say about universal grammar and deep structure in *Aspects* lends itself to this interpretation, which, as I say in the article, links up with certain traditional views on universal grammar.

3 It may be worth reproducing the original note, if only for historical purposes: "Since it is perhaps not immediately clear to all readers how the proposal being made here relates to the views of Chomsky, Lamb, Halliday and Shaumjan (and I may, in fact, be mistaken in my interpretation of these authors) an explanatory note may be helpful. As I understand Halliday (1966c) and Lamb (1964b; cf. also Gleason, 1964), they seem to be suggesting that the bracketing of constituents is confined to the 'surface' structure of sentences and that 'deep' structure is describable in terms of 'networks' of 'features' (Halliday) or 'sememes' (Lamb). Chomsky (1965), on the other hand, introduces both 'lexical categories' (e.g. NP, VP) and 'grammatical categories' (e.g. Aux, Copula) into the underlying constituent structure of sentences. In his most recent work, Shaumjan makes clear (1965: 361) the partial similarity between his 'abstract generator' and 'categorial' grammars of the kind studied by Bar-Hillel (1964: Chapters 5, 7, 14) and others. I should add that a number of points made in the

present article are also made, independently and with a good deal of additional syntactic argument, by Lakoff (1965)". This quotation makes it clear that it was a very eclectic approach to transformational grammar that I adopted and that I saw a good deal of merit in non-Chomskyan syntactic theory of the early 1960s (see Epilogue).

4 'Notional' has proved to be (in several respects) an unfortunate term. Two points are worth emphasizing here (which were not made in the text): (1) that the properties of universality and of being semantically based, which, following Jespersen, I associated with the term 'notional', are logically independent and should not be conflated; 'ontologically based' would have been a better term than 'semantically based' (see Epilogue and note 16).

5 This paragraph should not be read as implying a commitment to what Chomsky (1957) criticized as discovery procedures.

6 Sapir's argument, as formulated here, falls victim to the traditional failure to distinguish between the parts of speech as classes of lexemes (N, V, A, etc.) and as syntactically functioning expressions. It is NPs, not Ns, that are subjects of sentences and operate typically as referring expressions. There is a similar failure to distinguish between expressions and their referents, the term 'subject' being used for both. I myself similarly fail to distinguish between NPs and Ns in parts of the argument in the present article: see below.

7 At this point I would now draw a distinction between sentences and utterances (cf. Lyons, 1977a: 500 ff., 622 ff.).

8 I am here using 'Aristotelian' not to refer to Aristotle's own system as such, but rather to the system of traditional logic which developed out of it. Although Aristotle's own system of logic may not have included particular terms, they were introduced into what I am calling Aristotelian logic fairly early in the tradition (cf. Łukasiewicz, 1951). I am indebted to Robert M. W. Dixon for drawing my attention to this point (cf. Lyons, 1966b: 213).

9 The original note at this point ran as follows: "One might of course argue that the distinction between 'persons' and 'non-persons', or between 'animate' and 'inanimate' entities is independent of, and in certain respects prior to, the distinction of 'things' and 'non-things' (cf. 'some visible objects in our world, such as vertebrate animals, are genuine singulars, whereas in large parts of nature the visible entities are exclusively collections, unified only as objects for our perceptions': Hartshorne, 1966: 27). The present argument is unaffected by the particular metaphysical position one might adopt on this question. It may well be that lexical items denoting (classes of) 'animate beings', and in particular 'persons', should be regarded as the nuclear members of the syntactic class of nouns. (In the argument of this paper we have deliberately neglected, for simplicity, the connection between 'subject' and 'animacy' in many languages; we have also neglected the connection between 'subject' and 'definiteness'.)" (Lyons, 1966b: 213–214). I would now argue that lexemes denoting classes of animate beings and especially persons – i.e., denoting prototypical first-order

entities – should indeed be regarded as the nuclear, or prototypical, members of the lexico-syntactic class of (count) nouns. Much of the content of this paper has been further developed, and I trust more satisfactorily explained, in Lyons (1977a: Chapters 11 and 12). In my later treatment of the ontological primacy of nouns I emphasize the importance of not assimilating places to entities: this is something about which I said nothing in the present paper.

10 I am not of course suggesting that there is anything more fundamental about the structure Preposition + Noun than there is about what are traditionally classified as adverbs. Rather, what is being proposed is that both adverbs (of certain classes) and prepositional phrases should be derived from the same syntactic source. Indeed, I think that Chomsky's use of the term 'PrepPhrase' in *Aspects* for one of the putative substantive universals of syntactic theory was most unfortunate in this respect. Admittedly, names are arbitrary in a formal system; but prepositional phrases, as they are traditionally defined, are typologically very restricted in the languages of the world.

11 The term 'theme', regrettably, has been used in many different senses in linguistics, and I am sorry to have added to the potential confusion by employing it here. I much prefer, nowadays, to restrict it technically to the sense in which it opposes 'rheme' in the Prague School tradition (cf. Lyons, 1977a: 500ff.).

12 What follows was, as far as I know, the earliest published suggestion that a categorial grammar might replace a Chomskyan phrase-structure grammar in the base component of a transformational grammar of English and other languages. Categorial grammars and phrase-structure grammars were explicitly compared in Lyons (1968a: 230ff.).

13 This is of course my own *ad hoc* notation (which I also used in Lyons, 1968a). It is not particularly elegant. But I wanted to make directionality notationally more prominent than it is in the standard system which employs left-slanting and right-slanting 'fractional' obliques between the 'numerator' and the 'denominator'.

14 There are in fact many languages, including several West-African and American-Indian languages, in which the majority of nouns appear to be derived from verbs by means of productive syntactic processes. This fact was drawn to my attention originally by Keith Brown and Paul Postal (cf. Lyons, 1966b: 232). It does not, I think, go against the argument which follows.

15 The Epilogue is based on Section 2 of Lyons (1989a).

16 The term used in Lyons (1966b) was not 'semantically determined' but 'semantically based', which the advent of so-called generative semantics in the late 1960s made potentially ambiguous. 'Semantically determined' is, in any case, clearer – though not so precise as 'ontologically based'.

17 I am using 'substance' in the non-Aristotelian sense. In Aristotelian, and scholastic, terminology 'substance' is more or less synonymous with 'entity'. It is this by now almost obsolete sense of 'substance' which gave rise to the term 'substantive' for what, in modern terminology, are normally called nouns.

18 In Lyons (1989a) I argue that the traditional distinction between concrete and abstract nouns (and nominals) should be replaced by a more refined set of distinctions relating, on the one hand, to the difference between first-order and higher-order expressions and, on the other, to the difference between extensional and intensional expressions.

8 Deixis as the source of reference

1 This was originally published as Lyons (1975a). The present version is unchanged except for very minor adjustments to the notes. Much of its content (without the supporting detail) was introduced into Lyons (1977a). The formalism is *ad hoc*, eclectic and very much of its time: but what is formalized is unaffected by this and could, I think, be readily expressed in any one of several present-day models of (transformational or non-transformational) generative grammar. Several of the points made in the Epilogue to Chapter 7 are developed in Chapter 8. Except for introducing double quotation marks for quotations, I have kept the notation of the original published version, even though it is incompatible with that of the preceding chapter and also with that of Lyons (1977a) and of Chapters 1–5 of the present work.

2 It is one of a class of non-natural, but not unnatural, languages: see Chapter 4 above.

3 I also assume that equative structures underly such so-called cleft sentences as *The one who did this is John* (see Halliday, 1967a: 223).

4 On naturalness (in this sense) see now Chapter 4 above. On the topic–comment distinction and its relation to the definition of nouns (and nominals) in universal grammar see Chapter 7.

5 The etymology of such forms as *voici* and *voilà* in French is revealing in this connection.

6 Utterances like *There's a book* in English cannot be interpreted satisfactorily in terms of reference and predication. The function of the whole utterance is perhaps best described as quasi-referential (or quasi-predicative). It draws attention to an object (and by doing so it frequently introduces it as the topic about which a comment will then be made in subsequent utterances). But drawing attention to the object in such cases cannot be sharply distinguished from saying something about it. Quasi-reference is perhaps ontogenetically more basic than either reference or predication.

7 For a discussion of the meaning of such sentences and a formalization of some of the conditions of appropriate utterance associated with them, see Atkinson & Griffiths (1973).

8 Place-denoting nouns (whether common or proper) are not as fully assimilated to entity-denoting nouns in all languages as they are in the Indo-European languages. In Chinese, for example, place-nouns are distinguished from entity-nouns in that they can occur as locative adjuncts or complements without a postposed locative morpheme.

9 Quasi-English also generates such equative structures as $D_2 D_2$, which can be thought of as establishing an identity between two places. This is syntactically parallel to the identity established between two entities by $D_1 D_1$ (*That's it*, in English) or D_1 Nm (*That's John*). In English, of course, we say *This (place) is London* rather than *Here is London*. But a locative phrase can be in equative apposition with a deictic adverb in such sentences as *It is cold here in London*. It is arguable, therefore, that even in English we should admit such underlying equative structures as D_2 + Locative.

10 In principle, it could also be derived from the subject position of a predicative syntagm, [*That man [John Smith be very rich] be very rich*]; and perhaps also from the topic position of an equative syntagm, [*That man [John Smith be that man] be very rich*]. I will simply discount these alternatives.

11 A phrase like *on the table there* (in, say, *Put it on the table there*) is ambiguous with respect to the distinction between adjectivalization and predicate apposition; and this distinction is also neutralized in *on that table* and (in an appropriate context) *on the table*. More obviously distinct, semantically and syntactically, from either of these is a third interpretation of the phrase under which *there* is in equative apposition with the whole locative phrase *on the table*. In this case, however, it is perhaps more usual for the deictic adverb to precede the locative phrase (just as it is more usual for a deictic pronoun to precede an appositional noun-phrase). But *Put it there on the table* is itself structurally ambiguous. It can also mean, roughly, '*Put it on this part (of the surface) of the table*'. The grammatical rules presented here cannot account for this construction, which, I suspect, should be included among so-called inalienable possessives; and these I take to be a subclass of part–whole locatives.

12 There is no natural way of formalizing this process of amalgamation, as far as I can see, in Chomskyan transformational grammar. The best we can do is to substitute *that* for the string *that* + *there* (rather than simply to delete *there*) and this creates labelling problems for the derived phrase-marker.

13 In certain dialects of English *that there dog* is a perfectly grammatical phrase; and it is stressed in a way that suggests that *there* is enclitic. This does not seem to be the case for the Standard English *that dog there*, which, as the alternative correlated stress patterns would suggest, is interpretable as either '*that entity – the dog which is there*' or '*that entity – the dog – it is there*'. We have not dealt with the second interpretation (but see note 11).

14 There are certain differences between Sommerstein's (1972) and Thorne's (1973) proposals. Briefly (and to put it in my own terms), Sommerstein treats the definite article as a demonstrative pronoun and Thorne derives it by the adjectivalization of *there*. I believe that each of these proposals is correct, as far as it goes, but incomplete.

15 'Person' must here be understood to include a variety of personified individuals, not only supernatural beings and domestic pets, but also, under certain circumstances, ships, cars, and other artefacts. The grammar, or the rules of semantic interpretation, must also allow for the de-personification of babies

unfamiliar to the speaker. The details are more complex. One general principle seems to be that reference to an individual by name constitutes (or is evidence of) personification in English and precludes deictic or anaphoric reference to the same individual, by the same speaker, in a predicative utterance by means of a neuter pronoun: e.g. *The baby is a year old now and it/he/she is beginning to talk* vs. **Little Lesley is a year old now and it is beginning to talk.* In practice, one can of course know the name of a child or animal without knowing its sex; and this creates problems for the choice of *he* or *she*, which cannot be avoided, if the name is used, by simply employing *it.* There would seem to be further restrictions on the use of the demonstrative and personal pronouns with reference to infants (and animals?). *It* in *It's very good* (but not *that* or *this* in *That/this is very good*) can be used to refer to a baby, but not, I think, in such sentences as *It's very beautiful.*

16 Allan (1971) argues (against what he calls the Fillmore–Lyons hypothesis) that *there*$_1$ cannot be a thematic copy of the locative phrase in existential sentences because it differs syntactically and semantically from the locative proform *there*$_2$ and because there is another way of thematizing the locative phrase: namely by applying the independently motivated *have*-transformation. I cannot answer for Fillmore, but I at least never suggested that the preposed *there*$_1$ was an element which 'copied' all the features of the predicative locative phrase under thematization. It was an important part of my hypothesis that the predication of existence involved the extraction from the locative phrase of only the deictically neutral locative component and the copying (if copying is indeed the appropriate transformational mechanism) of this in the preposed *there*$_1$. I still believe that this gives a more satisfactory explanation of the meaning and function of *there*$_1$ in existential sentences than any alternative that I am aware of. Allan's own positive proposals fail to account for the formal identity of *there*$_1$ and *there*$_2$; and they depend upon the to me unacceptable notion of incorporating the existential operator in the deep structures of natural language (see below). As for the alternative means of thematization with the *have*-transformation, it should be obvious that what is 'thematized' in this case is the nominal part of the locative phrase: i.e., neither the whole phrase nor the locative element as such. *There is a book on the table* makes a predication about a book, whereas *The table has a book on it* makes a predication about the table. This distinction is unaffected by the fact that English also treats place-denoting nouns, syntactically, like entity-denoting nouns in a variety of constructions.

17 Some of these sentences are, of course, contradictory –*That*$_2$ *here dog big, This there*$_2$ *dog big*, etc.; and some are redundant – *This here dog big, That*$_2$ *there*$_2$ *dog big*, etc. We can obviously exclude either or both of these classes, if we wish to, by means of semantic rules. How we exclude these sentences (or their underlying structures), and indeed whether we exclude them or not, is irrelevant to the argument.

18 By a 'phrasal referring expression' I mean an expression which does not include an embedded clause (in terms of the traditional distinction between phrases and clauses).

19 This will have the effect of excluding as ungrammatical such strings as *he good man, *she girl, etc. There are other ways of excluding such strings.

20 In English that₁ and it are partly in complementary distribution and partly in free variation in particular syntactic environments. However, it is my assump'ion that the form of the non-proximate, non-distal, non-personal demonstrative pronoun that is used to refer to entities in the situation is always *it*.

21 To introduce the existential quantifier into the underlying structures of natural languages without giving it an interpretation in terms of some intuitive notion of existential predication is, to my mind, to put the cart before the horse; and I would suggest that the most satisfactory interpretation of existential quantification is in terms of a basically locative predicate, as proposed here. $(\exists x)(x = a)$, which Hintikka (1969) has put forward as an analysis of '*a* exists' (in connexion with Quine's famous dictum, that to be is to be the value of a variable), is interpretable intuitively as 'an x is there₁ which is identical with *a*'.

22 For extended discussion of this and related points see Chapter 9.

9 Deixis and anaphora

1 This chapter was originally published as Lyons (1978c). In the present context it can be seen as supplementing Chapter 8. For the other contributions to which reference is made in the text see Bullowa (1978), Halliday (1978) and Widdowson (1978).

Appendix: The scientific study of language. Inaugural Lecture, Edinburgh, 1965

1 This lecture was delivered before the University of Edinburgh on 19 January 1965 and subsequently published with copious notes and bibliographical references (Lyons, 1965a). An abbreviated version appears in Allen & Corder (1973: 162–177). In preparing the present version for publication, I have decided, after considerable initial hesitation, to leave the text of the lecture unchanged. I was at first tempted to remove some of the more local and more ephemeral comments and allusions, but, on reflection, felt that it would be more valuable to present-day and future historians of linguistics in Great Britain in the 1960s if I reprinted it in full and without any kind of revision. I have, however, shortened and amended the notes and removed most of the bibliographical references. A certain amount of the content of the lecture found its way into my *Introduction to Theoretical Linguistics* (1968), most of which was based on the lectures I gave to students enrolled for the postgraduate Diploma in General Linguistics in 1964/65, 1965/66 and 1966/67.

2 I was here assuming, perhaps wrongly, that the *Cratylus* (? c.385 BC) is earlier than the work of the great Indian grammarian Pāṇini.

3 It is no longer as unusual as it was in 1965 to emphasize the continuity between modern linguistics and traditional grammar. The historiography of linguistics has also made very considerable progress in the last twenty or so years. Many of

the bibliographical references that I gave in the original note have been superseded.

4 A more literal translation than the one I give in the text of the lecture would be: "Since I have put on the lion's skin I must not now be cowardly." (Few of my audience can have been expected to note the pun in the Greek, and I do not suppose that I would have done in an oral presentation.) Here, and elsewhere in the lecture, I was of course shamelessly trying to woo the classicists, partly for the more immediate purpose of soliciting their support for the new Department of General Linguistics and the support of other colleagues in the more traditional and long-established disciplines, but principally because I wanted to emphasize that, for me at least, there was no conflict between the more traditional, more philological, and the more recent, more scientific, approach to the study of language.

5 For an evaluation of Angus McIntosh's contribution to the study of English (modern and medieval), Scots and Linguistics in Edinburgh, reference may now be made to Aitken (1981) and J. M. Anderson (1981).

6 For an account of David Abercrombie's contribution to the development of phonetics in Edinburgh and more generally, reference may now be made to Asher & Henderson (1981b).

7 The Department of General Linguistics did, in fact, amalgamate with the Department of Phonetics, to form the Department of Phonetics and Linguistics, in 1967.

8 The Department of Applied Linguistics (which until 1964 had been the School of Applied Linguistics) was amalgamated with the Department of Phonetics and Linguistics, to form the Department of Linguistics, in 1970; and Pit Corder became Professor of Applied Linguistics. It was a condition of the amalgamation of what had been three independent departments that the three Professors should each retain academic responsibility for their own subject, but take turns as Head of Department for periods of three years.

9 The original note made reference at this point, for Celtic, to Jackson (1953); for Russian, to Ward (1963) – to which may also be added Ward (1965); for Middle English, to McIntosh (1956, 1963) – to which may now be added Benskin (1981) and McIntosh *et al.* (1986); for stylistics, to McIntosh & Halliday (1966), Thorne (1965); for the work of the Linguistic Survey of Scotland, to McIntosh (1952) – to which may now be added Mather & Speitel (1975), McClure (1982), McClure *et al.* (1980); for the *Dictionary of the Old Scottish Tongue*, to Craigie & Aitken (1963) – to which may now be added Aitken (1973–); for the *Scottish National Dictionary*, to Murison (1946–) – to which may now be added Murison (1972, 1977). Mention should have been made, explicitly and in the lecture itself, to the great contribution made to linguistics studies in Edinburgh, over a period of thirty years, by John Orr, by then Professor Emeritus of Romance Linguistics: cf. Orr (1933, 1953a, b, 1962a, b). Orr's influence, although I was not aware of this fact when I delivered my Inaugural Lecture, extended far

beyond Romance Linguistics, and he played an active role, with Angus McIntosh and David Abercrombie, in several of the projects referred to above: cf. Aitken (1981).

10 In preparing this version of my Edinburgh Inaugural Lecture for republication, I was tempted to omit or abbreviate the whole of this paragraph, but decided eventually to leave it unchanged as a record of the attitude that I and several of my British colleagues had at the time to what seemed to us to be a disturbingly parochial, not to say nationalistic, and even anti-American, trend that was discernible in a number of so-called neo-Firthian publications emanating from Edinburgh. (Incidentally, Firth himself was not entirely free from a certain misplaced nationalism: cf. Haas, 1958.) In the original notes at this point, I cited a number of recent works in which the terms 'British linguistics', 'Edinburgh linguistics' and 'the London School' had been used in the sense in question; and I made a number of critical comments about the way in which the proponents of these approaches to linguistics compared them, to my mind misleadingly, with other approaches, more particularly Chomskyan transformational-generative grammar. There seems little point in giving the same detailed references here. (For some contemporary reactions to one of the works I mentioned, cf. Haas, 1963; Lyons, 1963b; P. H. Matthews, 1965b.)

11 It was of course characteristic of linguists, at that time, that they should make rather strident and somewhat exaggerated claims about the scientific status of their discipline. For a more recent statement of the qualified sense in which I would nowadays interpret the terms 'scientific' in relation to linguistics, cf. Lyons (1981a: 37–46).

12 It is perhaps worth recording here that John Uldall, Hjelmslev's collaborator in the projected definitive formalization of Glossematics, only the first part of which was ever published (Uldall, 1957), had come to Edinburgh in 1950 (as a Lecturer in Linguistics in Angus McIntosh's Department) to work on the Linguistic Atlas of Scotland and, but for his untimely death in 1956, would no doubt have played a considerable role in the development of theoretical linguistics in Edinburgh.

13 When this lecture was delivered, undergraduates in the Faculty of Arts of Edinburgh, as at the other ancient Scottish universities, could take either an Ordinary (three-year) MA or an Honours (four-year) MA. Courses in the third and fourth year of an Honours curriculum were more specialized and were taught to smaller classes. But first-year and second-year courses were designed for both Ordinary and Honours students: i.e., both groups of students were taught together, often in quite large classes, and took various combinations of either First Ordinary (first-year) or Second Ordinary (second-year) courses. The First Ordinary Course in Phonetics had been started in 1950 and ran successfully for many years (cf. Abercrombie, 1958, 1966). With the formation of the amalgamated Department of Phonetics and Linguistics a full range of undergraduate courses was introduced, including a First and Second Ordinary

Course in Phonetics and Linguistics and several third- and fourth-year Honours courses leading to one or other of the several Joint Honours degrees in which Linguistics (including Phonetics) was combined with Anthropology, English, French, German, Psychology or Russian. Traditionally, I was told when I went to Edinburgh, the Professor's Inaugural Lecture was also the first lecture of his First Ordinary Course.

14 This passage, like several others in this lecture, was incorporated in Lyons (1968a), most of which was, however, based on teaching for the postgraduate Diploma in General Linguistics.

15 In making this assertion at that time (in 1965), I was almost certainly being too sanguine. It is still by no means universally accepted by linguists that written languages should be treated on their own terms independently of the spoken languages (if any) with which they are associated. That the language-system is independent of the medium in which it is manifest is, or course, one of the cardinal principles of (Saussurean) structural linguistics. It does, however, require some qualification: cf. Lyons (1968a: 66).

16 There are in fact several different senses in which speech can be said to have a certain priority in relation to writing – historical (or phylogenetic), structural, functional and biological (or ontogenetic): cf. Lyons (1981a: 11–17).

17 It seems to be very difficult to get across to some of the critics of modern linguistics the fact that an insistence upon the distinction between prescription and description does not, of itself, imply a *laissez-faire* attitude towards language. Recently, a pamphlet by Professor John Honey achieved a certain notoriety by accusing linguists of propagating the thesis that all languages and all dialects are equally suitable for all purposes and by supporting these accusations with a set of out-of-context and, for the most part, misconstrued quotations from a number of popular introductions to linguistics (cf. Honey, 1983). The question whether, or to what extent and up to what age, etc., one should use socially and regionally restricted non-standard vernaculars in school is a difficult (and politically sensitive) one. There can be no question, however, but that children in Britain should also be taught to understand and express themselves in standard English, if they are ever to gain access to the national and international culture to which standard English provides the key. (I and other linguists have made this, rather obvious, point on many occasions in print over the years: for a recent formulation by me, cf. Lyons, 1981a: 52–53, 329).

In this connexion, I may be permitted to quote one or two passages from an unpublished letter, dated 4 March 1983, which I wrote to *The Times* in response to what I described as a "foolish and intemperate commentary" on Honey, 1983, by John Vincent, published in *The Times* of 23 February 1983. Professor Vincent had not only, following Honey, misrepresented the principle of what he called linguistic egalitarianism, but also, gratuitously in this context, accused Chomskyan linguistics of being "a subject of little humane relevance". (The accusation was gratuitous because the principle in question is neutral between

Chomskyan and non-Chomskyan linguistics and is therefore not one that Chomsky has ever felt the need either to emphasize or to challenge. I imagine, but do not know for certain, that Chomsky's view is, in fact, very similar to mine.) My reply was:

> It is eminently humane, I would submit, in both senses of the term. On the one hand, it puts a commitment to human creativity and freedom and a hostility to mechanistic determinism at the very heart of its guiding theory and associated research programme; on the other, by insisting that, as I put it in my book [Lyons, 1970b: 15], the part of human nature that it studies is, on present evidence, 'common to all members of the species, regardless of their race or class and their undoubted differences in intellect, personality and physical attributes', it makes its distinctive contribution, in an academically responsible fashion, to the defence of a society whose members should be treated, with sympathy and compassion, as persons with equal rights at law and, as far as possible, with equal opportunities for the development and exploitation of their own potential.

Having corrected Professor Vincent on the answer that he gives to the question "What is Lyons really saying?", I continued:

> Clearly, standard English ought to be taught at school, though not in the way that it has been taught all too often in the past, by teachers inadequately trained for the purpose – I am in full agreement with Professor Vincent here. Whether, and to what degree, teachers should in addition tolerate or encourage the use of a non-standard local dialect in informal classroom discussion is an important question about which I have no firm view: it seems to me that there are both advantages and disadvantages, educationally, in the deliberate promotion of this kind of bilingualism (and biculturalism). But I do have very strong views about the arrogance and inhumanity of those who despise or ridicule, as persons, speakers of non-standard English, on the grounds that the various non-standard dialects of English (or the languages of the ethnic minorities) are, in all respects, inferior to standard English, and in so doing undermine their self-respect and their pride in their distinctive cultural identity. I have no reason to believe that Professor Vincent does this: I cannot but feel that his article confirms in their complacency and ignorance those who do.

18 Incidentally, it was on this occasion (in November 1963) that Chomsky informed me that he had been unaware of this connexion until he read of it in the copy of Lyons (1960) lent to him by the late Professor Bar-Hillel. (I first met Bar-Hillel at a conference at Indiana University in late 1960, just after I had submitted my Ph.D. dissertation, about which he made some very encouraging comments.) The connexion was obvious to anyone brought up in the European,

rather than the American, or more precisely post-Bloomfieldian, tradition: cf. Lyons (1958).

19 The original note cites Z. S. Harris (1951, 1952, 1954), Hockett (1954) and one of Chomsky's early, thoroughly neo-Bloomfieldian, articles (1953). Chomsky's neo-Bloomfieldianism has of course been played down in many accounts of the origins of transformational-generative grammar. For some interesting comments in this connexion, cf. P. H. Matthews (1986).

20 It is only in this sense, I suggested in the original note, that we can accept that "la grammaire scolaire constitue toujours le fonds commun des idées dont on part pour chercher par la discussion à les approfondir et à les corriger" (Hjelmslev, 1928: 297).

21 It is worth noting that it was not until some time in the early 1960s that generativists began to refer favourably to universal grammar. It is interesting, in this connexion, to read both the text ("A name is only a name, and the labels and symbols for a set of rules may be arbitrarily chosen ...") and the qualifying footnote ("I am ignoring here the important question of the possibility that at least some of the designations for syntactic classes will be supplied by general linguistic theory, i.e., by a set of universal categories like 'noun', 'verb' and so forth. The differences between languages have been stressed so much in recent years that we tend to overlook the very real similarities") in one of the earliest textbooks of generative grammar (Bach, 1964: 50). The footnote was written, presumably, after reading the preprint of Chomsky (1964a) and possibly an early draft of Chomsky (1965). For my own view of the relation between Chomskyan and traditional universal grammar, as I formulated it at the time, I may perhaps refer to my, rather critical, review of *Aspects* (Lyons, 1966d).

22 I am still not enamoured of these terms, but I have continued to use them in default of any other more generally accepted and more satisfactory terms: see Lyons (1981a). I borrowed them most directly from A. A. Hill (1958: 406). But they were more or less current in American linguistics at the time and, to the best of my knowledge, originated with Trager (1949), who, however, used the term 'macrolinguistics' somewhat differently.

23 This is how Saussure's 'langue', in its technical sense, is translated by W. S. Allen (1957b: 1), and it is by far the best translation.

24 This is a somewhat different definition of 'acceptability' from Chomsky's in *Aspects* (1965: 11), which had not yet been published, and is independent of the Chomskyan distinction between competence and performance (which, as formulated in *Aspects*, I have never accepted). I would now rewrite the whole of this section in the light of the distinction between semantics and pragmatics (cf. Lyons, 1981b).

25 It is worth quoting at this point the late Bernard Bloch's editorial comment in Postal (1966: 90):

An anecdote that Edward Sapir told me in 1937 is relevant here. Sapir was working once with a bilingual Navaho informant, an old woman who patiently recited paradigms for him. When he had heard several dozen forms, Sapir ventured to create new forms by extrapolation. The old woman shook her head in wonder, and looked at him respectfully. "You're a funny man," she said. "You say things in my language that I never heard before, AND THEY'RE RIGHT."

(See Langendoen, 1967: 746, who also quotes Bloch's editorial footnote.) Bloch's note is the more interesting in that he was, of course, closely associated with the post-Bloomfieldian movement in American linguistics, which, in its refusal to generalize or extrapolate beyond the corpus of attested utterances, if not in other respects, was at one with the Firthian and neo-Firthian schools of linguistics in this country.

26 Plato, *Republic* 592b: literally translated, "exemplar in heaven". The phrase comes from the passage at the end of Book 9 (the source of the Stoic and Christian idea of the City of God), where, after it has been conceded that the ideal city, whose constitution has just been described, "may not exist anywhere on earth" (though it is accessible to contemplation in the soul of the wise man), we are told that there may be "an exemplar of it in heaven for anyone wishing to contemplate it" and "whether it exists now or will ever exist is of no consequence", since the wise man will live by the principles that underly its constitution.

27 The original note at this point also referred to Katz & Postal (1964) with the comment "certain combinations of words may be specified as unacceptable both by virtue of the grammatical classification of the particular words in question and by virtue of their meaning. One may, of course, decide that if the grammatical description has already done a particular job there is no reason for the semantic description to repeat the work and then build this work into one 'integrated theory of linguistic descriptions'. This is another matter." It may be added that Lyons (1966c) was in press when this lecture was delivered. As for the substance of this passage in the lecture, it will be noted that I was still under the influence of distributionalism (though not to the point of espousing a distributionalist theory of meaning). I would not now talk about semantics as a third level of description taking over where grammar leaves off.

28 See also the final part of the second paragraph of note 17 above.

29 This is now known as the principle of compositionality; cf. Lyons (1981b: 144ff.).

30 I should perhaps draw attention to the fact that here I have coupled the two theoretically distinguishable ways in which, in my view then as now, language hooks onto the world: (i) in terms of what, in later terminology, I would call denotation and reference (cf. Lyons, 1977a); (ii) by virtue of being used in situations of utterance. Both linkages were coupled similarly, under the term 'application', in Lyons (1960 and 1968a: 434).

31 The original note ran as follows: "in saying that linguists have not provided a satisfactory theory of semantics, I do not mean to suggest that linguists have

contributed nothing of value in this field. Their contribution to the development of what in future might be a theory of semantics is twofold: (i) the construction of a formalised theory of grammatical structure which can be made the basis for semantic description, the theory of grammatical structure itself being set up independently of semantic considerations; (ii) the development of 'the structural approach' to language". For both (i) and (ii) I referred to Lyons (1960), which, as far as I know, constituted the first attempt to construct a theory of semantics on the basis of generative-transformational grammar and applied it to the analysis of a considerable body of material. Recent linguistic semantics has paid more attention to (i) than to (ii).

32 The original note ran as follows: "in saying that semantics is a field where progress depends necessarily upon the collaboration particularly of linguists and philosophers but also of linguists, anthropologists, sociologists and perhaps psychologists, I realise of course that the search for a unified and comprehensive theory of semantics – if semantics is interpreted as widely as it normally is – may turn out to be something of a wild goose chase. The only point that all those concerned with these questions seem to agree upon – philosophers, psychologists, anthropologists, sociologists and linguists alike – is that 'semantics' investigates 'meaning'. In expecting that everything referred to as 'meaning' should be handled within one theoretical framework, if we do have this expectation, we may simply be the victims of another of Ryle's 'systematically misleading expressions'. Distinctions must certainly be drawn and, when drawn, may lead to the inclusion of some aspects of what we now call 'meaning' in a new and narrower semantics and the exclusion of others from this branch of the scientific study of language. I do not believe, however, that there can be any lasting division of the field of semantics into 'microlinguistic' and 'macrolinguistic' semantics along the lines I have sketched such a division here." Although I still hold, in general, to the view expressed in this note, I see some virtue in formulating the somewhat different distinction between microlinguistic and macrolinguistic semantics (or, alternatively, between semantics in the narrower sense and pragmatics) in terms of a distinction between sentence-meaning and utterance-meaning: cf. Lyons (1981b).

33 This was of course a reference to the famous Whorfian hypothesis, the discussion of which dominated the psycholinguistics and ethnolinguistics of the 1950s. The pendulum has recently swung from relativism to universalism as the reigning orthodoxy. My own view has moved some way from the fairly extreme relativism that I expressed in articles of the time, but (as several of the chapters in this volume will have demonstrated) by no means as far as the currently fashionable universalism.

34 This now famous remark was quoted in Diebold (1964), a review article, which gives a perceptive and extraordinarily comprehensive account of early-1960s American psycholinguistics ('psycholinguistics' being very broadly interpreted). In the original, at this point, I referred to W. S. Allen (1957b: 4) for a similar view

on the desirability of restricting linguistics to what is here called microlinguistics, but added the comment: "notice that Allen includes 'situational events' as part of the linguist's data (p. 24). Here he follows Firth, and thus adopts a somewhat different view of language-systems from that of de Saussure and most linguists following him". Allen's synthesis of his modified Firthianism with Saussurean structuralism, on the one hand, and Chomskyan generative grammar, on the other, was very similar to my own – which is hardly surprising, since he was my first teacher of modern linguistics and introduced me to all three. Allen's Inaugural Lecture at Cambridge (1957b) was delivered in March 1957 and thus anteceded the publication of Chomsky (1957).

35 When I wrote this section, imbued with the optimism of youth and heady euphoria of the mid-1960s, a time of university expansion, I did not of course foresee the interpretation that would be given to this in itself eminently reasonable principle by the government in power in the early 1980s.

36 We are now experiencing the second wave of government support for computational linguistics, in this country and abroad, as part of what has come to be called information technology. It is to be hoped that it will not come to as abrupt an end as did the last wave of support, to which I was referring in my lecture.

37 For the work of the Department of Applied Linguistics (and subsequently of the Applied Linguistics section of the amalgamated Department of Linguistics: see note 8 above) during Professor Corder's time, cf. Allen & Corder, 1973, 1975; Corder, 1973).

38 The notes to the Appendix were compiled in the summer of 1987, and I have not revised them further. As this volume goes to press (in July 1990), I am poignantly aware that two of the scholars mentioned in the notes with whom I was very closely associated in Edinburgh have recently died: Pit Corder and James Thorne. So too has Peter Strevens, who had left Edinburgh before I arrived, but whose influence on the work of the Department of Applied Linguistics was still, and continued to be, very strong; and who was also a personal friend of mine. All three are sorely missed. For an appreciation of the work of Pit Corder and Peter Strevens in applied linguistics, see Selinker (1990) and Widdowson (1990); for my own tribute to Jimmy Thorne (as he was known to all his friends) see Lyons (1990b).

References

Aarsleff, Hans (1974). 'The Tradition of Condillac'. In Dell Hymes (ed.), *Studies in the History of Linguistics*. Bloomington, Ind,: Indiana University Press.

(1975). 'The eighteenth century'. In Sebeok (1975: 383–480).

(1976). 'An outline of Language-Origins Theory since the Renaissance'. In Harnad *et al.* (1976: 4–13).

Abercrombie, David (1949). 'What is a "letter"?'. (Reprinted in Abercrombie, 1965a: 76–95.)

(1958). 'The Department of Phonetics'. *University of Edinburgh Gazette* 20. 1–9.

(1963). 'Conversation and spoken prose'. *English Language Teaching* 18. 10–16. (Reprinted in Abercrombie, 1965a: 1–9.)

(1965a). *Studies in Phonetics and Linguistics*. London: Oxford University Press.

(1965b). 'On writing and the phoneme: two reviews (1954) and (1950)'. In Abercrombie (1965a: 131–136).

(1966). *Elements of General Phonetics*. Edinburgh: Edinburgh University Press; Chicago: Aldine.

(1968). 'Paralanguage'. *British Journal of Disorders of Communication* 3. 55–59. (Extract reprinted, as 'Paralinguistic communication', in Allen & Corder, 1973: 31–36.)

Adamczewski, H. (1974). 'BE + ING revisited'. In S. P. Corder & E. Roulet (eds.), *Linguistic Insights in Applied Linguistics*. Paris: Didier.

Admoni, V. G. (1964). *Osnovy Teorii Grammatiki*. Moskva & Leningrad: Izdatel'stvo 'Nauka'.

Adrados, Francisco (1965). Review of Lyons (1963a). In *Emerita* (Madrid) 33. 159–161.

Aitchison, Jean (1983). Review of Bickerton (1981). *Language and Communication* 3. 83–97.

(1987). *Words in the Mind: An Introduction to the Mental Lexicon*. Oxford: Blackwell.

Aitken, A. Jack (ed.) (1973–   ). *Dictionary of the Older Scottish Tongue*. Chicago & London: Chicago University Press.

References

(1981). 'Angus McIntosh and Scottish studies'. In Benskin & Samuels (1981: xix–xxvii).

& McArthur, T. (eds.) (1975). *Languages of Scotland*. (With a foreword by Angus McIntosh.) (Association for Scottish Literary Studies, Occasional Papers 4.) Edinburgh: Chambers.

, McIntosh, A. & Palsson, H. (eds.) (1973). *Edinburgh Studies in English and Scots*. London: Longman.

Ajdukiewicz, Kasimierz (1935). 'Die syntaktische Konnexität'. *Studia Philosophica* 1 (Warsaw). 1–28.

Akhmanova, O. S. (1968). Review of Lyons (1963a). In *Voprosy Jazykoznanija* 1968. 113–121.

, Mel'chuk, I. A., Frumkina, R. M. & Padučeva, E. V. (1961). *O Točnykh Metodakh Issledovanija Jazybkov*. Moskva: Izd. Moskv. Universities. (English trans. by David G. Hays & D. V. Mohr, *Exact Methods in Linguistic Research*. Berkeley & Los Angeles: University of California Press.)

Albert, Martin L. & Obler, L. K. (1978). *The Bilingual Brain*. New York: Academic Press.

Alinei, Mario (ed.) (1982). 'Le origini del significato: The origin of meaning'. *Quaderni di Semantica* 5. 89–131, 311–349.

Allan, Keith (1971). 'A note on the source of "there" in existential sentences'. *Foundations of Language* 7. 1–18.

(1972). 'In reply to "There$_1$, there$_2$"'. *Journal of Linguistics* 8. 119–24.

(1977). 'Classifiers'. *Language* 53. 285–311.

Allen, J. Patrick B. & Corder, S. P. (eds.) (1973). *Readings for Applied Linguistics*. (The Edinburgh Course in Applied Linguistics, vol. I.) London: Oxford University Press.

(1975). *Papers in Applied Linguistics*. (The Edinburgh Course in Applied Linguistics, vol. II.) London: Oxford University Press.

Allen, W. Sidney (1950). 'Notes on the phonetics of an Eastern Armenian speaker'. *Transactions of the Philological Society* 1950. 180–206.

(1951a). 'Phonetics and comparative linguistics'. *Archivum Linguisticum* 2. 126–135.

(1951b). 'Some prosodic aspects of retroflexion and aspiration in Sanskrit'. *Bulletin of the School of Oriental and African Studies* 13. 939–46. (Reprinted in Palmer, 1970a: 82–90.)

(1953). *Phonetics in Ancient India*. London: Oxford University Press.

(1954). 'Retroflexion in Sanskrit: prosodic technique and its relevance to comparative statement'. *Bulletin of the School of Oriental and African Studies* 16. 556–565.

(1956). 'Structure and system in the Abaza verbal complex'. *Transactions of the Philological Society* 1956. 127–76.

(1957a). 'Aspiration in the Hārauṭi nominal'. *Studies in Linguistic Analysis* 1957. 68–86.

241

(1957b). *On the Linguistic Study of Language: An Inaugural Lecture*. Cambridge: Cambridge University Press. (Reprinted, with 'Author's note [1965]', in Strevens, 1966b: 3–26; and (without notes or references), with '[Author's] Foreword [1971]', in Allen & Corder, 1973: 147–161.)

(1964). 'Transitivity and possession'. *Language* 40. 337–43.

Allerton, David J., Carney, E. & Holdcroft, D. (eds.) (1979). *Function and Context in Linguistic Analysis*. Cambridge: Cambridge University Press.

Alleyne, M. (1980). *Comparative Afro-American*. Ann Arbor, Mich.: Karoma Press.

Allport, D. Alan (1983). 'Language and cognition'. In R. Harris (1983a: 61–94).

& Funnell, Elaine (1981). 'Components of the mental lexicon'. In Longuet-Higgins *et al.* (1981: 183–196 [397–410]).

Anderson, John M. (1971). *The Grammar of Case: Towards a Localistic Theory*. London & New York: Cambridge University Press.

(1973a). *An Essay Concerning Aspect*. The Hague: Mouton.

(1973b). 'Maximi Planudis in memoriam'. In Kiefer & Ruwet (1973: 20–47).

(1977). *On Case Grammar*. London: Croom Helm.

(ed.) (1981). *Language Form and Linguistic Variation: Papers Dedicated to Angus McIntosh*. Amsterdam: Benjamins.

Anderson, Stephen R. (1985a). *Phonology in the Twentieth Century: Theories of Rules and Theories of Representations*. Chicago: University of Chicago Press.

(1985b). 'Typological distinctions in word formation'. In Shopen (1985c: 3–56).

Antinucci, F. (1974). 'Sulla deissi'. (Roma: Consiglio Nazionale delle Ricerche, Istituto di Psicologia.) *Lingua e Stile* 11. 223–247.

Appleton, Sir Edward (1956). *Science and the Nation*. (BBC Reith Lectures.) Edinburgh: Edinburgh University Press.

Arnold, Douglas G., Atkinson, R. M., Durand, J., Grover, C. & Sadler, L. (eds.) (1989). *Essays on Grammatical Theory and Universal Grammar*. London: Oxford University Press.

Aronoff, M. (1985). 'Orthography and linguistic theory'. *Language* 61. 28–72.

Asher, Ronald E. & Henderson, E. J. A. (eds.) (1981a). *Towards a History of Phonetics*. (Papers presented to David Abercrombie.) Edinburgh: Edinburgh University Press.

(1981b). 'Introduction' in Asher & Henderson (1981a: vii–xi).

Atkinson, R. M. (1979). 'Prerequisites for reference'. In Ochs & Schieffelin (1979: 229–249).

& Griffiths, P. (1973). 'Here's here's, there's, here and there'. *Edinburgh Working Papers in Linguistics* 3. 29–73.

, Kilby, David & Roca, Iggy (1982). *Foundations of General Linguistics*. London: Allen & Unwin.

Austin, John L. (1946). 'Other minds'. *Proceedings of the Aristotelian Society*, suppl. vol. 20. (Reprinted in Austin, 1970: 76–116.)

(1950). 'Truth'. *Proceedings of the Aristotelian Society*, suppl. vol. 24. 111–128. (Reprinted in Austin, 1970: 117–133.)

References

(1970). *Philosophical Papers*, 2nd edn, edited by J. O. Urmson & G. R. Warnock. London: Oxford University Press.

Bach, Emmon (1964). *An Introduction to Transformational Grammars*. New York: Holt, Rinehart & Winston.

(1968). 'Nouns and noun phrases'. In Bach & Harms (1968: 91–122).

(1974). *Syntactic Theory*. New York: Holt, Rinehart & Winston.

& Harms, R. T. (eds.) (1968). *Universals in Linguistic Theory*. New York: Holt, Rinehart & Winston.

Baker, Gordon P. & Hacker, Peter (1984). *Language, Sense and Nonsense*. Oxford: Blackwell.

Ball, Christopher (1967). Review of Bazell *et al.* (1966). *Bulletin of the School of Oriental and African Studies* 30. 757–758.

Bally, Charles (1932). *Linguistique Générale et Linguistique Française*. Paris: Ernest Leroux.

Banfield, Ann (1973). 'Narrative style and the grammar of direct and indirect speech'. *Foundations of Language* 10. 1–39.

Bar-Hillel, Yehoshua (1950). 'On syntactical categories'. *Journal of Symbolic Logic* 15. 1–16. (Reprinted in Bar-Hillel, 1964: 19–37.)

(1964). *Language and Information*. Reading, Mass.: Addison-Wesley.

(1969). Review of Lyons (1968a). In *Semiotica* 1. 449–459. (Reprinted in Bar-Hillel, 1970: 364–74.)

(1970). *Aspects of Language*. Jerusalem: Magnes.

, Malino, J. & Margalit, A. (1974). 'On logic and theoretical linguistics'. In Sebeok (1974a: 37–101).

Barthes, R. (1970). *S/Z*. Paris: Seuil.

Bartsch, Renate (1978). 'Comments on Lyons, "Basic problems of semantics" [Lyons, 1978a]'. In Dressler & Meid (1978: 22–27).

Bates, Elizabeth (1976). *Language and Context: Studies in the Acquisition of Pragmatics*. New York: Academic Press.

(1979). *The Emergence of Symbols: Cognition and Communication in Infancy*. New York: Academic Press.

, Camaioni, L. & Volterra, V. (1979). 'The acquisition of performatives prior to speech'. In Ochs & Schieffelin (1979: 111–129).

Bazell, Charles E. (1949a). 'Syntactic relations and linguistic typology'. *Cahiers Ferdinand de Saussure* 8. 5–20.

(1949b). 'On the problem of the morpheme'. *Archivum Linguisticum* 1. 1–15. (Reprinted in Hamp *et al.*, 1966: 216–226).

(1952). 'The correspondence fallacy in structural linguistics'. *Studies by Members of the English Department, Istanbul University* 1952: 138–145. (Reprinted in Hamp *et al.*, 1966: 271–298.)

(1953). *Linguistic Form*. Istanbul: Istanbul University Press.

(1958). *Linguistic Typology*. London: School of Oriental and African Studies. (Reprinted in Strevens, 1966: 29–49.)

References

(1959). Review of *Studies in Linguistic Analysis* (1957). In *Bulletin of the School of Oriental and African Studies* 22. 182–184.

(1962). 'Meaning and the morpheme'. *Word* 18. 132–142. (Reprinted in Kühlwein, 1973: 83–95.)

Catford, J. C., Halliday, M. A. K. & Robins, R. H. (eds.) (1966). *In Memory of J. R. Firth*. London: Longman.

Bellugi, Ursula & Klima, E. (1976). 'Two faces of sign: iconic and abstract'. In Harnad *et al.* (1976: 514–538).

& Studdert-Kennedy (eds.) (1980). *Signed and Spoken Language: Biological Constraints on Linguistic Form*. Deerfield Beach, Fla. & Basel: Verlag Chemie.

Belvalkar, K. (1915). *Systems of Sanskrit Grammar*. Poona.

Bennett, Jonathan (1976). *Linguistic Behaviour*. Cambridge: Cambridge University Press.

Benskin, Michael (1981). 'The Middle English Dialect Atlas'. In Benskin & Samuels (1981: xxvii–xli).

& Samuels, M. L. (eds.) (1981). *So Meny People Longages and Tonges: Philological Essays in Scots and Medieval English Presented to Angus McIntosh*. Edinburgh (Middle English Dialect Project, University of Edinburgh): Benskin & Samuels.

Benthall, Jonathan & Polhemus, Ted (eds.) (1975). *The Body as a Medium of Expression*. (Essays based on a course of lectures given at the Institute of Contemporary Arts, London.) London: Institute of Contemporary Arts.

Benveniste, Emile (1956). 'La nature des pronoms'. In Halle *et al.* (1956: 34–37). (Reprinted in Benveniste, 1966: 251–257.)

(1958). 'De la subjectivité dans le langage'. *Journal de Psychologie* 51. 257–265. (Reprinted in Benveniste, 1966: 258–66.)

(1959). 'Les relations de temps dans le verbe français'. *Bulletin de la Société de Linguistique* 54. 69–82. (Reprinted in Benveniste, 1966: 237–50.)

(1960). Review of Firth (1957a). In *Bulletin de la Société de Linguistique* 15. 18–19.

(1966). *Problèmes de Linguistique Générale*. Paris: Gallimard.

(1967). 'La forme et le sens dans le langage'. In *Actes du XIIIe Congrès de la Société de Philosophie de Langue Française* (Geneva, 1966). (Reprinted in Benveniste, 1974: 215–238.)

(1974). *Problèmes de Linguistique Générale*, vol. II. Paris: Gallimard.

Berry, Margaret (1973). *Introduction to Systemic Linguistics: Structure and Systems*. London: Batsford.

Berthoud, A.-C. (1979). 'Projet d'étude "La deixis en tant que problème d'apprentissage": étude de quelques verbes de mouvement'. *Travaux du Centre de Recherches Sémiologiques, Université de Neuchâtel* 33. 77–99.

Bever, Thomas G. (1971). 'The integrated study of language behavior'. In Morton (1971: 158–209).

(1982a). 'Broca and Lashley were right: cerebral dominance is an accident of growth'. In Caplan (1980: 186–230).

(1982b). 'Some implications of the nonspecific bases of language'. In Wanner & Gleitman (1982: 429–449).

Bickerton, Derek (1981). *Roots of Language*. Ann Arbor, Mich.: Karoma Press.

Black, Max (1968). *The Labyrinth of Language*. New York: Praeger. (British editions: London: Pall Mall, 1970; Harmondsworth: Penguin, 1972.)

Blakemore, Colin (1977). *Mechanics of the Mind*. Cambridge: Cambridge University Press.

Bleek, Wilhelm (1867). *Über den Ursprung der Sprache*. Kapstadt (als Manuskript gedruckt). (English edn, *On the Origin of Language*, ed. with a Preface by E. Haeckel and trans. from German by Thomas Davidson. New York: Schmidt, 1869.) (Facsimile reprint in Koerner, 1983: [xxix + 69pp.].)

Bloom, Lois (1970). *Language Development: Form and Function in Emerging Grammars*. Cambridge, Mass.: MIT Press.

Bloomfield, Leonard (1926). 'A set of postulates for the science of language'. *Language 2*. 153–164. (Reprinted in Joos, 1957: 26–31).

(1933). *Language*. New York: Holt, Rinehart & Winston; London: Allen & Unwin, 1935.

(1939). *Linguistic Aspects of Science*. (= vol. 1, no. 4, of Neurath *et al.*, 1939.) Chicago: University of Chicago Press.

Bolinger, Dwight (ed.) (1972). *Intonation*. Harmondsworth: Penguin.

(1977). *Meaning and Form*. London: Longman.

Bowerman, Melissa M. (1973). *Early Syntactic Development*. London & New York: Cambridge University Press.

Brandwood, Leonard (1965). Review of Lyons (1963a). In *Journal of Hellenic Studies* (London) 85. 206–207.

Bright, William (ed.). (1965). *Sociolinguistics*. (Proceedings of the UCLA Sociolinguistics Conference, 1964.) The Hague: Mouton.

Broadbent, Donald E. (1981). 'Perceptual experiments and language theories'. In Longuet-Higgins *et al.* (1981: 375–385 [161–171].)

Broca, Paul (1863). 'La linguistique et l'anthropologie'. *Bulletin de la Société d'Anthropologie de Paris*. Année 1863. 264–319.

Brøndal, Viggo (1948). *Les Parties du Discours*. Copenhague: Munksgaard. (Danish original, 1928.)

Brough, John (1951). 'Theories of general linguistics in the Sanskrit grammarians'. *Transactions of the Philological Society 1951*. 27–46.

Brown, E. Keith (1984). *Linguistics Today*. London: Fontana/Collins.

& Miller, J. E. (1980). *Syntax: A Linguistic Introduction to Sentence Structure*. London: Hutchinson.

& Miller, J. E. (1982). *Syntax: Generative Grammar*. London: Hutchinson.

Brown, Gillian (1972). Review of Palmer (1970a). In *Lingua 29*. 84–88.

& Yule, George (1983). *Discourse Analysis*. Cambridge: Cambridge University Press.

Brown, Penelope & Levinson, S. C. (1987). *Politeness: Some Universals in Language*

References

Use. Cambridge: Cambridge University Press. (First edn, in Esther N. Goody, *Questions and Politeness*, 1978.)

Brown, Roger (1970). *A First Language.* London: Allen & Unwin.

   & Gilman, A. (1960). 'The pronouns of power and solidarity'. In Sebeok (1960: 253–276). (Reprinted in Fishman, 1968; Giglioli, 1972; Laver & Hutcheson, 1972.)

Bruner, Jerome S. (1974/5). 'From communication to language'. *Cognition* 3. 255–287.

   (1983). *Child's Talk.* New York: Norton.

Bublitz, W. (1978). *Ausdrucksweisen der Sprechereinstellung im Deutschen und Englischen.* Tübingen: Niemeyer.

Bühler, Karl (1934). *Sprachtheorie.* Jena: Fischer.

Bullowa, Margaret (1978). 'Infants as conversational partners'. In Myers (1978a: 44–60).

   (1979). *Before Speech: The Beginnings of Interpersonal Communication.* Cambridge: Cambridge University Press.

Bursill-Hall, Geoffrey N. (1961). 'Levels of analysis: J. R. Firth's theories of linguistic analysis (Part 2)'. *Journal of the Canadian Linguistic Association* 6. 164–191.

   (1962). 'The linguistic theories of J. R. Firth'. *International Journal of American Linguistics* 28. 256–257.

Bynon, Theodora & Palmer, F. R. (eds.) (1986). *Studies in the History of Western Linguistics: In Honour of R. H. Robins.* Cambridge: Cambridge University Press.

Campbell, Robin N. (1986). 'Language acquisition and cognition'. In Fletcher & Garman (1986: 30–48).

Caplan, David (ed.) (1980). *Biological Studies of Mental Processes.* Cambridge, Mass.: MIT Press.

Carnap, Rudolf (1939). *Foundations of Logic and Mathematics.* (=vol. I, no. 3, of Neurath *et al.*, 1939.) Chicago: University of Chicago Press.

   (1955). 'Meaning and synonymy in natural languages'. *Philosophical Studies* 6. 33–47. (Reprinted in Carnap, 1956: 233–47.)

   (1956). *Meaning and Necessity,* 2nd edn, Chicago: Chicago Univerity Press.

Carnochan, John (1951). 'A study of quantity in Hausa'. *Bulletin of the School of Oriental and African Studies* 13. 1032–1044.

   (1952). 'Glottalization in Hausa'. *Transactions of the Philological Society* 1952. 17–109.

   (1957). 'Gemination in Hausa'. *Studies in Linguistic Analysis.* 149–81.

Catford, John C. (1961). 'J. R. Firth and British linguistics'. In A. A. Hill (1961: 218–228).

Chao, Yuen Ren (1934). 'The non-uniqueness of phonemic solutions of phonetic systems'. *Bulletin of the Institute of History and Philology, Academia Sinica* 4. 363–397. (Reprinted in Joos, 1957: 38–54.)

References

(1962). 'Models in linguistics and models in general'. In Nagel *et al.* (1962: 528–550).

Chomsky, Noam (1953). 'Systems of syntactic analysis'. *Journal of Symbolic Logic* 18. 242–256.

(1955a). 'Logical syntax and semantics'. *Language* 31. 36–45.

(1955b). 'Semantic considerations in grammar'. Round Table on Languages and Linguistics, Monograph 8: 141–153. Washington, DC: Institute of Languages and Linguistics.

(1956). 'Three models for the description of language'. *IRE Transactions on Information Theory* IT–2. 113–124. (Reprinted, with corrections, in Luce *et al.*, 1963: 105–124.)

(1957). *Syntactic Structures*. The Hague: Mouton.

(1959a). Review of Skinner (1957). In *Language* 35. 26–58.

(1959b). 'On certain formal properties of grammars'. *Information and Control* 2. 137–167. (Reprinted in Luce *et al.*, 1963: 125–155.)

(1962). 'Explanatory models in linguistics'. In Nagel *et al.* (1962: 125–155.)

(1963). 'Formal properties of grammars'. In Luce *et al.* (1963: 323–418).

(1964a). 'The logical basis of linguistic theory'. In Lunt (1964: 914–978). (Revised and expanded, and published separately as Chomsky, 1964b, and, in part, in Fodor & Katz, 1964: 50–188.)

(1964b). *Current Issues in Linguistics*. The Hague: Mouton.

(1965). *Aspects of the Theory of Syntax*. Cambridge, Mass.: MIT Press.

(1966). *Cartesian Linguistics*. New York: Harper & Row.

(1968). *Language and Mind*. New York: Harcourt, Brace & World.

(1970). 'Remarks on nominalization'. In Jacobs & Rosenbaum (1970: 184–221). (Reprinted in Chomsky, 1972: 11–61.)

(1972). *Studies on Semantics in Generative Grammar*. The Hague: Mouton.

(1975a). *The Logical Structure of Linguistic Theory*. New York: Plenum Press.

(1975b). *Reflections on Language*. New York: Random House.

(1976). *Reflections on Language*. London: Temple Smith.

(1980a). *Rules and Representations*. Oxford: Blackwell.

(1980b). 'Human language and other semiotic systems'. In Sebeok & Umiker-Sebeok (1980: 287–330).

(1981). 'Knowledge of language: its elements and origins'. In Longuet-Higgins *et al.* (1981: 223–234 [9–20]).

(1982). *The Generative Enterprise: A Discussion with Riny Huybregts and Henk van Riemsdijk*. Dordrecht: Foris.

(1986). *Knowledge of Language: Its Nature, Origin and Use*. New York & London: Praeger.

& Halle, Morris (1968). *The Sound Pattern of English*. New York: Harper & Row.

& Miller, G. A. (1958). 'Finite state languages'. *Information and Control* 1. 91–112. (Reprinted in Luce *et al.*, 1963: 125–155.)

References

& Miller, G. A. (1963). 'Introduction to the formal analysis of natural languages'. In Luce *et al.* (1963: 269–321).

Christy, T. Craig (1983). *Uniformitarianism in Linguistics*. Amsterdam: Benjamins.

Clements, George N. (1977). 'The autosegmental treatment of vowel harmony'. In Dressler & Pfeiffer (1977: 111–120).

Cohen, L. Jonathan (1981). 'Some remarks on the nature of linguistic theory'. In Longuet-Higgins *et al.* (1981: 235–243 [21–28]).

Cole, Peter (ed.) (1981). *Radical Pragmatics*. New York: Academic Press.

Collinge, Neville E. (1965). Review of Lyons (1963a). In *Archivum Linguisticum* 17. 53–55.

Comrie, Bernard (1976). *Aspect*. London: Cambridge University Press.

Cornish, Francis (1986). *Anaphoric Relations in English and French: A Discourse Perspective*. London: Croom Helm.

Coseriu, Eugenio (1952). *Sistema, Norma y Habla*. Montevideo: Universidad de la Republica. (Reprinted in Coseriu, 1962: 11–113.)

(1954). *Forma y Sustancia en los Sonidos del Lenguaje*. Montevideo: Universidad de la Republica. (Reprinted in Coseriu, 1962: 115–234.)

(1958). *Sincronia, Diacronia e Historia. El Problema del Cambio Linguistico*. Montevideo: Universidad de la Republica.

(1962). In *Teoria del Lenguaje y Lingüística General*. Madrid: Gredos.

(1973). *Lezioni di Linguistica Generale*. Torino: Boringheri.

Coulmas, Florian & Ehlich, K. (eds.) (1983). *Writing in Focus*. Berlin, New York & Amsterdam: Mouton.

Craigie, William A. (1937–). *A Dictionary of the Older Scottish Tongue*, vols. I & II. Chicago: Chicago University Press; London: Oxford University Press.

& Aitken, A. J. (1963). *A Dictionary of the Older Scottish Tongue*, vol. III. Chicago: Chicago University Press; London: Oxford University Press.

Crymes, Ruth (1968). *Some Systems of Substitution Correlations in Modern American English*. The Hague: Mouton.

Crystal, David (1975). *The English Tone of Voice*. London: Arnold.

(ed.) (1982). *Linguistic Controversies: Essays in Linguistic Theory and Practice in Honour of F. R. Palmer*. London: Arnold.

(1986). 'Prosodic development'. In Fletcher & Garman (1986: 174–197).

Culioli, Antoine, Fuchs, C. & Pêcheux, M. (1970). 'Considérations théoriques à propos du traitement formel du langage'. Centre de Linguistique Quantitative, Université de Paris VII.

Culler, Jonathan (1975). *Structuralist Poetics: Structuralism, Linguistics, and the Study of Literature*. Ithaca, NY: Cornell University Press.

Curtius, Ernst R. (1953). *European Literature and the Latin Middle Ages*. (Trans., by W. R. Trask, of *Europäische Literatur und Lateinisches Mittelalter*, Bern: Francke, 1948.) London: Routledge & Kegan Paul.

Darwin, Charles (1859). *Origin of Species*. London: Murray.

(1871). *The Descent of Man*. London: Murray.

References

(1872). *The Expression of the Emotions in Man and Animals.* London: Murray.

(1877). 'A biographical sketch of an infant'. *Mind* 2. 285–294.

Darwin, Christopher J. (1987). 'Speech perception and recognition'. In Lyons *et al.* (1987: 59–81).

David, Jean & Martin, R. (eds.) (1976). *Modèles Logiques et Niveaux d'Analyse Linguistique.* Paris: Klincksieck.

Derrida, Jacques (1967). *De la Grammatologie.* Paris: Minuit.

(1972). *La Voix et le Phénomène: Introduction au Problème du Signe dans la Phénoménologie.* Paris: Presses Universitaires de France.

Desclés, J.-P. (1976). 'Description de quelques opérations éconciatives'. In J. David & R. Martin (eds.), *Modèles Logiques et Niveaux d'Analyse Linguistique.* Paris: Klincksieck.

des Places, Edouard (1964). Review of Lyons (1963a). In *Revue des Etudes Grecques* (Paris) 77. 345.

(1965). Review of Lyons (1963a). In *Revue de Philologie* (Paris) 39. 321.

Détienne, Marcel (1967). *Les Maîtres de Vérite dans la Grèce Archaïque.* Paris: François Maspero.

Deuchar, Margaret (1984). *British Sign Language.* London: Routledge & Kegan Paul.

(1985). 'The implications of sign language research for linguistic theory'. In William Stokoe & Virginia Volterra (eds.), *Proceedings of the Third International Symposium on Sign Language Research.* Silver Spring, Md.: Linstok Press; Rome: Istituto di Psicologia CNR, 293–346.

(1987a). 'Sociolinguistics'. In Lyons *et al.* (1987: 296–310).

(1987b). 'Sign language'. In Lyons *et al.* (1987: 311–335).

Diebold, A. Richard (1964). Review of Saporta (1961). In *Language* 40. 197–260.

Dimond, Stuart J. & Blizard, D. A. (eds.) (1977). *Evolution and Lateralization of the Brain.* (Annals of the New York Academy of Sciences.)

Dinneen, F. P. (1967a). *An Introduction to General Linguistics.* New York: Holt, Rinehart & Winston.

Dixon, Robert M. W. (1963). *Linguistic Science and Logic.* The Hague: Mouton. (Extract, pp. 40–49, reprinted as 'Linguistics as a science', in Kühlwein, 1973: 43–52.)

(1968). 'Noun classes'. *Lingua* 21. 104–125.

(1971). 'A method of semantic description'. In Steinberg & Jakobovits (1971: 436–471).

(1977). 'Where have all the adjectives gone?' *Studies in Language* 1. 19–80. (Reprinted in Dixon, 1982.)

(1980). *The Languages of Australia.* Cambridge: Cambridge University Press.

(1982). *Where Have All The Adjectives Gone? And Other Essays in Semantics and Syntax.* The Hague: Mouton.

Donnellan, Keith (1966). 'Reference and definite descriptions'. *Philosophical Review* 75. 281–204. (Reprinted in Steinberg & Jakobovits 1971: 100–114.)

Donzella, Carlo (1980). 'Storia e bibliographia del campo glossematico'. In Zinna (1986: 113–127).

References

Dressler, Wolfgang U. & Meid, W. (eds.) (1978). *Proceedings of the Twelfth International Congress of Linguists* (Vienna, 1977). (PICL 12.) Innsbrucker Beiträge zur Sprachwissenschaft. Innsbruck: Institut für Sprachwissenschaft der Universität Innsbruck.

Ducrot, Oswald & Todorov, T. (1972). *Dictionnaire Encyclopédique des Sciences du Langage*. Paris: Seuil. (English edn, Oxford: Blackwell, 1980.)

Dummett, Michael (1973). *Frege: Philosophy of Language*. London: Duckworth.

Durand, Jacques & Robinson, D. (eds.) (1974). *La Linguistique en Grande Bretagne dans les Années Soixante*. (*Langages* 34.) Paris: Larousse-Didier.

Eco, U. (1976). *A Theory of Semiotics*. Bloomington, Ind. & London: Indiana University Press.

Eddington, Arthur S. (1935). *The Nature of the Physical World*. (The Gifford Lectures, 1927.) London: Dent (Everyman Library). (First published, Cambridge, 1928.)

Ellis, Jeffrey (1966). Review of Lyons (1963a). In *Linguistics* 24. 83–115.

Emeneau, Murray B. (1955). 'India and linguistics'. *Journal of the American Oriental Society* 75. 143–153.

Engler, Rudolf (1967–). *Edition Critique du "Cours de Linguistique Générale" de F. de Saussure*. Wiesbaden: Harrassowitz.

 (1975). 'European structuralism: Saussure'. In Sebeok (1975: 829–886).

Fillmore, Charles H. (1968). 'The case for case'. In Bach & Harms (1968: 1–88).

Firth, John R. (1930). *Speech*. London: Benn. (Reprinted in Firth, 1964: 139–211.)

 (1935a). 'The technique of semantics'. *Transactions of the Philological Society* 1935. 36–72. (Reprinted in Firth, 1957a: 7–33.)

 (1935b). 'The use and distribution of certain English sounds: phonetics from a functional point of view'. *English Studies* 17. 2–12. (Reprinted in Firth, 1957a: 34–46.)

 (1937). *The Tongues of Men*. London: Watts. (Reprinted in Firth, 1964: 1–136.)

 (1946). 'The English school of phonetics'. *Transactions of the Philological Society* 1946. 92–132. (Reprinted in Firth, 1957a: 92–100.)

 (1948a). 'The semantics of linguistic science', *Lingua* I, 393–404. (Reprinted in Firth, 1957a: 139–147.)

 (1948b). 'Atlantic linguistics'. *Archivum Linguisticum* 1. 95–116. (Reprinted in Firth, 1957a: 156–172.)

 (1948c). 'Sounds and prosodies'. *Transactions of the Philological Society* 1948. 127–152. (Reprinted in Firth, 1957a: 121–139; Palmer, 1970a: 1–26; Hamp *et al.*, 1966: 175–191; Jones & Laver, 1973: 47–65; Makkai, 1972: 252–263.)

 (1950). 'Personality and language in society'. *Sociological Review* 42. 37–52. (Reprinted in Firth, 1957a: 177–189; extract in Allen & Corder, 1973: 15–21.)

 (1951a). 'Modes of meaning'. *Essays and Studies of the English Association* (New Series) 4. 118–149. (Reprinted in Firth, 1957a: 190–215.)

 (1951b). 'General linguistics and descriptive grammar'. *Transactions of the Philological Society* 1951. 69–87. (Reprinted in Firth, 1957a: 216–28.)

 (1956). 'Linguistic analysis and translation'. In Halle *et al.* (1956: 133–39).

References

(Reprinted in Firth, 1968a: 84–95.)

(1957a). *Papers in Linguistics, 1934–1951*. London: Oxford University Press.

(1957b). 'A synopsis of linguistic theory, 1930–1955'. *Studies in Linguistic Analysis* 1957: 1–32. (Reprinted in Firth, 1968a 168–205; extract in Kühlwein, 1973: 24–27.)

(1957c). 'Ethnographic analysis and language with reference to Malinowski's views'. In Raymond Firth (ed.), *Man and Culture: An Evaluation of the Work of Bronislaw Malinowski*. London: Routledge & Kegan Paul. (Reprinted in Firth, 1968a: 137–167.)

(1957d). 'Applications of general linguistics'. *Transactions of the Philological Society* 1957. 1–14. (Reprinted in Firth, 1968a: 126–136.)

(1964). *The Tongues of Men and Speech*. (=Firth, 1937 & 1930, edited by Peter Strevens.) London: Oxford University Press.

(1968a). *Selected Papers of J. R. Firth, 1952–1959*. (Edited by F. R. Palmer.) London: Longman.

(1968b). 'Linguistic analysis as a study of meaning'. In Firth (1968a: 12–26).

Fischer, Susan D. (1978). 'Sign language and creoles'. In Siple (1978: 309–331).

Fishman, Joshua A. (ed.) (1968). *Readings in the Sociology of Language*. The Hague: Mouton.

Fletcher, Paul & Garman, Michael (eds.) (1986). *Language Acquisition*. (2nd edn) Cambridge: Cambridge University Press. (1st edn, 1979.)

Fodor, Janet D. (1981). 'Does performance shape competence?'. In Longuet-Higgins et al. (1981: 285–295 [71–81]).

Fodor, Jeremy A. (1975). *The Language of Thought*. New York: Cromwell; Hassocks, Sussex: Harvester Press.

(1981). *Representations*. Hassocks, Sussex: Harvester Press.

(1983). *The Modularity of Mind*. Cambridge, Mass.: MIT Press.

& Katz, J. J. (eds.) (1964). *The Structure of Language: Readings in the Philosophy of Language*. Englewood Cliffs, NJ: Prentice Hall.

Foster, Mary L. & Brandes, Stanley H. (eds.) (1980). *Symbol as Sense*. London & New York: Academic Press.

Fowler, Roger (1966). Review of Firth (1964). *Linguistics* 23. 121–123.

Fried, Vilem (ed.) (1960). *The Prague School of Linguistics and Language Teaching*. London: Oxford University Press.

Friedman, Lynn A. (ed.) (1977). *On the Other Hand: New Perspectives on American Sign Language*. London & New York: Academic Press.

Friedrich, Paul (1966). 'Structural implications of Russian pronominal usage'. In Bright (1965: 214–259).

(1974). *On Aspect Theory and Homeric Aspects*. (Indiana University Publications in Anthropology and Linguistics; Memoir 28 of *International Journal of American Linguistics*.) Bloomington, Ind.: Indiana University Press.

Fries, Charles C. & Pike, K. L. (1949). 'Co-existent phonemic systems'. *Language* 25. 29–50.

References

Fromkin, Victoria A. (1965). 'On system-structure phonology'. *Language* 41: 601–609. (Reprinted in Makkai, 1972: 283–289.)

Fuchs, C. & Rouault, J. (1975). 'Towards a formal treatment of the phenomenon of aspect'. In Keenan (1975: 373–388).

Fudge, Erik C. (ed.) (1973). *Phonology*. Harmondsworth: Penguin.

Garcia, Erica C. (1970). 'British-style descriptive linguistics'. (Review article on F. R. Palmer, 1970a.) In *Romance Philology* 24. 612–625.

Gardiner, Alan H. (1932). *The Theory of Speech and Language*. London: Oxford University Press. (2nd edn, 1951.)

Garvin, Paul L. (1961). 'The Prague School of linguistics'. In A. A. Hill (1961a: 229–239).

(1964). *On Linguistic Method: Selected Papers*. The Hague: Mouton.

Gibson, Kathleen R. (1983). 'Comparative neobehavioral ontogeny and the constructionist approach to the evolution of the brain, object manipulation and language'. In Grolier (1983: 37–61).

Giglioli, Pier Paolo (ed.) (1972). *Language and Social Context*. Harmondsworth: Penguin.

Gleason, Harold A. (1964). 'The organization of language: a stratificational view'. In Stuart (1964: 75–95).

Godel, Robert (1957). *Les Sources Manuscrites du Cours de linguistique générale de F. de Saussure*. Genève & Paris: Droz.

(1961). *L'Ecole Saussuriene de Genève'*. In Mohrmann *et al.* (1961: 294–299).

(ed.) (1969). *A Geneva School Reader in Linguistics*. Bloomington, Ind. & London: Indiana University Press.

Goldsmith, John A. (1976). *Autosegmental Phonology*. New York: Garland.

Gonda, Jan (1966). Review of Lyons (1963a). In *Mnemosyne* (Leiden) 19. 416–420.

Goody, Jack (ed.) (1968). *Literacy in Traditional Societies*. London & New York: Cambridge University Press.

(1977). *The Domestication of the Savage Mind*. Cambridge: Cambridge University Press.

(1983). 'Literacy and achievement in the ancient world'. In Coulmas & Ehlich (1983: 83–97).

(1986). *The Logic of Writing and the Organization of Society*. Cambridge: Cambridge University Press.

& Watt, I. (1963). 'The consequences of literacy'. *Comparative Studies in Society and History* 5. 304–45. (Reprinted in Goody, 1968: 27–68.)

Gray, Louis H. (1939). *Foundations of Language*. New York: Macmillan.

Greenbaum, Sidney, Leech, G. N. & Svartvik, J. (eds.) (1980). *Studies in English Linguistics* (for Randolph Quirk). London: Longman.

Greenberg, Joseph H. (1963). *Universals of Language*. Cambridge, Mass.: MIT Press.

Osgood, C. & Jenkins, J. (1961). 'Memorandum concerning universals'. In Greenberg (1963: 255–264).

Greenberg, Joseph H. (1954). 'A quantitative approach to the morphological typology of languages'. In Robert E. Spencer (ed.), *Method and Perspective in Anthropology*. Minneapolis, Minn.: University of Minnesota Press.

Greene, Judith (1972). *Psycholinguistics: Chomsky and Psychology*. Harmondsworth: Penguin.

Greimas, A. J. (1966). *Sémantique Structurale*. Paris: Larousse.

Grice, H. Paul. (1968). 'Utterer's meaning, sentence-meaning and word-meaning'. *Foundations of Language* 4. 225–242.

(1981). 'Presupposition and conversational implicature'. In Cole (1981: 183–198).

Grillo, Ralph D., Pratt, J. & Street, J. V. (1987). 'Anthropology, linguistics and language'. In Lyons *et al.* (1987: 268–295).

Grolier, Eric de (ed.) (1983). *Glossogenetics: The Origin and Evolution of Language*. New York: Harwood.

Gruber, J. S. (1967). 'Topicalization in child language'. *Foundations of Language* 3. 37–65.

Haas, William (1954). 'On defining linguistic units'. *Transactions of the Philological Society* 1954. 54–84.

(1958). Review of Firth (1957a). In *Bulletin of the School of Oriental and African Studies* 21. 668–671.

(1963). Review of Dixon (1963). In *Archivum Linguisticum* 15. 216–217.

(1964). 'Semantic value'. In Lunt (1964: 1066–1077).

(1967). 'Grammatical prerequisites of phonological analysis'. In Josef Hamm (ed.), *Phonologie der Gegenwart*. Graz & Wien: Bohlaus.

(1970). *Phono-graphic Translation*. Manchester: Manchester University Press.

(1973a). 'Meanings and rules'. *Proceedings of the Aristotelian Society* 1972/73. 135–155.

(1973b). Review article, 'John Lyons' "Introduction to Theoretical Linguistics"'. *Journal of Linguistics* 9. 71–113.

(1976a). 'Writing: the basic options'. In Haas (1976b: 131–208).

(ed.) (1976b). *Writing Without Letters*. Manchester: Manchester University Press.

(ed.) (1981). *Standard Languages, Spoken and Written*. Manchester: Manchester University Press.

(1983). 'Determining the level of a script'. In Coulmas & Ehlich (1983: 14–29).

Haeckel, Ernst H. (1867). *Natürliche Schöpfungsgeschichte: Gemeinverständliche Wissenschaftliche Vorträge*. Berlin: Reimer. (English trans., *The History of Creation*. London: King; New York: Appleton, 1876.)

Haiman, John (1985). *Natural Syntax*. Cambridge: Cambridge University Press.

Hall, Robert A. (1950). *Leave Your Language Alone!* New York: Doubleday. (Revised 2nd edn, reprinted as *Linguistics and Your Language*. New York: Doubleday, 1975.)

(1968). *An Essay on Language*. Philadelphia & New York: Chilton.

Hall, Roland (1965). 'Parts of speech'. *Proceedings of the Aristotelian Society*, suppl. vol. 39. 173–188.

References

Halle, Morris, Lunt, H. G., McLean, H. & Schooneveld, C. H. van (eds.) (1956). *For Roman Jakobson: Essays on the Occasion of his Sixtieth Birthday*. The Hague: Mouton.

Halliday, Michael A. K. (1957). 'Some aspects of systematic description and comparison in grammatical description'. *Studies in Linguistic Analysis* 1957. 54–67.

(1959). *The Language of the Chinese "Secret History of the Mongols"*. (Publications of the Philological Society, 17.) Oxford: Blackwell.

(1961). 'Categories of the theory of grammar'. *Word* 17. 241–92. (Extract reprinted in Halliday, 1976: 52–72.)

(1962). 'Linguistique générale et linguistique appliquée à l'enseignement des langues'. In *Etudes de Linguistique Appliquée*. Publications du Centre de Linguistique Appliquée, Université de Besançon. Paris: Didier. 1. 5–48.

(1966a). 'Intonation systems in English'. In McIntosh & Halliday, 1966: 111–133.

(1966b). 'Lexis as a linguistic level'. In Bazell *et al.* (1966: 150–161). (Extract reprinted, as 'Lexical relations', in Halliday, 1976: 73–83.)

(1966c). 'Some notes on "deep" grammar'. *Journal of Linguistics* 2. 57–67. (Extract reprinted in Halliday, 1976: 8–98.)

(1967a). *Intonation and Grammar in British English*. The Hague: Mouton.

(1967b). 'Notes on theme and transitivity in English: Part 1'. *Journal of Linguistics* 3. 37–81.

(1967c). 'Notes on theme and transitivity in English: Part 2'. *Journal of Linguistics* 3. 199–244.

(1967d). *Grammar, Society and the Noun*. (Inaugural lecture.) London: H. K. Lewis (for University College, London). (Extract reprinted in Kühlwein, 1973: 96–116.)

(1969). 'Options and functions in the English clause'. *Brno Studies in English* 8. 81–88. (Reprinted in Householder, 1972: 248–257.)

(1970a). 'Language structure and language function'. In Lyons (1970a: 140–165).

(1970b). 'Functional diversity in language as seen from a consideration of modality and mood in English'. *Foundations of Language* 6. 322–365. (Extract reprinted, as 'Modality and modulation in English', in Halliday, 1976: 189–213.)

(1971). Review of Firth (1968a). In *Bulletin of the School of Oriental and African Studies* 34. 664–667.

(1973). *Explorations in the Functions of Language*. London: Arnold.

(1976). *System and Function in Language: Papers*, edited by Gunther Kress, London: Oxford University Press

(1978). 'Development of texture in child language'. In Myers (1978a: 72–87).

Strevens, P. D. & McIntosh, A. (1964). *The Linguistic Sciences and Language Teaching*. London: Longman. (Extract, pp. 12–14, reprinted as 'The relation between observation and theory', in Allen & Corder, 1973: 209–211.)

Hamburger, K. (1968). *Die Logik der Dichtung*. Stuttgart: Klett.

Hamp, Eric P. (1961). 'American schools of linguistics (other than generative-transformational)'. In A. A. Hill (1961a: 239–249).

Householder, F. & Austerlitz, R. (1966). *Readings in Linguistics II*. Chicago: Chicago University Press.

Harman, Gilbert (ed.) (1974). *On Noam Chomsky*. New York: Doubleday.

Harnad, Stevan R., Steklis, H. D. & Lancaster, Jane (eds.) (1976). *Origins and Evolution of Language and Speech*. (Annals of the New York Academy of Sciences, 280.) New York: Academy of Sciences.

Harris, Roy (1980). *The Language Makers*. Ithaca, NY: Cornell University Press.

(ed.) (1983a). *Approaches to Language*. Oxford, New York, etc.: Pergamon.

(1983b). 'Language and speech'. In Harris (1983a: 1–15).

(ed.) (1988). *Linguistic Thought in England 1914–1945*. London & New York: Routledge.

Harris, Zellig S. (1944). 'Simultaneous components in phonology'. *Language* 20. 181–205. (Reprinted in Joos, 1957: 124–138; Makkai, 1972: 115–133.)

(1951). *Methods in Structural Linguistics*. Chicago: University of Chicago Press. (Republished as *Structural Linguistics*, 1961.)

(1952). 'Discourse Analysis'. *Language* 28. 1–30.

(1954). 'Distributional Structure'. *Word* 10. 775–793. (Reprinted in Fodor & Katz, 1964: 33–49; Harris, 1970: 775–794; Katz, 1985: 26–47.)

(1957). 'Co-occurrence and transformation in linguistic structure'. *Language* 33. 283–340. (Reprinted in Householder, 1972: 151–185.)

(1970). *Papers in Structural and Transformational Linguistics*. Dordrecht: Reidel.

Hartmann, Peter (1962). Review of *Studies in Linguistic Analysis* (1957). In *Biblioteca Orientalis* 19. 2320–2340.

Hartshorne, Charles (1966). 'Some reflection on metaphysics and language'. *Foundations of Language* 2. 20–32.

Hattori, Shiro & Inoue, K. (eds.) (1983). *Proceedings of the Thirteenth International Congress of Linguists* (Tokyo, 1982.) (PICL 13.) Tokyo & The Hague: CIPL.

Haugen, Einar (1958). Review of Firth (1957a). In *Language* 34. 498–502.

(1965). 'Linguistics and language planning'. In Bright (1965: 50–71).

Havelock, E. A. (1976). *Origins of Western Literacy*. Toronto: Ontario Institute for Studies in Education.

Hays, David G. (1964). 'Dependency theory: a formalism and some observations'. *Language* 40. 511–525. (Reprinted in Householder, 1972: 223–240.)

Heilmann, Luigi (ed.) (1974). *Proceedings of the Eleventh International Congress of Linguists* (Bologna, 1972). (PICL 11.) Bologna: Mulino.

Henderson, Eugenie J. A. (1949). 'Prosodies in Siamese'. *Asia Major* (New Series) 1. 189–215. (Reprinted in Palmer, 1970a: 27–53.)

(1951). 'The Phonology of loanwords in some South-East Asian languages', *Transactions of the Philological Society* 1951. 131–158. (Reprinted in Palmer,

1970a: 54–81.)

(1952). 'The main features of Cambodian pronunciation'. *Bulletin of the School of Oriental and African Studies* 14. 149–174.

Hertzfeld, Michael & Melazzo, Lucio (eds.) (1988). *Semiotic Theory and Practice*, 2 vols. (Proceedings of the 3rd International Congress of the International Association for Semiotic Studies, Palermo, 1984.) Berlin: Mouton de Gruyter.

Hewes, Gordon W. (1973). 'Primate communication and the gestural origins of language'. *Current Anthropology* 14. 5–32.

(1976). 'The current status of the gestural theory of language origin'. In Harnad *et al.* (1976: 482–584).

(1983). 'The invention of phonemically-based language'. In Grolier (1983: 143–162).

Hill, Archibald A. (1958). *Introduction to Linguistic Structures: From Sound to Sentence in English*. New York: Harcourt, Brace & World.

(ed.) (1961a). *Linguistics Today*. New York & London: Basic Books.

(1961b). 'Suprasegmentals, prosodies, prosodemes: comparison and discussion'. *Language* 37. 457–468.

Hill, Jane H. (1974). 'Possible continuity theories of language.' *Language* 50. 134–150.

(1978). 'Apes and language'. *Annual Review of Anthropology* 7. 89–112.

& Most, R. B. (1978). Review of Harnad *et al.* (1976). *Language* 54. 647–660.

Hill, Trevor (1966). 'The technique of prosodic analysis'. In Bazell *et al.* (1966: 198–226).

Hinde, Robert A. (ed.) (1972). *Non-Verbal Communication*. London & New York: Cambridge University Press.

Hintikka, Jaako (1969). *Models for Modalities: Selected Essays*. Dordrecht: Reidel.

Hirst, Graeme (1981). *Anaphora in Natural Language Understanding: A Survey*. Berlin: Springer.

Hjelmslev, Louis (1928). *Principes de Grammaire Générale*. Copenhagen: Host & Son.

(1935). *La Catégorie des Cas*. Aarhus: Universitetsforlaget.

(1943a). *Omkring Sprogteoriens Grundlaeggelse*. Aarhus. (English trans., Francis Whitfield, *Prolegomena to a Theory of Language*. Madison, Wis.: University of Wisconsin Press, 1953. (Revised edn, 1961.) Extract, from Sections 2 to 6, pp. 10–19, reprinted, as 'The aim of linguistic theory', in Allen & Corder, 1973: 202–208.

(1943b). 'Langue et parole'. *Cahiers Ferdinand de Saussure* 2. 29–40. (Reprinted in Hjelmslev, 1959.)

(1947). 'The structural analysis of language'. *Studia Linguistica* 1. 69–78. (Reprinted in Katz, 1985: 163–71.)

(1954). 'La stratification du langage'. *Word* 10. 163–188. (Reprinted in Hjelmslev, 1959: 36–68.)

(1959). *Essais Linguistiques*. (Travaux du Cercle Linguistique de Copenhague, 12.) Copenhagen. (2nd edn, Paris: Minuit, 1971.)

References

(1963a). *Sproget: En Introduktion*. København: Berlingske Forlag. (English trans., Francis Whitfield, *Language: An Introduction*. Madison, Wis.: University of Wisconsin Press. French trans., Michel Olsen (with 'Préface' by A. J. Greimas), *Le langage: Une Introduction*. Paris: Minuit, 1966.)

(1963b). *Essais Linguistiques*, 2. (Travaux du Cercle Linguistique de Copenhague, 16.) Copenhagen. (Republished, in part, as *Nouveaux Essais*. Paris: Presses Universitaires de France, 1985.)

(1975). *Résumé of a Theory of Language*, edited by F. J. Whitfield. (= Travaux du Cercle Linguistique de Copenhague, 16. Copenhagen.) Madison, Wis.: University of Wisconsin Press.

Hockett, Charles F. (1949). 'Two fundamental problems in phonemics'. *Studies in Linguistics* 7. 29–51.

(1954). 'Two models of grammatical description'. *Word* 10. 210–233. (Reprinted in Joos, 1957: 386–399.)

(1958). *A Course in Modern Linguistics*. New York: Macmillan.

(1960a). 'Logical considerations in the study of animal communication'. In Wesley E. Lanyon & William N. Tavogla (eds.), *Animal Sounds and Communication*. Washington, DC: American Institute of Biological Sciences, 392–430.

(1960b). 'The origin of speech'. *Scientific American* 203: 88–96.

(1963). 'The problem of universals in language'. In James H. Greenberg (1963: 1–22).

(1968). *The State of the Art*. The Hague: Mouton.

(1977). *The View from Language: Selected Essays*. Athens, Ga.: University of Georgia Press.

& Altmann, S. A. (1968). 'A note on design features'. In T. A. Sebeok (ed.), *Animal Communication*. Bloomington, Ind.: Indiana University Press, 1968, 61–72.

& Asher R. (1964). 'The human revolution'. *Current Anthropology* 5. 135–168.

Hoenigswald, Henry M. (1965). Review of Lyons (1963a). In *Journal of Linguistics* 1. 191–196.

Hoijer, Harry (1961). 'Anthropological Linguistics'. In Mohrmann *et al.* (1961: 110–127).

Honey, John (1983). *The Language Trap: Race, Class and the 'Standard English' Issue in British Schools*. Kenton, Middlesex: National Council for Educational Standards.

Honey, P. J. (1956). 'Word classes in Vietnamese'. *Bulletin of the School of Oriental and African Studies* 8. 534–544. (Reprinted in Hamp *et al.*, 1966: 276–286.)

Hook, Sidney (ed.) (1969). *Language and Philosophy*. New York: New York University Press.

Hope, T. E. *et al.* (eds.) (1981). *Language, Meaning and Style: Essays in Memory of Stephen Ullman*. Leeds: Leeds University Press.

Householder, Fred W. (1952). Review of Z. S. Harris (1951). In *International Journal of American Linguistics* 18. 260–268.

(1957). 'Rough justice in linguistics'. *Georgetown University Round Table on Language and Linguistics* 1957. Washington, DC: Georgetown University Press.

References

157–173.

(1962a). Review of Hoenigswald (1960). In *International Journal of American Linguistics* 28. 69–79. (With comments by Hoenigswald.)

(1962b). 'On the uniqueness of semantic mapping'. *Word* 18. 173–185.

(1971). *Linguistic Speculations*. Cambridge: Cambridge University Press.

(ed.) (1972). *Syntactic Theory, 1: Structuralist*. Harmondsworth: Penguin.

(1973). 'On arguments from asterisks'. *Foundations of Language* 10. 365–376.

Humboldt, Wilhelm von (1836). *Über die Verschiedenheit des Menschlichen Sprachbaues und ihren Einfluss auf die Geistige Entwicklung des Menschengeschlechts*. (Also published as an Introduction to *Über die Kawisprache auf der Insel Java*. Berlin, (1836–39.) Berlin. (Gesammelte Schriften, Band 7. 1–344. Berlin: Königliche Preussische Akademie der Wissenschaften, 1907) (Reprinted, Darmstadt: Claassen & Roether, 1949.)

Husserl, Edmund (1900/1). *Logische Untersuchungen*. Halle: Niemeyer.

Huxley, Renira (1970). 'The development of the correct use of subject personal pronouns in two children'. In G. B. Flores d'Arcais & W. J. M. Levelt (eds.). *Advances in Psycholinguistics*. Amsterdam: North Holland.

Hymes, Dell H. (1972). Review of Lyons (1970b). *Language* 48. 416–427. (Reprinted in Harman, 1974: 316–333.)

& Fought, J. (1975). 'American structuralism'. In Sebeok (1975: 903–1176). (Also published separately, with 'Epilogue'. The Hague: Mouton, 1981.)

Ingram, David (1989). *First Language Acquisition*. Cambridge: Cambridge University Press.

Innis, Robert E. (ed.) (1985). *Semiotics: An Introductory Anthology*. Bloomington, Ind.: Indiana University Press.

Isard, S. (1975). 'On changing the context'. In Keenan (1975: 287–296).

Ivić, Milka (1963). *Pravci u Lingvistiki*. Ljubljana: Dravna Zalozba Slovenije.

(1965). *Trends in Linguistics* (English trans., by Muriel Heppel, of Ivić, 1963.) The Hague: Mouton.

Jackson, Kenneth H. (1953). *Language and History in Early Britain*. Edinburgh: Edinburgh University Press.

Jakobson, Roman (1932). 'Zur Struktur des russischen Verbums'. In *Charisteria Guilelmo Mathesio Quinquagenario*, Prague. (Reprinted in Vachek, 1966: 347–359; Hamp et al., 1966a: 22–30.)

(1960). 'Linguistics and poetics'. In Sebeok (1960: 359–77). (Reprinted, with editorial Introduction, in Innis, 1985: 145–175. Extract reprinted, as 'Functions of language', in Allen & Corder, 1973: 53–57.)

(1963). 'Implications of language universals for Linguistics'. In Greenberg (1963: 208–19).

& Halle, M. (1956). *Fundamentals of Language*. The Hague: Mouton.

Jarvella, Robert J. & Klein W. (eds.) (1982). *Speech, Place and Action: Studies in Deixis and Related Topics*. New York: John Wiley.

Jespersen, Otto (1922). *Language: Its Nature, Development and Origin*. London: Allen & Unwin.

258

References

(1929). *The Philosophy of Grammar*. London: Allen & Unwin.

Jones, William E. & Laver, J. (eds.) (1973). *Phonetics in Linguistics: A Book of Readings*. London: Longman.

Joos, Martin (ed.) (1957). *Readings in Linguistics*. Washington, DC: American Council of Learned Societies. (Republished as *Readings in Linguistics 1*. Chicago: Chicago University Press, 1966.)

(1964). *The English Verb*. Madison, Wis.: University of Wisconsin Press.

Jurgens, V. & Von Cramon, D. (1982). 'On the role of the anterior cingulate cortex in phonation. A case report'. *Brain and Language* 15. 234–248.

Juszczyk, Peter W. (1981). 'Infant speech perception: a critical appraisal'. In P. D. Eimas & J. L. Miller (eds.), *Perspectives on the Study of Speech*. Hillsdale, NJ: Erlbaum, 113–164.

(1983). 'On characterizing the nature of speech perception'. In Jacques Mehler & R. Fox (eds.), *Neonate Cognition: Beyond the Blooming, Buzzing Confusion*. Hillsdale, NJ: Erlbaum.

Karmiloff-Smith, Annette (1987). 'Some recent issues in the study of language acquisition'. In Lyons *et al.* (1987: 367–386).

Katz, Jerrold J. (1972). *Semantic Theory*. New York: Harper & Row.

(1976). 'A hypothesis about the uniqueness of natural language'. In Harnad *et al.* (1976: 33–41).

(1981). *Language and Other Abstract Objects*. Oxford: Blackwell.

(1984). 'An outline of Platonist grammar'. In Thomas Bever, J. M. Carroll & L. A. Miller (eds.) *Talking Minds: The Study of Language in Cognitive Science*. Cambridge, Mass.: MIT Press, 1984, 1–33. (Reprinted in Katz, 1985: 172–203.)

(ed.) (1985). *The Philosophy of Linguistics*. London: Oxford University Press.

& Fodor, Jeremy, A. (1963). 'The structure of a semantic theory'. *Language* 39. 170–210. (Reprinted in Fodor & Katz, 1964.)

& Postal, P. M. (1964). *An Integrated Theory of Linguistic Description*. Cambridge, Mass: MIT Press.

Kavanagh, James R. & Mattingley, I. G. (eds.) (1972). *Language by Ear and by Eye. The Relationship between Speech and Writing*. Cambridge, Mass.: MIT Press.

Keenan, Edward L. (1972). 'On semantically based grammar'. *Linguistic Inquiry* 4. 413–461.

(ed.) (1975). *Formal Semantics of Natural Language*. (Papers from a Symposium sponsored by King's College Research Centre, Cambridge.) Cambridge: Cambridge University Press.

Kempson, Ruth M. (1985). 'C. E. Bazell: Obituary'. *Bulletin of the School of Oriental and African Studies* 48. 340–342.

Kenny, Anthony J. P. (1981). 'Language and the mind'. In Longuet-Higgins *et al.* (1981: 245–251 [31–37].)

Kent, R. D. (1981). 'Articulatory–acoustic perspectives on speech development'. In R. E. Stark (ed.), *Language Behavior in Infancy and Early Childhood*. New York: Elsevier/North Holland.

Kiefer, Ferenc & Ruwet, N. (eds.) (1973). *Generative Grammar in Europe*. Dordrecht: Reidel.

259

References

Kilby, David A. (1977). *Deep and Superficial Cases in Russian*. Frankfurt A. M.: Kubon & Sagnar.

(1981). 'On case markers'. *Lingua* 54. 101–133.

Klima, Edward S. & Bellugi, U. (1979). *The Signs of Language*. Cambridge, Mass.: Harvard University Press.

Koerner, E. F. Konrad (ed.) (1983). *Linguistics and Evolutionary Theory: Three Essays by August Schleicher, Ernst Haeckel, and Wilhelm Bleek*. Amsterdam: Benjamins.

Krantz, G. S. (1980). 'On sapientization and speech'. *Current Anthropology* 21. 773–792.

Krashen, Stephen D. (1975). 'The development of cerebral dominance and language learning: more new evidence'. In Daniel P. Dato (ed.), *Developmental Psycholinguistics: Theory and Applications*. Washington, DC: Georgetown University Press.

(1976). 'Cerebral asymmetry'. In H. Whitaker & H. A. Whitaker (eds.), *Studies in Neurolinguistics*, vol. 2. London & New York: Academic Press.

Kristeva, Julie (1969). Σημειωτική: *Recherches pour une Sémanalyse*. Paris: Seuil.

(1971). 'Du sujet en linguistique'. In J. Kristeva (ed.), *Epistémologie de la Linguistique*. Paris: Didier & Larousse. (Reprinted in J. Kristeva, *Polylogue*. Paris: Seuil, 1977.)

Milner, J.-C., & Ruwet, N. (eds.) (1975). *Langue, Discours, Société: Pour Emile Benveniste*. Paris: Seuil.

Kühlwein, Wolfgang (ed.) (1973). *Linguistics in Great Britain. Vol. 2: Contemporary Linguistics*. Tübingen: Niemeyer.

Kuroda, S. Y. (1973). 'Where epistemology, grammar and style meet – a case study from Japanese'. In Stephen R. Anderson & P. Kiparsky (eds.), *Festschrift for Morris Halle*. New York: Holt, Rinehart & Winston. (French trans. in Kuroda, 1979: 235–260.)

(1974). 'On grammar and narration'. In C. Rohrer & N. Ruwer (eds.), *Actes du Colloque Franco-Allemand de Grammaire Transformationelle*. Tübingen: Niemeyer. (French trans. in Kuroda, 1979: 261–272.)

(1975). 'Réflexions sur les fondements de la théorie de la narration'. In Kristeva *et al.* (1975: 260–300). Paris: Seuil. (English version in T. van Dijk (ed.), *Pragmatics of Language and Literature*. Amsterdam: North Holland, 1976.)

(1979). *Aux Quatre Coins de la Linguistique*. Paris: Seuil.

Kuryłowicz, Jerzy (1960). *Esquisses Linguistiques*. (Prace Językoznawcze 19.) Wrocław-Kraków: Polska Akad. Nauk.

(1964). *The Inflexional Categories of Indo-European*. Heidelberg: Carl Winter Universitätsverlag.

(1972). 'The role of deictic elements in linguistic evolution'. *Semiotica* 5. 174–183.

Lakoff, George (1965). *On the Nature of Syntactic Irregularity*. (Report NSF-16, Mathematical Linguistics and Automatic Translation.) Cambridge, Mass.: Harvard University Computation Laboratory. (Reprinted as *Irregularity in Syntax*. New York: Holt, Rinehart & Winston, 1970.)

References

Lamb, Sidney M. (1964a). 'The sememic approach to structural semantics'. *American Anthropologist* 66. 57–78. (Revised version in Makkai & Lockwood, 1973: 207–228.)

(1964b). 'On alternation, transformation, realization and stratification'. In Stuart (1964: 105–122). (Reprinted in Makkai, 1972, 595–605.)

Lancaster, Jane (1975). *Primate Behavior and the Emergence of Human Culture*. New York: Holt, Rinehart & Winston.

Langendoen, D. Terence (1964a). Review of *Studies in Linguistic Analysis* (1957). In *Language* 40. 305–321.

(1964b). 'Modern British linguistics: a study of its theoretical and substantive contributions' (MIT Ph.D. dissertation: see Langendoen, 1968.)

(1967). Review of Dixon (1963). In *Language* 43. 742–750.

(1968). *The London School of Linguistics: A Study of the Linguistic Theories of B. Malinowski and J. R. Firth*. Boston, Mass.: MIT Press. (Revised version of 1964b with Appendix to Chapter 3, pp. 69–75: 'The views of J. Lyons in structural semantics'.)

(1969). Review of Bazell *et al.* (1966). In *Foundations of Language* 5. 391–408.

(1971). Review of Firth (1968a). In *Language* 47. 180–181.

Lass, Roger (1984). *Phonology*. Cambridge: Cambridge University Press.

Laver, John & Hutcheson, S. (eds.) (1972). *Communication in Face to Face Interaction*. Harmondsworth: Penguin.

Leech, Geoffrey N. (1983). *Principles of Pragmatics*. London & New York: Longman.

Lees, Robert B. (1957). Review of Chomsky (1957). In *Language* 33. 375–407.

(1960). *The Grammar of English Nominalizations*. (*International Journal of American Linguistics* 26; 3, Part 4.) (= Indiana University Research Center in Anthropology, Folklore and Linguistics, Publication 24.) Baltimore: Waverley Press.

Lejewski, Czesław (1958). 'On Leśniewski's ontology'. *Ratio* 1. 150–176.

(1975). 'Syntax and semantics of ordinary language'. *Proceedings of the Aristotelian Society*, suppl. vol. 49. 127–146.

(1979). 'Idealization of ordinary language for the purposes of logic'. In Allerton *et al.* (1979: 94–110).

Lenneberg, Eric H. & Roberts, J. M. (1953). *The Language of Experience*. Bloomington, Ind.: Indiana University Press.

Le Page, Robert B. (1964). *The National Language Question: Linguistic Problems of Newly Independent States*. London: Oxford University Press.

(1989). 'The concept of "a language"'. In K. Sornig (ed.), *Festgabe für N. Denison*. Graz: Institut für Sprachwissenschaft der Universität Graz.

Lepschy, Giulio C. (1970). *A Survey of Structural Linguistics*. London: Faber & Faber. (Revised English version of *La Linguistica Strutturale*. Torino: Einaudi.) (2nd edn, London: André Deutsch.)

Leroy, Maurice (1963). *Les Grands Courants de la Linguistique Moderne*. Bruxelles: Presses Universitaires de Bruxelles; Paris: Presses Universitaires de Paris.

(1967). *Main Trends in Modern Linguistics*. (English trans., by Glanville Price, of Leroy, 1963.) Berkeley & Los Angeles: University of California Press.

References

Leśniewski, S. (1930). 'Über die Grundlagen der Ontologie'. *Comptes Rendus des Séances de la Société des Sciences et des Lettres de Varsovie*, Classe 3, 23ème Année (Warsaw).

Levelt, Willem J. M. (1981). 'The speaker's linearization problem'. In Longuet-Higgins *et al.* (1981: 305–314 [91–100].)

Lewis, David (1972). 'General semantics'. In Davidson & Harman (1972: 169–218).

Lieberman, Philip M. (1975). *On the Origins of Language: An Introduction to the Evolution of Human Speech*. New York: Macmillan.

— (1976). 'Interactive models for evolution: neural mechanisms, anatomy, and behaviour'. In Harnad *et al.* (1976: 660–672).

— (1983). 'On the nature and evolution of the biological bases of language'. In Grolier (1983: 91–114).

— & Crelin, E. S. (1971). 'On the speech of Neanderthal man'. *Linguistic Inquiry* 11: 203–222.

—, Crelin, E. S. & Klatt, A. H. (1972). 'Phonetic ability and related anatomy of the newborn and adult human, Neanderthal man, and the chimpanzee'. *American Anthropologist* 74. 287–307.

Lightfoot, David (1982). *The Language Lottery: Toward a Biology of Grammars*. Cambridge, Mass.: MIT Press.

Limber, J. (1980). 'Language in child and chimp'. In Sebeok & Umiker-Sebeok (1980: 197–220).

Lochner-Huttenbach, Fritz von (1966). Review of Lyons (1963a). In *Anzeiger für die Altertumswissenschaft* (Innsbruck) 19. 242–244.

Lock, Andrew J. (ed.) (1978). *Action, Gesture and Symbol: The Emergence of Language*. London & New York: Academic Press.

Longuet-Higgins, H. Christopher, Lyons, J. & Broadbent, D. A. (eds.) (1981). *The Psychological Mechanisms of Language*. London: Royal Society & British Academy. [=Transactions of the Royal Society, Series B. 295. 215–423.]

Love, Nigel (1988). 'The linguistic thought of J. R. Firth'. In R. Harris (1988: 148–164).

Luce, R. Duncan, Bush, R. R. & Galanter, E. (1963). *Handbook of Mathematical Psychology*, vol. II. New York & London: John Wiley.

Łukasiewicz, Jan (1951). *Aristotle's Syllogistic: From the Standpoint of Modern Formal Logic*. [Based on the texts of 'Organon'.] (2nd edn, enlarged, 1957.) Oxford: Clarendon Press.

Lunt, Horace (ed.) (1964). *Proceedings of the Ninth International Congress of Linguists* (Cambridge, Mass., 1962) (PICL 9.) The Hague: Mouton.

Lyons, John (1958). Review of Chomsky (1957). In *Litera* (Istanbul) 5. 109–115.

— (1960). 'A structural theory of semantics and its application to some lexical subsystems in the vocabulary of Plato'. (University of Cambridge, Ph.D. dissertation: see Lyons, 1963.)

— (1961). Review of Hoenigswald (1960). In *Bulletin of the School of Oriental and African Studies* 23. 621–622.

References

(1962a). 'Phonemic and non-phonemic phonology'. *International Journal of American Linguistics* 29. 127–133. (Reprinted in Fudge, 1973: 190–99; Jones & Laver, 1973: 229–39; Makkai, 1972: 275–289. Reprinted, with extensive notes and an Epilogue, as Chapter 6 of the present volume.)

(1962b). Review of Mohrmann *et al.* (1961). In *American Anthropologist* 64. 1118–1124.

(1962c). 'A structural theory of semantics'. (Revised version of part of a paper, entitled 'Structural semantics with special reference to Greek', delivered to the Philological Society on 24 November 1961.) Previously unpublished: revised version in Lyons (forthcoming c).

(1963a). *Structural Semantics.* (Publications of the Philological Society, 20.) Oxford: Blackwell.

(1963b). Review of Ziff (1960). In *International Journal of American Linguistics* 29. 82–87.

(1963c). Review of Dixon (1963). In *Lingua* 12. 431–444.

(1965a). *The Scientific Study of Language.* (University of Edinburgh, Inaugural Lectures, 24.) Edinburgh: Edinburgh University Press. (Extract reprinted in Allen & Corder, 1973: 162–77. Reprinted, with extensive notes, in the present volume as an Appendix.)

(1965b). Review of Mohrmann *et al.* (1963). In *Journal of Linguistics* 1. 87–92.

(1966a). 'Firth's theory of meaning'. In Bazell *et al.* (1966: 288–302). (To be reprinted, with new notes, in Lyons, forthcoming c.)

(1966b). 'Towards a "notional" theory of the "parts of speech"'. *Journal of Linguistics* 2. 209–36. (Reprinted, with extensive notes and an Epilogue, as Chapter 7 of the present volume.)

(1966c). Review of Katz & Postal (1964). In *Journal of Linguistics* 2. 119–126.

(1966d). Review of Chomsky (1965). In *Philosophical Quarterly* 16. 393–395.

(1967a). 'A note on possessive, existential and locative sentences'. *Foundations of Language* 3. 390–396. (Revised version to be reprinted, with Lyons, 1968b, in Lyons, forthcoming c.)

(1967b). Review of Admoni (1964). In *Archivum Linguisticum* 17. 183–187.

(1967c). Review of Martinet (1964). In *Archivum Linguisticum* 17. 187–190.

(1968a). *Introduction to Theoretical Linguistics.* London & New York: Cambridge University Press.

(1968b). 'Existence, location, possession and transitivity'. In B. Rootselaar & J. F. Staal, (eds.), *Logic, Methodology and Philosophy of Science,* III. Amsterdam: North Holland. (Revised version to be reprinted, with Lyons 1967a, in Lyons, forthcoming c.)

(1969a). Review of Ivić (1965). In *Lingua* 22. 278–286.

(1969b). Review of Langendoen (1968). In *American Anthropologist* 71. 713–714.

(1969c). Review of Leroy (1967). In *Language* 45. 105–108.

(1969d). Contribution to 'Formal logic and natural languages: a symposium'. *Foundations of Language* 5. 269. (=Staal, 1969: 269.)

References

(ed.) (1970a). *New Horizons in Linguistics*. Harmondsworth: Penguin. (Italian edn, Torino, Einaudi, 1975; Portuguese edn, Sao Paolo: Cultrix, 1976.) (Reprinted as *New Horizons in Linguistics* 1, 1987.)

(1970b). *Chomsky*. London: Collins/Fontana; New York: Viking. (2nd edn. 1977.)

(1972). 'Human language'. In Hinde (1972: 49–85).

(1973). 'Structuralism and linguistics'. In Robey (1973: 5–19).

(1975a). 'Deixis as the source of reference'. In Keenan (1975: 61–83). (Reprinted as Chapter 8 of the present volume.)

(1975b). *Nuevos Horizontes de la Linguistica*. (=Lyons, 1970a.) (Version española de Conxita Lleo con la colaboración de Pedro Albertelli y Delia Suardiez.) Madrid: Alianza Editorial.

(1975c). Review of Lepschy (1970). In *Modern Language Review* 70. 840–841.

(1975d). 'The use of models in linguistics'. In Lyndhurst Collins (ed.). *The Use of Models in the Social Sciences*. London: Tavistock Press.

(1977a). *Semantics*, 2 vols. London & New York: Cambridge University Press.

(1977b). 'Statements, questions and commands'. In Zampolli (1977: 255–280).

(1977c). Review of Harman (1974). In *Modern Language Review* 72. 137–139.

(1977d). Review of Ian Robinson, *The New Grammarians' Funeral* (London & New York: Cambridge University Press). In *Modern Language Review* 72. 131–132.

(1978a). 'Basic problems of semantics'. In Dressler & Meid (1978: 13–21).

(1978b). Review of Hockett (1977). In *Journal of Linguistics* 14. 323–328.

(1978c). 'Deixis and anaphora'. In Myers (1978a: 88–103). (Reprinted as Chapter 9 of the present volume.)

(1979a). 'Knowledge and truth: a localistic approach'. In Allerton *et al.* (1979: 111–141). (To be reprinted in Lyons, forthcoming c.)

(1979b). Review of Martin (1976). In *Etudes Anglaises* (Paris) 32. 220–222.

(1979c). Review of David & Martin (1976). In *Etudes Anglaises* (Paris) 32. 222–224.

(1979d). 'The pros and cons of formal semantics'. (Paper delivered to the Linguistics Association of Great Britain on 24 September 1979.) Previously unpublished: revised version in Lyons (forthcoming c).

(1980a). 'Pronouns of address in 'Anna Karenina': the stylistics of bilingualism and the impossibility of translation'. In Geoffrey N. Leech & S. Greenbaum (eds.), *Studies in English Linguistics*. London: Longman, 1980. (Slightly revised version in Lyons, forthcoming c.)

(1980b). Review of Rey-Debove (1978). In *Journal of Linguistics* 16. 292–300.

(1981a). *Language and Linguistics*. London & New York: Cambridge University Press.

(1981b). *Language, Meaning and Context*. London: Fontana/Collins.

(1981c). 'Language and speech'. In Longuet-Higgins *et al.* (1981: 215–222 [1–8]). (Expanded and revised version reprinted as Chapter 1 of the present volume.)

(1981d). 'Sentence meaning and propositional content'. (Paper delivered to the

References

Philological Society on 24 November 1961.) Previously unpublished: revised version in Lyons (forthcoming c).

(1981e). *'Structural Semantics* in retrospect'. In Hope *et al.* (1981: 73–90).

(1982). 'Deixis and subjectivity: Loquor, ergo sum?'. In Jarvella & Klein (1982: 101–124). (To be reprinted in Lyons, forthcoming c.)

(1984). 'La subjectivité dans le langage et dans les langues'. In Serbat (1984: 131–140). (Revised English version in Lyons, forthcoming c.)

(1987a). 'Origins of language'. In Andrew Faber (ed.), *Origins.* Cambridge: Cambridge University Press. (Expanded and revised version reprinted as Chapter 5 of the present volume.)

(1987b). 'Introduction'. In Lyons *et al.* (1987: 1–29).

(1987c). 'Semantics'. In Lyons *et al.* (1987: 152–178).

(1988). 'Theoretical semiotics and theoretical semantics'. In Hertzfeld & Melazzo (1988: 672–688).

(1989a). 'Semantic ascent: a neglected aspect of syntactic typology'. In Arnold *et al.* (1989: 153–186).

(1989b). 'The last forty years: real progress or not?'. *Georgetown University Round Table on Languages and Linguistics 1989.* Washington, DC: Georgetown University Press, 13–38.

(1990a). 'Linguistics: theory, practice and research'. *Georgetown University Round Table on Language and Linguistics 1990.* Washington, DC: Georgetown University Press, 11–30.

(1990b). 'In memoriam: James Peter Thorne, 1933–1988'. In Sylvia Adamson, V. Law & N. Vincent (eds.), *Papers from the Fifth International Conference on Historical Linguistics (Cambridge, 6–9 April, 1987).* Amsterdam & Philadelphia: Benjamins.

(forthcoming a). *Principles of Semantic Theory.* Cambridge: Cambridge University Press.

(forthcoming b). Review of R. Harris (1988). In *Albion.*

(forthcoming c). *Semantics, Subjectivity and Localism: Essays in Linguistics Theory, Volume II.* Cambridge: Cambridge University Press.

Atkinson, R. M., Griffith, P. D. & Macrae, Alison (1975). 'The linguistics development of young children'. Final Report to the Social Sciences Research Council (London).

Coates, R. Deuchar, M. & Gazdar, G. (eds.) (1987). *New Horizons in Linguistics 2.* London: Penguin & New York: Viking.

& Wales, R. J. (eds.) (1966). *Psycholinguistics Papers.* Edinburgh: Edinburgh University Press.

McClure, J. Derrick (1973). Review of Palmer (1970a). In *International Review of Applied Linguistics* 11. 97–101.

(ed.) (1982). *Scotland and the Lowland Tongue: Studies in the Language and Literature of Lowland Scotland, in Honour of David D. Murison.* Aberdeen: Aberdeen University Press.

References

, Aitken A. J. & Low, J. T. (eds.) (1980). *The Scots Language: Planning for Modern Usage*. Edinburgh: Ramsay Head.

McIntosh, Angus (1952). *An Introduction to a Survey of Scottish Dialects*. (University of Edinburgh, Linguistic Survey of Scotland Monographs 1.) Edinburgh: Edinburgh University Press.

(1956). 'The analysis of written Middle English'. *Transactions of the Philological Society* 1956: 26–55. (Reprinted in Lass, 1969: 35–57.)

(1958). Review of Firth (1957a). In *Archivum Linguisticum* 10. 54–58.

(1961a). '"Graphology" and meaning'. *Archivum Linguisticum* 13. 107–20. (Reprinted with additional notes and references in McIntosh & Halliday, 1966: 98–110.)

(1961b). 'Patterns and ranges'. *Language* 37. 325–37. (Reprinted in McIntosh & Halliday, 1966: 183–99.)

(1963). A new approach to Middle English dialectology'. *English Studies* 44. 1–11. (Reprinted in Lass, 1969: 392–403.)

(1966a). 'Linguistics and English studies'. In McIntosh & Halliday (1966: 42–55).

(1966b). 'Some thoughts on style'. In McIntosh & Halliday (1966: 83–97).

& Halliday, M. A. K. (1966). *Patterns of Language*. London: Longman.

, Samuels, M. L. & Benskin, M. (eds.) (1986). *A Linguistic Atlas of Late Middle English*. Aberdeen: Aberdeen University Press.

McNeill, David (1971). 'Explaining linguistic universals'. In Morton (1971: 53–60).

Magnusson, Rudolf (1954). *Studies in the Theory of The Parts of Speech*. (Lund Studies in English, 24.) Lund: Gleerup; Copenhagen: Munksgaard.

Makkai, Valerie B. (ed.) (1972). *Phonological Theory: Evolution and Current Practice*. New York: Holt, Rinehart & Winston.

Makkai, Adam & Lockwood, D. G. (eds.) (1973). *Readings in Stratificational Linguistics*. University, Ala.: University of Alabama Press.

Malmberg, Bertil (1964). *New Trends in Linguistics: An Orientation*. Stockholm & Lund: Naturmetodens Språkinstitut. (English trans. of 1st edn. of *Nya Vägar inom Språkforskningen: En Orientering i Modern Lingvistik*. Stockholm, 1959. 2nd edn, 1962; 3rd edn, 1966.)

Marcos Marin, Francisco (1974). *Aproximación a la Gramatica Española*, 2nd edn. Madrid: Cincel.

Marler, Peter (1976). 'An ethological theory of the origin of vocal learning'. In Wanner & Gleitman (1978: 386–395).

(1977). 'The evolution of communication'. In Sebeok (1977a: 45–70).

Marshack, Alexander (1976). 'Some implications of the Palaeolithic symbolic evidence for the origin of language'. In Harnad *et al.* (1976: 289–311).

Marshall, John C. (1971). 'Can humans talk?'. In Morton (1971: 24–52).

(1980a). 'Clues from neurological deficits'. In Bellugi & Studdert-Kennedy (1980: 275–290).

(1980b). 'On the biology of language acquisition'. In Caplan (1980: 104–148).

References

Marslen-Wilson, William. D. & Tyler, L. K. (1981). 'Central processes in speech understanding'. In Longuet-Higgins et al. (1981: 103–118 [317–332]).

Martinet, André (1960). Eléments de Linguistique Générale. Paris: Armand Colin.

(1962). A Functional View of Language. (The Waynflete Lectures, 1961.) Oxford: Clarendon Press.

Martlew, Margaret (1983). 'The development of writing: communication and cognition'. In Coulmas & Ehlich (1983: 257–275).

Mather, James Y. & Speitel, H. H. (eds.) (1975). Linguistic Atlas of Scotland: Scots Section, vol. I. (With a Foreword by Angus McIntosh.) London: Croom Helm.

Matthews, G. S. (1965). Hidatsa Syntax. The Hague: Mouton.

Matthews, Peter H. (1965a). 'The inflexional component of a transformational grammar'. Journal of Linguistics 1. 139–171.

(1965b). Review of Dixon (1963). In Journal of Linguistics 1. 61–68.

(1968). Review of Bazell et al. (1966). Language 44. 306–317.

(1979). Generative Grammar and Linguistic Competence. London: Allen & Unwin.

(1981). Syntax. Cambridge: Cambridge University Press.

(1986). 'Distributional syntax'. In Bynon & Palmer (1986: 245–277).

Mattingly, Ignatius G. (1972). 'Reading, the linguistic process, and linguistic awareness'. In Kavanagh & Mattingly (1972: 133–148).

& Liberman, Alvin M. (1986). 'Specialised perceiving systems for speech and other biologically significant sounds'. In G. M. Edelman, W. E. Gall & W. M. Cowan (eds.), Functions of the Auditory System. New York: John Wiley.

Mehler, Jacques (1981). 'The role of syllables in speech processing'. In Longuet-Higgins et al. (1981: 332–353 [119–138]).

Meillet, Antoine (1921). Linguistique Historique et Linguistique Générale. Paris: Honoré Champion.

Miller, George A. (1962). 'Some psychological studies of grammar'. American Psychologist 17. 748–762.

& Johnson-Laird, P. N. (1976). Language and Perception. Cambridge: Cambridge University Press.

Miller, James (1985). Semantics and Syntax. Cambridge: Cambridge University Press.

Milner, E. (1976). 'Central nervous system maturation and language acquisition'. In H. Whitaker & H. A. Whitaker (eds.), Studies in Neurolinguistics, vol. I. London & New York: Academic Press.

Mitchell, Terence F. (1953). 'Particle-noun complexes in a Berber Dialect (Zuara)'. Bulletin of the School of Oriental and African Studies 15. 375–390.

(1957a). 'Long consonants in phonology and phonetics'. Studies in Linguistic Analysis 1957. 182–205.

(1957b). 'The language of buying and selling in Cyrenaica: a situational statement'. Hesperis 44. 31–71. (Reprinted in Mitchell, 1975a: 167–200.)

(1958). 'Syntagmatic relations in linguistic analysis'. Transactions of the Philological Society 1958. 101–118.

(1965). On the Nature of Linguistics and its Place in University Studies. (Inaugural

References

Lecture delivered on 26 April 1968.) Leeds University Press.

(1971). 'Linguistic "goings-on": collocations and other lexical matters arising on the syntagmatic record'. *Archivum Linguisticum* (New Series) 2. 35–65.

(1975a). *Principles of Firthian Linguistics*. London: Longman.

(1975b). "Not of the letter, but of the spirit; for the letter killeth, but the spirit giveth life". In Mitchell (1975a: 33–74).

Mohrmann, Christine, Sommerfelt, A. & Whatmough, J. (eds.) (1961). *Trends in European and American Linguistics 1930–1960*. Utrecht & Anvers: Spectrum.

Norman, F. & Sommerfelt, A. (eds.) (1963). *Trends in Modern Linguistics*. Utrecht & Anvers: Spectrum.

Montague, Richard (1974). *Formal Philosophy: Selected Papers of Richard Montague*, edited with an Introduction by R. Thomason. New Haven, Conn.: Yale University Press.

Moore, Terence & Carling, Christine (1982). *Understanding Language: Towards a Post-Chomskyan Linguistics*. London: Macmillan.

Morris, Charles W. (1938). *Foundations of the Theory of Signs* (= vol. 1, no. 2 of Neurath *et al.*, 1939: 77–138.) (Reprinted in Morris, 1971: 17–74.)

(1971). *Writings on the General Theory of Signs*. The Hague: Mouton.

Morton, John (ed.) (1971). *Biological and Social Factors in Psycholinguistics*. London: Logos Press.

Morgan, Lewis (1877). *Ancient Society*. New York: Holt.

Motsch, W. (1965). 'Untersuchungen zur Apposition im Deutschen'. *Studia Grammatica* 5. 87–132.

Murison, David D. (1972). 'The Scottish National Dictionary'. In *University of Edinburgh Journal* 25. 305–309.

Myers, Terry (ed.) (1978a). *The Development of Conversation and Discourse*. Edinburgh: Edinburgh University Press.

(1978b). 'Verbal and non-verbal interactivity'. In Myers (1978a: 1–43).

Nagel, Ernest, Suppes, P. & Tarski, A. (eds.) (1962). *Logic, Methodology and the Philosophy of Science*. Stanford: Stanford University Press.

Nencioni, Giovanni (1983). 'Lingua e linguistica'. In Segre (1983: 11–26).

Neurath, Otto, Carnap, R. & Morris, C. (eds.) (1939). *International Encyclopedia of Unified Science*. Chicago: University of Chicago Press.

Newmeyer, Frederick J. (1980). *Linguistic Theory in America*. New York: Academic Press.

(ed.) (1988). *Linguistics: The Cambridge Survey*, 4 vols. Cambridge: Cambridge University Press.

Ochs, Elinor & B. Schieffelin (eds.) (1979). *Developmental Pragmatics*. New York: Academic Press.

Orr, John (1933). *French, the Third Classic*. (Inaugural Lecture given at the University of Edinburgh, 10 October 1933.) Edinburgh & London: Oliver & Boyd.

(1953a). *Words and Sounds in English and French*. Oxford: Blackwell.

(1953b). *Studies in Romance Philology and French Literature Presented to John Orr by*

References

Pupils, Colleagues and Friends. Manchester: Manchester University Press.

(1962a). *Three Studies on Homonymics*. (Reprinted from Orr, 1953a.) Edinburgh: Edinburgh University Press.

(1962b). *Old French and Modern Idiom*. Oxford: Blackwell.

Otto, Ludwig (1983). 'Writing systems and written language'. In Coulmas & Ehlich (1983: 45–62).

Palmer, Frank R. (1955a). 'The "Broken Plurals" of Tigrinya'. *Bulletin of the School of Oriental and African Studies* 17. 548–566.

(1955b). '"Openness" in Tigre: a problem of prosodic statement'. *Bulletin of the School of Oriental and African Studies* 18. 561–577. (Reprinted in Palmer, 1970a: 153–73.)

(1957a). 'The verb in Bilin'. *Bulletin of the School of Oriental and African Studies* 19. 131–159.

(1957b). 'Gemination in Tigrinya'. *Studies in Linguistic Analysis* 1957. 139–148.

(1957/8). 'Linguistic hierarchy'. *Lingua* 2. 226–241. (Extract reprinted in Kühlwein, 1973: 27–43.)

(1964). '"Sequence" and "order"'. In Stuart (1964: 123–130). (Reprinted in Householder, 1972: 140–147.)

(1968a). Review of Firth (1964). *Foundations of Language* 4. 84–86.

(1968b). 'Introduction'. In Firth (1968a: 1–11).

(ed.) (1970a). *Prosodic Analysis*. London: Oxford University Press.

(1970b). 'Introduction'. In Palmer (1970a: ix–xvi).

(1974). *The English Verb*. London: Longman.

(1986). *Mood and Modality*. Cambridge: Cambridge University Press.

Pandit, P. B. (1970). Review of Firth (1968a). In *Journal of Linguistics* 6. 280–284.

Passingham, R. E. (1981). 'Broca's area and the origins of human vocal skills'. *Proceedings of the Royal Society*, Series B, 292. 167–175.

Pateman, Trevor (1982). 'Realism and language change'. *Language and Communication*. 2. 161–78. (Revised version, 'A realist theory of linguistics', in Pateman, 1987a: 18–42.)

(1983). 'What is a language?'. *Language and Communication*. 3. 101–127. (Revised version in Pateman 1987a: 43–80.)

(1985). 'From nativism to sociolinguistics: integrating a theory of language growth with a theory of speech practices'. *Journal for the Theory of Social Behaviour* 15. 38–59. (Revised version in Pateman, 1987a: 81–104.)

(1987a). *Language in Mind and Language in Society*. Oxford: Oxford University Press.

(1987b). 'Philosophy of linguistics'. In Lyons *et al.* (1987: 249–267).

Pike, Kenneth L. (1952). 'More on grammatical prerequisites'. *Word* 8. 106–121. (Reprinted in Makkai, 1972: 211–223.)

Popper, Karl R. (1933). *The Logic of Scientific Discovery*. London: Hutchinson.

(1963). *Conjectures and Refutations*. London: Routledge & Kegan Paul.

(1972). *Objective Knowledge*. London: Oxford University Press.

References

Postal, Paul M. (1966). Review of Dixon (1963). In *Language* 42. 84–93.

(1967). 'On so-called "pronouns" in English'. Georgetown University Monograph Series on Languages and Linguistics. 1. 177–206.

(1968). *Aspects of Phonological Theory*. New York: Harper & Row.

Potter, Simeon (1959). Review of *Studies in Linguistic Analysis* (1957). In *Modern Language Review* (1959). 54. 80–81.

Powell, Mava Jo (1985). 'Conceptions of literal meaning in speech act theory'. *Philosophy and Rhetoric* 18. 133–157.

(1986). 'Purposive vagueness: an evaluative dimension of vague quantifying expressions'. *Journal of Linguistics* 21. 31–50.

(1987). 'Benveniste's notion of subjectivity in the active metaphors of ordinary language'. *Semiotica* 67. 39–59.

Quine, Willard V. (1953a). *From a Logical Point of View*. Cambridge, Mass.: Harvard University Press. (2nd edn, 1961.)

(1953b). 'Meaning in linguistics'. In Quine (1953a: 47–64).

(1960). *Word and Object*. Cambridge, Mass.: MIT Press.

Récanati, François (1979). *La Transparence et l'Enonciation*. Paris: Seuil.

Recherches Structurales (1949). (Travaux du Cercle Linguistique de Copenhague, 5.) Copenhague.

Reeder, Ken (1978). 'Reflections on the Symposium'. In Myers (1978a: 104–117).

Reid, T. B. W. (1970). 'Verbal aspect in modern French'. In T. G. S. Combe & P. Rickard (eds.), *The French Language: Studies Presented to Lewis Charles Harmer*. London: Harrap.

Reinhart, Tanya (1983). *Anaphora and Semantic Interpretation*. London: Croom Helm.

Rey-Debove, Josette (1978). *Le Métalangage*. Paris: Le Robert.

(1979). *Lexique: Sémiotique*. Paris: Presses Universitaires de France.

Ridjanović, M. (1976). *A Synchronic Study of Verbal Aspect in English and Serbo-Croatian*. Cambridge, Mass.: Slavica Publishers.

Rist, John M. (1966). Review of Lyons (1963a). In *Classical Philology* (Chicago) 61. 280–282.

Roberts, E. W. (1972). 'A critical survey of Firthian phonology'. *Glossa* 6. 3–73.

Robey, David (ed.) (1973). *Structuralism: An Introduction*. Oxford: Clarendon Press.

Robins, Robert H. (1951). *Ancient and Medieval Grammatical Theory in Europe*. London: Bell.

(1952a). 'Notes on the phonetics of the Georgian word' (with Natalie Waterson). *Bulletin of the School of Oriental and African Studies* 14. 55–72.

(1952b). 'Noun and verb in universal grammar'. *Language* 28. 209–298. (Reprinted in Robins, 1970: 25–36.)

(1952c). 'A problem in the statement of meaning'. *Lingua* 3. 121–137.

(1953a). 'The phonology of the analysed verbal forms in Sundanese'. *Bulletin of the School of Oriental and African Studies* 15. 138–45. (Reprinted in Palmer, 1970a: 104–111; Robins, 1970: 227–236.)

270

References

(1953b). 'Formal divisions in Sundanese'. *Transactions of the Philological Society* 1953. 109–142. (Reprinted in Robins, 1970: 237–272.)

(1957a). 'Vowel nasality in Sundanese: a phonological and grammatical study'. *Studies in Linguistic Analysis* 1957. 87–103. (Reprinted in Robins, 1970: 273–291.)

(1957b). 'Aspects of prosodic analysis'. *Proceedings of the University of Durham Philosophical Society* I, Series B (Arts). 1–12. (Reprinted in Palmer, 1970a: 186–200; Robins, 1970: 207–226; Makkai, 1972: 264–272.)

(1959). 'In defence of WP'. *Transactions of the Philological Society* 1959. 116–144. (Reprinted in Robins, 1970: 49–77.)

(1961). 'John Rupert Firth'. (Obituary article.) *Language* 37. 191–200.

(1963). 'General linguistics in Great Britain 1930–1960'. In Mohrmann *et al.* (1963: 11–37). (Reprinted in Robins, 1970: 155–180; extract in Kühlwein, 1973: 3–24.)

(1964a). 'Grammar, meaning and the study of language'. *Canadian Journal of Linguistics* 9. 98–114. (Reprinted in Robins, 1970: 81–97.)

(1964b). *General Linguistics. An Introductory Survey.* London: Longman. (3rd edn. 1979.)

(1966). 'The development of the word-class system of the European grammatical tradition. *Foundations of Language* 2. 3–19. (Reprinted in Robins, 1970: 185–203.)

(1969). Review of Langendoen (1968). In *Language* 45. 109–116.

(1970). *Diversions of Bloomsbury: Selected Writings on Linguistics.* Amsterdam & London: North Holland.

(1979). *A Short History of Linguistics*, 2nd edn. London: Longman & Bloomington Ind.: Indiana University Press. (1st edn, 1967.)

(1982). 'Condillac et l'origine du langage'. In Jean Sgard (ed.) (1985), *Condillac et les Problèmes du Langage*. Genève & Paris: Slatkine, 95–101; 55–72.

Robinson, David B. (1965). Review of Lyons (1963a). In *Classical Review* (London) 15. 311–314.

Russell, B. (1940). *An Inquiry into Meaning and Truth.* London: Allen & Unwin.

Sadock, Jerrold M. & Zwicky, A. N. (1980). 'Sentence types'. In Stephen R. Anderson, T. Givón, E. Keenan, T. Shopen, & S. Thompson (eds.), *Language, Typology and Syntactic Field Work.*

Saljö, R. (ed.) (1986). *The Written Code and Conceptions of Reality.* (Proceedings of the Symposium held at Sydkoster, Sweden, August 1985.) Linköping.

Sampson, Geoffrey R. (1985). *Writing Systems: A Linguistic Introduction.* London: Hutchinson.

Sanders, Carol S. (1987). 'Applied linguistics'. In Lyons *et al.* (1987: 200–224).

Sandmann, M. (1954). *Subject and Predicate.* Edinburgh: Edinburgh University Press.

Sankoff, Gillian (1980). *The Social Life of a Language.* Baltimore: Pennsylvania University Press.

Sapir, Edward (1921). *Language*. New York: Harcourt, Brace & World.

Saussure, Ferdinand de (1916). *Cours de Linguistique Générale*, edited by Charles Bally & Albert Séchehaye. Paris: Payot. (English translations: (1) by Wade Baskin: *A Course in General Linguistics*. New York: Philosophical Library, 1960. (Revised edn, with Introduction by Jonathan Culler, London: Fontana/Collins, 1974.). (2) by Roy Harris, *Course in General Linguistics*, with Introduction and annotations. London: Duckworth, 1972.)

Schachter, Paul (1985). 'Parts-of-speech systems'. In Shopen (1985a: 8–61).

Schank, Roger & Abelson, Robert (1977). *Scripts, Plans, Goals and Understanding*. Hillsdale, NJ: Erlbaum.

Schleicher, August (1863). *Die Darwinische Theorie und die Sprachwissenschaft*. Weimar: Bohlan. (English trans., *Darwinism Tested by the Science of Language*, translated from the German, with Preface and Additional Notes, by A. V. W. Bikkers, London; John Camden Hotten, 1869. Facsimile reprint in Koerner, 1983: [71 pp.].)

Schrödinger, Erwin (1944). *What is Life? The Physical Aspect of the Living Cell*. Cambridge: Cambridge University Press.

Schubiger, Maria (1965). 'English intonation and German modal particles: a comparative study'. *Phonetica* 12. 65–84. (Reprinted in Bolinger, 1972: 175–193.)

Schuchardt, Hugo (1928). *Hugo-Schuchardt Brevier*, 2nd edn, edited by L. Spitzer. Halle.

Searle, John R. (1969). *Speech Acts*. London & New York: Cambridge University Press.

Sebeok, Thomas A. (ed.) (1960). *Style in Language*. Cambridge, Mass.: MIT Press.

(ed.) (1965). *Current Trends in Linguistics, vol. 1: Slavic and East European Linguistics*. The Hague: Mouton.

(ed.) (1968). *Current Trends in Linguistics, vol. 3: Theoretical Foundations*. The Hague: Mouton.

(ed.) (1973). *Current Trends in Linguistics, vol. 4: Ibero-American and Caribbean Linguistics*. The Hague: Mouton.

(ed.) (1974a). *Current Trends in Linguistics, vol. 12: Linguistics and the Adjacent Arts and Sciences*. The Hague: Mouton.

(1974b). 'Semiotics: a survey of the art'. In Sebeok (1974a: 211–264).

(ed.) (1975). *Current Trends in Linguistics, vol. 13: Historiography of Linguistics*. The Hague: Mouton.

(ed.) (1977a). *A Perfusion of Signs*. Bloomington, Ind. & London: Indiana University Press.

(1977b). 'Ecumenicalism in semiotics'. In Sebeok (1977a: 180–206). Also in Sebeok (1979: 61–83).

(ed.) (1977c). *How Animals Communicate*. Bloomington, Ind.: Indiana University Press.

(1977d). 'Zoosemiotic components of human communication'. In Sebeok (1977c: 1055–1077).

References

(1979). *The Sign and its Masters*. Austin, Tex. & London: University of Texas Press.

& Umiker-Sebeok J. (eds.) (1980). *Speaking of Apes: A Critical Anthology of Two-Way Communication with Man*. New York: Plenum Press.

Segre, Cesare (ed.) (1983). *Intorno alla Linguistica*. Milano: Feltrinelli.

Selinker, Larry (1990). 'Pit Corder'. In *Georgetown University Round Table on Language and Linguistics 1990*. Washington DC: Georgetown University Press, 33–34.

Selkirk, Elisabeth O. (1980). 'Prosodic domains in phonology: Sanskrit revisited'. In M. Aronoff & Mary Louise Kean (eds.) (1980), *Juncture*. Saratoga, Calif.: Anna Libri.

Sharp, Alan E. (1954). 'A tonal analysis of the disyllabic noun in the Machame dialect of Chaga'. *Bulletin of the School of Oriental and African Studies* 16. 157–69.

Shaumjan, Sergej K. (1965). *Strukturnaja Lingvistika*. Moskva: Izdatel'stvo 'Nauk'.

Shopen, Timothy (ed.) (1985a) *Language Typology and Syntactic Description*, vol. I: *Clause Structure*. Cambridge: Cambridge University Press.

(ed.) (1985b). *Language Typology and Syntactic Description*, vol II: *Complex Constructions*. Cambridge: Cambridge University Press.

(ed.) (1985c). *Language Typology and Syntactic Description*, vol III: *Grammatical Categories and the Lexicon*. Cambridge: Cambridge University Press.

Siertsema, Bertha (1955). *A Study of Glossematics*. The Hague: Mouton.

Siple, Patricia (ed.) (1978). *Understanding Language Through Sign Language Research*. London & New York: Academic Press.

Skroka, Kazimierz A. (1972). Review of Firth (1968a). In *Linguistics* 78. 78–109.

Smith, F. & Spencer, F. (eds.) (1984). *The Origins of Modern Humans*. New York: Liss.

Smith, John Maynard (1975). *The Theory of Evolution*. 2nd. edn. Harmondsworth: Penguin.

Smith, Neil V. & Wilson, Deirdre (1979). *Modern Linguistics: The Results of Chomsky's Revolution*. Harmondsworth: Penguin.

Soll, Ludwig (1974). *Gesprochenes und Geschriebenes Französisch*. Berlin: E. Schmidt.

Sommerfelt, Alf (1960a). Review of Firth (1957a). In *Norsk Tidskrift for Sprogvidenskap* 19. 704–707.

(1960b). Review of *Studies in Linguistic Analysis* (1957). In *Norsk Tidskrift for Sprogvidenskap* 19. 707–708.

Sommerstein, Alan H. (1972). 'On the so-called definite article'. *Linguistic Inquiry* 3. 197–209.

(1977). *Modern Phonology*. London: Arnold.

Spang-Hanssen, Henning (1954). *Recent Theories of the Linguistic Sign*. (Travaux du Cercle Linguistique de Copenhague, 9.) Copenhague.

(1961). 'Glossematics'. In Mohrmann et al. (1961: 128–162).

Spencer, John (ed.) (1963). *Language in Africa*. London: Oxford University Press.

Sperber, Dan & Wilson, Deirdre (1986). *Relevance: Communication and Cognition*. Oxford: Blackwell.

Sprigg, R. K. (1954). 'Verbal phrases in Lhasa Tibetan'. *Bulletin of the School of Oriental and African Studies* 16. 134–56, 320–50, 566–591.

(1955). 'The tonal system of Tibetan (Lhasa Dialect) and the nominal phrase', *Bulletin of the School of Oriental and African Studies* 17. 134–53. (Reprinted in Palmer, 1970a: 112–132.)

(1957). 'Junction in Spoken Burmese'. *Studies in Linguistic Analysis* 1957. 104–138.

Staal, Jan F. (ed.) (1969). 'Formal logic and natural languages: a symposium'. *Foundations of Language* 5. 256–285.

Stam, James H. (1976). *Inquiries into the Origin of Language: The Fate of a Question.* New York: Harper & Row.

Stark, Rachel E. (1986). 'Prespeech segmental feature development'. In Fletcher & Garman (1986: 149–173).

Starosta, Stanley (1971). Review of Lyons (1968a). In *Language* 47. 429–444.

Steinberg, Danny D. & Harper, H. (1983). 'Teaching written language to a deaf boy'. In Coulmas & Ehlich (1983: 327–354.)

Stephany, Ursula (1984). *Aspekt, Tempus und Modalität: Eine Studie der Entwicklung der Verbalgrammatik in der Neugriechischen Kindersprache.* Tübingen: Narr.

(1986). 'Modality'. In Fletcher & Garman (1986: 375–400).

Stockwell, Robert P. (1959). Review of *Studies in Linguistic Analysis* (1957). In *International Journal of American Linguistics* 25. 254–259.

Stokoe, William C. (1972). *Semiotics and Human Sign Languages.* The Hague: Mouton.

(1973). 'Classification and description of sign languages'. In Sebeok (1973: 345–371).

(1978). *Sign Language Structure.* Silver Spring, Md.: Linstok.

Strang, Barbara M. H. (1962). *Modern English Structure.* London: Arnold. (2nd edn, 1968.)

Strawson, Peter F. (1959). *Individuals: An Essay in Descriptive Metaphysics.* London: Methuen.

(ed.) (1971). *Philosophical Logic.* London: Oxford University Press.

(1975). *Subject and Predicate in Logic and Grammar.* London: Methuen.

Strevens, Peter D. (1964). 'Editor's preface'. In Firth (1964: vii–x).

(1966a). 'The study of the present-day English language'. (Inaugural Lecture, University of Leeds, 1962.) In Strevens (1966b: 105–129.)

(ed.) (1966b). *Five Inaugural Lectures.* Oxford: Oxford University Press.

Stuart, C. I. J. M. (ed.) (1964). (Georgetown University Round Table on Language and Linguistics.) *Monograph Series on Language and Linguistics* 17. Washington, DC: Georgetown University Press.

Stubbs, Michael (1980). *Language and Literacy: The Sociology of Reading and Writing.* London: Routledge & Kegan Paul.

Studies in Linguistic Analysis (1957). (Special [unnumbered] Volume of the Philological Society.) Oxford: Blackwell.

References

Tarski, Alfred (1944). 'The semantical conception of truth'. *Philosophy and Phenomenological Research* 4. 341–375. (Reprinted in Tarski, 1956: 152–295.)

(1956). *Logic, Semantics, and Metamathematics*. London: Oxford University Press.

Tauli, Valter (1964). 'Practical language planning'. In Lunt (1964: 605–609.)

Terrace, H. S. & Bever, T. G. (1976). 'What might be learned from studying language in the chimpanzee? The importance of symbolizing oneself'. In Harnad *et al.* (1976: 579–588). (Reprinted in Sebeok & Umiker-Sebeok, 1980: 182–189.)

Tesnière, Lucien (1959). *Eléments de Syntaxe Structurale*. Paris: Klincksieck.

Testa, Aldo (1967). *La Struttura Dialogica del Linguaggio*. Bologna: Capelli.

Thieme, Paul (1956). 'Pāṇini and the Pāṇiniyas'. *Journal of the American Oriental Society* 76. 1–23.

Thorne, James Peter (1965). 'Stylistics and generative grammar'. *Journal of Linguistics* 1. 49–59.

(1972). 'On the notion "definite"'. *Foundations of Language* 8. 562–8.

(1973). 'On non-restrictive relative clauses'. *Linguistic Inquiry* 3. 552–6.

Todorov, Tvetzan (ed.) (1970). *L'énonciation*. (Langages 17.) Paris: Didier & Larousse.

Tolstoy, L. N. (1953). *Anna Karenina*. Moskva: Gosudartstv. Izd. (First published, 1877.)

Trager, George L. (1949). *The Field of Linguistics* (Studies in Linguistics, Occasional Papers, 1.) Norman, Okla.: Battenbury Press.

& Smith, H. L. (1951). *An Outline of English Structure*. (Studies in Linguistics, Occasional Papers, 3.) (Reprinted, Washington, DC: American Council of Learned Societies, 1957.)

Trudgill, Peter (1974). *Sociolinguistics: An Introduction*. Harmondsworth: Penguin.

Tylor, Edward B. (1871). *Primitive Culture*. London: Murray.

(1881). *Anthropology: An Introduction to the Study of Man and Civilization*. London: Murray.

Uldall, Elizabeth (1981). 'Bibliography: the published works of David Abercrombie'. In Asher & Henderson (1981a: 283–288).

Uldall, Hans J. (1944). 'Speech and writing'. *Acta Linguistica* 4. 11–16. (Reprinted in Hamp *et al.*, 1966: 147–151.)

(1957). *Outline of Glossematics, 1: A Study in the Methodology of the Humanities with Special Reference to Linguistics*. (= Part 1 of Louis Hjelmslev & H. J. Uldall, *Outline of Glossematics*.) (Travaux du Cercle Linguistique de Copenhague, 10.) Copenhague: Nordisk Sprog- og Kulturforlag.

Ullendorff, E. (1971). 'Is Biblical Hebrew a language?'. *Bulletin of the School of Oriental and African Studies* 34. 241–255.

Vachek, Josef (1945/9). 'Some remarks on writing and phonetic transcription'. *Acta Linguistica* 5. 86–93.(Reprinted in Hamp *et al.*, 1966: 152–157.)

(1959). 'The London group of linguistics'. *Sbornik Praci Filosoficke Fakulty Brnenske University* 8 (A7). 106–113.

(1966a). *A Prague School Reader in Linguistics*. Bloomington, Ind.: Indiana

References

University Press.

(1966b). *The Linguistic School of Prague*. Bloomington, Ind.: Indiana University Press.

(1973). *Written Language*. The Hague: Mouton.

Van Riemsdijk, Henk & Williams, E. (1986). *An Introduction to the Theory of Grammar*. Cambridge, Mass.: MIT Press.

Vihman, Marilyn M., Macken, M. A., Miller, R., Simmons, H. & Miller, J. (1985). 'From babbling to speech'. *Language* 61. 397–445.

Voegelin, Carl F. & Ellinghausen, M. E. (1943). 'Turkish structure'. *Journal of the American Oriental Society* 63. 34–60.

Waaub, Jean-Marie (1967). 'The Firthian school of linguistics: Notes on In Memory of J. R. Firth'. (Review article on Bazell *et al.*, 1966.) *Revista Portuguese de Filologia* 6. 43–72.

Wackernagel, J. (1920). *Vorlesungen über Syntax*. Basel: Emil Birkhauser.

Wanner, Eric & Gleitman, L. R. (eds.) (1982). *Language Acquisition: The State of the Art*. Cambridge: Cambridge University Press.

Ward, Denis (1963). *In Pursuit of a Modern Language*. (Inaugural Lecture delivered on 17 November 1963.) Edinburgh: Edinburgh University Press.

(1965). *The Russian Language Today: System and Anomaly*. London: Hutchinson.

Warrington, Elizabeth K. (1981). 'Neuropsychological studies of verbal semantic systems'. In Longuet-Higgins *et al.* (1981: 197–209 [411–423]).

Washburn, S. L. & McCown, E. R. (eds.) (1978). *Human Evolution: Biosocial Perspectives on Human Evolution*, vol. IV. Menlo Park, Calif.: Benjamin Cummings.

Waterson, Natalie (1956). 'Some aspects of the phonology of the nominal forms of the Turkish word'. *Bulletin of the School of Oriental and African Studies* 18. 578–91. (Reprinted in Palmer, 1970a: 174–87.)

Weinrich, Harald (1964). *Tempus: Besprochene und Erzählte Welt*. Stuttgart: Kohlhammer. (French edn, *Le Temps*. Paris: Seuil, 1964.)

(1970). 'Tense and time'. *Archivum Linguisticum* (New Series) 1. 31–41.

Weissenborn, Jurgen & Klein, Wolfgang (eds.) (1962). *Here and There: Cross-Linguistic Studies on Deixis and Demonstration*. Amsterdam: Benjamins.

Weist, Richard M. (1986). 'Tense and aspect'. In Fletcher & Garman (1986: 356–374).

Westcott, Roger W. (ed.) (1974). *Language Origins*. Silver Spring, Md.: Linstok.

Whitney, William D. (1872). *The Life and Growth of Language*. New York: Appleton. (London: King, 1875.)

Whorf, Benjamin L. (1938). 'Some verbal categories in Hopi'. *Language* 14. 275–286. (Reprinted in Whorf, 1956: 112–124.)

(1945). 'Grammatical categories'. *Language* 21. 1–11. (Reprinted in Whorf, 1956: 87–101; Householder, 1972: 103–114.)

(1956). *Four Articles on Metalinguistics*. Cambridge, Mass.: MIT Press.

Widdowson, Henry G. (1978). 'Rules and procedures in discourse analysis'. In

References

Myers (1978a: 61–71.)

(1990). 'Peter Strevens'. In *Georgetown University Round Table on Language and Linguistics 1990*. Washington DC: Georgetown University Press. 32–33.

Wilkins, David A. (1976). *Notional Syllabuses*. London: Oxford University Press.

Wind, Jan (1982). 'On sapientization and speech'. *Current Anthropology* 23. 107.

(1983). 'Primate evolution and the emergence of speech'. In Grolier (1983: 15–35.)

Wittgenstein, Ludwig von (1922). *Tractatus Logico-Philosophicus*. London: Routledge & Kegan Paul.

(1953). *Philosophical Investigations* (trans. by G. Elizabeth Anscombe). Oxford: Blackwell.

Wolpoff, M. H. (1980). *Palaeoanthropology*. New York: Knopf.

Wood, Bernard, Martin, L. & Andrews, P. (eds.) (1986). *Major Topics in Primate and Human Evolution*. Cambridge: Cambridge University Press.

Wunderlich, Dieter (1972). *Linguistische Pragmatik*. Frankfurt: Athenäum.

Wundt, Wilhelm (1901). *Sprachgeschichte und Sprachpsychologie*. Leipzig: Engelmann.

(1912). *Völkerpsychologie*. Leipzig: Engelmann

Zampolli, Antonio (ed.) (1977). *Linguistic Structures Processing*. Amsterdam: North Holland.

Zgusta, Ladislav (1963). Review of *Studies in Linguistic Analysis* (1957). In *Archiv Orientalní*. 325–328.

(1968). Review of Lyons (1963a). In *Archiv Orientalní* 36. 149.

Ziff, Paul (1960). *Semantic Analysis*. Ithaca, NY: Cornell University Press.

Zinna, Alessandro (ed.) (1986). *Louis Hjelmslev: Linguistica e Semiotica Strutturale*. (Versus 43.) Milano: Bompiani.

Subject index

278

Names index

Names index

Lakoff, G. 226
Lamb, S.M. 110, 140, 225
Langendoen, D.T. 104, 22, 237
Lass, R. 104
Laver, J. 104, 218
Le Page, R.B. 200, 203
Lees, R.B. 138
Lejewski, C. 140
Lenneberg, E.H. 197
Leroy, M. 194
Leśniewski, S. 140
Levelt, W.J.M. 8
Lewis, D. 140
Lieberman, P.M. 85, 87
Lisker, L. 183
Lock, A.J. 85, 88
Longuet-Higgins, H.C. 202
Łukasiewicz, J. 226

Macaulay, D. 225
McClure, J.D. 232
McCown, E.R. 80, 85
McGivney, J. 206
McIntosh, A. 180, 186, 204, 232, 233
Makkai, V.B. 104
Marshall, J.C. 7, 203
Martinet, A. 66, 105, 194, 206
Mather, J.Y. 232
Matthews, P.H. 112, 225, 233, 236
Mehler, J. 7
Meillet, A. 118
Meinhof, U. 206
Miller, G.A. 194, 198
Miller, J. 143
Milner, E. 92
Mitchell, T.F. 218, 223
Montague, R. 54, 56, 61, 65, 140
Morgan, L. 79
Morris, C.W. 19
Most, R.B. 89, 91, 93
Motsch, W. 153
Murison, D.D. 232

Nencioni, G. 211
Nida, E.A. 154

Obler, L.K. 90
Orr, J. 232–3
Otto, L. 206

Palmer, F.R. 104, 106, 129, 204, 218,
    219, 221, 223, 224
Pāṇini 231
Passingham, R.E. 87, 89
Pateman, T. 46, 47, 206, 209, 213
Peirce, C.S. 204
Piaget, J. 178

Pike, K.L. 102
Plato 117, 118, 134, 180, 201, 237
Popper, K.R. 18, 208, 213
Postal, P.M. 121, 125, 127, 155, 221,
    225, 227, 236, 237
Priscian 185

Quine, W.V. 134, 143, 146, 213, 231

Rey-Debove, J. 210
Roberts, J.M. 197
Robins, R.H. 79, 104, 112, 113, 118,
    123, 134, 215, 218, 219, 222, 223,
    224
Russell, B. 148, 214
Ryle, G. 196, 238

Saintsbury, G. 189
Sampson, G.R. 204, 206
Sanders, C.S. 206
Sandmann, M. 149
Sankoff, G. 203
Sapir, E. 112, 141, 224, 226, 236–7
Saussure, F. de 10, 11, 12–13, 18, 19, 23,
    27, 31, 35–42, 49, 55, 187, 189, 191,
    211, 212, 219, 223, 236, 239
Schachter, P. 141
Schleicher, A. 2, 55, 215
Schuchardt, H. 134
Scott, N.C. 218
Searle, J.R. 163
Sebeok, T.A. 92–3, 200
Selinker, L. 239
Selkirk, E.O. 205
Sharp, A.E. 218
Shaumjan, S.K. 110, 139, 140, 225
Shopen, T. 64
Siple, P. 7
Smith, H.L. 236
Smith, N.V. 203
Sommerstein, A.H. 104, 146, 155, 156,
    157, 223, 229
Speitel, H.H. 232
Spencer, J. 200
Sperber, D. 79, 80–1, 216
Sprigg, R.K. 218
Staal, J.F. 224
Stam, J.H. 75
Stark, R.E. 84, 91
Starosta, S. 28
Stephany, U. 88
Stokoe, W.C. 84
Strang, B.M.H. 131
Strawson, P.F. 115, 135, 169
Street, B. 206
Strevens, P.D. 182, 213, 239
Swadesh, M. 141

289